D0569829

AN ORDINARY MARRIAGE

An Ordinary Marriage

THE WORLD OF A GENTRY FAMILY
IN PROVINCIAL RUSSIA

Katherine Pickering Antonova

For Dr. Whittaker —
In thanks for
your advice &
support! Best wishes,
Kate

OXFORD
UNIVERSITY PRESS

OXFORD
UNIVERSITY PRESS

Oxford University Press is a department of the University of Oxford. It furthers the University's objective
of excellence in research, scholarship, and education by publishing worldwide.

Oxford New York
Auckland Cape Town Dar es Salaam Hong Kong Karachi
Kuala Lumpur Madrid Melbourne Mexico City Nairobi
New Delhi Shanghai Taipei Toronto

With offices in
Argentina Austria Brazil Chile Czech Republic France Greece
Guatemala Hungary Italy Japan Poland Portugal Singapore
South Korea Switzerland Thailand Turkey Ukraine Vietnam

Oxford is a registered trade mark of Oxford University Press in the UK and certain other countries.

Published in the United States of America by
Oxford University Press
198 Madison Avenue, New York, NY 10016

Library of Congress Cataloging-in-Publication Data

Antonova, Katherine Pickering, 1975-
  An ordinary marriage: the world of a gentry family in provincial Russia / Katherine Pickering Antonova.
    pages ; cm
  Includes bibliographical references and index.
  ISBN 978-0-19-979699-1 (hardback : alkaline paper) 1. Chikhachev family. 2. Families—Russia
(Federation)—Vladimirskaia guberniia—History—19th century. 3. Gentry—Russia (Federation)—
Vladimirskaia guberniia—History—19th century. 4. Gentry—Russia (Federation)—Vladimirskaia guberniia—
Social life and customs—19th century. 5. Marriage—Russia (Federation)—Vladimirskaia guberniia—History—
19th century. 6. Sex role—Russia—History—19th century. 7. Women in real estate—Russia (Federation)—
Vladimirskaia guberniia—History—19th century. 8. Real estate management—Russia (Federation)—Vladimirskaia
guberniia—History—19th century. I. Title.
  HQ637.A58 2012
  306.8094709'034—dc23   2012013100

9 8 7 6 5 4 3 2 1

Printed in the United States of America on acid-free paper

This book is for the people who made it possible: Christine Smit Pickering, Daniel R. Pickering, Sergei A. Antonov, and Anya Antonova.

Contents

Acknowledgments

RESEARCH FOR THIS book was funded primarily by a Fulbright grant, and additional short research trips were funded by the Harriman Institute and PSC-CUNY. I am grateful to all the archivists, librarians, and museum curators who helped me access sources. Most of all, I thank the staff of the State Historical Archive of Ivanovo Oblast (GAIO). The generous collegiality of the director of GAIO, L. N. Lisitsyna, the deputy director, N. A. Murav'eva, and the research department head, O. I. Zakharova, were crucial in making this book possible, while the pleasant company and patient advice of E. B. Manertseva, the reading room archivist, eased my labors considerably. I also thank Professor Kirill Baldin and N. G. Remizova at Ivanovo State University for their support, and the university librarians for allowing me to photograph articles from several of their periodicals. The kind curators of the Shuia Regional Museum (Shuiskii Kraevdcheskii Muzei) shared their collection of Chikhachev letters and bound periodicals annotated with Andrei's own marginalia. The staff of the Russian Museum in St. Petersburg was especially responsive and helpful in arranging permission to reproduce two images from their collection.

My stay in Ivanovo was enriched by the kindness of Ludmila Leonidovna Burlakova, her son Igor, and Regina Chumakova. Igor and Regina arranged and accompanied me on our adventures into the countryside to explore the Chikhachevs' home and other local highlights. I am grateful beyond words to Galina Petrovna, Liubov Borisovna, and Zoia Aleksandrovna, teachers in the village school in Dorozhaevo, for treating us to two wonderful afternoons in the village once owned by the Chikhachevs. I will never forget our time spent there, especially the feast we shared in what had once been Natalia Ivanovna's bedroom. I also thank Vladimir Smirnov, the priest of the village church in Zimenki, for his tour and conversation. My several research trips to Russia were made much more comfortable by the Shashkov family.

My graduate advisors at Columbia University, Professors Richard S. Wortman and Mark L. von Hagen, have been supportive guides throughout the PhD program and generous readers of the dissertation. In addition, I have greatly benefited from the support and criticism of Professor Barbara Alpern Engel of the University of Colorado, Boulder. Susan Smith-Peter of the College of Staten Island not only told me about the Chikhachevs in the first place but has been equally generous with her knowledge and friendship as the project has progressed over many years. Michelle Lamarche Marrese, whose book first made me ask these questions, generously shared her ongoing work and excellent advice (and obtained for me a Xerox from Helsinki in a case of dire emergency). Bella Grigoryan has been a stimulating colleague and great friend, whose work is always inspiring. Professors Alice Kessler-Harris and Irina Reyfman of Columbia University and Professor Cynthia Whittaker of Baruch College provided invaluable advice on the dissertation, which has greatly informed my revisions. While at Columbia I also benefited from the lively discussions of dissertation group workshops led by Professors Kessler-Harris and Bradley Abrams. I am grateful to all of my graduate school comrades, and most of all Aline Voldoire for her attentive reading of drafts, generous comments, and her unstinting friendship and support. Moreover, I am grateful to Aline for several translations from the French; whatever errors remain lie at my door. I also thank the participants of the Columbia University Seminar on Slavic Studies and the Russian Studies Workshop of the Harriman Institute, as well as the attendees at the several conferences where portions of this work have been presented, for their helpful comments.

Crucial time needed to revise my dissertation into this book was provided by Queens College, of the City University of New York. I also enormously appreciate the moral and practical support of the faculty and secretaries of the history department. Revisions were also enriched by the anonymous reviewers of Oxford University Press, and especially by the generous and thoughtful editing of Nancy Toff and Sonia Tycko.

My absorption in this project tested the patience of many friends and family members. I thank Chris Smit Pickering, Daniel Pickering, Galina Antonova, Aleksandr Antonov, and my daughter Anya, especially, for putting up with me. This book may never have been completed without the emotional and intellectual generosity of Sergei A. Antonov. He has been my sounding-board, editor, critic, cheerleader, and greatest comfort at every step of the way. All translations from the Russian, unless otherwise noted, are by Sergei A. Antonov and me, although responsibility for errors of translation or deficiencies of any other kind is of course mine.

Preface

SOMETIME IN THE 1970s, in the obscure Soviet town of Kovrov, a factory worker and son of a Red Army veteran, Oleg Chikhachev, was made an "honored veteran of labor." Oleg was an unremarkable Soviet citizen, but just two generations earlier his forebears had owned several country estates. His father, Anatoly, the son of a nobleman, became a mathematics teacher after being discharged from the Red Army with the conclusion of the Civil War in the early 1920s. Oleg's Aunt Elena had helped to convert the family's manor house into a village school, and was a teacher there until she married. Many of the former nobility assimilated into the new Soviet regime as Oleg's family did. These people included noble families who did not have the means or influence to emigrate after the Revolution of 1917, those who were not specifically targeted by the Bolsheviks or by vengeful local peasants, and those who were not useful enough to be actively co-opted into the new regime as "bourgeois specialists."[1]

In the turbulent years of Revolution and Civil War a great deal of Russia's local and national historical heritage was destroyed, but by the mid-1920s something of a fad for local history arose, probably as a reaction to the recent loss of so much tradition.[2] In 1925, someone deposited a collection of Chikhachev papers in the newly established State Historical Archive of Ivanovo Region. Several books belonging to a long-dead Chikhachev ancestor were also deposited with the Shuia local museum. These donated papers represent what is so far the most extensive and elaborate archive of gentry family papers preserved in provincial Russia.

Anatoly and Elena's father, Konstantin Alekseevich Chikhachev, died in early 1918, just missing news of the Bolshevik Revolution. As a young man in the 1880s Konstantin had kept a diary in imitation of his venerable and beloved grandfather, Andrei Ivanovich Chikhachev. By the time of Konstantin's boyhood, Andrei was a local legend for his newspaper articles and philanthropy. Among other ventures, Andrei had founded the first free public library in the province (the books that were given to the Shuia museum in the 1920s were what remained of that library). But as Konstantin knew, even more extraordinary than Andrei's public work was his private writing and that of his wife Natalia and their son Aleksei (Konstantin's father).

The documents deposited at the Ivanovo archive consist of hundreds of pages of private writing by Andrei, Natalia, and Aleksei, covering much of the period from 1830 to 1866, with scattered documents also from the 1820s and 1870s. Together, these documents make up an astonishingly rich history of mid-nineteenth-century provincial gentry life. Even in the United States or western Europe, where historical records were not ravaged by Revolution and aggressive censorship as they were in Russia, a family archive of this type from this period would be a remarkable find.

In addition to diaries by several people covering several years and sometimes overlapping chronologically, besides hundreds of letters received by Andrei, and the business and legal papers that establish many of the factual circumstances of the family, there is also a series of books containing what the family referred to as their notebook correspondence. In the 1830s, the Chikhachevs lived for part of every year on an estate neighboring the one owned by Natalia's brother and Andrei's close friend, Yakov Chernavin. While they were neighbors, each "side" of these two families kept a notebook for immediately recording whatever thoughts occurred to them for sharing with the other "side." Whenever a servant or member of the family was passing from one estate to the other, the notebooks would be exchanged. The resulting correspondence is less like an exchange of posted letters and more like a recorded conversation, with colloquial exchanges of quips, commiserations, ruminations, jokes, and all the details of everyday life.

These documents are now located in the State Archive of Ivanovo Region, in the city of Ivanovo, about a five-hour drive northeast from Moscow. Although squarely in the heart of European Russia, the village of Ivanovo was incorporated as the town of Ivanovo-Voznesensk only in 1871. A center of the textile industry and home of the famous strike that, in Soviet historiography, started the "first Russian Revolution" in 1905, Ivanovo (as it was renamed in 1932) has always been associated with industry, and in imperial times with the merchantry that dominated textile trade there. Thus, historians who visit the Ivanovo archive are generally looking for documents about industry, business, revolution, or the merchantry. Historians looking for documents about the provincial landowning gentry generally go anywhere but Ivanovo. And, until 1991, foreign historians have had trouble visiting Ivanovo at all (not far from the city is a major military base, Ivanovo Severny).

The extraordinary Chikhachev archive rested almost untouched from the time it was deposited, in 1925, until the mid-1990s, when several local historians discovered it and began to publish articles about Andrei and his writing.[3] A few years later, an American historian, Susan Smith-Peter, came upon the archive in her search for provincial members of the Moscow Agricultural Society; she has since published an article on Andrei's founding of his public library and other works relating to Andrei's participation in regional civil society.[4] It was Susan Smith-Peter who alerted me to the Chikhachev archive and specifically the presence there of diaries by Natalia Chikhacheva, when I asked her about finding women's diaries in the provinces.

I sought documents written by provincial, land-owning women who were not from the small number of wealthy and highly educated families, who often produced the writers of the time (and who usually paid outsiders to manage their property). I wanted to understand families who did not produce the cultural imagery of the day but instead those who consumed it. Unfortunately, documents by obscure women are notoriously unlikely to survive in archives. The Chikhachev archive, however, contains several extensive diaries by a woman landowner no one had ever heard of by the name of Natalia Ivanovna Chikhacheva (it was at first incidental that this Natalia Chikhacheva had a husband who is quite interesting in his own right, and that he, too, wrote a great deal). I spent nine months in the reading room of the Ivanovo archive, reading nearly every word of the Chikhachev family *fond* and copying most of it out by hand (since other forms of duplication were barred for anything more than a few pages).[5] The following book is the product of that research.

A Note on Language

RUSSIAN WORDS HAVE been transliterated according to a modified Library of Congress standard; apostrophes to indicate soft signs have been omitted, names familiar to English-speaking readers are in their Anglicized forms, and names beginning with "Ia" have been rendered as the more easily pronounced "Ya." The notes and bibliography follow the Library of Congress method strictly.

The name "Chikhachev" is pronounced "Chee-khuh-CHYOFF" with the "ch" as in "cheese" and the "kh" like the German "ch" in "liebchen." The standard form of address for Russian nobles was by first name and patronymic, a form of middle name based on the individual's father's name with an ending added to indicate "daughter of" (*-vna*) or "son of" (*-vich*). The Chikhachev family members are often referred to here by first name only for convenience. Others are referred to in the way they were mentioned by the Chikhachevs or by full formal name. Most Russian names also had diminutive equivalents used to show familiarity or closeness of relationship. Thus, the family is quoted referring to Aleksandra as "Sasha" or "Sashonochka," Aleksei as "Alesha" (pronounced "Al-YO-shuh"), and Andrei sometimes refers to Natalia as "Natasha." Some serfs were referred to by different diminutives conveying condescension, such as "Sashka" instead of the neutral "Sasha" for a serf named Aleksandr. The children usually referred to their parents as "Papinka" and "Maminka," now-archaic diminutives for "Papa" and "Mama."

Variations in spelling and idiosyncrasies of grammar have been rendered into correct modern English, except where idiosyncrasies are significant. Translations attempt to render the original tone and style, though in some cases particularly extensive repetition or circuitous syntax have been simplified for the sake of intelligibility. Unusual punctuation has been retained when it is particularly expressive, as Andrei Chikhachev's often was. Underlining and all-caps used for emphasis are given as they appeared in the original.

Nineteenth-century dates are given in the Old Style, following the Julian calendar in use in imperial Russia before 1918. To compare these dates to events happening simultaneously outside the Russian Empire, add twelve days. Dates after 1918 follow the New Style, or Gregorian calendar.

The geographical unit *guberniia* has been translated as province, according to convention, while *uezd*, sometimes translated as "district" is here rendered as "county." Some key terms are given in the original, since exact English equivalents do not exist. These are defined when they are first used, except for units of measure. The metric equivalents of these are as follows:

Arshin—measurement of length, equal to 28 inches

Chetvert—dry measure equal to 5.95 bushels, or a land measure equal to one half a *desiatina*

Chetverik—dry measure, 1/8 of a *chetvert*

Desiatina—land measure equal to 2.7 acres

Funt—measure of weight equal to 0.9 pounds, rendered here as the American pound

Pud—weight equal to 40 *funty,* or 36 pounds

Talik—idiosyncratic spelling of *talek*, a ball of linen yarn made from one *funt* of flax

Versta or (plural) *verst*—measure of length/distance equal to .66 miles or 1.067 kilometers.

Chikhachev Family Tree

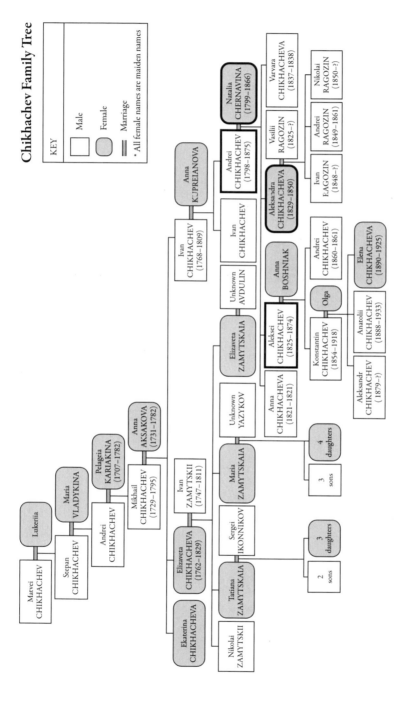

KEY

☐ Male

▢ Female

━ Marriage

* All female names are maiden names

This family tree shows Andrei Chikhachev's ancestors and descendants. All women are indicated with their maiden names, and birth and death dates are given when they are known. This tree shows that Andrei's family was well documented for many generations before the nineteenth century. It also shows his family ties with the Zamytskii, Ikonnikov, and Yazykov families, who figure prominently in the Chikhachev documents.

Natalia's Ancestry

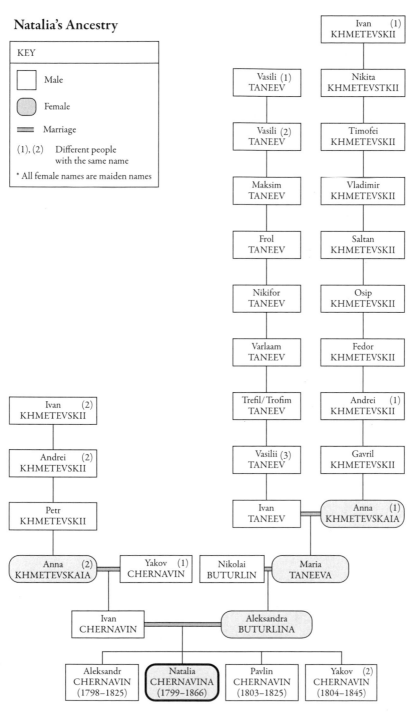

This is a simplified tree showing the known direct ancestors of Natalia Chikhacheva (née Chernavina). All women are indicated with their maiden names, and birth and death dates are given when they are known. Although the Chernavin family line was not well documented, Natalia was connected to the Taneev and Khmetevskii families, both of which were ancient, with a long-standing presence in Vladimir province.

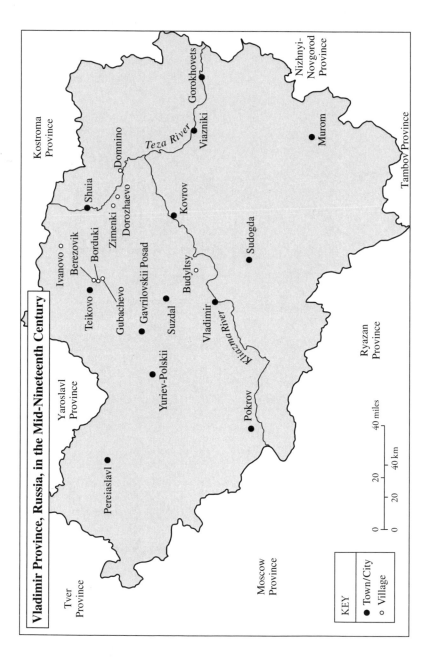

Vladimir Province, Russia, in the Mid-Nineteenth Century

Kostroma Province

Tver Province

Yaroslavl Province

Nizhnyi-Novgorod Province

Tambov Province

Ryazan Province

Moscow Province

Teza River

Kliazma River

Gorokhovets

Viazniki

Murom

Domnino

Shuia

Zimenki

Dorozhaevo

Kovrov

Sudogda

Ivanovo

Berezovik

Borduki

Teikovo

Gubachevo

Gavrilovskii Posad

Suzdal

Budyltsy

Vladimir

Yuriev-Polskii

Pereiaslavl

Pokrov

KEY

● Town/City

○ Village

0   20   40 miles

0   20   40 km

This map of Vladimir province, Russia, in the nineteenth century shows the location of the Chikhachevs' residential villages, Dorozhaevo and Borduki, in the *upper right* quadrant. The Chikhachevs' villages were conveniently located in a relatively populous region, a comfortable distance from the provincial capital city, Vladimir, and the closer market towns of Kovrov and Shuia.

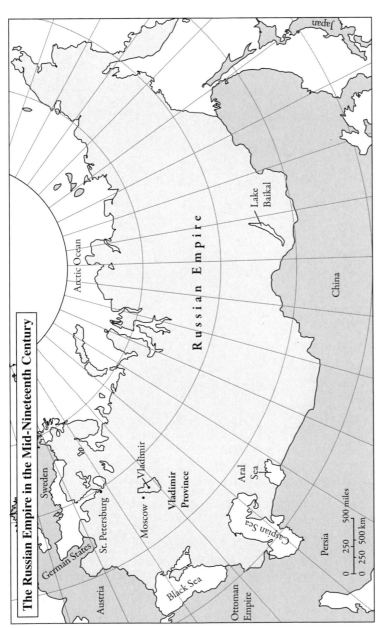

The Russian Empire in the Mid-Nineteenth Century

This map of the Russian empire in the mid-nineteenth century shows the position of Vladimir province within the empire: east of Moscow and part of the "Golden Ring" of ancient cities that make up the heartland of European Russia. This was a relatively more populous part of the country, within reasonable traveling distance of the lively trade economy of Moscow.

Introduction

IN PROVINCIAL RUSSIA in the middle of the nineteenth century, a woman named Natalia Chikhacheva spent most of her adult years managing all the everyday details of several complex agricultural estates, including the labor of hundreds of serfs. While she did this, her husband Andrei concentrated his energies on raising their two children. This arrangement strikes a modern reader as surprising for its time and place, yet it was not considered unusual by the Chikhachevs or their neighbors and friends. In fact, many of their peers may have had similar marital arrangements.

Their case appears surprising because it seems to contradict the tenets of domestic ideology, the notion that women belonged in the home, mothering their children, while men worked in the wider world beyond the home. Domesticity in its historical sense refers to this well-established rhetoric about "separate spheres" for women and men, and about how an ideal woman should behave. The ideal woman was supposed to be modest, virtuous and pleasant, and focus her energies on being an "angel of the house," making a home for her family and nurturing her children. This rhetoric began to appear in western European literature and advice manuals as industrialization increasingly pushed middle-class men into work in offices, enterprises, and institutions instead of family businesses, which in the pre-industrial period had often operated out of the home, with help from the woman of the house. The rhetoric of domesticity was—and to a much lesser degree remains—powerful. But it was and is rhetoric, not reality.

Even as western middle classes grew in numbers and influence, and most middle-class men increasingly worked outside the home, these changes did not occur overnight, and many people's lives countered the trend in various ways. Most importantly, the behaviors

and beliefs of real people were far more complicated than prescriptive literature suggested. The rhetoric helped to create a gender norm, which real men and women might
follow, fight, or disregard.[1] Many middle-class fathers remained devoted to their children,
for example, and many middle-class women worked outside the home or otherwise acted
against the idealized model of the angel of the house (though they sometimes paid a
social price when these actions were perceived as transgressing against a norm represented by the rhetoric of domesticity).[2]

Literature scholar Diana Greene has written on the ubiquity of domestic ideology in
the Russian periodic press in the 1830s and '40s, demonstrating that European ideas of
domesticity were available to Russian provincial gentry readers like the Chikhachevs.
Contrary to some other scholars, this book argues that ideas about domesticity, though
widely read and even repeated privately by many provincial Russians, could not be
easily or quickly digested by a society that developed in very different economic and
political conditions than the societies of western Europe where these ideas were born.[3]
Motherhood, especially, was differently understood in serf-owning provincial families,
and this alternate model of motherhood had crucial implications for the everyday
experience of marriage and parenting, and understandings of men's roles. These (seemingly) peculiar gender arrangements made the importation of western European ideas
about domesticity complicated in Russian provincial homes.

Critical to understanding the gendered family dynamics of the nineteenth-century gentry
is a book by Michelle Lamarche Marrese on Russian noblewomen's ownership of property.[4]
Marrese established through extensive research in legal documents and memoirs that, unlike
in western Europe where married women were legally barred from property ownership, Russian married women were not only legally permitted to own property but regularly exercised
this right, managing their own property separately from their husbands in many cases, and in
still other cases managing their husband's property along with their own. These women represented themselves and their interests in court, and sometimes successfully sued to protect
their property rights against wastrel husbands. Further, Marrese's research in memoir literature showed that many eighteenth- and early nineteenth-century Russians remembered
women property owners as commonplace, as unquestioned in their authority as property
owners, and often as admirable managers (even though, interestingly, such women were
often portrayed in fiction in much less positive terms). Marrese argues that this situation was
made possible by the Russian gentry's understanding of estate management, broadly defined,
as a natural extension of domestic economy.

Given that so many Russian married women were managing their own property separately from their husbands', or were managing all the family property, the Chikhachev
story is intended to show what influence that fact could have on such women's marriages,
on the ways such men and women were able to understand their roles as spouses and
parents, and on how the educated Russian public received western European ideas about
a wife and mother as an angel of the house and a husband and father as having his "natural" role in the public sphere when their own circumstances were often very different.

The reception of ideas such as domesticity by readers is a notoriously elusive subject. For lack of other evidence it is generally assumed that an overwhelming presence of certain ideas in popular literature means that readers absorbed the ideas, in ways and degrees unknowable. Accordingly, historians who have previously examined the dissemination of western European domestic ideology in Russia have concluded that the prevalence of these ideas not only in the periodic press but also in popular fiction and private writings indicates that significant numbers of Russian readers embraced these ideas; the principal question these historians have asked is why they did so despite significant institutional and cultural differences between mid-nineteenth-century imperial Russia and western Europe, and how these ideas spread so quickly.[5]

My study of the Chikhachev documents suggests that these questions may be premature. The Chikhachevs read much of the vast literature, creative and prescriptive, that promoted domestic ideology, and Andrei's own writing reflects some of the language of domesticity.[6] But Natalia Chikhacheva's acknowledged sphere was far wider than that accorded to women in popular literature or occupied by most real women in the West, and her sphere also took a different form. Financial affairs were decidedly within Natalia's realm; the moral upbringing of children decidedly was not. Even while Andrei aped the language of domesticity in his diaries, he also promoted in the local newspaper the importance of a wife as financial manager and supervisor of estates. Natalia's own diaries testify to the reality of her role as Andrei promoted it, and to the fact that this role was the primary one by which Natalia identified herself: a role she took pride in. This book thus joins those of scholars of western Europe in mapping out ways in which domestic realities differed from domestic ideology. This would not be a particularly significant finding on its own—it is, after all, hardly surprising to say that people did not necessarily use the periodic press as a direct guide to behavior. More significant are the several implications of the particular reality seen in the Chikhachev marriage.

The Chikhachev family was not noticeably unusual among the middling provincial gentry, aside from the fact that they wrote so much and that so many of their papers happened to survive: their income was middling for provincial landowners, and they led their lives much the way their neighbors and relations did. But of course no one family can accurately stand in for all families (with respect to Tolstoy, no families are "all alike," happy or not). As a microhistory, this book seeks to understand one family in as much depth as possible, so that it may serve as a yardstick by which to measure greater or lesser variation in other cases that are often far less thoroughly documented but which can be better understood in light of it. Simon Dixon's important recent survey of the literature on Russian nobility called for studies that could "relate personality to place by situating . . . individual life-writings and correspondence . . . more precisely in the social and cultural environment in which their authors lived."[7] That is exactly the intention of this book. A synthesis of the Chikhachev material with other, still emerging, evidence to create a whole portrait of the nineteenth-century nobility would be a quite different project.

That an arrangement of gendered marriage roles like the Chikhachevs' was available and accepted without comment or criticism is significant even if such a marriage was not typical of the middling gentry (though there is reason to suppose that it may have been at least fairly common within that slice of the population). The Chikhachev case, though singular, is extraordinarily rich and has significant light to shed on several broad areas of inquiry, including the history of gender and family, serf ownership, the middling gentry, and the reception of ideas, from domesticity to Romanticism and nationality.

One primary reason why gendered marital roles in Russia differed from those promoted by Western literature lay in nineteenth-century Russia's peculiar political and economic realities. Most importantly, Russia's most powerful propertied class in this period was not a commercial or professional middle class, but a landed nobility, and noble identity was closely linked with the ethos of state service and the institution of serfdom. All Russian nobles—from grand aristocrats to middling gentry like the Chikhachevs to penniless petty gentry who made a living as best as they could—enjoyed significant legal privileges: freedom from most personal taxation and corporal punishment, and even freedom from personal service obligations (secured by Peter III's Charter to the Nobility of 1762 and confirmed by Catherine II in 1785).[8] However, while the nobility was no longer *required* to serve the state, it was still *expected* to do so (and often had to whenever income from land was insufficient). By the nineteenth century many middling landowners served only for a few years and then retired to their estates. State service required men to be absent from their estates and families for long periods of time, and in such cases many wives managed estates by default (other less attractive options would be to hire an expensive professional manager, entrust a relative with a power of attorney, or turn over this considerable responsibility to a serf elder).[9] In the Chikhachev case, the husband lived at home from the beginning of the marriage, but the notion that he was primarily the tsar's loyal servitor was never far from his mind while his wife managed their estates.

The second important noble privilege was the exclusive right to own land with serfs.[10] Whether or not they chose to serve away from their estates, the middling gentry depended on income from serf-based agriculture and were obliged in turn to ensure the basic material welfare of their serfs. Serf management was a complex, time-consuming task with a great deal at stake and many risks; it formed one of the primary occupations of any serf-owning family.

Serving the state, governing landed estates, and, for better-educated individuals, participating in Russia's cultural life nearly exhausted Russian nobles' opportunities for meaningful activity. Alternative avenues for masculine occupation were effectively closed for most noblemen. For example, political participation in this period was nearly nonexistent, because Russia did not have a central representative body until 1906, and limited local self-government bodies (*zemstva*) were established only in 1863. Prominent positions in the bureaucracy were generally limited to the most elite noble families. Commercial and industrial development during the reign of Nicholas I (1825–55) were purposefully discouraged for fear of social turmoil. Although technically nobles could establish factories on their estates and enroll in merchant guilds, the Russian economy as a whole lacked sufficient capital for investment and innovation, and institutional and legal structures were designed to discourage speculative activity, hampering entrepreneurship and risk taking.[11] While Russian "gentlemanly capitalism" did exist, investing in land or depositing cash at a state-owned bank were more attractive options in the first half of the century.[12]

Retiring from state service after only a few years in the army and lacking the connections or capital to engage in political or commercial activity, Andrei Chikhachev justified his own role as moral educator and intellectual because he considered these roles "public" in the sense that they brought him (mentally and symbolically) beyond the estates. Someone, however, still had to engage in the vital task of everyday management. This was Natalia. Andrei identified her role as a private one ("within the home"), thereby defining multiple estates containing several serf villages as the "home," as was a common assumption among provincial gentry throughout the eighteenth and nineteenth centuries.[13]

Andrei wrote about the village as an extension of the family as was common in the mid-nineteenth century, but the Chikhachev case provides a window into the life behind the rhetoric: in this case the village was indeed an extension of their family in almost every possible way. Just as Natalia mothered her children by concerning herself chiefly with their material welfare, she understood her duties toward serfs the same way. And as Andrei was his children's moral educator, he considered himself to play the same role with regard to his serfs. From the perspective of the owners, at least, the hierarchy of the village "family" went from parents to children to other dependents, and the latter category was composed of many layers, from privileged nannies to hired tutors to free clergy to household servants and field workers. Each was dependent on the others by degrees that varied, sometimes greatly.

About 90 percent of serf owners in imperial Russia were not wealthy enough to hire estate managers or to live for any significant time away from their estates. The historical literature on Russian serfdom has nevertheless had to concern itself almost exclusively with the wealthiest 3.4 percent of landowners, because hired estate managers left behind extensive reports to and correspondence with owners, and because the documents of the empire's wealthiest landowners were usually preserved in the central archives, which have been most accessible and complete.[14] The several most important studies on Russian serf ownership are based on wealthier estates that differ in many meaningful ways from the Chikhachevs' property, but the Chikhachevs' estates were the more common type. Similarly, work on aristocracy in Russia has, due to the same problems with sources, mostly dwelt on the upper 3.4 percent of noblemen. The

Chikhachev evidence, then, cannot be in direct conversation with the existing literature on serf ownership and aristocracy since it concerns quite different people and estates. Instead, this book addresses related questions in the historiography of Russia, centered around the seeming absence of a coherent middling, conservative landed class.

In other contexts, a landholding class enjoying moderate income and legal privileges is expected to be conservative: it is precisely these people who have the greatest stake in upholding the status quo. Based on the western European model, it is also expected that a middling, propertied, privileged class would grow in influence over the course of the nineteenth century. In Russia, however, the conservative, middle-income, landed gentry never generated much influence on the government or educated public opinion, and in the historical literature they seem almost to have slipped away some time after the emancipation of the serfs in 1861, becoming increasingly indistinguishable from other groups. Many blended in with the rising numbers of late-nineteenth-century professionals; others became impoverished and, despite their legally superior status, lived more or less the same as townsmen or peasants.[15] The chief cultural legacy of the provincial gentry has been to serve as the basis for comic caricatures in the writing of Nikolai Gogol, Anton Chekhov, and other literary masters.[16]

Historians, though, have a growing sense that this seeming absence of the middling gentry in the broader narrative of the Russian empire must be explained. Why did they not serve as that conservative backbone that supports a monarchy or otherwise resists or ameliorates the excesses of either the radical socialism of the intelligentsia or the wanton materialism and superfluity of the aristocratic elite?[17]

This book adds to a body of empirical evidence on this question of the middling gentry by examining the values, ideas, and family structure of one middling gentry family and the village on which they based their ideas about society and nationality. Andrei Chikhachev published dozens of testimonials to the values and virtues of the provincial village that he believed should form the basis of a healthy and ordered national character. These ideas were based on Andrei's understanding of the village as a family, and family for him implied a mother-manager and a father-educator. Andrei valued order and duty, and believed both came from God and therefore could not be meddled with.

Like an upside-down pyramid, his notion of order expanded upward from the male and female parental roles to the village as family, and finally to the nation as a family of villages. Thus, when the emancipation of serfs unraveled the order of life in the village in 1861, Andrei's understanding of nationhood collapsed with it. If the assumptions about order and nature common to those who had no interest in questioning the status quo can define Russia's "conservative backbone," then that conservatism was undermined by the government itself when it emancipated the serfs on terms that forced the sons of middling provincial landlords increasingly out of landholding and into the professions. The "importance of the woman of the house" (Andrei's words) was that the wife and mother as estate manager was the point of the upside-down pyramid on which the weight of the provincial gentry's ordered view of the world rested, and that model, too, collapsed with the emancipation of the serfs and a great part of the mother's role.

1

A Provincial World

NATALIA IVANOVNA CHERNAVINA married Andrei Ivanovich Chikhachev in 1820. She was twenty-one years old, he was a year older. They had probably known each other most of their lives, since they were both raised in the same circle of gentry families residing on rural estates in Vladimir province. At twenty-two, Andrei Chikhachev was already retired from military service in the empire's capital, St. Petersburg, and had inherited his family's ancestral property, centered on their residential estate of Dorozhaevo. Andrei was an orphan, raised by relations after his parents' premature deaths. By the time of his marriage he was in the process of taking over full control of the family estates from his older brother, Ivan, who had been declared a "wastrel." The takeover required a complex legal struggle, but ultimately Andrei won control of the property by assuming an enormous loan to buy out his brother's share, leaving him with a mortgage on 90 percent of the serf "souls" now belonging to him.[1]

Natalia's family background was more stable: she was one of four children and the only daughter of a navy captain. Natalia was raised on an estate called Berezovik; when she married she was given substantial properties as her dowry, including a small estate bordering Berezovik called Borduki. She and Andrei spent time there each year, staying close to the Chernavin side of the family. At the time of her marriage, Natalia's younger brother Yakov was probably not yet in service, and he may have already been friends with Andrei Chikhachev, possibly helping to facilitate the match with his sister. In any event, at least by 1830 Andrei considered Yakov a dear friend as well as a brother-in-law. After Yakov retired from the navy and came home to Vladimir province in 1833, he settled at Berezovik and enjoyed regular visits and correspondence with the Chikhachevs until his death.[2]

Andrei and Natalia endured many trials in the first few years of their marriage. In addition to the arduous process of settling Andrei's inheritance after his "wastrel" brother died, they lost their first child, Anna, in infancy in 1821. The next year, Natalia's father died. In 1823 they moved temporarily to Moscow, to pursue ongoing legal battles over Andrei's inheritance, now including a separate case related to his aunt's property.³ By 1824 Andrei recorded that they had the "happiness" to see Emperor Alexander I in person in Vladimir, indicating that they had moved back home by this time. In 1825, the same year that Emperor Alexander I died and a group of elite army officers revolted over the matter of succession and a constitution, the Chikhachevs welcomed their first surviving child, Aleksei, in early September. A few months earlier, in April, Natalia's two eldest brothers, Aleksandr and Pavlin, died in a boating accident (ironically, after they had both retired from the imperial navy). Three years later, in January 1828, Natalia's mother Aleksandra Nikolaevna died. The only member of Natalia's family living in Vladimir province at this time was an enigmatic figure named Timofei Ivanovich Krylov, who was referred to as "uncle" by the Chikhachevs and by Yakov Chernavin, though his exact relationship to the family is unknown. He may have been Aleksandra Nikolaevna's second husband, and thus Natalia's stepfather. Whatever the relationship, he was a part of the family until his death, in the late 1830s or early 1840s.⁴ By the end of the first decade of their marriage, Natalia and Andrei welcomed their second surviving child, Aleksandra (on October 26, 1829), and embarked on a second stage of their lives together, bringing to a close the family sorrows of the 1820s.

In the 1830s and '40s, the two decades most thoroughly documented in the surviving diaries and correspondence, the Chikhachevs concentrated on raising their children and paying off the debts encumbering Andrei's inheritance. At this time Andrei described himself to Yakov as "your dashing brother with a broken tooth, graying sideburns and a small ginger mustache."⁵ He was also nearsighted and wore spectacles.⁶ No description of Natalia or the children survives, although they sat for a family portrait painted by a local artist, Ivan Ilich Orekhov, in 1831 and daguerreotypes were done in 1842; none of these have surfaced.⁷ By Andrei's description, Yakov was a "small, stout, corpulent little man."⁸ Six years younger than Andrei, he was a lifelong bachelor. Andrei teased Yakov about his unmarried state, joking of buying his brother-in-law "a marital grammar with a 'land-map' attached. The price is nothing, and we'll have a laugh and a discussion, huh? Do you agree? Truly so. Alright, I donate a ruble, you should donate one as well." Yakov responded, "As to the marital grammar, it's n-o-t n-e-e-d-e-d! If god brings me to marry, then the marital grammar will be more engaging—a <u>practical one</u>, but not at all theoretical!"⁹ When Yakov Chernavin retired from the navy and moved back home to Berezovik, he completed the family circle whose activities, values, and ideas are reflected with astonishing detail.

The Chikhachevs' home province had a population in the mid-nineteenth century of just over one million people, making it the twenty-first most populous of the forty-nine provinces of European Russia. Vladimir was located in the northeast quadrant of the giant circle around Moscow considered the heartland of Russia. The provincial capital was the historic town also called Vladimir. A capital city of the medieval northeastern Rusian principalities, it is located 171 *versts* northeast of Moscow (183 kilometers or 114 miles), and in the mid-nineteenth century was considered "near" Moscow as the two cities were connected by an "excellent highway."[10] Other cities in the area include Suzdal, Yaroslavl, Kostroma, and Rostov "the Great," which are all part of the "Golden Ring" of medieval Russian cities with rich historical and religious associations, then and now.

In addition to the medieval cathedrals of Vladimir and other cities, the province's two most prominent landmarks were Lake Pleshcheevo, where Peter the Great learned to sail, and the town of Aleksandrov, where Ivan the Terrible cloistered himself with his *oprich-niki* (a private police force, infamous for conducting a civil war against his nobles). The nearest towns to the Chikhachev estates were Shuia (famous for clean water and vodka) and smaller Kovrov; both towns were also county capitals. The Chikhachevs' main residential estate, Dorozhaevo, was on the east side of the "large country road" from Kovrov to Shuia and was listed in reference sources as relying on ponds and wells for its water supply (it was also not far from a small branch of the Teza river, which the government was trying to make navigable in the 1850s).[11] In a letter to a friend, Andrei described Dorozhaevo as conveniently located, "only 20 *versts* [twenty-one kilometers or thirteen miles] away from Shuia, where you can get whatever you want."[12]

Kovrov lies thirty-one *versts* to the south of Dorozhaevo on the road to Vladimir (55.5 *versts* farther on). The Chikhachevs stopped at Kovrov regularly on the way back and forth to Vladimir, sometimes to visit their friend and religious mentor, Father Sila, and made separate trips there to visit the fair and bazaar. Thanks to Kovrov's present-day local historian, N. V. Frolov, we know something about this town in the first half of the nineteenth century, during which it was mentioned often in the Chikhachev documents. According to Frolov, "the old village of Kovrov was transformed into a county capital town in 1778 by the *ukaz* of Empress Catherine II. Under Emperor Paul I, Kovrov lost its county center status . . . but in 1804 was [again] formally raised to the status of a county center," this time for good.[13] One can understand why the authorities questioned its status, quite aside from Emperor Paul's habit of undoing anything his mother had done: for example, in 1808 Kovrov had only 853 inhabitants. In 1817, well after securing its position as county town, it was still a place of only 117 households, with three stone buildings and four streets. By 1849 the population grew to 1,844, and by 1852 there were 231 households, ten stone buildings, and six streets. This was still very small compared to other towns in the province—less than one-sixth the size of Murom—but "in terms of merchant shops Kovrov took third place in the province up to 1840, behind that same Murom and Pereslavl-Zalesskii."[14]

The presence of these shops would have been no small matter to the Chikhachevs. Their location in this relatively densely populated area, between Shuia and Kovrov with Suzdal and Vladimir not far beyond, meant that they were not as isolated as other provincial landowners and were able to buy daily necessities or find medical care within a relatively easy drive by carriage. Of course, the state of the roads made distances seem greater than they actually were. The Chikhachevs traveled more often and more easily in summer when the roads were dry (albeit dusty) or in winter, when packed snow and sleighs made for a smoother ride. In summer, Shuia was about a two-hour carriage drive away. Several gentry families lived in the immediate vicinity of Dorozhaevo, but the Chikhachevs' closest friend, Natalia's brother Yakov, lived a twelve-hour carriage drive away in Berezovik, surrounded by another cluster of friendly neighbors, so that when the Chikhachevs made this trip, as they did frequently, they visited with families in the town of Teikovo, or at Gubachevo, the estate of the Ikonnikov family (Andrei's cousins). To get to Vladimir, the Chikhachevs traveled for twenty-four hours, including one brief stop to feed their horses and an overnight stop to rest. The trip to Moscow from Dorozhaevo was twice as long, requiring two stops to feed the horses and two overnight stays.

In terms of culture, Kovrov must have been fairly typical of many small towns in central Russia. Frolov provides a vivid description from the diary of Prince Ivan Mikhailovich Dolgorukov, a governor of Vladimir from 1802 to 1812, who mentioned passing through Kovrov in 1813. Upon arrival in the town, Prince Dolgorukov was invited to a merchant's "town house" for refreshments, and there the prince was greeted by "all" the town's "clerks and officials." Though the officials were polite, the governor grumbled that "every one of them had something different on their tongues than in their minds." He went on to describe the town's "beautiful" placement on a hill "washed by the Kliazma," a river at its foot. The town was laid out "sufficiently well, but the buildings [were] in general very poor." He claimed that a "long stone trading row" and a stone building for "Government Offices" were built since he had become governor, and he lauded himself on the speech he gave at the opening for the government building. He then mentioned a "quite new" custom of various social estates giving speeches at town celebrations, a custom already fading again. Finally, the governor was escorted to the outskirts of the town by city magistrates. He stayed that night in a village twenty-five *versts* away called Voskresenskoe, which was "owned by several landlords."[15] Although there were several villages in the area with that common name, the Chikhachevs were one of multiple owners of one of them.

The countryside of Kovrov county was a place of smaller-than-usual villages, averaging around twenty-four households in the 1850s. The county was also known for peddlers, called the *Ofenia*, who sold the products of the province's industries and were famous for their intelligence and craftiness, which extended to the invention of an artificial language to keep their trade secrets from outsiders.[16] On a larger scale than modest Kovrov was Suzdal, a sizable town figuring prominently in the Chikhachev archive. Though smaller than Vladimir at this time and lacking its political importance as a capital, Suzdal shared with Vladimir a rich medieval history and, in the nineteenth century, Suzdal still maintained a flourishing religious culture. It was located sixty-eight *versts* from Dorozhaevo, on the Nerl River. Home to four monasteries and an ancient *kremlin* (fortress), Suzdal also boasted a number of shops and two annual fairs.

By comparison to Shuia, Kovrov, or even Suzdal, the provincial capital at Vladimir was a metropolis. It is situated on top of a long, narrow hill overlooking the Kliazma River, with the twelfth-century "Golden Gates" at the western end and the architecturally and historically significant St. Dmitry and Assumption cathedrals at the eastern end, near the Noble Assembly building, which was a regular stop for Andrei on his trips there. The city was founded by the great medieval prince Vladimir Monomakh, after whom it was named, and was first mentioned in chronicles in 1108; by 1157 it had taken over from Suzdal as the administrative center of northeast Rus. In the twelfth century the Grand Duchy of Vladimir-Suzdal replaced Kiev as the most powerful Rusian principality, but by the fourteenth century it had given way to the growing Muscovite state.

Although imperial Russia's economy was overwhelmingly based on agriculture, this central heartland region was known for poor soil and low crop yields compared to the fertile black earth provinces to the south. Vladimir province in particular contained a mix of reasonably good and quite poor soil for agriculture, with the Chikhachev estates lying in the poorer regions. The province had therefore boasted a disproportionate concentration of small industry since the eighteenth century. Many serfs worked seasonally in these small workshop-factories (in this period, such workshops employed only a few workers each), making yearly or semi-yearly payments in cash or kind to their owners on the *obrok* (quitrent) system, rather than or in supplement to working labor days on their owner's fields (known as *barshchina* or corvée). Much of the land in this area was used for sheep grazing and, where possible, growing flax, which was then turned into linen textiles in the small noble- and merchant-owned workshops. The Chikhachevs raised several food grains and flax for their own consumption and for sale, but most of their serfs appear to have been on the quitrent system, paying in cash, kind, or some combination of both in accordance with the local pattern.

Compared to other provinces, Vladimir struggled economically, but this disadvantage was outweighed by its central location. Describing a visit to the family's remote properties in Simbirsk province, Aleksei wrote to his parents in 1861 that the Simbirsk lands could "be very profitable for us," and—in the midst of witnessing the Emancipation announcement—appeared to him to be their "only hope," since "the land of Vladimir province is not to be expected to bring any income even with a most sincere wishing[.]" However, in "other aspects" their "cranberry province" could not be compared to Simbirsk, where "the land is not enlightened—neither black [peasants'] nor landlords' houses have toilets, and taking a walk out into the field is—with all due respect—not very convenient."[17]

Together Andrei and Natalia owned somewhere between 240 and 350 total "souls" or male serfs, which were legally divided, approximately equally, between husband and wife.[18] These serfs lived in villages throughout Vladimir province, as well as a few scattered villages in Yaroslavl and Simbirsk provinces. Inhabited lands comprised only about half of the Chikhachevs' mutual property. The other properties were forests or uninhabited fields, some of them shared with other landlords, and located, again, in scattered patches throughout the region. An undated listing of Andrei's uninhabited properties stated that out of thirty-three and one-third parts Andrei owned fourteen and three-twelfths. Each part included seven *desiatins,* or approximately nineteen acres. A remaining two and one-half parts were owned by still more "multiple" individuals.[19] Only two of the Chikhachevs' villages, Dorozhaevo and Borduki, featured small manor houses. These were constructed of wood until they finished building a stone house in Dorozhaevo in 1843. By 1863 Dorozhaevo had a recorded population of 142 people, divided into sixteen households. In the same year, Kovrov had a population of more than two thousand people; Suzdal had more than six thousand (with an impressive twenty-five churches and four monasteries); Shuia more than eight thousand (with only six churches); and Vladimir more than thirteen thousand people and twenty-six churches.[20]

The Chikhachevs' secondary residential estate, Borduki, was the one originally attached to the main Chernavin family estate, Berezovik; it came into Chikhachev possession as part of Natalia's dowry. The estates were divided by the small but beautiful Viazma River, and were accessed from the postal road running between Suzdal and Shuia. In 1863, when it was owned by Andrei and Natalia's son Aleksei, Berezovik was credited with thirty-two households, consisting of 92 men and 108 women, and two churches (one of which was probably actually in Borduki, which had been rejoined with Berezovik when Aleksei inherited both properties).[21] One brick church still stands in Berezovik today, but both manor houses are gone without a trace. The Chernavin house had been built by Natalia and Yakov's father, Ivan Yakovlevich Chernavin, in 1809–10. A floor plan of it shows a front façade supported by columns, with the balcony on the back of the house (facing the river). The main floor contained a dining room, study, billiard room, ballroom, bedroom, and sitting room, as well as closets, rooms for servants, a large corridor, and entrance foyer. The second floor featured two unheated rooms and a foyer without windows.

This description indicates that the Chernavin house was comparable in size to the house Andrei and Natalia eventually built in Dorozhaevo. Both houses were no doubt two or three times larger than the largest peasant hut in the village, but they were by no means grand mansions. Nonetheless, they did boast all the necessary comforts for country life. In the years before Andrei and Natalia began building their house, Andrei recorded some of his plans, with accompanying sketches, in the "notebook correspondence" he kept with his brother-in-law, Yakov. Near his plan for the main floor (featuring a half-circular hall, which became the entrance hall of the finished house), he listed his requirements:

First, it must be made of stone, with an iron roof, because this is for posterity, which must value Dorozhaevo for the reason that it was granted to my ancestor by the tsar (as I recall). 2. The house must be as comfortable as possible, so that no lack would be felt if 5 guests stay overnight and so that it does not arouse by its excessive size a vain desire for luxury in our descendants. 3. Don't forget a little pantry, as we did at

Borduki. 4. Heated retiring rooms for both sexes. 5. A sturdy vault for storing papers. 6. Laid out in such a way that if it becomes crowded for some future descendent, there will be room to build. 7. I would like an *Orangerie* in the house, but I'm afraid to allow myself the fancy. But maybe I'll allow it.[22]

Andrei's accompanying drawing features four large rooms in addition to the half-circular "hall, drawing room, every-room"—rooms for himself, his wife, the maids, and an entrance hall. The finished house would also contain a billiard room. Andrei referred often to his own and his wife's "hermitage," which apparently was another way of describing "his" and his "wife's" rooms.[23] In his plan for "his" hermitage, Andrei drew two long "Turkish couches" with small tables, a stone stove, a pipe rack, stools and chairs, two screened-off corners—one for guests' belongings and the other a space for guests to change clothes in, where books and papers would also be kept—and indicated that the floor would be painted. There would be engravings and "portraits of famous people" on the walls, while light in the evening would be provided by lamps.[24] In 1850, after settling in to the new house, Andrei drew a map of his study, where he confessed that he was constantly moving the furniture around (he labeled the map to illustrate the places where furniture had been, and where it was moved to). The room contained a divan and desk, shelves for books and papers, doors into the billiard room, an alcove with a writing stand on a cabinet, a door into the corridor, a stove built into the corridor wall so it could be filled from outside the room, and a mirror.[25] Andrei's ambition for an orangerie was not outlandish; in 1852 the military-statistical survey of Vladimir province reported that "because fuel [was] cheap, any garden of any size has an orangerie with pineapples, peaches, grapes, oranges, lemons, [and] winter strawberries."[26] In short, the Chikhachev house was comfortable and efficiently outfitted for the family's needs, but it was not luxurious.

Beyond Andrei's extraordinarily detailed description of the layout, we even know something about the atmosphere inside the Chikhachevs' home from an 1845 article Andrei published in the *Agricultural Gazette* called "On Indoor Air." He explained that he and his family suffered from stuffy, unclean air for years, battling the problem with incense or *potpourri,* until their daughter's German governess came to live with them. To their astonishment, the German woman threw open all the windows of her room to air it out, every single day, even in winter. But they soon learned, as Andrei took pains to describe, that the difference made by fresh air on the family's health and the pleasantness of the house was well worth such drastic measures as they thereafter took (but always being careful to close themselves up in another, warm room while the airing-out was taking place).[27]

In a "notebook correspondence" with a friend, Vladimir Kopytovskii, in 1850, Andrei drew a map of his estate and described Dorozhaevo's placement as "the very, very least advantageous. Almost flat all around, surrounded almost entirely by forest." The disadvantageous placement of the village is evident to the casual summer visitor today; the area suffers from an unusually intense infestation of mosquitoes and biting flies. Andrei's map of the estate is not clear—the scale is wildly inaccurate—but it gives the viewer a sense of the layout of the estate and lists the principle outbuildings. Andrei showed the house in the center, with a yard and gates in front, facing onto a road leading west and north. Behind the house was a very large "garden" (more than ten times the size of the house, by this drawing), and the whole was surrounded by a bigger box labeled "my estate" (*usad'ba*), meaning their demesne land. Outside this box, across the road fronting the house, there were two very large threshing barns and granaries. On the other side of these, farther to the southeast, were a line of barns for drying wheat; beyond these on both the southeast side and the northeast side were forests. To the south, the forest was combined with swampland. To the east of the threshing barns Andrei drew two "streets" meeting at a wide angle, with a pond between them. To the north of the "estate" proper was another line of barns for drying wheat. Directly to the north, he labeled the next village as Stolbtsy, 1 and one-half *versts* away. To the northwest was the village of Gvozdevo, one *verst* away, and Fateevo was two *versts* away to the west. To the southwest was the village of Senino, 1 and one-half *versts* away, and to the south was the village of Moloshno, one *verst* away. The Chikhachevs owned serfs in Moloshno and Senino, and probably owned fields or parts of forests in nearly every direction.[28]

In an undated note that appears to have been written much earlier than the map, Andrei listed the width and length of several parts of Dorozhaevo, and the number of steps between major points, in the process naming many of the other, smaller landmarks of the estate. The distance from the Dorozhaevo garden gates to the granaries was 104 steps, but his other measurements cannot be reconstructed without more information. Among the landmarks listed are: a "cross-wise allée," a firewood yard, birches, a sundial, "the place where there used to be cherries," vegetable plots, raspberry bushes, a well, blackcurrant bushes, an "apple plantation" (measuring thirty by twenty-one steps), a "covered allée," a carriage house, a cattle yard, and the *banya* (bathhouse), which was thirty steps from the animal-feed barn and sixteen steps long.[29] In their diaries, the Chikhachevs also mentioned a mill, a weaver's shed and other small outbuildings, and various fields for different grains. Today, in addition to the village houses (a few dating back almost to Andrei and Natalia's time), only the Chikhachevs' stone house stands of the buildings that comprised the estate, although a limewood allée is still recognizable, leading to the northwest from the house toward the still-extant pond. The villagers re-member where the main barns once stood, beyond the area that used to contain the garden and which still has a few unusual "English" blooms scattered among the wild-flowers. The church built by Andrei and Natalia's grandson Konstantin was razed to its foundations after the 1917 Revolution and rebuilt into a community center, which is still the building's function.[30] The Chikhachev family grave markers have disappeared, though the villagers claim they were not far from the church.[31]

Despite their provincial existence, the Chikhachevs were not unfamiliar with Moscow. In 1825 Andrei wrote a petition on Natalia's behalf to the Suzdal County Court, which lists her residence as the Prechistenka precinct in central Moscow, in the parish of

Sts. Athanasius and Cyril, under No. 24, "in [her] own house."[32] Since the Chikhachevs lived in Moscow soon after they married, it is possible the house mentioned here was theirs, whether it was inherited or purchased. As late as 1836 they were still trying to sell their Moscow house, as Andrei complained to Yakov that a potential buyer had changed her mind.[33]

Inexplicably, considering both that they were hoping to sell a house in Moscow and Andrei's emphatic views on the advantages of country over city life, Andrei dreamed in 1831 about building a house in Moscow, "which I would build somewhere on the outskirts of the city, God willing. For example, in the vicinity of the Cadet Corps. First, it's close to the Palace Garden. Second, the air is cleaner and safer during epidemics. Third, the land is much cheaper and the house can be bigger."[34] Apparently he contemplated needing a house there someday (probably while their children were in school there) and hoped at least to move to the outskirts that offered fewer disadvantages. They did live there briefly to monitor their children's schooling in 1842, and in 1860 the family contemplated a more permanent move. A letter from their Muscovite friend Praskovia Melnikova told them to rent rooms first and then look for an apartment, since apartments "are very expensive[;] a tiny apartment has no stables and a barn to put carriage and this you need and it will be better as I am advising you to come and rent something and then we can talk where would be better."[35] However, ultimately these plans came to nothing.

The level of detail in Andrei's descriptions of his home represents only a tiny fraction of the documentation left by this family. Andrei wrote more compulsively than any of the others, and it was he who urged their son Aleksei to keep his own diaries. But the record-keeping began before Andrei was born; Natalia's father Ivan Chernavin kept a series of enormous books in which he made detailed notes about the weather and his ship's activities for nearly every day of his naval career.[36] Natalia's brother Yakov was also a compulsive note taker, usually in the form of lists and charts rather than diary entries, until the 1830s when at the instigation of his brother-in-law he began to keep the "notebook correspondence" that passed between the two families almost daily from 1834 to mid-1837. Each household—the Chikhachevs on one hand and Yakov and Timofei Krylov on the other—kept one notebook of a matching pair, so that each had a place to write down any thoughts as they occurred, periodically exchanging the notebooks and commenting on each other's writing. Andrei (the army man) referred to the notebooks on their title pages as the right and left "flanks," while Yakov (the navy man) titled them the "port" and "starboard" notebooks.

Natalia began her record-keeping career with simple accounting lists of credits and debits but eventually expanded these into a series of diaries recording—in addition to the expenses and credits described now in prose—notes on purchases, her own work and the estate work she oversaw, her health, and the comings and goings of her family and visitors. In his turn, their son Aleksei began diary-keeping at his father's behest on his tenth birthday and picked up the habit again during his first summer vacation home from boarding school.[37] He kept one additional diary during his first year of military service abroad, in

Vilno (Vilnius, now the capital of Lithuania). Their daughter Aleksandra, however, is almost absent from the family archive except for references to her in her family's diaries and letters. Most likely her papers were handed down to her sons and were lost. As a result, there are only two documents in her hand: nearly identical, formulaic notes written to her uncle Yakov in the notebook correspondence in 1836, when Aleksandra was seven years old.[38] Some of the later letters in the Chikhachev archive refer to letters she had written, but none of these were preserved.

Andrei explained one purpose of his diaries when he inscribed his short memoir of his religious seclusion (dated 1852–57) with the words, "I beg my descendants to preserve this manuscript, so that perhaps in time it will inspire in someone a desire to emulate [it]."[39] Much earlier, when Andrei invented the "notebook correspondence," he recorded its purpose more modestly, as his first entry in the notebook (February 3, 1834): "No. 1. So it is that these notes can with the passage of time be of interest; and in that case [it would be] very sad if they [were to be] lost; and for this I founded [this] book, which I will always send so that the responses would be written here. And I beg you, *"R-U-D-A-R,"* to start your response here right now."[40] To this Yakov replied, "Eh! *bien, soit* N[o]. 1." A few days later Andrei congratulated himself on his new toy, and presciently noted how interesting these papers could be to posterity:

> Truly I'm a <u>wonder</u> at inventing!!! Look here at all these filled notebooks, and they'll be very interesting for us; and for our children??? and for our grandchildren??? and great-grandchildren???? In 1934, every sheet of our joke <u>Postal Correspondence</u> will be valued at a few rubles. . . . How will this enrich our descendants?? Chernavins and Chikhachevs will be millionaires!!!![41]

Presumably Andrei wrote these words with a touch of irony, having had no idea how true his prediction would become, though not at the time he specified and without enriching anyone. In any case, a little over a year later Andrei disclaimed any interest in being remembered for his own sake, saying, "Would I like to live on in the memory of later generations? But what for? Will it make it any softer for my bones, lying in the ground? Or would it still be possible to hear what people say [of one]?"[42]

Eternal fame, sought or unsought, was not the only purpose or benefit of the correspondence colorfully described by Andrei as their "encyclopedic-mosaic manuscript, or postal notebook."[43] The notebooks also allowed Andrei, Yakov, and Natalia to break out of the strictures of polite epistolary formulas of the time, formulas to which they all adhered in any letters not bound into a notebook, even those written to each other. Andrei, characteristically, found these strictures particularly confining; he was most apt to break them, and even to mock them:

> Well! How very true that our notebook correspondence is sweeter than any formal letters? For me it's true, just so. I can't stand these "kind sirs," "dear friend," "I remain

forever," and so on. What kind of banalities [are these]. It's a different matter to prance around in the paragraphs of our notebook correspondence? Dashingly-wonderfully-importantly-gloriously-miraculously-amusingly-honestly-sweetly-gallantly and forty times trakh-tara-rakh-trakh-trakh!!!!—Ha! Ha! Ha! you kill me, dammit![44]

When his fellow writers lapsed into more formal habits, Andrei admonished them: in 1835 Andrei berated Yakov for using officious language in the notebooks (Yakov had sent some books and used the word "herewith")—"Sir, you must begin more joyfully, more solemnly, more interestingly (don't always be in a hurry, think about it, etc.)"[45] Andrei was draconian perhaps because this informal correspondence was a central part of his life, as he made clear when he wrote the following to Yakov in 1835: "Just imagine this: as soon as I get out of bed, before even washing . . . I take up my pen to manufacture a little article and send it to Berezovik." He anticipated that Yakov would respond, "But isn't it possible to do without this?" and answered the imaginary question, "No, not possible, Sir!"[46]

Early in 1835 Andrei and Yakov realized that they were on to a good thing, and Andrei proposed that they expand on the notion by keeping bound books for their personal notes and records as well as the correspondence (their personal notes had apparently been kept on loose-leaf before this time). These new books would eventually evolve into the "parallel diaries" they would each keep in the late 1830s and, in Andrei's case, through-out most of the 1840s, in which they recorded each day's events in columns divided by year, so that each entry could be compared with the same day in previous years. As usual, the instigator was Andrei, telling Yakov, "If you notice that a Diary is not a bad thing, then would you be well-disposed toward keeping one in a bound book next year (if God allows us to be still living)[?]" Andrei then added a list of the benefits to be had from binding the diaries and keeping them in parallel columns: that it would allow a comparison to previous years, the pages would not get bent, it would "have a respectable look," and if the book were thick enough, it could also be used as a household register.[47] A household register was the kind of book both men had kept previously, which included such information as an index of their libraries, gardening records, drawings and schematics, and reference material copied out of books and periodicals. Yakov responded to Andrei's suggestion with enthusiasm: "I'm entirely in agreement with you that it's much more comfortable, more respectable, more beautiful to keep a book for daily notes in a bound volume! And I find that the thing must necessarily be done." But characteristically he added a slightly dampening note: "It's too bad only that no matter how much I saw such books in Suzdal and Shuia, they all were made of less than medium quality."[48] Quality was important: these books were meant to last, and to be used frequently in the near term.

These entries from the notebook correspondence come only a few pages after Andrei wrote that he had been re-reading his old diaries, and after he summarized a week of entries in his current one for his brother-in-law's benefit. Several references indicate that

Andrei regularly re-read his own papers, and also read Aleksei's diaries. And although Yakov may have gone along with his eccentric brother-in-law at first merely to humor him, he soon adopted a similar enthusiasm for saving and re-reading family papers. In early 1835 he told Andrei how he happened to come across an old "bag" of letters from his mother, brother, sister, "uncle" (Timofei Krylov), and his close friend Nikolai Yakovlevich Cherepanov, adding, "being gladdened by this discovery, I've started re-reading them all, absolutely all of them. It's true this is entirely pleasant—and now from experience I see how good and useful it is to save letters, especially from beloved ones."[49]

Testifying to the self-conscious nature of this family's diary keeping (and the fact that one of Andrei's grandsons, at least, heard his pleas to emulate it), Aleksei's son Kostya (Konstantin) also kept a diary from 1883 to 1885. He began it in fulfillment of a promise to a friend, Nikolai Ivanovich, even though he doubted his own patience and "time and circumstance." He had tried and failed before, when he was "urged on by the example of [his] grandfather" to no avail and "to [his] shame," admitting, "the reason is my foolish laziness." He went on to assure himself, however, that he was as ever "convinced that to write down one's life and all that surrounds one is entirely and completely useful and instructive; writing all the details and even all the mistakes and misdeeds perfects one without one's will, because sometime in the future [one looks back on it] and tries to change oneself." In addition, a diary "helped one to remember thoughts that would otherwise be forgotten, and to try to think about [them] from every side, and if it is necessary then the thought brings about some kind of fulfillment." Konstantin concluded: "I beg, don't judge me too harshly, I will write as I may, although sometimes it will be not very well composed, but hopefully I won't be judged. I write for myself and Nik[olai] Iv[anovich] And so I say in truth I do not at all desire, that anyone [else] would read [this]. K. Chikhachev, 14th of August, 1883."[50] Unfortunately, Kostya's discipline proved less strong than Andrei's, and he gave up on his rather spotty diary after two years, as it turned out to be "very boring."[51] With those words, Kostya brought to an end the family tradition that began with Ivan Chernavin's first naval diary in 1793.

Most of the surviving Chikhachev documents were written between 1830 and 1850, which constitutes most of the reign of Nicholas I. Nicholas has gone down in history as, variously, a despot, an inept micromanager, a family man staunchly upholding the same values made famous by his contemporary in England, Queen Victoria, and a weak, unschooled, unintelligent bigot.[52] He was, arguably, all these things. Nicholas began his reign under a cloud known as the Decembrist rebellion, in which a small group of nobleborn elite officers organized a revolt on the occasion of Alexander I's death, demanding a constitution and the accession of Alexander's second brother, Constantine, in place of his third brother, Nicholas. Unbeknown to the rebels, Constantine had signed a secret document relinquishing his claim to the throne, and Nicholas took his brother's place with the greatest reluctance. He began his reign by ordering his men to fire on the cream of the nobility and officer corps, then sentenced five leaders of the rebellion to hanging, and the rest to imprisonment in Siberia. The hanging or exile of these idealistic young men sent shock waves through the aristocracy. When the exiles' wives voluntarily abandoned their privileged lives (and their children) to join their husbands in Siberia, the Decembrists' aura of tragic heroism took firm root in ground made fertile by the rising popularity of Romantic literature.

Nicholas's reign never fully recovered from this rocky start. Under his predecessor Alexander I, the empire had faced invasion and emerged triumphant as the victor over Napoleon and an unquestioned Great Power in Europe. Domestically, Alexander had failed to live up to his youthful promises to liberalize the monarchy (a prime factor motivating the Decembrists), but Alexander's image remained largely that of the "Blessed One" whose face was used as a model for the angel atop the Alexander Column on Palace Square, named for the tsar and erected in memory of his victory over Napoleon. By contrast Nicholas was seen as rigid and cold. He was particularly despised by intellectuals who resented his restrictive censorship policies. Commercial and industrial investment in his reign stagnated under his conservative finance minister Egor Kankrin, which created a sense of falling behind the rapidly industrializing West. Though Nicholas did recognize the economic imperative to expand Russia's universities, especially in technical fields, the expansion of education was accompanied by stifling censorship and surveillance. Ironically, universities became notorious for producing secretive self-study "circles" of students increasingly open to ideas that the regime found seditious.

Nicholas codified his status quo with the slogan, "Autocracy, Orthodoxy, Nationality," naming the three pillars propping up the empire and known together as "Official Nationality." Implicit in this slogan were the essentially xenophobic nature of "Orthodoxy and Nationality" as the basis for what had been from ancient times a multiethnic and religiously diverse empire, and the fact that the autocracy depended on its military might and ultimate domestic authority to survive. Nicholas managed to avoid major international conflict for most of his reign, but he won enemies all over Europe for his brutal treatment of Polish rebels in 1830–31 (his son and successor reinforced this reputation with a similar response to another Polish rebellion in 1861–63). The Poles wanted liberal reforms and independence; those rebels who survived and emigrated to the West (mostly youthful, idealistic, and Romantic noblemen) brought their accusations of mistreatment to the salons of England and France. Part of the same process that brought on the two Polish rebellions was the so-called springtime of nations in 1848, when nationalists and liberals attempted, but ultimately failed, to topple absolute monarchies across Europe. The rebellions were put down and the old order restored, but sitting monarchs could not but feel less secure on their thrones in the aftermath.

Although no rebellion occurred in Russia in 1848, Russia's monarch had cause to feel even more threatened than others. First, Nicholas enjoyed less restricted personal power than any other European monarch and, along with that, a more notorious reputation for despotism. Second, the Russian empire was the last state in Europe to permit unfree labor on its soil. Although the United States was still a slave society at this time, Anglo-American abolitionism was transitioning from a fringe movement in the early 1830s into a conventional sentiment (outside the American South, at least) by 1860, the eve of emancipation in both the United States and Russia. While Nicholas sat on a throne that was in many ways supported by serfdom, the idea that both absolute monarchy and unfree labor were morally indefensible was becoming widespread in Russia as well as in the West. Yet Nicholas remained to his death in denial that change would come. Instead he held ever tighter to the path of resistance to change on general principle, thus becoming synonymous with European Reaction. At the end of Nicholas's life when the Crimean War (1853–56) demonstrated the apparent ineptitude and decrepitude of the imperial army and navy, his reign came to seem a sham, a facade of bluff imperial chauvinism hiding weakness and incompetence. His heir, Alexander II, was forced to tacitly acknowledge this and usher in the "Great Reforms" of the 1860s, which brought emancipation of the serfs, a modernized judiciary with jury trials, and other liberalizing changes.

Andrei Chikhachev's well-connected friend Aleksandr Merkulov, who served in the War Ministry's Department of Inspection, wrote on the eve of Nicholas I's twenty-fifth jubilee, "this is a great celebration for every Russian." Merkulov's sentiments are comically out of sync with the way historians would remember Nicholas's reign: "How many events have marked this reign; how many reforms carried out, especially in the military—one can say not a single stone remained unturned; how many notable buildings: St. Isaac's is close to being finished; a permanent bridge across Neva—a wonder of art—will be opened on Nov 20; the railroad [between St. Petersburg and Moscow] will be finished by November 1851; how many official buildings are erected everywhere; one can't name everything; history will certainly place this reign along those of Peter I and Catherine II."[53] Far from placing Nicholas alongside Peter and Catherine, history has remarked on the singular *lack* of reform in his reign, the disastrously slow pace of economic investment, particularly in railroads, and even on the remarkable ugliness of St. Isaac's Cathedral. Such is the difference in perspective between conservative people of no particular distinction and the cultural elites who are the sources for much of our history.

The Chikhachevs expressed only unswerving admiration for the monarchy and for the entire imperial family, viewing public events of the 1830s, '40s, and '50s in an entirely different light than the intellectuals of Petersburg or Moscow (or Paris or London or Warsaw). There is nothing in their documents from the mid- to late 1820s referring to the Decembrist rebellion, but given their attitude of reverence whenever anything related to the imperial family was mentioned, news of the rebellion must have been greeted with horror and confusion. The aristocratic youths implicated in the rebellion were very remote from a family as modest as the Chikhachevs. Compared to their provincial lifestyle, the lives of the scions of Russia's wealthiest families were almost unimaginably cosmopolitan, which in Andrei's eyes equated to excess and decadence.

During the period of the first Polish uprising, a cholera epidemic swept Vladimir province; Andrei had his hands full serving as a county health inspector, yet in his diary he followed events in Poland closely, through reports in newspapers like the *Northern Bee* and the periodical for army retirees, the *Russian Invalid*. Later, during the revolutions of

1848 when Aleksei was serving with the Russian army in Poland, the family would anxiously monitor news from abroad. What is more significant than the family's brief commentaries on current affairs in their diaries and correspondence is the fact that they were kept regularly up to date on European events. The spread of periodical publications into the provinces is one of the major developments of the middle nineteenth century that changed the lives of people like the Chikhachevs and their neighbors.[54] While a handful of Russian intellectuals like Alexander Herzen emigrated, resenting their inability to publish their ideas in Russia, provincial readers were for the first time enjoying the privilege of reasonably current access to news, fiction, advice, and fashion trends. That all this reading matter was heavily censored was probably not of much interest to people whose parents had never had access to so many sources of information before, and whose values and beliefs about the world were for the most part already consistent with Nicholas's Official Nationality.

The Chikhachevs' world was largely disconnected from those central political events that form the master narrative of imperial Russian history. The social and cultural historians of recent decades have striven to illuminate many other aspects of Russian society, broadening the narrative to include diverse perspectives. The Chikhachevs' diaries and correspondence add to this endeavor, offering a unique window into provincial gentry society.

2

Society

GENEALOGICAL TABLES OF the Russian nobility include the Chikhachevs among those untitled noble families who could trace their ancestry back to the sixteenth century.[1] The pre-revolutionary *Encyclopedic Dictionary* of Brokgauz and Efron recounts that the Chikhachev family's common ancestor was one Daniil Chikhachev (or Chikhachov) of the late fifteenth and early sixteenth centuries, who owned land in Pskov and Voronezh provinces and was listed in the sixth book of noble genealogy, making him part of the old, prestigious Muscovite nobility. From this Daniil Chikhachev can be traced three branches: one remaining in Pskov and Voronezh, the second appearing in Vladimir province in the early seventeenth century, and the third eventually appearing in Yaroslavl and Vologda provinces. One descendent of Daniil was documented as a general under Ivan the Terrible; this likely marked the highest rank achieved by any of Andrei's ancestors.[2]

In a family tree drawn in his own hand on a page of the notebook correspondence, Andrei traced his branch of the family back seven generations, to an Ivan Chikhachev who lived in the late sixteenth century. This family tree has been confirmed through official demographic and military records as far as five generations before Andrei, to the Matvei Chikhachev who lived in the late seventeenth century and was a landowner in Pustorzhevskii county. He was probably the son of a Stepan Ivanovich Chikhachev who was "killed by Lithuanians at Drutsa" in 1633 and buried in the monastery of the caves at Pskov. Matvei inherited his properties from his childless uncle Luka, brother of Stepan Ivanovich, according to Frolov.[3] Matvei's son Stepan, next in the line, is already listed in official records as a landowner in Suzdal county, Vladimir province, one of the same counties in which Andrei inherited property a century later. This Stepan Matveevich had three brothers; two were also landowners in Suzdal county, and the third served as a mid-level military officer. One of Stepan Matveevich's sons, Andrei Stepanovich, who was born in Peter the Great's reign and died shortly after Catherine the Great took the throne, is the first Chikhachev known to have lived on the estate at Dorozhaevo; he was Andrei's great-grandfather.[4] When Andrei wrote that his new stone house was "for posterity," he emphasized that the value of the Dorozhaevo estate was in part due to its history, beginning as a gift from the tsar and handed down from son to son, each generation hopeful of adding improvements.[5] The Chikhachev to whom the tsar granted Dorozhaevo might have been this same Andrei Stepanovich. Not much else is known about the man, but information becomes more detailed with his son, Andrei's grandfather, Mikhail Andreevich Chikhachev.

Mikhail Andreevich was born in 1729 and died sometime in the last years of the eighteenth century, shortly before his grandson Andrei's birth in 1798. He had been a sergeant of the Nevskii infantry regiment, from which he retired at the age of twenty-three, and he was a landowner in Suzdal and Vladimir counties. He was married to Anna Afanasevna, née Aksakova, the daughter of Afanasii Gavrilovich Aksakov (and thus distantly related to the family that would later boast two famous Slavophiles and a novelist). Mikhail Andreevich and Anna Afanasevna's first surviving child was a daughter, Elizaveta, and their next, their only surviving son, was Andrei's father, Ivan Mikhailovich, born in 1768. He was followed by a second daughter, Ekaterina.

Ivan Mikhailovich Chikhachev served for twelve years in the prestigious life-guards Preobrazhensky Regiment, but retired as an army captain in the entirely unprestigious Vladimir garrison battalion in 1794. The Preobrazhensky Regiment was traditionally officered by scions of old Muscovite families like the Chikhachevs who were not necessarily wealthy but had ancient connections (the wealthiest young men preferred showier regiments, such as the Horse Guards). It was common for officers of the Imperial Guard to transfer to a less prestigious army regiment before retiring, because this allowed them to skip two ranks (one after 1884) and thus retire with a higher rank.[6] Since one's rank was recorded along with one's name in any official documents, and also associated officially with one's wife and children, it was of great social importance. This practice may account for Ivan Mikhailovich's transfer, although he may also have simply wished to be stationed nearer to home.

Ivan married Anna Semenovna Kupreianova and was a deputy of the nobility (subordinate to the marshal) for Suzdal county from 1794 to 1796. He served again in the same capacity for Kovrov county in 1804–05 and was elected for the 1809–11 term, but died in the first year of it. He was a landowner in Kovrov and Suzdal counties of Vladimir province, and in Saratov province.[7] Anna Semenovna died not long after Andrei's birth on February 20, 1798. Ivan and Anna had had one older son before Andrei, Ivan Ivanovich Chikhachev—the "wastrel"—who died in young adulthood. He is hardly mentioned in the surviving family documents. The elder Ivan's property had been divided between

Andrei and Ivan the younger in 1816, but the younger Ivan's portion was taken into trust-eeship in 1818, on the grounds of his "dissolution."[8]

Because of the early deaths of his parents, Andrei was raised—probably from infancy, shortly after his mother's death—by his widowed paternal aunt, Elizaveta Zamytskaia. Her deceased husband, Ivan Glebovich Zamytskii, had been of comparable rank to Andrei's father. He was a retired second-major in 1782, later ranked in the civil hierarchy as a collegiate assessor, and he served Viaznikovskii county as marshal of the nobility (1784–85); he was assessor of the second department of the Vladimir superior *zemskii* court in 1789 and deputy of the nobility for Vladimir county in 1791–96, overlapping for part of that time with Ivan Mikhailovich Chikhachev, then serving as the deputy from Suzdal county. The Zamytskiis owned land in Kovrov as well as Viazniki counties and so were neighbors to the Chikhachev lands.[9] Andrei grew up referring to the Zamytskiis' son Nikolai as his "brother" and remained close also to at least two of the three Zamytskii daughters and their families (they married an Avdulin, a Yazykov and an Ikonnikov, respectively; the latter two families lived near the Chikhachevs and were frequently mentioned).

Andrei would later complain that he had been badly educated, but in fact his educa-tion at a private *pansion* in Moscow was rather impressive for his time and position. As the son of a Preobrazhensky Guards officer, Andrei ought to have had a good chance to join that regiment, but since he entered service in 1813 when vacancies were few (because of the Napoleonic wars, every eligible man was serving), he may have decided he stood a better chance of seeing active duty by taking advantage of his relatively thorough educa-tion. Most regiments required cadets to study academic subjects; the highly regarded Noble Regiment was established in 1808 for young men who were able to pass academic exams immediately, and provided only a crash-course in military arts to allow their cadets to move on to their commissions more quickly.[10] By the time Andrei achieved his com-mission, the fighting against Napoleon was concluded; during the Hundred Days he was briefly commissioned in a bridging company and marched west but went only as far as Poland.[11] So Andrei's "military service" consisted mainly of staying on as a teacher in the same school after his own graduation. In 1818, he retired with the lowly rank of second lieutenant and returned to the estate he had inherited two years before, at Dorozhaevo. His willingness to teach—and his unwillingness to remain longer in the post-Napoleonic army as it suffered through a period of "paradomania" where officers spent most of their time polishing their buttons for parade (to the point that the Semenovskii Guards revolted in 1820)—all attests to Andrei's early interest in education as his vocation.

The Chernavin family, though traced only three generations back from Natalia and Yakov on their family tree, was closely connected to the enormous Khmetevskii and Taneev clans. Both of these families were able to trace their noble names even farther back than the Chikhachevs (twelve and eleven generations, respectively, from Natalia) and had many interconnected branches still living in Vladimir province, so that the names of various Chernavin connections appear regularly in the documents. Through the

Chernavins, Natalia was related to the local Buturlin, Oshanin, and Karabin families, and even distantly related to an Aleksei Nikolaevich Chikhachev, who must have been descended from either the Pskov/Voronezh or Yaroslavl/Vologda lines of Chikhachevs.

Natalia Chernavina was born on August 26, 1799, and grew up on the Chernavin family estate at Berezovik. There is no surviving record of her education, but a comparison of handwriting and syntax suggests that she did receive some formal, secular education at least relative to her mother, Aleksandra Nikolaevna, née Buturlina. Natalia's father, Ivan Yakovlevich, was a naval captain of the second rank (equivalent to lieutenant colonel of the army) and cavalier of the order of St. Vladimir, fourth class. Thus Natalia's background was very similar to that of her husband, both families being comparably ancient but also comparably modest by the turn of the nineteenth century.

Possessing documented noble pedigrees, a coat of arms, and lands granted to their ancestors by the tsar, the Chikhachevs recognized their membership in a community of privilege. At the same time, they also recognized their exclusion from the worldly "society" of the capitals and the empire's wealthiest aristocrats. The Chikhachevs' engagement with their social estate and the larger world beyond their estates was limited. They depended on their connections to the noble patronage network for at least one highly important need: the launching of their children into schools, marriages, and military service. Aside from this vital purpose, however, the Chikhachevs' association with their social superiors in the capitals and in the tsar's service was almost nonexistent. Although their legal rank was the source of their right to own land and serfs, the Chikhachevs' identification with the noble estate was, for the majority of their daily lives, limited to their participation in a much smaller social network composed mainly of the provincial landowning gentry.

This provincial network, maintained by complicated ties of friendship, family, favors, debt, and commerce, in meaningful ways extended beyond its gentry leadership to include state officials, merchants, petty industrialists, doctors, students, teachers, people of religious vocation, and impoverished nobles without land or serfs. Although non-nobles interacted with the landed gentry on deferential terms and largely in connection with commercial, religious, or official transactions, such transactions also took on a social aspect in the insular world of the provinces, and together the gentry and the other free estates in the provinces shared common interests, needs, and fears.

Russian society in the nineteenth century was legally divided into an estate-based hierarchy with the emperor (*imperator* or *tsar*) and his family at the top, followed by: the hereditary and personal nobility (*dvorianstvo*); townspeople (*gorodskie obyvateli*), including "honorary citizens," merchants, "burghers," called *meschane*, and artisans; non-noble but free persons falling between the cracks of the official ranks, known as the *raznochintsy*; and peasants (*krestianstvo*, a category which included state peasants, "palace peasants," noble-owned serfs, and some free settlers of remote areas or non-Russian regions).[12] Nobles were further subdivided according to the fourteen ranks of the official Table of Ranks adopted in 1721 (ranks one through eight conferred hereditary nobility in the early nineteenth century, while the remaining ranks conferred only personal nobility). The Table of Ranks included a parallel hierarchy for the military and the imperial court. The clergy (known collectively as the *dukhovenstvo*) had ranks ranging from the patriarch down to village priests, deacons, and various ecclesiastical servants like bell-ringers.

Technically, all the nobility, regardless of place in the Table of Ranks, fell into the legal category "*dvorianstvo*," which does not correlate exactly to either the English "aristocracy" or "gentry"; thus the Russian word is most accurately translated as the more general "nobility" in parallel to the terms used for continental European privileged classes.[13] In the middle of the nineteenth century, the total number of Russian nobles was more than 900,000, or "one noble for about every eighty inhabitants in the empire."[14] This catch-all legal category of "nobility" was divided by income, lifestyle, and social and professional opportunity into (1) an urbanized aristocracy; (2) a landed gentry; and (3) a service elite whose incomes frequently did not match their officially high legal status. The middle group, which included the Chikhachevs, grew throughout the nineteenth century and is often described more accurately in Russian works as the *pomestnoe dvorianstvo* (provincial gentry) the Russian label conveys the crucial fact that these people's lifestyles and incomes derived from their estates, or *pomestie*.[15] Those nobles who owned approximately five hundred or more serf "souls" (a legal term meaning one male serf), and who were thus likely to live away from most of their estates and probably part-time in cities, made up about 3 percent of the total noble population, or almost four thousand landowners. The middling category, those who owned between one hundred and five hundred souls, were approximately 16 to 22 percent of nobles, or between 17,000 and 20,000 individual owners. The remaining roughly 80 percent of all nobles were those who owned fewer than 101 souls, and could thus be described as poor (between 80,000 and 100,000 individuals). Many of the people in this third category would have been "personal nobles," who earned their rank through service and whose nobility was not hereditary.[16]

In Vladimir province, the total number of nobles in 1852 was 5,104, making up only 0.004 percent of the total provincial population of more than one million. This group was divided almost in half between hereditary and personal nobles, but these numbers include the children of personal nobles (who were not technically noble themselves). Of the 2,610 hereditary nobles in the province, only 320 had the right to vote in noble elections (this right depended on service records and property ownership). According to the nineteenth-century guidebook that provided these numbers, the majority of hereditary nobles in Vladimir province owned property "only in this province, and have their residential estates there." The majority of these residential landlords were also retired from service, "mostly occupying themselves with their estates."[17]

Outside of the circle of relations and neighbors living in the immediate region, the Chikhachevs maintained ties through correspondence with a vast network of extended relations and old friends in distant places. Beyond ties of affection and family connection, this network served to extend their reach into the circles of patronage that were necessary to social and financial advancement (through both service careers and marriage), to the guarantee of help in cases of disaster, and to the successful navigation of any complex bureaucratic endeavor (such as civil court cases, property transfers, or for some nobles, securing a government contract or concession). Andrei maintained his place in this all-important network through daily correspondence and by granting favors as well as asking for them. The first certain instance in which Andrei called upon the gentry patronage network was to make sure that Aleksei would get a place in the fairly prestigious Noble Institute, a school in Moscow (Aleksei wrote at the time: "In the evening Papinka wrote many letters about me to Moscow").[18] In this realm, Andrei's letter-writing talents were an invaluable asset to the family (when Yakov's abrasive neighbor Kashcheev went personally to St. Petersburg in 1837 to "grab" an officer's commission for his son, Yakov remarked disparagingly that "it is unlikely that he will succeed!").[19]

After Aleksei finished his formal schooling, Andrei started his second letter-writing campaign to secure his son a place in an army regiment. The first step, apparently, was to provide Aleksei with a respectable official post, a boon for which Andrei was willing to pay cash. In December 1845, he used his connections in the Kovrov town government to assign the twenty-year-old Aleksei to a position at the Chancery of Kovrov County Court as an "Honorary Inspector of Shuia County Schools"; in exchange Andrei agreed "to disburse annually for the benefit of the Shuia County School 200 silver rubles" (an amount that could double the annual salary of a regular county-level civil servant).[20]

Not long after, Andrei called upon his mother's family, specifically General Pavel Kupreianov, to get Aleksei assigned to a regiment stationed with Kupreianov's headquarters in Vilno, where the general could continue to keep a watchful eye on Aleksei's welfare and eventually appoint the boy as his adjutant. Kupreianov was the son of Andrei's mother's first cousin, but Aleksei called him "dear uncle."[21] Aleksei was not actually permitted to enter service, however, until Andrei submitted his own service list or discharge orders to the Department of Inspections.[22] It seems Alekei's entrance into a good regiment depended not only on having contemporary connections to that regiment but also on the service record of his father.

Although Andrei's efforts achieved a fair measure of success where Aleksei's career was concerned, there was a limit to how high he was able to reach. In 1860 Andrei sent a letter to Princess Sofia Grigorievna Volkonskaia, a member of one of imperial Russia's wealthiest and most influential families. The Volkonskiis owned estates in Vladimir province but rarely visited them, and it is likely that Andrei never personally encountered any of the family. On this particular occasion, he wrote to inform the princess that one of her peasants had "insulted" his son. He received the following reply:

Dear Sir Andrei Ivanovich,
Her Highness Princess Sofia Grigorievna, being not entirely in good health, delegated to me to respond to your letter from 20th day of past January, in which you complain about the insults inflicted on Your son by her peasant Nikolai Alekseev.

In this regard, I have the honor to inform You, that, not having found it necessary to conduct a special investigation of this matter, given that I quite have confidence in the circumstances described by You,—I at the same time gave the necessary instructions towards the satisfaction of Your son, of which he is notified by a separate letter.

With sincere respect I have the honor of being Your, Dear Sir, humble servant.

Steward-in-chief of Her Highness' estates

Moscow, 10 march 1860

This document is notable in a number of respects. First, it seems strange that Andrei should consider an "insult" inflicted on a nobleman by a peasant as worthy of notice, or, if so, that it could not be handled satisfactorily when it occurred (although the word "insult" may imply a physical assault, perhaps sufficient cause to demand formal redress). Second, the princess did not deign to reply personally to Andrei's letter, even though she might as easily have signed a letter composed by a secretary in her name. Even though Andrei appealed to her personally at her residence in Moscow, she ordered her steward to respond; this unequivocally positions Andrei's complaint as that of a person of lower order—it was a business matter rather than a personal, social matter in the eyes of the princess.

Although she and Andrei unquestionably shared the same legally privileged status, the princess just as clearly did not consider a man of Andrei's low rank and wealth to be her equal. Even the princess's property manager apparently considered his position high enough to look down on Andrei: his description of Andrei's letter as a complaint is condescending, as is the manner in which he generously explained that he would accept Andrei's word on the matter against that of a serf, when Andrei's legal rank alone should have made that acceptance automatic. Finally, it is significant that Andrei wrote this letter on his son's behalf about a matter that involved only Aleksei, who at the time was thirty-five. Allowing for the fact that as an adult Aleksei remained somewhat dependent on his father, it seems likely that when one called upon the patronage network, one used the best ammunition one had to hand; the highest ranking or most well-connected individual would be more likely to succeed in a request than someone with lower status. In this case, it appears, Andrei's status was sufficient to reach a resolution, but not so great as to avoid being further insulted in the process.

Another example involves a friendly relationship rather than a conflict and reinforces the substantial difference in status between wealthy nobles and the provincial gentry. On an 1861 trip to the family's Simbirsk properties, Aleksei described the people he became friendly with on his long journey. These included the retired Guards officer Nikolai Toparin and his son Petr, who at fifteen had just entered Kazan University. The father, an owner of three thousand serfs, had recently returned from a trip abroad with his son and was joining him in Kazan, leaving his wife and daughter behind in St. Petersburg. Aleksei enthused naively that Toparin's house (in Kazan) was "better than the governor's mansion in Vladimir." Aleksei enjoyed getting to know this much wealthier man, who for some reason was traveling second-class: "it was so pleasant for me to spend three days with them in the second-class compartment that you can't even imagine, we talked and played cards, and laughed at all kinds of things, everything was plenty, Nikolai Fedorovich himself is a great talker and orator, surpassing our Bezobrazov and likewise for a while served as the County Marshal of the Nobility, but did not get along with provincial authorities."[23] Toparin seems to have been happy to patronize the younger nobleman; certainly Aleksei's attitude is one of awe and admiration, not just at Toparin's entertaining conversation but his mansion, and, reading between the lines, his generosity toward the more modest provincial.

It appears that just two aristocratic clans—the Naryshkins and the Saltykovs—with their many connections and lesser branches ruled over the entire noble patronage network, requiring even the lowliest nobles to seek protection under one of the two great umbrellas in order to contract advantageous marriages, obtain services positions, pursue law suits or in other myriad ways navigate the old regime system.[24] As the Volkonskaia letter shows, there was certainly a hierarchy within the noble estate, and those who did not know their place in it would be made to see it. The wealthiest and most powerful nobles patronized lesser gentry like the Chikhachevs much the same way that Andrei patronized the most responsible of his serfs, and probably as his serf patriarchs patronized the lesser members of their own households and villages. The nature and structure of authority was replicated at every level of society, and it was enacted, justified, and constantly renewed through the complex negotiation of favors, rewards, and loans—and through the punishments incurred by those who did not play the game of give-and-take according to the unwritten but well-understood rules. Middle-level families like the Chikhachevs must have known that it was the 5 percent of wealthiest noble families— owning more than half the serfs in the empire—who, while they did not control the state itself, certainly did control the daily operation of patronage, the army, and the bureaucracy. And it could not have been clearer to these much less wealthy gentry families that their own status, outside their villages, was decidedly farther down the scale.

Patronage was hardly unique to the Russian nobility, of course. Patronage as "generalized sponsorship" is common to almost all societies, especially societies with marked degrees of inequality.[25] Perhaps the chief difference between Russian patronage and the system that operated in contemporary Britain, for example, was the centrality of politics in the latter setting. The misuse of patronage for political advantage has been the basis of negative public perceptions of the concept.[26] Although patronage certainly could be political in Russia, far larger numbers of people had a great deal more experience of patronage as a helpful way of navigating an under-administered society.

A letter from Andrei, written in 1866, demonstrates again the vast distance between a modest provincial landowner and an urban noble with greater status, in this case a Moscow doctor holding the rank of a general of the second or third class, Vasilii Pavlovich (Vlasov or Basov, the signature is unclear). Andrei began his letter obsequiously: "The seventy-year-old elderly man writing this is kneeling and begging You about a great favor." Andrei sought the opportunity to visit the general in Moscow to show him his grandson, Ivan Rogozin, then eighteen, who was severely debilitated by a leg injury caused by a fall from a carriage a year previously. Closing with the hope that the doctor would at least be able to relieve an old man's mind, Andrei added a postscript, sincere but also clearly calculated to play on the doctor's sympathies. Only two days previously, Andrei wrote, he had lost his wife of forty-six years, his family's "care-giver," and "[o]n her deathbed she grieved much that her grandson had to stay a cripple for his entire life. Akh, I wish that God gave her joy at least in the heavenly abode by the possible assistance to him, through beneficent science, through which you have dedicated yourself to suffering humanity." The doctor returned Andrei's letter with a note in the margin: "I have the honor to respond that in all likelihood in December I will be in Moscow. Your obedient servant." The doctor's note was politely phrased, but the simple annotation to a long, heartfelt, supplicatory letter is evidence of an unbridgeable social distance between the two men.[27]

Patronage failed Andrei completely on another occasion, presumably due to his lack of connections and his unwillingness to spring for a bribe. When Andrei sought to explore his family's ancestry through the Heraldry Office, he wrote, "I think that . . . my documents will be put away for a while: for without an adjective you will not find a noun." This was his quaint way of saying the office would expect something more from him. Though Andrei had the required certificate from his local Marshal of the Nobility and the thirty-ruble fee, "at the Heraldry they won't take the white twenty-five ruble note. There you'll need digits with two zeroes; and this won't do for me."[28] One's ability to use the patronage network was limited by one's pocketbook as well as one's relative rank.

Compared to the aristocratic high nobility, much less is known about more modest nobles like the Chikhachevs and their friends who lived exclusively in the country and exercised little or no influence in state affairs (young country-bred men usually serving in the lower ranks of the officer corps and retiring early). By putting together anecdotal references in the Chikhachevs' papers and the letters they saved from their friends and family, along with the data collected by Andrei, reference books of the period, and work published by Andrei's twentieth-century counterpart N. V. Frolov, it is possible to formulate a fairly wide-ranging picture of life for this provincial gentry society.

The nobility of Vladimir province was a vanishingly small portion of the overall population, and only half of them were hereditary nobles, comparable in rank to the Chikhachevs. The majority of these were what Andrei called "men of rather medium means," referring to province-bound noblemen like himself.[29] Landowners in Vladimir province were overshadowed by merchants and industrialists, but seven noble estates were highlighted in 1852 as the "best cultivated" in the province, including two owned by Chikhachev relatives (Taneev's village of Kstovo and Yazykov's Minakovo). These were singled out in part for their large amounts of livestock, which helped to enrich the soil, in some places improving its quality enough to match even "black earth" regions. At an 1846 exhibition, Taneev and a few other outstanding landowners (including a Prince Golitsyn) received prizes or commendations for successfully producing heavy-weight grain crops.[30] A different Taneev estate, Marinino, was described by Frolov as "one of the main centers of social life in the district." This estate's mistress, Natalia Taneeva, had an impressive library on her estate and was a donor to an 1832 project to establish a provincial library.[31] Though heavily outnumbered, these modest nobles were not without pride or innovative spirit.

In 1850, in his notebook correspondence with Astrakhan landlord Vladimir Kopytovskii, Andrei copied for his friend a list of all the villages and landowners of Kovrov county, providing an invaluable demographic picture of the noble population in this much smaller geographical unit, the equivalent of an English or American county.[32] Andrei listed a total of seventy populated villages, of which twenty were owned by the state. Speaking of both the state-owned and privately owned villages together, Andrei added that some of these con-tained as many as 650 peasant households, but that most contained from three to fifty households. The fifty villages owned by private landowners were divided among 159 families (villages were often broken up into households, fields, and forests owned by different people due to partible inheritance and the sale of partial properties). Andrei noted that of these 159 landlords, only thirty were resident (including the Chikhachevs). However, the 129 "absen-tee" landlords included five names belonging to people who were certainly resident in their villages in bordering counties.[33] The absentee list also included a Count Sheremetev (a member of the wealthiest family in the empire) and ten princes or princesses from other leading families (Volkonskii, Vorontsov, Viazemskii, Golitsyn, Gorchakov, Dolgorukii, Shakhovskaia, Trubetskaia, and Dashkova) and Princess Eletskaia, the last surviving member of an ancient but not particularly wealthy or influential clan. Also among the absentees were members of the well-known Musin-Pushkin and Pestel families. Only one titled owner (a Princess Gundorova) was listed as a resident landlord. From the entire list, twenty-six names are also mentioned regularly elsewhere in the Chikhachev archive as acquaintances, friends, or relations. Of this group, ten were residents and sixteen listed as absentee.

Andrei recorded each of these names in either the feminine, masculine, or plural form. Since he listed his own family in the plural, it seems likely that the female names on the list indicate widows, unmarried women, or women whose husbands were not present because of abandonment or state service rather than women who controlled their own separate estates or their family's estates while their husbands were present, as Natalia did. Of the total list of 159 landowners, seventy-four were male, forty-seven female, twenty-eight (including the Chikhachevs) were listed in the plural, and ten are foreign-derived names that cannot be declined according to gender or number. These data confirm sev-eral suppositions about landownership in nineteenth-century Russia: (1) most villages were owned by several unrelated persons; (2) many landowners were at least technically absentee (though only a small percentage of them were the extremely wealthy absentee landlords who may never have seen most of their estates and lived very far away); and (3) a large proportion of landowners were female.[34] The fact that Andrei distinguished between masculine names and plural ones also demonstrates that he acknowledged the fact of joint ownership by married spouses, perhaps hinting that other wives, like Natalia, were managers as well as owners.

Of the families that appear most frequently in the Chikhachev archive, there were neighbors like Maria Petrovna Izmailova—whose estate bordered Berezovik and who was apparently a widow—and the Kashcheevs (a family with several "young ladies" who frequently visited the bachelor Chernavin), the Pozharskiis, the Cherepanovs, and the Ikonnikovs, who also lived near Berezovik, and the Kultashevs who owned the village of Zimenki, 6.5 *versts* from Dorozhaevo. All of these families were mentioned as frequent visitors and friends. The Ikonnikovs and Yazykovs were the Chikhachevs' closest friends, owing some of their closeness to their blood relationship by way of the Zamytskii clan.[35] The one son of that family—Nikolai Zamytskii—was a bachelor, always referred to as "brother" by Andrei and Natalia and "uncle" by their children. His estate at Domnino was also only a few *versts* away from Dorozhaevo, in the opposite direction from Zimenki. His three sisters married into local families, and two of these were the Ikonnikovs and Yazykovs.[36] Both the Ikonnikov and Yazykov families were large, and their many children were the companions of Aleksei and Aleksandra Chikhachev.

From the account of historian Nikolai Frolov a detailed picture can be reconstructed only of the Kultashevs of Zimenki, which draws a picture of family life so different from the Chikhachevs' that it is revealing as a contrast. The Kultashevs' home, neighboring Dorozhaevo, boasted two brick churches by 1850, the second built thanks to Andrei's fund-raising, as well as Andrei's public library (founded in 1854), housed in a separate building between the two churches. Frolov writes that in the 1830s and 1840s two brothers, Vasilii Mikhailovich and Ivan Mikhailovich Kultashev, were living in Zimenki with their families; both of their names appear regularly in the Chikhachev documents. The generation before and after these brothers were both quite scandalous. Mikhail Vasilevich Kultashev (1747–1824) was the father of the brothers Vasilii and Ivan. Mikhail was a county marshal of the nobility for two years, and it was he who built the first stone church in the village. Mikhail never married, but he produced five children by four different household serf women. He acknowledged all five children, and they all inherited property as children of a legitimate marriage would have done, and were recognized as members of the noble estate. Vasilii and Ivan were the sons of a woman whose name is recorded only as "Pelageia." They had two half-brothers and one half-sister, each of whom had a different serf mother recorded by first name in their documents.[37] Ivan Kultashev (born 1798, died after 1847) married Anna Aleksandrovna Merkulova and had a son named Mikhail Ivanovich, born in 1820 (a contemporary of Aleksei Chikhachev). Mikhail Ivanovich grew up to become a lieutenant in the Belevskii infantry regiment, retire, and marry a Vera Apollonovna. Mysteriously, on December 25, 1851, he was killed in a duel. His opponent, a bachelor named Vasilii Evlampievich Kashintsev (also born in 1820 and a member of a family well-known in the district), was "fatally wounded" in the duel, dying on April 8, 1852, after an extended illness. The duel is not mentioned by any of

the Chikhachevs so there is no way of knowing how the neighborhood scandal was received at the time.[38] What is certain is that whatever taint may or may not have attached
to the products of alliances between nobles and serf women, it did not prevent friendly
and open relations between the Chikhachevs and their neighbors, or apparently Ivan
Kultashev's ability to contract a respectable marriage—unless his marriage was what pro-
voked the duel.

Life in these rural counties was not untouched by the long arm of the imperial government. Provincial governors were the highest representatives of state authority in the
provinces. They came and went, and were often not local residents. To be effective in
implementing the circulars they were constantly receiving from the central government in
St. Petersburg, they depended on locally elected representatives ("marshals") of the
nobility. Most respected provincial noblemen would serve at one time or another as a
marshal at least at the county level and those of greater local reputation at the provincial
level. They were elected by their peers, though candidates had to be approved by the
governor in order to take office. Andrei's father had served as a county marshal of the
nobility, and so did his adopted father, his uncle Ivan Glebovich Zamytskii. Other marshals
of the nobility for Vladimir province included members of several other families related to
or friendly with the Chikhachevs.[39] Andrei himself, seemingly too much a homebody and
amateur scholar to involve himself in active politics, nevertheless avidly followed and
voted in county and provincial elections, and during the cholera epidemic in 1831 he served
his county as a temporary health inspector.[40] A letter from Aleksei from the spring of 1861
notes that his in-laws, the Boshniaks, were particularly successful in attaining public office:
Aleksei's brother-in-law Nikolai Konstantinovich was a representative of the government
in the Kostroma provincial peasant committee, while his father-in-law Konstantin
Boshniak was a peace mediator (these were noblemen appointed by governors to ensure
the smooth implementation of the serf emancipation of 1861 by apportioning land, serving
as local justices, and supervising local peasant communities). Aleksei remarked simply,
"These Boshniaks have me beat!"[41] The family Aleksandra married into, the Rogozins,
were similarly active, though usually only as county marshals of the nobility.[42]

The Chikhachevs and Chernavins, however, followed provincial affairs from the sidelines, which apparently involved being occasionally pumped for cash. In 1837 Yakov
received a letter from the provincial marshal of the nobility asking for donations to build
a guard house for a local monument: Peter the Great's boat, at Pleshchevo Lake near
Pereiaslavl. Yakov was happy enough to comply to the tune of "3 blue banknotes" (fifteen
rubles), but, typically, he couldn't send the money until the road dried up. "[N]ow the
road is at a standstill—they say—it's very, very bad!"[43]

The provincial gentry were also involved, increasingly over the nineteenth century, in
local associations such as agricultural societies, Bible societies, "patriotic" charitable societies, and others that were neither political nor truly independent but were nonetheless
lively gatherings of like-minded men, and even sometimes women. The Women's Patriotic Society, for example, was founded in St. Petersburg in 1812 and soon branched out

into several provincial capitals; it lasted as a continuous entity until 1825.[44] Andrei was a member of the Vladimir branch of the Moscow Agricultural Society, a large-scale voluntary organization devoted to spreading the gospel of rational agriculture and, beginning in the 1840s, increasingly interested in supporting peasant literacy; it was this group that provided significant support and inspiration for Andrei's founding of the public library.[45]

Writer and historian Nikolai Karamzin famously claimed that "even those who are wealthy do not purchase newspapers."[46] In fact, the provincial gentry were thoroughly engaged in public intercourse through an active and independent print culture. They read all the major journals and sometimes contributed articles or letters, mainly to lesser journals published in their provincial capitals. In addition to the Chikhachevs' own reading, Andrei and Natalia left a record in the "notebook correspondence" of a constant sharing of periodicals and books among a wide circle of acquaintances. One issue might be passed along to as many as six or more different readers, including acquaintances outside the immediate family circle such as Honorary Citizen Karetnikov, and Andrei was known to exchange books with everyone from the Marshal of the Nobility to the parish dean.[47] The Chikhachevs and their neighbors valued having access to a constant supply of news and literature, some of it foreign. In addition to periodicals, they also ordered books by mail from merchants in Moscow or St. Petersburg, or commissioned friends to buy them.[48]

Reading must have served in many ways to compensate for the fact that private travel beyond one's home province was expensive and usually limited to occasional journeys to Moscow for those who lived in the central provinces. During their military service the sons of the provincial gentry were likely to see the two Russian capitals, if not to travel extensively abroad with the army or, as Yakov Chernavin did, with the navy.[49] Aleksei Chikhachev would eventually see much of Poland during his military service, being stationed for a year in Vilno, several months near Warsaw, and another month in Liublin province.[50] The Chikhachevs lived in Moscow temporarily twice; the first time early in their marriage, and the second time in 1842 when their children were attending schools there. In addition, Natalia traveled there with the Ikonnikovs for a shopping trip in 1831, and Andrei sometimes accompanied Aleksei there when he went to attend school, and they probably took other occasional short trips there that went unmentioned. On only one occasion, in 1842 after their debts were paid, the Chikhachevs were able to take a significant unnecessary journey with only a single purpose: their family pilgrimage to Kiev. Financial constraints would have prevented most families of comparable income from traveling more extensively than the Chikhachevs did, and very likely many families traveled less; not everyone would have been as much of an enthusiast for travel as Andrei was. When Andrei recorded every significant journey he had made in his life, he also complained of the discomfort of having had to do all this traveling in a carriage—suggesting another reason why the middling gentry, less able to command luxury in vehicles and accommodations, was less likely to travel widely than their wealthier counterparts.[51]

Letters served as a way for the gentry to associate with one another when travel was impractical or prohibitively expensive. Letters served to keep scattered relatives and acquaintances informed of family news, conveyed formal congratulations and good wishes on every major religious holiday, birthday, and name day, and were a means of exchanging news about local politics, gossip, or events such as weddings, deaths, or fires.[52] A study of epistolary fiction in Russia has suggested that the postal system was less reliable across the enormous distances and bad roads of imperial Russia than it was in western Europe at the same time (and that for this reason epistolary culture was not as well-developed there).[53] Judging by the Chikhachev documents, however, the postal system had either vastly improved since the eighteenth century (though the roads did not), or this was a mistaken assumption. Certainly, complaints about the unreliability of postal systems are common wherever such systems exist, and no doubt letters did occasionally go missing or take too long to travel the hundreds of miles separating Russian towns and villages. However, the Chikhachevs and their neighbors sent letters, packages, and even cash by mail regularly—letters at least were sent or received several times a week—and their concern about the fate of these mailings was minimal.[54] They were also able to send letters and packages privately, via serfs or friends who happened to be traveling in the desired direction. Given that they owned serfs in scattered villages, there was almost always someone traveling from Dorozhaevo on any given day when the roads were in good condition. This method saved the cost of the official post and made the most sense for messages sent short distances (the nearest post office was in Shuia), but apparently it was rather less reliable than the postal service, since the courier in question (whether serf or noble) was liable to be delayed or distracted by other errands.[55]

Those of the middling gentry who desired to compete with their richer peers in material consumption must certainly have fallen quickly into the category of impoverished nobility or, like Andrei's brother, perhaps left their debts to be paid by others, as some husbands in this situation chose to disappear, leaving their wives with the burden of debt.[56] Andrei and Natalia owned a respectable number of serfs, but they lived in an agriculturally unproductive region, and as a result their income seems to have been just sufficient to support a modest provincial lifestyle similar to that of their neighbors and relations (requiring occasional small loans to bridge the gaps between seasonal windfalls). One 1822 financial calculation made by Andrei gives a snapshot of their finances. He listed incoming sums totaling 14,786.50 rubles for the month of March. From this, 2,451 rubles were needed to make their debt payments to the state and to an Avdotia Semenovna, leaving 12,335 rubles "left for living expenses." The sums in the credit column varied from 644.50 assignat rubles in cash on hand (gold, "old rubles," and small change were not counted), to 110 rubles of "arrears from Foma, ransom for girl," to payments due from various peasant villages for unlisted reasons, ranging from 40 to 1,157 rubles, to more than 6,000 rubles due for winter quitrents (a portion of which was overdue since September), to small debts paid by various people, probably peasants, but also one Konstantin Petrovich (200 rubles) and 50 rubles of "Mother's debt," as well as 2,287 rubles for "canvas, rams, mushrooms and sieves."[57] A less detailed evaluation from early 1834, in Natalia's account book, shows that at that time she had 1,265.85 rubles in cash. In addition, each child had their own savings—Aleksei had 127.24 rubles and Aleksandra had 120.35.[58]

However limited their income was compared to the wealthiest Russians, Andrei claimed in a letter to his brother-in-law that the necessary sacrifices were a worthwhile price to pay for country life. Underlining the words, "Too bad, that I'm not rich, and [it's] good that I'm not rich," he continued, "I have one saying: 'All for the best!' To grow up in the fields of Dorozhaevo or Borduki is gold, pearls, diamonds . . . if only I don't have to buy my bread or argue with the Board of Trustees [who administered the Chikhachevs' largest debts], I will buzz, 'All for the best!'"[59] Beyond the mere words, enthusiastic as they are, the fact that Andrei continued to make sacrifices in lifestyle and to extol his comfortable rural existence after his debts were paid off suggests that he sincerely valued rural peace over riches. In an article written for more public eyes, Andrei wondered who had time for fashion, and then stressed the imprudence of overspending in circumstances where unplanned expenses could arise at any time: "buy this, buy that in the most favorable time, and what if someone falls sick, or there is a bad harvest, or something burns down! My God! How can one even think about wasting money and wasting time?"[60]

Despite their prudence and economy the Chikhachevs managed to enjoy some imported goods, particularly the occasional bottle of champagne or other French wine; usually they drank "ordinary" red or white wine, purchased in Shuia, locally produced fruit or honey wines, or vodka.[61] Natalia prized small cigars and snuff obtained in Moscow. Andrei and Yakov preferred pipes and were not so choosy about tobacco, but Andrei was a connoisseur of unusual seeds and flower bulbs from the empire's commercial capital. In May 1836 Andrei asked Yakov to loan him some "white Holland paper in the large format," for writing "lengthy" letters or to important officials. Yakov sent him the required paper, adding, "I'm certain you'll be pleased; it's so good, you could even write to the tsar. I bought it in Naples."[62]

In 1835 Yakov sent his father's mirror to Andrei as a birthday present. At the same time he also sent "a pair of 'Voltaire's chairs'" for Andrei and Natalia. The first gift, at least, was a family item and so might the chairs have been. Gift-giving was not an occasion for conspicuous consumption here.[63] Even less so on another occasion, when a sweet "surprise" made by Timofei Krylov for Yakov was the lettering of the cover for Andrei and Yakov's signal book for their homemade telegraph system—it said "Telegraph" in gold. Yakov was "delighted."[64]

Occasional luxuries were indulged in, as when in Vilno Aleksei got a sample of "a new fashionable mantilla" to send to his "dear sister to show what is being worn here."[65] But even luxuries were purchased on a modest scale. The same artist who painted the family's portrait was commissioned to paint St. Mitrofan for both the Chikhachevs and for Yakov. Calling the painter, whose proper name was Orekhov, the more familiar "Orekhych," Yakov asked Natalia how much she had paid "Raphael" because the painter was coming soon and Yakov could not remember the agreed-upon price. Natalia replied that he should pay "three quarters," only seventy-five silver kopeks.[66]

With so few indulgences, these were clearly not people who defined social success or status in terms of expensive foreign goods. In fact, there is no indication in any of the Chikhachevs' writings that they ever bought an item, or considered one superior, by virtue of its foreignness alone. It was accepted that some goods were made best in certain places (champagne in France, paper in Holland, vodka in Shuia), but most goods could satisfactorily be obtained locally, including most of the materials for their clothing, some of which were created on their own estate, and almost all of which were sewn up or knitted there, sometimes by Natalia herself. On one of the rare occasions when Andrei confessed to a spending spree, the purchases included a "wonderful vest made of black silk," and the goods totaled a significant 180 rubles, but they were bought from a Leontii Fedorov, a peddler from nearby Suzdal.[67] On another occasion, a food peddler visited the estate on Palm Sunday, and Andrei celebrated by buying "caviar, lox, capers and olives," concluding in his note to his brother-in-law: "Come by to have some!"[68] The Chikhachevs' table, at least on holidays, did not suffer from monotony, but as imported luxuries go, capers and olives are modest and may have been grown in one of the southern parts of the empire rather than abroad. The sense of excitement was similar when the twenty-two-year-old Aleksei purchased, on his way to Vilno, an "entire case" of gingerbread cookies made in Viazma, which, with those from Tula, were among the most famous gingerbread cookies of the time.[69] In still another instance, Andrei declined an opportunity to purchase from a peddler "marvelous" rugs that had been produced in Chernigov province and ranged in price from one hundred to four hundred rubles. Andrei's grounds for saving his money appear to have been moral: the peddler, Efim Filipych Gromov, "with a huge mustache and a very long beard," was "drunk to the extreme."[70]

The fact that the Chikhachevs bought relatively few imported goods, then, was as much a result of conscious preference as financial constraint. Or rather, the two factors were inextricably linked. Foreign luxury goods were, naturally, tempting, but the excess of spending on imported luxury items reportedly so characteristic of aristocratic dandies and ladies in St. Petersburg was beyond them, while local goods usually provided sufficient pleasure. So they prioritized their major expenditures, and often the purchases that were most important to them conferred basic comfort and security rather than outward status. Andrei confirmed this explicitly in his article about the building of their "stone house in the country," in which he explained that the undertaking was motivated in part by Natalia's health, apparently compromised by the drafts and other discomforts of their original wooden home. He concluded his article with an assessment of what he sacrificed in order to build the house—"[c]hampagne, pineapples, English blood horses, works by Italian artists tempt me just as much as any other person"—and why the long period of sacrifice was worth it: "I don't dare resolve to do anything without my treasure-box [Natalia]. I prefer her health to all fun little diversions; whenever she has spasms and hysterics, I can't do a thing."[71] The Chikhachevs considered the stone house necessary to their basic comfort and so they sacrificed luxuries to achieve it.

The exchange of errands and commissioning of purchases among friends as well as servants was an intrinsic part of daily life in this rural environment. For regular transactions, Natalia commissioned her husband, a trusted serf (male or female), or a friend who happened to be traveling in the required direction (or even, in at least one instance, the local stationmaster).[72] This system of exchange was effective and socially gratifying; the participants had surprisingly easy access to a wide variety of material goods through this extension of each family's reach, and they obviously enjoyed the many short, neighborly visits that the system entailed. When the Chikhachevs were at Borduki, the exchange system was made more efficient by the homemade telegraph they shared with Yakov at Berezovik (the system was arranged on their balconies, which faced each other across a small river; signals were raised like flags on a ship and read through a telescope on the other side; later they invented a nighttime version, using candlelight for signals).[73] The Chikhachevs also relied on their immediate social network for small loans, influence, advice and help of all kinds during times of financial hardship or ill-health. Advice went both ways: in 1850 Andrei received letters from two "nephews," brothers Mikhail and Nikolai Fedorovich Stepanov of the village Dobrokhotovo, near Kineshma, who hoped to engage Andrei's attorney Zarubin for their upcoming litigation.[74]

The Chikhachevs borrowed money from friends like the Ikonnikovs and, especially in their later years, they also loaned money to friends and relatives.[75] In 1833 Natalia listed her debtors in her account book. Altogether she was owed 117 rubles from six different people, with sums ranging from eight to fifty rubles. The man who owed fifty rubles is also the only name that is recognizable from the Chikhachevs' social circle—Dmitry Vasilevich Chernev. This suggests that Natalia loaned money to people she did not necessarily know well, and to people from different social estates, very likely including peasants (one name on the list, "Gus," seems a likely candidate, the others are too abbreviated to allow for an educated guess as to social origin).[76] Recent research into imperial Russia's debt culture confirms that people who were not necessarily close by relationship or status commonly borrowed money from one another.[77] Other debts were family matters; in addition to the debts the Chikachevs inherited from Andrei's "wastrel" brother, they took on a debt owed by Natalia's mother to the Board of Trustees at the time of her death. This debt was finally repaid sometime before July 1850, and an overpayment of 41.08 silver rubles was sent back to Natalia in August.

In 1860 Aleksei related to his parents how a friend, Nikulin, had given him one hundred silver rubles to deliver to Liudmila Vasilevna Kultasheva, but Aleksei, living in Vladimir for a week and a half "with horses"—that is, at considerable expense for their maintenance in town stables—was forced to spend the cash placed in his care and wrote to his parents begging them to forward the amount to Kultasheva themselves, subtract it from his allowance, and send him the receipt.[78] By the 1860s Andrei and Natalia, then in their sixties, had become respected elders of their community, and many of the letters they received in those years requested favors or advice from one or the other of them, depending on their realms of expertise, as in the following letter from a Kultasheva (possibly the same Liudmila Vasilevna whose money Aleksei was spending), which conveyed to Natalia a complicated dilemma involving a wet nurse. Liudmila Vasilevna was responding to an inquiry from Natalia asking "whether we are happy with our wet nurse": Natalia was perhaps looking for a new wet nurse for her latest grandson. Liudmila Vasilevna reported, "the old one left, and God with her, they say she is of bad behavior—she has a lover in Shuia, who does not allow her to be a wet nurse." But this unsatisfactory woman had already been replaced with a new one; "this [other] woman seems to be good and quiet, I don't know what will happen next."[79] She hoped Natalia could advise her.

The friendly interdependence between the Chikhachevs and Chernavin illustrates how people in the provinces managed without the institutions and intermediaries present in towns. In April 1836 Yakov wrote to the Chikhachevs (specifically addressing both Andrei and Natalia), asking to borrow fifty rubles to pay the sawyers "immediately," because "they finished their work and want to go!" Yakov apparently had sufficient cash ("by your grace," so possibly thanks to a previous loan), but it was "under arrest" in his dresser, the key to which he had misplaced. Natalia replied that she was sending "with great pleasure" a curious mixture of coins: eight ruble-coins, three half-rubles, seven thalers, and one five-ruble gold coin. Yakov replied with "many thanks" and updated his sister to say he had paid the sawyers but still could not find his key. Then, presumably in part to show his gratitude, he invited the Chikhachevs over for a meal, and sent a carriage to pick them up.[80]

Although interdependence among provincial neighbors conferred many advantages, it could also cause conflict. Astrakhan landlord Vladimir Kopytovskii's ownership of some of his lands was contested by a neighbor in the early 1830s, and in connection with that dispute, the "guardians of that estate cut down some wood"; as a result Kopytovskii reported being "in trouble with the forest service" as late as 1850.[81]

Sometimes conflicts were raised to the level of tragedy. A particularly pathetic example of noble debt is provided by Andrei and Natalia's creditor, A. Nosova. In March 1850 Nosova wrote to Andrei to beg him to pay the interest he owed, or even to repay the principal on his debt early. She hoped to engage Andrei's sympathy on her behalf, and her list of problems is extreme indeed. As she wrote, "this . . . was the time of my grievous existence; in six months I lived through over 10 years' worth of misfortunes and everything terrible that a human mind can imagine has happened to me." Her troubles began with a month-long fever, then "a bilious inflammation from which [she] almost died." While she was ill a servant girl left her alone in a huge house that was "cold like Siberia." Her hands and face were "covered in scales," probably chilblains. On the advice of her doctor Nosova then moved, encountering several other troubles in the process. Then at the new house she allowed ("because of [her] stupid nature") a visit from a "Nikitina from Voronezh" who owed her money. Nikitina's servant girl robbed Nosova "of everything," including jewelry and 550 rubles in cash. Nosova was "unable to find any kind of justice anywhere." Making the rounds of various authorities, she encountered only "all kinds of rudeness, saw all kinds of humiliation," as well as suffering hunger and exhaustion from her efforts. This drove her even to feel "like little ants were running on [her] head," and she was again living in very cold quarters, requiring her to sleep in heavy outerwear. She tried several inns, which were expensive, and one had wet firewood.

This astonishing list of troubles, Nosova assured Andrei, was "only a brief description of [her] life." She was borrowing money to support herself, and listed at least 450 silver rubles owed at 35 percent interest to, variously, a doctor, a priest, a "salon," "Meshcherskii," a shop owner "on Ilinka," and the "Zakharins." She had already pawned her silver and shawls, getting six hundred rubles for them. She feared imprisonment for debt if Andrei did not pay her what he owed early. Moreover, she had lost status as well: "people will never value me now I don't have . . . linens, . . . don't have dishes, don't have dresses, and don't even have my daily bread." Nosova concluded her sad story with a claim that she not only ate from a wooden spoon—as opposed to silver—but that the spoon was frequently empty.[82]

Nosova appealed also to Natalia, sending her respects and promising to write, and she wrote that she had even cornered the Chikhachevs' son Aleksei during a chance encounter in Moscow (he was then just twenty-five and unable to help her). Andrei's sympathy was engaged—but his lawyer told him that even if he repaid the principal it would not help Nosova, as the money would go straight to her creditors and could not be used to help with her living expenses. Despite two letters on the matter from Efim Zarubin, Andrei's attorney, which were passed back and forth through Agrafena Vasilevna Kultasheva, it is not clear in the end when Andrei paid off his debt to the unfortunate lady.[83]

The Chikhachevs related to their neighbors, friends, and relations according to an exchange of give and take that allowed all the participants to make better use of the available resources in their relatively small world of the province. However, relations among fellow landowners were only one part of this network of exchanged goods and services. Equally active in it, though operating according to more complicated rules involving deference and commercial transactions that overlapped with purely social exchanges, were the large numbers of people who held mixed or blurred social rank.

In the country, families like the Chikhachevs socialized not in high-profile salons but informally, in their own drawing rooms. And, more often than with fellow nobles, they talked and read aloud with serf nannies, village priests, tutors, and governesses. Some of the nobles they knew were not local landlowners but military men who passed through (Yakov once wrote tellingly, "Drunk hussar. Drunk hussars.")[84] They also did business and socialized with doctors, lawyers, merchants, and industrialists. Such people were a large segment of the local population. In Kovrov county in 1852, there were 130 male merchants, 472 male *meshchane* (burghers), and 39 persons "without rank" of both sexes; five foreigners were living in rural areas, suggesting they were probably tutors, governesses, or stewards. The Military-Statistical Survey of the province distinguished between a long-established, multigenerational merchant population from Murom, Viazniki, and

Melenki counties, and newly rich merchants of peasant origin centered in the area where the Chikhachevs lived, around Shuia, Ivanovo, Teikovo, and other industrial villages. The older merchants specialized in linen and leather works, but their businesses were declining by mid-century. The newly enriched peasant-merchants, according to the survey, owed their success to the relocation of factories to their region from Moscow after the great fire of 1812. Cotton manufacture was brought to Shuia county (depending on cotton imported from England) and spread outward from there. The survey was critical of the "*hauteur* and luxury" indulged in by the *nouveau riche*, which it claimed brought some to bankruptcy. This official criticism may or may not have been connected to the fact that many of the merchants were Old Believer sectarians, while local feasts still evinced signs of pagan roots.[85]

In her study of nineteenth-century advice literature in Russia, cultural historian Catriona Kelly identified a process of social "homogenization" in which the tastes and activities of Russians who were educated and owned property—but who were not part of titled aristocratic society—tended increasingly to merge into a common culture of "gentility" comparable to that which emerged in Georgian England in a slightly earlier period.[86] There is considerable evidence for this phenomenon in the Chikhachev documents: the family associated as frequently with the clergy, doctors, merchants, artisans, students, "honorary citizens," petty bureaucrats, officials, legal practitioners, and manufacturers of nearby small towns as they did with their social peers outside of their own family and closest circle of friends. Many of their interactions with non-nobles would have been on matters of business, but as in the English case, the lines between business and socialization were blurred when a merchant or clerk came to a rural estate to conduct his business, and his visit therefore involved considerable time and the informal chat, refreshments, and civility that such occasions demanded.[87]

Yakov recounted in the notebook correspondence how he first met "Mr. Bistrom," physician to the vastly wealthy Count Sheremetev. The count had invited his doctor to Ivanovo, but his instructions for him had not yet arrived, so the physician did not know what to do and was traveling around the area acquainting himself with local landowners (presumably to build up a practice), and in this context called upon Yakov. To Chernavin's consternation, the doctor stayed on and on through the afternoon, then, finally, took Yakov aside and asked to borrow twenty-five rubles to pay his hired driver. Yakov refused, but notably he did so on the grounds that he did not know enough about the physician, rather than his inferior rank: country relations were based on reputation and the interdependence of those who lived together in relative isolation from outsiders.[88] Yakov later wrote in his diary that he had dinner with Bistrom and his wife, so they grew closer with time.[89]

In May 1850 a letter from Andrei's lawyer, I. Gruzinov, contained an offer to make purchases for the Chikhachevs because the lawyer was able to get a "good price" from vendors by buying bulk. In the same letter Gruzinov responded to two inquiries from Andrei, one related to his delivery of a refund from the Board of Trustees, and the other about whether the board was aware that Andrei had given part of his property (including sixty-nine souls) to Aleksandra as her dowry, which would reduce the amount Andrei owed.[90] Another letter in June was accompanied by a quarter-pound each of five types of tea, along with a note stating prices for coffee and sugar.[91] It is not clear whether it was considered normal for a lawyer to carry out unrelated errands, or if the Chikhachevs were friendly enough with Gruzinov that the lawyer was doing them a personal favor, as a friend or neighbor of their own rank often did. Either possibility is striking.[92]

In other cases, there is not enough context to know the nature of relations between the Chikhachevs and a visitor from the middling ranks, as when Andrei briefly noted that "The Jew from Shuia has fixed the wall clock" in 1837.[93] Or when a "free practicing land surveyor" named Ivan Nikonorov Speranskii was mentioned as living in Shuia the same year.[94] But thanks to Aleksei's boyhood interest in the emerging industrialization of the region between Vladimir and Yaroslavl, his reports of his family's visits with people from the merchant or industrial world do exist. In one instance, he mentioned visiting an Honorary Citizen, Stepan Ivanovich Karetnikov, in Teikovo, a small town. On another occasion Aleksei noted that on the way home from a journey to Berezovik the family stopped to "ha[ve] tea in the village of Voskresenskoe with the manufacturer Levikov."[95] And on a trip to Shuia to see off "Dear Uncle" Yakov and bring Aleksandra to see a doctor there, they "stopped by the cotton mill of the merchant Posylin, where everything is run by steam engine."[96]

What is most notable in these notations is that, at least in the first two examples, the visits were social: they "went to . . . Karetnikov's" and "had tea" with the "manufacturer Levikov." In the third case it is clear that their attraction was the steam-driven cotton mill, and they may not have been directly acquainted with the "merchant Posylin" before this visit (not to mention the clearly professional visit to the doctor, presumably at his office, though his office was likely also his home). The visits with Karetnikov and Levikov suggest, though, that it would not have been impossible for the Chikhachevs to simply socialize with the merchant or the doctor. In any case, these examples, together with Chernavin's narrative of the traveling doctor's visit, imply that much more than straightforward, impersonal commercial transactions lay behind the hundreds of other instances throughout the Chikhachev and Chernavin papers when individuals of middling rank were mentioned without description of the nature of their visits. Significantly, the majority of such individuals were mentioned as visiting the Chikhachevs or Chernavin at their homes, not vice versa; such visits, even if motivated entirely by official business, necessitated at a minimum that the visitors be offered refreshments. If the visitor had traveled far enough to need to spend the night, he might also be entertained and given a bed.

In addition to their relations with merchants, townspeople, and officials, there was another category of people with whom the Chikhachevs interacted daily, often with some degree of intimacy, who ranked below the nobility and above the peasants—the local clergy and their families. The Military Statistical Survey of 1852 listed 16,727 clerical

persons in Vladimir province, of whom "very few" were of noble origin.[97] Natalia
frequently recorded visits from the wives of the priests of Dorozhaevo, Zimenki, Borduki,
or Berezovik, both during the day and in the evening when the whole family was present.
Both Chikhachevs corresponded regularly with Father Sila from Kovrov, a well-known
figure in the area.[98] And Andrei frequently mentioned consulting, arguing, or just passing time with various clerics on his travels. Not all the priests—probably not most of
them—were able or willing to engage with Andrei philosophically, but inarguably they
were part of the social landscape. In 1837 Yakov mentioned a priest from Afansevo who
had stopped by Berezovik on his way back from Teikovo, "he came already tipsy, just
before dinner, and after eating left right away."[99] One is tempted to assume that his timing
in arriving just before dinner was not accidental. A few years later, Andrei wrote of comradeship between himself and Father Aleksei, the village priest of Zimenki (where Andrei
would found his library)—Andrei had been retired from the army and resident in Dorozhaevo already thirty-two years, and the priest had been installed in Zimenki for forty
years. This probably made the two of them the elders of the neighborhood. Andrei also
noted proudly that he read church books so often that Father Aleksei asked him to do the
reading for services rather than the designated deacon.[100] And in 1859 Andrei published
an article called "Village order: On the subject of bringing together nobles and clergy."[101]

In October 1834 Yakov recounted a tale involving several local priests: a Father Matvei
traveled to Vladimir, hoping to witness a visit from the sovereign. While there he bumped
into Vasilii (probably a serf), who told him Father Ivan was hoping to do the same.
Matvei, knowing it was his week for services, "lost his courage . . . fearing that in the
absence of them both there would be some religious need," so he left Vladimir without
seeing the sovereign. As it turned out, Father Ivan never intended to go anywhere. This
left Matvei's wife with "a horrible grievance against him that he did not get the business
done and spent a considerable amount of money." Besides suggesting that gentry women
were not the only wives with their hands on the purse strings, the anecdote portrays these
local priests as responsible and well-meaning, in contrast to much nineteenth-century
literature that used village priests as comic figures (a device common also to Jane Austen,
so hardly a commentary on Russian peculiarities).[102]

Still another category of rural residents with whom the Chikhachevs interacted were
what they called "poor nobles." The Chikhachevs' relations with these people were charitable, not social. In her account book for 1831–34, Natalia noted small sums given out to
poor nobles, such as the 2.31 rubles given to a "poor officer" in December 1831.[103] And in
August 1840, Yakov gave 1.75 rubles for [or to] "poor nobles," as compared to the 2.50
rubles he spent in September for six jars of pomade.[104] Charity to poor nobles was not
always in cash. In November 1835 Natalia gave a poor noblewoman ten *arshins* of canvas
and two rolls of thread as well as eighty-eight kopeks. A different poor noblewoman,
Aleksandra Gavrilovna Khreshchova of Kostroma province, was invited to stay with the
Chikhachevs.[105] The distance between those who had means and those who did not
clearly was more salient than their technically identical legal status.

Nobles whose status had even recently been equal but whose fortunes had changed soon found themselves outside the society of property owners. In 1850 Andrei's friend Vladimir Kopytovskii of Astrakhan province discussed the prospects and background of his eldest daughter's potential suitor. Wanting to find out "what kind of dashing fellow this is," Kopytovskii made inquiries. Some news was good—the twenty-five-year-old "local nobleman" had studied at the University of St. Petersburg and held the rank of Collegiate Secretary (tenth in the table of fourteen ranks), serving as "senior aid to the secretary of the Astrakhan military governor," with a salary of six hundred silver rubles. This meant to Kopytovskii that the young man had "a head on his shoulders rather than a watermelon." Unfortunately for the young man, however, he had "nothing more than that." Kopytovskii discovered that the man's father had lost his fortune in "speculations related to fisheries," rendering the son no longer eligible.[106]

Andrei's childhood friend, Pavel Timiriazev, gave an account of his life in a letter from 1850 that gives a more detailed example of how easily one's status could tumble. Timiriazev was the father of seven children; three sons were commissioned officers, the fourth a cadet. Two daughters were in a school in Moscow "under their mother's oversight." But their father stated that he had not seen his children—nor presumably his wife—in five years, and his youngest daughter had been "taken up by her [maternal] grandparents" from the age of two. The grandparents provided for the girl and, Timiriazev added, "for different circumstances we do not recognize each other when we meet." Timiriazev had lost his estate "through misfortune." He had attempted to buy a village "for half price" by assuming an existing mortgage with the Board of Trustees of the Imperial Orphanage. He signed the papers, but it turned out that the estate was already under trusteeship (presumably for delinquent debt), making any private sale illegal, a fact that was "concealed" from him. He moved to the new estate with all his property four months before the sale was final, having paid thirteen thousand rubles (it seems Timiriazev sold his own "family estate" to a Mr. Novikov before attempting to buy the other). He was then "dragged around the courts," and in the end the estate was sold to another buyer and all Timiriazev's property "disappeared." With all of his property gone, Timiriazev was hoping to make a living as a police chief in some town. He had been wounded in his army days but had not asked for a pension; he hoped under these circumstances he would be granted a position instead. He concluded his letter hoping he could rekindle his friendship with Andrei, but hesitated, not knowing if Andrei would "be glad to see him."[107]

In short, the Chikhachevs' relationships with the community of free persons around them was a curious mixture of egalitarian and hierarchical currents. On the one hand, they engaged in the traditional Russian world of extended noble clans, whose more successful branches comprised the aristocratic nobility of the capitals. Middling landowners like the Chikhachevs were legally equal, as members of the noble estate, to any Volkonskii, Golitsyn, or Buturlin. At the same time, their interactions were thoroughly unequal, for the Chikhachevs had to rely on their more powerful acquaintances to provide for their children's educations and to secure their careers or marriages. In turn, the wealthier nobility could and did treat families of the Chikhachevs' rank in much the same way as Andrei treated his more reliable serfs. The provincial landowning gentry who were the Chikhachevs' equals in all respects were the people with whom the Chikhachevs engaged in a lively intercourse through informal sociability, travel, letters, and reading culture (although even within this group there were subtle differences of rank bestowed by age or experience). The middling landed nobility were the natural leaders of their provincial world as masters of their serfs and as the occupiers, especially after the reforms of the 1860s, of a variety of elected offices. They enjoyed superior legal rank and privilege over their non-serf and non-gentry neighbors like merchants, industrialists, professionals, clergy, or lower-level state officials or poor nobility, but at the same time they shared with those people a common culture and interests.

3

The Village

THE NOBLE PATRIMONIAL estate—including the landlord's household with its farm holdings as well as serf-populated villages—was the center of the Chikhachevs' world. For Natalia, the estate delineated the sphere of her authority as *khoziaika*, or lady estate manager. For Andrei's male world, rural village life was the mainstay of any moral, or as he put it himself, "conscientious" existence, and it was the source of his uniquely Russian identity. In the social order of the small Russian village with resident landlord, the landlord's paternalistic authority was complemented by the equally essential and strictly defined responsibilities of the *khoziaika* and also by a number of intermediary figures who occupied places of more limited power. The estate thus comprised a continuum of authority, with the male patriarch at the top of a many-layered hierarchy. The well-established roles through which the noble family channeled its authority imposed significant limitations on each person's exercise of power and thereby contributed to social stability throughout the empire.

To be sure, the power of noble estate-owners like the Chikhachevs over their dependents was immense, including a formidable array of disciplinary measures. Technically, Russian serfs were not enslaved: they owed taxes and military service to the government and thus had a different legal status from slaves elsewhere. By law they were officially tied to the land they worked, rather than directly to their landlords. Serfs could be legally mortgaged, sold, gifted, or inherited by their landlords, but by this time only by households and together with the land (although loopholes, of course, existed). Legal niceties aside, the incomes of people like the Chikhachevs derived from the labor of unfree people, and Andrei was aware of the moral dilemma upon which his idealized village rested. He did not romanticize the peasants or their plight, as some Slavophiles or anti-serfdom advocates did. Unlike either of those groups, Andrei lived closely with most of the peasants he owned. His writings show that he recognized the complexity and precariousness of a serfdom-based economy and social order, while remaining dependent on it and acknowledging that his power to alter this system was limited.[1] He recognized above all that social order, safety, and prosperity were all dependent on a system of negotiations and compromises, which, while fundamentally upholding the authority of the serfowner, nevertheless limited his authority in practice by demanding that he adhere to unspoken but well-established hierarchies, fulfill certain obligations, and limit his demands.

The Chikhachevs lived exclusively on the fruits of their serfs' labor and, like other landowners, were fully aware of their vested personal interest in making their serfs as productive as possible. In particular, Andrei was aware of having inherited his estates from a long line of ancestors and felt strongly his own obligation to pass this property on to his heir in as good or better condition than he had inherited it.[2] The Chikhachevs evinced the "enlightened seigniorialism" that inspired wealthier landlords to vast projects of improvement, regularization of rules, and formalized hierarchy on estates in the late eighteenth century, though naturally this Enlightenment impulse took a somewhat different and more direct form in the more modest context.[3] However, most prominent of all in these documents is a deeply felt paternalism that colored all the Chikhachevs' relations with their peasants and justified, at least in Andrei's mind, his ownership of human beings, while also motivating him to strive to improve the lot of the whole village—which he understood as the larger unit encompassing nobles, clergy, and peasants.[4]

When Andrei set out to describe his way of life in the village for readers of the *Agricultural Gazette*, he did it in terms that portray Dorozhaevo as an oasis of paternal (and sometimes maternal) benevolence and friendly communal relations. "On our land," he began, "everyone bows [in politeness]: you will meet neither an old man nor a boy, who, when meeting you, will not take off his hat and bow. This custom I support— How?—with my own bow, with a loud greeting—so that the others may hear it." He described how involved he was with his peasants and everyone else in the village: "I get into a conversation not only with my peasants, but with others as well," offering advice ("[I] constantly tell them—'when you are at a loss about what to do, come to me, talk about it, I will not misadvise you'") and worrying when someone failed to make a regular appearance ("I send a messenger"). In cases of illness, it was his lady's place to intervene: "Whenever someone falls sick, the mistress gives the medicine." Natalia was also noted as a benefactor to children: "Our youngsters don't hide in the corner, rare among them [is one who] does not have a ring from the mistress, or earrings, a belt, a kerchief, a red shirt."

Andrei claimed that village life was symbiotic: "Having condemned myself to permanent life in a village in order to avoid debts and needless worry, we have long become close to the common folk; we know each other well and see significant mutual advantages." The landlords opened their doors to the village regularly, at "[e]ach first day of the month, at the blessing of the waters, and before one of the twelve feasts [of the Orthodox calendar] or the tsar's day, [when] there is an all-night vigil at our house." Concluding his account, Andrei gave in to hyperbole, "I don't think there is anything more majestic than an orderly, neat, religious management of one's property," explicitly attributing this "majestic" management at least in part to "mix[ing] with the gray-coats [peasants]." Further, he "must do them full justice for evaluating our kind without error," but he did not specify what the peasants' evaluation was, precisely; he only corrected himself, saying that he referred specifically to peasant elders, "who are sober, energetic, having earned the respect of their kind; and in this land they are not rare."[5]

It is significant that Andrei's account of village life emphasized "mutual advantages," "respect," "religion," "order," and "neatness." Although this description must be understood to represent Andrei's ideal rather than a reality the peasants might have recognized, the passage is nevertheless striking as a form of rhetoric about serfdom that was not employed by wealthy absentee landlords (much less so by their paid managers). This was a point of view that could be entertained only by a landlord who lived among his peasants, and indeed Andrei stated that his understanding was based directly on his lived experience in the village. Similarly, he claimed that his peasants' respect for him was based also on their experience of his treatment of them.

Clearly the purpose of publishing this account was, essentially, to advertise Andrei's point of view—to urge that other landlords consider their estates in the same light. However, Andrei's voice was far from a lone sound in the darkness. The *Agricultural Gazette* had many contributors like Andrei, most of whom were preaching attitudes similar to his. And his own attitude had not developed solely from his direct experience; he discussed conditions and strategies with his neighbors, and eventually with the other members of the Vladimir branch of the Moscow Agricultural Society. In the 1830s and 1840s, many middling landlords like Andrei, having imbibed the Enlightenment-based rationality of the cultural leaders of the previous generation, were elaborating and adapting these ideas to suit their own experiences, with the help of the booming provincial print culture of this period.[6] They concluded that village life, with the proper attentions of a benevolent landlord, could be rationalized and thereby improved. Andrei, at least, also believed that rationalization, in bringing order to the estate, brought other virtues such as piety and respect.

The relative closeness of relations between master and serf—or the distinction between absentee and resident landlords—was, however, far from the only relevant factor determining attitudes and social order on private estates. Edgar Melton suggests another important distinction, between estates run on the *barshchina* or corvée system, and those run on *obrok* or quitrents.[7] Those serfs who worked three days of every week on their lord's land necessarily required much more intense supervision and control than those who were merely required to pay a certain amount in cash or kind, and were often free to acquire those dues in whatever way they could. Melton's work emphasizes the rent-based estates of the poor soil regions where agriculture was relatively unproductive, and serfs therefore worked a variety of unskilled or semi-skilled jobs in the many and varied small industries and crafts of these regions. The Chikhachevs lived in the central industrial zone of which Melton speaks, and most of their income derived from quitrent payments. As Andrei mentioned in his article, though, they also required labor days to cultivate the fields of grain and flax that provided their estates with most of their food and clothing. It is unclear whether only the peasants of Dorozhaevo had labor obligations and the others, residing on outlying or partial estates, paid only quitrents, or if duties were divided in a more complicated fashion. What is clear is that the Chikhachevs' records of quitrent payments were extensive and elaborate, while labor was supervised personally by peasant elders and Natalia, apparently without elaborate record keeping.[8]

The system was further complicated by the largely hereditary distinction between so-called household serfs and the field peasants. The former category (approximately forty people in Dorozhaevo) included not only those who worked in the house but also many others holding specialized jobs, such as those who worked in outbuildings or on certain kinds of projects, like builders. The number of "household people" who acted as domestic servants was considered a luxury item: "[We had] a conversation about the small number of household servants upon elimination of [unnecessary] luxury."[9] Whether they worked indoors or outdoors, these were the people with whom the Chikhachevs interacted most.

More remote were the field serfs, who were officially (for tax purposes) divided into husband-and-wife labor teams, although in practice Natalia usually wrote of "the women" working the vegetable gardens while "the men" were in the fields or engaged in construction. These peasants would have lived in the village of Dorozhaevo together with the "household" workers, and they attended the same village church (along with the Chikhachevs and the priest's family). Andrei claimed to have known all these people, and since their total numbered only about 140, it seems likely.[10]

In a private letter to his friend Kopytovskii Andrei admitted to not knowing even the total number of serfs he owned on some of his outlying estates, much less their names or anything more about them.[11] This statement probably did not refer to Borduki, the small estate bordering Berezovik where they spent some months of every year while Yakov was resident at Berezovik. They had some cultivated fields or at least vegetable gardens in Borduki, certainly some household servants (if only part-time), and it is likely that they were familiar with the small number of villagers there. The remainder of the serfs they owned resided in villages that, while mostly lying within Vladimir province or just over the border in Yaroslavl province, were distant enough that the Chikhachevs visited them only occasionally and usually in passing. They had no residences in these places, and in most cases their peasants resided in villages that were also home to peasants belonging to other landlords.

The dividing of villages among various owners was common in Russia because of the tradition of partible inheritance, but it made the control of serfs immensely complicated.[12] These outlying villages owned by the Chikhachevs, different as they were from Dorozhaevo, just as little resembled the villages of wealthier "absentee" landlords; rather, they represent another category altogether. These kinds of villages were very small and relatively independent communities who owed only quitrent dues to their various landlords, and received in return some guarantees that their welfare would be looked after in times of crisis, and that they could turn to the landlord in case of serious disputes. Serfs in such villages were free of hired intermediaries and were governed largely by their own elected serf elders. They had rights to a small plot of land surrounding their houses, but most probably earned the cash or goods to pay their quitrent by working, at least seasonally, in the many small factory workshops of the region. Some also engaged in animal husbandry; a significant portion of the Chikhachevs' (and their household's) meat intake came from the sheep raised by such serfs. In addition, the Chikhachevs sent for extra labor from these outlying estates during harvest and to complete large construction projects, presumably counting this labor as part of the quitrent dues. In short, there was a strikingly wide variety of conditions and degrees of relationship and control for a landlord of this level, one who was both resident and absentee and lacked paid intermediaries.

A survey of the peasants of Vladimir province from 1852 confirms the impression made by the Chikhachevs of considerable diversity in conditions from village to village. Factory owners were said to pay barely a subsistence wage, and so the peasants of Shuia county who were most likely to work in factories were "even poorer" than agricultural workers. Peasants who engaged in crafts such as masonry, joinery, construction, painting, peddling, or icon-making were more successful. Contradicting themselves, the writers of the survey also claimed that agricultural peasants were "the poorest ones" and even admitted that the "oppression" of work in the fields impaired peasants' mental development. At the same time, there were compensations to village life: agricultural workers were more likely to maintain a "regular family life" and preserve morality and "a complete religious faith." Proto-industrialization had brought other changes that affected all peasants: homespun clothing had already been replaced by factory-made ware by midcentury, and festival clothing was described as "gaudy and tasteless but flashy." The county surrounding the provincial capital was "known for its love of luxury clothing."[13]

Andrei regarded himself, ultimately, as lord and master of his small realm (when he wrote the line "Gavr[il] Mikhailovich is telling stories about 'my courtiers,'" he was referred to himself semi-ironically as a little tsar, with his peasants as 'courtiers')[14], and it would be surprising if he had not seen himself this way, given that this attitude and the social reality accompanying it had been bred in families like his for generations. In a summary of the attitudes of eighteenth-century landlords of Andrei's level written by historian Wilson Augustine, the estate held significance far beyond its meaning as a source of revenue; in addition and perhaps even primarily it was a "social organism" in which the owner "enjoyed the power, authority and dignity of ruling over a small self-contained world." Both power and moral responsibility for the people in the landowner's care were sanctioned by tradition. "However imperfectly a lord might fulfill the requirements of tradition," what mattered was that the model existed for landlords to live up to, to fail by, or to be compared to by others.[15]

Andrei was as fully aware of his traditional "moral responsibility" toward his peasants as he was aware of his own social status as a noble landowner. As a year-round resident of the countryside for many decades, he was also fully aware of the forms of indirect resistance practiced by peasants (though of course he did not see them in those terms): he frequently witnessed drunkenness, conflicts, petty thievery, and general disobedience, and so he quoted approvingly an assessment of peasant behavior on holidays that emphasized "their attachment to feasting, vodka and carousing."[16] Yet Andrei, a man who enjoyed the occasional shot of vodka himself, recognized and encouraged the talents of individual serfs, referring to them in his diaries respectfully, and going to considerable lengths to further the literacy and skill-levels of all the peasants in his power. He was also painfully aware that his family's survival depended on the continued goodwill of these people, and this factor no doubt contributed to his attitude of relative benevolence, though it cannot account for it entirely (the peasant view of Andrei's relative benevolence might well have been very different, but their voices are not directly present in these documents, and most peasants who left memoirs were never field serfs).[17]

Knowing as he did that the serfs' survival was to a large degree dependent on him, Andrei claimed that his response, undertaken soon after first settling on the estate and adhered to throughout his life, was to negotiate a practical compromise that met the minimum self-interest of all parties, as he claimed to have explained in detail to the peasants when he first took over the estate. As he recounted the story almost thirty years after the fact, "having taken a look around at everything we had," Andrei and Natalia "gathered all our folk of both sexes, household serfs and peasants alike, read them out the sum total of our debts, *which were not created by us*." They (Andrei used the plural pronoun) then explained how much they needed for their own living expenses and bringing up their children, "if all the possible proprieties were to be observed." The degree to which the serf audience might have agreed on how many of these proprieties were truly necessary is undocumented. In any case, Andrei and Natalia then factored in unforeseen expenses, "which occur almost every year," and concluded that they depended on the "diligence" of the peasants and their own "prudence" to make ends meet. They assured their audience that they had no intention of increasing dues or work obligations, but would be forced to make sure their income was protected: "we nonetheless can't fail to monitor constantly and attentively whether the circle of economic pursuits was going properly, in order to obtain the bottom line of periodic expectancies." Further, using examples "that were most clear to common folk," as Andrei condescendingly reported it, he and Natalia "applied to their own everyday life" a metaphor of an "unbreakable chain" of household management, observing that "poor performance in one task will harm other links also, and two damaged links will harm the entire affair."[18]

Only after going into all this detail about finances did Andrei turn to his own role apart from his wife: "Then it was my turn, to speak about *all our responsibilities to them as their landlords*, and that in the activities that we expect of them, we will try to constantly set them an example." Then Andrei addressed himself directly to the priest, the "Holy Father" whose role in the village was "without any pretension . . . to remind, educate, teach, reason, forbid." He asked that the priest serve as a witness to the Chikhachevs' promises to their peasants, and, "because without asking for God's blessing no affair should be consummated," Andrei concluded by asking the priest to conduct a mass.[19]

This story as Andrei published it in the *Agricultural Gazette* in October 1848 curiously mirrors an essay published by Nikolai Gogol a year earlier, in his *Selected Passages from Correspondence with Friends*, in which he advised landlords to "gather the peasants and explain to them" that a landlord rules over them not to profit from their labor but because it is his God-given role and God would punish him for doing otherwise.[20] Although Andrei did not specifically mention reading this particular work, it is very possible that he had read the essay and equally possible that he borrowed from Gogol the rhetorically powerful image of a landlord gathering all his peasants to explain his and their roles. However, there is also no reason to presume that Andrei and Natalia did not actually also address at least some of their higher-ranking peasants at Dorozhaevo on an occasion of this nature. In any case, there are important differences in the content of Gogol's essay and Andrei's version. Where Gogol suggested to landlords that they actually burn money before the peasants' eyes to prove to them how little it mattered, Andrei naturally did no such thing. Rather, he claimed to have explained to the peasants the enormous burden of his indebtedness and to have appealed to them on the grounds that it was in *their* interest as well as their lords' to work efficiently and prosperously, to pull the whole village and all its inhabitants away from the collective danger of foreclosure. In Gogol's version, the landlord and peasants are adversaries, and the landlord must reconcile the peasants to their relative powerlessness on the grounds that the arrangement is God's will. Andrei, while firmly believing in the heavenly ordained nature of social hierarchy, did not deny the importance of financial self-interest. Instead he tried to portray himself and his peasants as economically bound together—what was prosperity for one was prosperity for all and, likewise, ruin for the landlord spelled ruin and possibly dislocation and the separation of families for the peasants.

So much for rhetoric. As a matter of daily existence, it was Andrei and Natalia who decided the proportion of the estate's income that went to their own needs, and that went to satisfy the needs of the peasants. One day in 1834 Andrei and Yakov compared the quality of food given to serfs and to sailors. "I said that in our navy sailors receive a pound of meat every Sunday and on other days except for Wednesdays and Fridays they get 60 *zolotniks* [nine ounces] of meat, and you were amazed at the sailors' excellent upkeep. [I]ndeed, my friends, it is excellent: you know yourself what an infantry soldier receives, and from the attached note you will see what our sailor receives every day." Attached was a list including rum or gin, peas, grains, meat, butter, rye biscuits, malt biscuits, and salt. Yakov concluded, "Don't you think this is quite plentiful, huh?" Andrei responded that "a sailor is worth it!" He then listed what his own peasants received (whitened cabbage soup and kasha, meat twice a week, and on holidays a piece of pie), admitting that it was not as much: "I really like to give my people good upkeep, and deeply regret that I don't yet have the means for that."[21]

Andrei was explicitly paternalist—in 1849 he described peasants as "our children according to God's word," and claimed that these "children" were "inseparable from our [nobles'] happiness," a phrasing that would seem more appropriate for a literal parent to say of his own child than for an employer or owner to say of his servant.[22] Andrei's paternalist view of his peasants was not racialized, since for the most part his peasants would have looked very much like himself. How then, did he account for what he saw as their childishness and dependence on the moral guidance of landlords? The source, for Andrei, of peasant disobedience was the same as the source of cruelty in landlords, and this source was also the solution: *vospitanie*, or moral education. Andrei believed that traditional peasant upbringing and the habits of generations caused peasants to behave irrationally or counterproductively, and he believed, therefore, that education and moral guidance also had the power to make peasants (and landlords) better.

Using the example of a weaver, Andrei wrote that the child of a skilled weaver would learn "how it could be possible to weave some more during the time that is free from other domestic tasks," while the child of someone interested only in selling for profit (as opposed to the skilled work of creating a cloth) learned "how to undermeasure, underweigh, get rid of the goods, to know how to go up, to bring in, to serve, to show, to inquire, to seem to honor, to give in, to make a necessary expression and so on." Selling only for the sake of profit was apparently associated with dishonesty in Andrei's mind. Each child grew up to apply the ideas heard in childhood, Andrei summarized, in the process summing up his rather simplistic interpretation of the Enlightenment understanding of childhood.[23]

Andrei's fervent belief in the power of moral education to form the character of children made him as strong a supporter of serf education as of education for nobles. His ideas on this point can be usefully contrasted to a famous Russian conservative who freed his own serfs and generated a great deal of newsprint romanticizing the peasantry. Sergei Glinka, editor of the popular journal *Russian Messenger*, deeply feared the prospect of an educated peasantry, according to historian Alexander Martin: "[t]he availability of inexpensive libraries . . . was giving the lower classes access to dangerous ideas; this was particularly alarming in cases when the people involved had no fixed place in the social order to begin with, 'for instance, noble-owned serfs who engage in commerce and are neither peasants nor merchants.'"[24] Andrei founded his public library precisely for such people, and all the other serfs in his region, in the belief that only education and greater access to both practical knowledge and the spiritual benefits of religious and artistic literature could make the peasants better and more productive people. More optimistic than Glinka, Andrei rested his faith in education on the notion that the "right" ideas were strong enough to overcome the "dangerous" ones. In short, his interpretation of the Enlightenment led him to idealize a community in which serfs were literate (and reading his own articles in the provincial newspapers), and in which the family's nanny, the serf bailiff, paid tutors, and priests all took part in the "reading aloud in the home" every evening.[25]

Other documents also confirm that Chernavin and the Ikonnikovs shared Andrei's belief in the improvement of serf conditions through education, through what must have been a fairly common practice on quitrent estates in the central-industrial region of apprenticing promising serf boys to skilled craftsmen. In 1841 Chernavin, for example, "gave for apprenticeship in the craft of joiner" his household serf boy Spiridon Isakov to a joiner named Radim Nikitin of Teikovo. The term of the apprenticeship was five years, and the conditions were that Nikitin teach the boy his craft "as well as" the master himself "possessed" it. The master had also to provide "food, shoes, bath, and laundry," while Chernavin provided "clothing, both outer and inner" and paid Radim (referred to by his first name in the document) three assignat rubles at the end of each year, for a total of fifteen rubles. For his part, the boy Spiridon was required to be "entirely obedient to the master" and "not leave his household without his permission!"[26] This document was accompanied by a similar one apprenticing Kapiton Isakov to a tailor in Teikovo. Presumably the boys were brothers, and it is possible that they may have been orphaned or for some similar reason required special provision. Although it is equally possible that these boys simply happened to be unusually promising. Similarly, in the same notebook there is a record of the apprenticeship of Vasilii Matveev from the Ikonnikovs' village of Bolshoe Gubachevo, to the grinding mill in Ivanovo, signed by Sergei Andreevich Ikonnikov.[27]

Terms for these apprenticeships were negotiated, as were terms for corvée labor and quitrents, peasant marriages and living circumstances, workloads, and even salaries, since landowners frequently paid serfs from other estates to do specialized jobs. Yakov's cook Gavrila, for example, was hired, at a salary of 120 rubles per year, with his food coming from whatever he cooked for Yakov.[28] In 1834 Andrei described his village of Rykovo as "contested," apparently among other claimants to the property. One day the peasant Prokofii, formerly the miller at Dorozhaevo, came for a visit, bringing a *chetverik* of peas as a gift. Andrei wrote of the peasants in Rykovo, "they have their own politics": he interpreted Prokofii's gift as an attempt to ingratiate his family with the Chikhachevs. "But if we will not end up belonging to him," Andrei imagined Prokofii thinking, "then the horse cart [for the trip] and the peas are no great loss!!"[29]

When Yakov commissioned the building of a new grain storage barn for his peasant, he hired the same contractor who had built a previous barn and an addition on his house. The contractor promised a building "done in the same way as at Khmetevskii's." The charge to the peasant was three hundred rubles. At this point Yakov stepped back from the proceedings: "I left the bargaining to the peasants, surely they will be better able to preserve their interests."[30] It seems Yakov had a healthy respect for his peasants' bargaining powers, which must have been based on experience.

Other evidence confirms that the Chikhachevs and Yakov negotiated terms with the peasants on a variety of other issues. In the mid-1830s Andrei "voluntarily took upon [himself] . . . a distribution to churches and to the poor" of thirteen hundred rubles, as part of the resolution of a lawsuit over a disputed piece of property. Andrei's peasants argued with him about the settlement, and Andrei commented bitterly, "[s]tupid peasants don't want to hear anything about [the voluntary nature of his settlement] being the truth. No! they say, we will be free."[31]

Negotiations went in the landlord's favor consistently only in matters within the estate, under a landlord's complete authority. In 1843 Yakov noted the arrival of a man with "two machines" hired to sow late barley and flax, at fifteen silver kopeks per *chetverik*. Yakov paid a total of five paper rubles for the job but thought it was too expensive, since the man took only five hours, less time than expected. So Yakov judged the labor by how long it took; the man's efficiency only led Yakov to resolve to try to pay less next time.[32] And in 1861 on his inspection trip to the family's Simbirsk properties, Aleksei discovered that the peasants there were paying his mother only fifty-five paper rubles in quitrent rather than the sixty-seven per male-female pair that they were supposed to pay. He "convinced them to pay up."[33] Aleksei did not specify his methods, and no opposing accounts from the peasants exist to give their side of any of these negotiations.

Letters show that these kinds of negotiations were common on other estates. In 1860 a neighbor wrote to Andrei to ask about a man called Alesha Kiteev, a free peasant who worked as a gardener and who threatened to give notice in a couple of weeks. The writer, named Maria (last name illegible), worried that her orangerie would be abandoned, so she asked Andrei, with whom Kiteev was apparently then working, what he "want[ed]" to be paid. She added that she believed Kiteev would be "better off stay[ing]" with her family, "for wages of course," because that was the village "where he was born and grew up."[34]

Finally, in an unprecedented situation with a great deal at stake, Aleksei also negotiated emancipation terms with the Simbirsk peasants. He recorded for his parents details of his attempts to reach a settlement, which he conducted with a draft copy of the Emancipation Contract in hand. However, "the agreement with the peasants did not take place." At issue was insufficient plow land to create a full allotment for the peasants, who would not agree to supplement it with woodland. The land due to the peasants could only be calculated approximately, which did not help matters. Finally, they reached a deal with Aleksei: the Chikhachevs' plow land would be given to the peasants for one year to enable them to pay their quitrent arrears. After that point, the land would revert to the Chikhachevs' use (they would rent it out to any willing taker, and Aleksei told his parents there were "many willing persons").[35]

As in all other aspects of his life, Andrei owed much of his understanding of serfdom to the influence of sentimentalism and Romanticism. Such texts must certainly have reinforced Andrei's instinctive and experiential sense that agricultural life was a more moral, and thus more rewarding life, for *all* those who were privileged to live it, even as a serf.[36] In this vein, Andrei focused in his diaries on his own affectionate condescension toward peasant behavior ("I received the grain owed from the peasants at the reserve storage, and then the peasants packed up the snow in the courtyard, which was amusing to watch"), and sometimes a sincere pity for the uglier sides of peasant life ("It was a pity to see the peasants from Urvanovo, two splendid fellows who came with their father the headman Platon Antonov; one of them has to be conscripted").[37] Despite such twinges of sympathy, he considered himself powerless to change these circumstances—with some reason. Instead, he did what he could to further his own and his peasants' interests, often doing more than other landlords might, probably out of his intense faith in the possibility of improving human behavior: "[A] conversation in the living room with Sergei Andreevich [Ikonnikov] about peasants and household servants—I must confess I don't like to listen to frequent complaints about them. One ought to be sensible—moderate in one's desires, lenient; and to treat [them] in a fatherly way, which means not to demand everything; but sometimes to be lenient."[38]

Naturally, this "fatherly" course of moderation and occasional leniency was also the wisest way to protect a landlord's income, and Andrei's negotiations with the peasants were never so generous as to be altruistic: educating one's peasants arguably improved their value as workers (so did attending to their health—Andrei inoculated his serfs for smallpox).[39] But at the same time, the Chikhachevs did their best to be "gracious and just" in the way they wielded power over their dependents—terms used by Aleksei when he appealed to his parents to grant the requests of two peasants in their charge—because they saw this power as a duty as well as a privilege.[40]

The Chikhachevs and Chernavin allowed their serfs to buy their freedom for 100 to 200 rubles per person.[41] In 1844 Chernavin recorded a complex and legalistic negotiation in which he agreed to sell a vacant house to a free peasant only on the condition that the buyer took into his household a soldier's wife who, because of her husband's absence with the army, was without a household of her own. The freed peasant, Egor Dmitriev, was a former household serf of a neighbor, Madame Merkulova. He wanted to buy from Chernavin a peasant house with an extra room and courtyard located in Afanasevo, a Chernavin family property. The house was vacant following the death of one Nikita Ivanovich, presumably one of Chernavin's peasants. Chernavin agreed to a purchase price of 25 assignat rubles, to be paid in two increments ("10 rubles by Shrovetide and the rest by Easter"). Oddly, Chernavin included a provision that if he ordered the buildings sold to someone else before receiving the money, Dmitriev would still have the right to live in the house for one year without payment. Either way, Dmitriev would be required to allow Marfa, wife of the soldier Efim, to live in the house with his family. As this example shows, it was the landlord's responsibility to make sure that every peasant belonged to a productive household unit. This unit determined how land and dues were distributed, and formed the most basic unit of social order (in the form of each patriarch's absolute authority over the several younger generations of his household).

For several decades it had been illegal for landlords to split up peasant households through sale.[42] Yet, the manner in which this dilemma was generally avoided and minimal prosperity guaranteed for serf households was that landlords and peasant heads of households colluded to arrange marriages that, they believed, would result in productive husband-and-wife labor units and healthy offspring.[43] In a series of entries from Andrei's parallel diary from 1845, he recorded the process of inspecting potential serf couples to determine whether they "suited" and could be given his permission to marry. First, the young men and women from distant properties trickled into Dorozhaevo: "Grooms and brides from Vladimir county arrived and came into the reception room—we are waiting for those from Rykovo."[44] Once all the peasants arrived, "The inspection of grooms and brides [took place] in the stone house and then in the landlady's bedroom."[45] The process took days; another later entry recorded, "Looked at a groom, Stepka, and a bride, Variukha, but they don't suit each other."[46]

It appears from these entries that Andrei was trying to breed his peasants, in much the same way that he and other amateur scientists of the Enlightenment period tried to cultivate superior strains of plants and breed healthier, stronger animals. To Andrei this was the application of science and reason to better the lot of benighted humanity (he also judged new acquaintances, of any rank, according to their "physiognomy," which was understood as scientific in Enlightenment Europe). Of course, inherent in his reasoning was his belief in his own superiority over his peasants—just as he had the right to arrange his children's marriages because he supposed himself to know their interests better than they could, he also explained away every kind of peasant behavior of which he did not approve as the actions of a child who does not know better because he or she has not been taught to know better.[47]

But on some occasions peasants did exert their own wills with regard to marriage. An adult Aleksei wrote to his parents on behalf of two peasants, one of whom requested permission to marry a certain bride, the other sought a groom. "Please do not refuse them," asked Aleksei. The male peasant apparently already had Natalia's permission to take "a free bride," and "in justice we must help him." The price to "ransom" a girl was sixty silver rubles. Aleksei proposed that his parents send him the money, which Aleksei would give to the peasant, minus the quitrent he owed. "This would be gracious and just."[48] Exit letters were formal documents that permitted one's serf to marry a serf belonging to another landlord or a free person. This was usually done in exchange for payment. Yakov mentioned writing exit letters for two girls on May 1, 1836, and asked Andrei to witness the documents.[49] In other cases, a favored serf was not necessarily consulted about his marriage but was given a cash gift to start him off in married life. Nikolai, the Chikhachevs' former yardman from Moscow (a man who took care of the courtyard but also acted as a doorkeeper and guard, an important and relatively privileged position) was going to be married off to someone referred to as "Kondrat's grandaughter." He was to be given 1.84 rubles, more than the usual amounts of charity Natalia gave to poor nobles.[50]

In a microhistorical account of serfdom on a set of estates in Tambov province, historian Steven Hoch describes at length the role of serf patriarchs in maintaining social control, which was especially crucial when landlords were absentee (given that hired managers were distrusted by both sides). This pivotal role reserved for elected elders might have been less important on estates like Dorozhaevo, but there remained a formalized hierarchy in the village that necessarily contributed to maintaining order (and sometimes to generating conflict) on such estates.[51]

Above and separate from this hierarchy was a second non-serf family, the clergy, who held an influential place in the community, albeit with no earthly authority. In Dorozhacvo, the priest and his wife socialized regularly with the Chikhachevs while also playing a leadership role in the village. A brief reference from Andrei's parallel diary shows that village priests also played a patronage role, in which they could advocate for certain serfs in times of trouble: "In the morning received a letter from Rykovo's priest, in which he is exercising patronage with regard to Ivan Petrov who was conscripted, requesting that he be replaced."[52] In this case the priest was not successful in his bid to help Petrov, but it is notable that he tried.

Next after the priest's family in the social hierarchy but often carrying more weight and influence were the children's nanny and the serf bailiff, who were treated in many ways as members of the family and could act as intermediaries between the nobles and other serfs. "Nanny" was frequently mentioned in both Andrei's and Natalia's diaries as a valued companion ("Since yesterday another year has passed since our good, dear nanny has lived with us");[53] she sat with the family in the evenings, especially when there were no guests, and she spent many hours knitting or sewing alongside Natalia. When Natalia was absent in Moscow in 1831, Andrei was dependent on Nanny for company ("I played at 'idiot' with Nanny 5 times").[54] It is also clear from financial accounts that Nanny was permitted to travel regularly, apparently to visit her family members on other estates, and was given money to do so. Yakov once warned Andrei that he had had to hire a carter to take Nanny back to Berezovik—he worried about whether the carter was too expensive—but left Andrei with the plea that Nanny was "in much hurry to get to you, she wanted to leave today, but she would still have to spend the night on the road, and so she stayed until tomorrow."[55]

In 1861 a letter written to Andrei and Natalia by "Nanny Uliana Vasileva"—probably the nanny to Aleksei's children—actually states explicitly that a nanny could be placed as literal intermediary between nobles and other serfs, and explains that this situation could also be the source of friction. Aleksei had left the village of Berezovik, which he now owned, in Nanny's charge by means of a power of attorney. Before leaving, Nanny explained, Aleksei had asked his household peasants "very strongly" to serve him well while he was away and not to quarrel among themselves or mistreat Uliana, "an intermediary person between them and the landlord and observing the benefit of the landlord in accordance with his power of attorney." Aleksei's entreaties were at the time of Nanny's writing already half-forgotten: "poor me, as an outsider among strangers, [I] am not allowed to say a single word in support of the lord." Nanny asked anxiously whether an insider would be preferable: "Would it not be better to select whomever you would desire from among them to oversee them instead of me; and to let me go to my place, as someone who is an outsider to them and hated by everyone, of which I beg you with tears." In this case, at least, Nanny disclaimed her ability to act as intermediary on the grounds that her outsider status made it impossible for other serfs to listen to her. Her place was truly between nobles and serfs, part of neither group.

A postscript to Nanny's letter, written by mysterious "humble servants of the village Beriozovik, D. Vasilii and Anastasis [or Anastasiia] Vylinskiie," suggests that the problems Nanny described were not limited to this particular incidence, but were a common phenomenon, "the same as in the past," in which lower-ranking serfs resented the privilege of those bearing the family's trust. They claimed that this conflict was particularly sharp between female household servants and nannies:

> Hatred of household servants, especially women, toward a nanny observing the interests of the landowner was the same in the past. Their malice does not appear anew and develop in the absence of Aleksei Andreevich; it is only spoken out and proven more boldly and sharply. The reasons for that are obvious and mean that whoever was [put] in the nanny's place with the landlord's power of attorney, it [would be] all the same, [that person] would experience the same attitude from the household serfs as both now and always. In this sense I reason with Nanny herself, when she comes to me to tell me her woe and, at Aleksei Andreevich's request, I ask her not to cease to be faithful as usual to her beloved lord, to serve him at least until his return and not to pay any attention to capricious whims of the women.[56]

Nanny's loyalties were at the center of a tug-of-war between the household servants and the noble family, both of whom felt she owed them her loyalty.

Much more secure in his authority as an intermediary between noble family and laborers was Grigorii Alekseev, nicknamed "Rachok," the Chikhachevs' longtime serf bailiff. Rachok was an extraordinarily talented man who related to Andrei on terms of friendship throughout his career. He appears in the diaries in affectionate terms ("A reprimand to Rachok for not visiting Dorozhaevo for a long time"), was entrusted with errands that sent him as far as Moscow, and was always asked to give advice with regard to any major project on the estate.[57]

The largest project on which the Chikhachevs ever embarked was their building of a new house at Dorozhaevo; upon its completion Andrei wrote an article about the process for the *Agricultural Gazette*, in which he explained Rachok's central role in detail and even recorded what he claimed to be Rachok's actual words. First Andrei explained how several obstacles to the building "comprised the foundation and a warp for a densely woven curtain, which closed up for me a marvelous vision of the well-being of the landowners of Dorozhaevo who would come after me." Andrei feared taking on such a huge expense and worried that a brick house could be unhealthy. But, "[t]he person who ripped aside this curtain was my serf peasant, Grigorii Alekseev, nicknamed Rachok." Andrei summoned Rachok initially to discuss what should be done with the "emptied, rotten, tall wooden house of my parents, from the rooms of which one could sometimes make astronomical observations, and not merely out of the windows[.]"

Rachok's suggestion was to "saw off" the most sturdy part of the house for the family to live in temporarily while the rest was burned to bake bricks, and, "having prayed to God, why don't we get started on a little stone house?" (The term "stone" was used in opposition to "wooden"; the house, like many Russian structures of the period, would be built of brick covered with plaster and stucco.) Andrei recounted that he was shocked at the suggestion, quoting himself saying, "Are you out of your mind, Grigorii? A stone house!" Rachok "slavishly" heard Andrei out, and then systematically dispelled every argument. Timber to build or repair a wooden house would have to be bought from a great distance, and carpenters would need to be hired (experienced bricklayers and plasterers were already numbered among Andrei's peasants, from property he owned in Vladimir county). A new wooden house would have to be finished in only one summer so that all the wood would season evenly. A masonry construction would be more solid and less vulnerable to fire. And finally, a masonry house could be unhealthy only if it were shoddily built, "[b]ut in your case, lord, your serf stonemasons from Vladimir will do a good job," Rachok assured.

As an economy, Rachok further argued that the work could be done by only those laborers who did not spend all their time working in Moscow, who instead "stay home twice a year or so, after the spring and fall planting." These men were impressively experienced: according to Rachok, "[e]ach of them has worked, whatever it's worth, for at least 15 years in Moscow on private or government construction projects." In short, "They won't mess it up." Materials for a brick house were made to seem more reasonable than buying timber (Andrei and Natalia owned several plots of forest land, so this seems strange): "Lime, even brought from 30 *versts* away for long periods costs no more than 12 kopeks in assignats per *pud*. Bricks are made locally including the firing, not more than 6.5 rubles per thousand." According to Rachok, it was cheaper to build slowly, and as time passed during the building process, he said, "[m]other-winter and father-summer will freeze out and burn out all the moisture, and the walls will be nice and sound." Rachok even demolished a further objection that Andrei had not voiced, but which would have been characteristic of him, given that Andrei had a habit of constantly speculating about his own death: "If God does not will it for you to see the end of this project, then your son, who will have seen what's been started by the parent, will be obliged to finish what was started."

As Andrei stated in response to these impressive arguments, "[t]here was nothing to say to contradict this." Construction was begun with the foundation trench in May 1835.

Progress was slow, "[s]ometimes an *arshin* per year, sometimes even less," but by October 1843, the family moved into their snug new home. Andrei concluded his article by attesting to the fulfillment of all his serf's predictions: "Rachok's arguments turned out to be true by the very result: the walls were sound as a bell, the air in the whole house marvelous without any incense and without platinum wire."[58]

Andrei relied on and trusted Rachok's judgment, allowing his own reservations to be overruled in light of Rachok's input. The serf bailiff knew and understood Andrei well, meeting unvoiced objections as well as explicit ones. Another surprising facet of Andrei's relationship with Rachok is that according to Andrei's transcription of their conversations, Rachok addressed his "lord" with the informal "you" (*ty* not *vy*, the equivalent of the French *tu* as opposed to *vous*). The formal "you" was borrowed into Russian from the West and was adopted only inconsistently in this period. Among the peasant classes in the nineteenth century *vy* usually signified difference in rank, while among the more educated classes it could also signify relative closeness of relationship (for example, children came increasingly to address their parents with the informal *ty* rather than *vy*). The formal form of address when used by a peasant toward his landlord would have been a recognition of hierarchy, implying that while Rachok addressed his superiors with *vy*, he would be similarly addressed by those beneath him in the hierarchy. That Rachok seems actually to have addressed Andrei informally suggests a recognition of patriarchy over hierarchy. That is, Rachok deferred to Andrei's authority more as a child to a parent, adopting the pose of humility (real or affected) before a father-figure rather than an observation of rank that would have been the same at any level of the hierarchy, including between Rachok himself and a lower-ranking serf.[59] This confirms Andrei's own understanding of the village hierarchy as a metaphorical family, rather than a command hierarchy analogous to military or business organizational patterns.

A few other serfs were especially trusted. "M. Serge," or Sergei the carpenter, belonged to Yakov but Andrei occasionally borrowed him to fix furniture and the telegraph, and wrote about him with affection for his unusual skill.[60] And as a young man Aleksei brought a serf servant with him to Vilno also named Aleksei, but called Aleshka (a condescending diminutive, as opposed to the affectionate "Alesha" that gentry used for someone of their own class). On the servant's name day, he brought his master a pastry, and Aleksei gave him fifty kopeks.[61] And on a different occasion, Aleksei went out with this mentor Vasilii Andreevich "to pick out new clothes for Aleshka."[62]

When Andrei received news of the death of a particularly admired peasant from one of his estates, he wrote the following poem, titled "True Story":

I have received another push by Fate
Right before the New Year
A wonderful peasant in Rykovo
Has closed his mouth for the ages

His name was Osip Stepanych
And he was dedicated to us with his soul.
Having found out—believe me—I screamed
He was quiet, kind, and never quarreled with anyone.[63]

Osip Stepanych was not prominently mentioned in other documents—perhaps because he lived in Rykovo rather than Dorozhaevo—but Andrei's grief appears sincere, suggesting his emotional attachment to individual serfs may have extended to others beyond the handful who were frequently mentioned as part of the Chikhachevs' daily lives.

After those few privileged serfs who worked very closely with the family, the next important hierarchical distinction in the village was between household serfs in general and those who worked the fields, who were considered beneath their more specialized counterparts. In the early 1820s Andrei listed thirty adult household serfs: fourteen men, seven "wives," and nine unmarried women, including two widows. Of these, only a coachman and a *skotnitsa* (a woman in charge of cattle) were named by their occupation. In addition, there were eight boys and girls, two infants, and another four persons marked as on *mesiachina*, a monthly payment in food and clothing given to peasants who did not have their own land allotments. These persons were identified as two men who worked with cattle, and their wives.[64] Other documents mention serving "girls," cooks, as many as three coachmen, a gardener, weavers, a wet nurse, carpenters, bricklayers, plasterers, those in charge of each major outbuilding (the cow barn, grain barns, and so on), and other specialized persons. Some of these people might have fulfilled multiple roles, while others may have come or gone over time.

Probably belonging to the latter category was Nazar, a musician, mentioned by Andrei: "Nazar the musician wants to go for a visit home."[65] It is curious to note that Nazar's desire for a visit home was an important enough consideration for Andrei to mention it in his diary; indeed, the requests of the higher-ranking or more intimately familiar servants such as Nanny and the cooks and coachmen to go on visits or errands frequently found their way into both Andrei's and Natalia's diaries. Finally, also among the ranks of higher-level and specialized servants were the laborers who were hired on particular occasions when the Chikhachevs' own serfs were not able to meet a need, as in this instance: "Both our mills have broken, and there is a lot of work to do around them, [we] will have to hire a master; ours say they don't know how to do it."[66]

An item on one of Andrei's ubiquitous to-do lists reminded him to "[d]emand a morning and evening report: from Rachok, from the Dorozhaevo elder, from Akulina, from the gardener and from all three coachmen,"[67] This may be seen as a list, but not necessarily a complete one, of the most important serfs: from bailiff to village elder to Akulina (probably the housekeeper), the gardener, and coachmen. Among the specialized serfs, rank accrued according to the closeness of the servant to the family's everyday life and to the level of responsibility they had over essential tasks (resembling a medieval royal household). A limited number of field peasants thus also achieved significant rank as elected elders, drawn from the various available heads of households. Elders bore considerable responsibility for overseeing peasant discipline, ensuring that corvée labor was carried out and that land, goods, and privileges were distributed evenly to each household. Regular letters written to the Chikhachevs from the elders of their outlying villages show that most but not all were literate.[68] No doubt because such a great weight of responsibility rested on the shoulders of the elders, Andrei made a point of getting to know them: "I turned my attention to Yaroslavl peasants. The headman is a completely [sober? advanced?] man and pleases me with his instructions [to the peasants]."[69] The elders consulted each other in a formal way, in "assemblies," but it is not clear from the short notes in Andrei's diary about such meetings whether Andrei or Natalia would have been present: "Rachok, Agafon and the other elders went home, and their assembly is scheduled by 10th March."[70]

The elder of one of Andrei's villages, Dimakovo, wrote Andrei that he was being asked by the police for the loan payment Andrei owed to the Board of Trustees (Andrei had sent it by mail). Clearly, the expectation of the police was that Andrei's serf elder frequently handled such weighty matters as cash payments on government loans.[71] In 1859 Andrei and Natalia received a report from the elder of Chekalino, Vasilii Egorov. Egorov's handwriting was European in style and practiced-looking, yet not as stylized as that of an official scribe. Besides a number of pious sayings, the letter noted that that year had seen the "greatest bad harvest everywhere," which had caused great hardship. "[W]e might as well turn beggars to a man, but most of us became poor a very long time ago, both in bread, but also there are no crafts or trade of any kind, as to hiring ourselves out [as day laborers], even then no one is taking us on, only for daily sustenance." Lest his readers think he exaggerated for effect, Egorov added, "may God strike [him] if [he was] lying." He then concluded with a report of quitrents paid, except for one individual who "is begging to wait" because of a large family with small children. Altogether Egorov sent 475 paper rubles (136 silver rubles). Unpaid arrears amounted to 437.50 paper rubles. Closing in humble terms, Egorov added, "Hereby we earnestly request you as our father [otecheski], if you don't believe us, then believe God, wait up for a while."[72]

Parallel to the hierarchy in rank among peasants were distinctions by gender. Most notably, female peasants had to live up to much higher standards of morality. In 1850 Father Sila begged Natalia for a female servant who could be relied upon, "whether it's the cheapness of bread, or immorality of these transient [female] workers, but nearly every day [we have a] new slave [raba] and one is worse than the other." He begged, "[d]o you happen to have, mother Natalia Ivanovna, in your household or in the village a woman of good behavior who you could dispense with, who can do no more than wash clothes, cook cabbage soup and porridge, in other words, without large pretensions, as long as she would do the dirty work around the house?" If found, Father Sila undertook to pay the woman four rubles per month, "if she would have her own clothes, which is the custom both for me and around the town." If her clothes were to be provided, as was the custom in the village, then her monthly wage would be lowered to account for "outer clothing and shoes."[73] In a follow-up letter a month later Father Sila sent his thanks to Rachok, who had delivered to him "a laborer," as well as to Andrei and Natalia: "The woman, it seems, is very modest; we are happy with her; at first she is feeling wild and bored; but I hope that time and our treatment of her will weaken the first impression. Now my wife and I are contented."[74]

Hierarchy implies discipline: inasmuch as the condition of peasants on these estates varied greatly in responsibility and privilege, landowners would necessarily confront conflicts, even outright resistance to the system itself. In the same article in which Andrei described his relationship with his peasants as friendly and full of "mutual advantages," he acknowledged that no community is perfect, and explained cheerfully how he handled serf discipline:

> But is there no slack to swindles and tricks? I am only vengeful with respect to these things. A joke is a joke, but to someone who attempts to cheat me, and then begins to act all contrite, I think I will not be ashamed to remind him in the presence of everyone else about his "deeds of long gone days, and even the tale of deep antiquity."

The quote from Pushkin that ends that passage was only one way that Andrei "reminded" his peasants of what he expected from their behavior. He also employed the lash, once admitting to "beating" several household serf girls indiscriminately when they allowed a young Aleksei to be scalded by the samovar:

> While I was occupied with Kultashev's letter, Alesha ran up with cheeks scorched by the samovar. My God, how I was scared and furious. I beat all the girls, both the guilty and the innocent. Thank God they rubbed [him] with grated potatoes, and although Alesha was very scared and cried, nevertheless he has gotten better.[75]

When Andrei re-read this incident in his notebook later, he remonstrated with himself for his temper, but other documents attest that this was not an isolated incident. Far more than Andrei's benevolent paternalism, the events that stand out most prominently among the mentions of serfs in the family diaries are problems with peasant discipline and—frequently—Andrei's outbursts of temper aimed at his servants. One typical case involved whipping a carter from Budyltsy for something as seemingly minor as "disorderly delivery of a package."[76] Another time, Andrei "[b]erated the Yaroslavl elder for allowing the peasants to divide up [their households] among themselves," an offense apparently made worse by the fact that the elder "himself divided up [his household] with his brother without asking his landlords for permission."[77]

On another occasion, Andrei wrote that he "became extremely, and unusually, angry," as soon as he rose for the day, because he walked into the dining room and discovered that several of his workers had not cleaned up after weaving ropes and making matting in that room several weeks previously: "the lazy do-nothings still don't want to throw out the entire project and the workbench and clear out the dining room."[78] Another incident is remarkable for how minor an infraction merited an angry mention in writing. Andrei, annoyed because he had missed his chance to send his notebook over to Yakov across the river, wrote, "I told your scoundrel Sokratka to let me know when he was going home, he did not listen to me, the son of a dog!!"[79] Yakov later reported that "it has been commanded through Sokratka's parents" that he would get the "strictest" reprimand "for his absentmindedness."[80] That labor on the Chikhachev estates was no idyll is confirmed by a comment Andrei made to Yakov about his serfs working in rainy weather: "because the air is not cold, and Russians are not made of sugar and will not melt."[81]

There were consequences when an owner went too far with his serfs. Runaway serfs were a common problem but not so common that Yakov knew what he was supposed to do to address it. He turned to Andrei: "You write that you are submitting a petition about your serfs that have previously run away, then my friend I think that I should also submit about my [runaways;] teach me my friend how this is to be done; I truly don't know anything about it."[82] A serf might also, if conscripted, run back to the village to escape the army. It was then the landlord's duty to turn him in, making desertion yet another discipline problem for landlords. In one publicized case, a deserter was turned in by his own father, as recounted in the *Agricultural Gazette's* tale about the "loyal peasant Aleksei Rudenko." Rudenko's son, Makar, had been conscripted seven years earlier, returned home pretending he was on his way to guard duty in Kiev. The father saw through the lie and "remembering in his consciousness the duty of a loyal subject, immediately presented the runaway to the local police." In return for his loyalty, Rudenko was rewarded with the Order of St. Anna, "for zeal," and the sovereign further ordered that the peasant's deed be announced in the provincial newspaper.[83]

As with taxes and conscription into the army, the state occasionally reached its long arm into the village in other ways, which led to disgruntlement or worse. Local landlords then had to respond to the situations that arose. In 1836 Andrei reported that his servants from Dorozhaevo had come to Borduki to tell them that "some general came to the canal lock and said that its width must necessarily be doubled," presumably by peasant labor. "There you go!!" wrote Andrei to Yakov: "So, on that occasion it is good to remember Peter the First's stick." Andrei was referring to Tsar Peter the Great's reputation for personally beating recalcitrant subjects. This is a singular but notable instance when Andrei shows some awareness of the Russian government's long-standing habit of progress through coercion, and perhaps even a modicum of resentment about its effects on the village.[84]

The constant frustrations with servants that Andrei recorded suggest that the Enlightenment notion of bettering the lot of the peasants through "reason" without altering the basic nature of serfdom (a notion aggressively propagated in Russia through the Free Economic Society, founded in the eighteenth century) was largely a failed one. This failure left landlords to constantly find other, ad hoc means to respond to open or tacit resistance. It is important to note, however, that Andrei also employed the lash against his son in at least one recorded instance, and wrote similarly hasty and frustrated remarks about Aleksei's disobedience in his diaries. This comparison is significant given that Andrei viewed his serfs as children, over whom he had the same moral duty to exercise what he probably saw as salutary discipline. In a study of the middling gentry in the eighteenth century, Wilson Augustine noted that paternalistic authority over serfs differed from other disciplinary systems in which familial ties were not employed to justify or shape relations precisely according to the fact that familial relationships allowed as much "tenderness and forgiveness" as they did "violence, particularly uncontrolled and angry violence, in contrast with cold and measured punishment."[85]

Of field serfs historians know much less. Yet this group, much more so than the household servants and elders whom Andrei mentioned in his diaries, actually represented the most likely source of threat to the stability and physical security of the village. Although field peasants' resentment might have often been directed at the peasant patriarchs who gave most of their orders, a resident landlord was less shielded from such threats than an absentee. The Chikhachevs and Chernavins were relatively attentive, competent, and prosperous landlords, and they were (at least by their own record) rarely arbitrary. Still, they encountered serious serf unrest from more than one quarter, suggesting that a realistic specter of serf unrest must have hovered threateningly on the horizon of every estate.[86] One peasant memoir, in explaining an exceptional case of a landlord who inspired only love and trust in his peasants, among whom he lived closely, the more "common opinion" was given that "as soon as the master loosens the reigns, the peasants will begin to make him small dirty tricks: to steal his property, cut down wood, set their animals loose in his grain and meadows."[87]

In 1826 Aleksandra Nikolaevna Chernavina, Andrei, and Yakov were called upon to deal with a frightening incidence of unrest on one of the Chernavin estates. With Andrei's help, the Chernavins were able to avert outright rebellion, but a series of letters from January 1827 records the stealing of timber, failure to pay quitrent, and incitement of other peasants perpetrated by a small group of serfs from the village of Afanasevo (owned jointly by Aleksandra Nikolaevna, Yakov, and their neighbor and friend, Nikolai Yakovlevich Cherepanov).

Cherepanov berated the peasants involved "for their rudeness," and local magistrates ordered them to be whipped, but neither measure had any effect. Andrei then wrote to his absent brother-in-law that the only recourse was to file an official complaint, "binding them over to judgment under the utmost strictness of the laws," which would result in their being whipped by knout and sent to Siberia (and thus the loss of Yakov's property). Andrei reasoned that in the four years since Chernavin's father's death these peasants had paid only four hundred rubles' worth of canvas cloth ("never mind any sheep!"), and destroyed over one thousand rubles' worth of timber (chopping timber at random and selling it for their own profit, refusing "out of spite" to take it from those nearer sections of forest designated for their use). They would therefore not be much of a loss if sent away, and their absence would put an end to the bad influence on Aleksandra Nikolaevna's peasants, who had also begun to refuse to pay quitrent. At this point in the affair, Andrei, Aleksandra Nikolaevna, Nikolai Cherepanov, and even Timofei Krylov (who chimed in with his own letter, noting that the felled timber was being ruined by rain) all awaited Yakov's verdict before taking the final, drastic measure of turning the peasants over to the authorities. The 1827 episode ends here.

Yakov's response was not preserved, but the serfs were not sent to Siberia because the same trouble again reared its head in Afanasevo in July 1836. On the fourth of that month, Andrei addressed Yakov as "[m]y worried brother," using the affectionate diminutive *bratikoska*, and saying "I'll call you [that] because of the unpleasantness in Afanasevo."[88] The next day, he continued with some specific advice: "Teach them a lesson, my brother, teach them a lesson, and teach them well." He then compared the rebellious peasants to "the ancient Novgorodians," referring to the once independent medieval republic of Novgorod, famous for its proto-democratic government by town assembly, or *veche*; the city was ultimately conquered, its ruling class deported, and even the archives of the *veche* destroyed by Ivan III, ruler of the rising Muscovite state, in 1478. Andrei claimed that the Afanasevo peasants, too, had an assembly like the one in ancient Novgorod, and "like that one, it has to be destroyed."[89]

Andrei's plan of attack was to begin by sending the offending peasants "to the assessor Smirnov and to the Vladimir workhouse," and if that failed, "down the Nizhny Novgorod road," which was to say, to Siberia. Further, he averred that "in every community there are almost always one, at most two, who are ringleaders, rabble-rousers," and recommended that Chernavin deal first with those individuals: "my habit is to [pull] out by the root, and then immediately everything will quiet down as if it never happened." Andrei concluded, in an apparent effort to push a hesitating Yakov into action, by noting that there are some instances "when one must act without haste, indirectly and carefully," but other cases "to the contrary, require the greatest haste," and this was clearly such a situation. Yakov must act, he urged, "without hesitation, resolutely, even if it involves a tangible loss."[90]

Andrei spoke from personal experience. There was a similar but unrelated incident on the Chikhachevs' estate a few years earlier involving household serfs. In a letter from Andrei's neighbor Aleksei Alekseevich Kascheev,[91] dated January 1830, Kascheev warned Andrei of the "evil of your people." Kascheev had heard "from two faithful people" that some of the house serfs of Dorozhaevo were expressing "dissatisfaction." He added that there was in fact a "conspiracy" among the Chikhachevs' house serfs "to complain to the government a second time," but apparently they had not yet done so because they were unsure of the procedure.[92] Kascheev advised Andrei (because he "loved" him) to remove the "less well-meaning serfs" from his proximity.[93] Andrei's response to the incident does not survive, although it may be obvious from the opinions he expressed to Yakov in 1836. In his diary he did refer once (February 16, 1831) to what must have been the preceding incident (the first "complaint to the government"), which presumably was not repeated in early 1830, as Kascheev had warned. This diary entry illustrates, though, how the incident continued to haunt Chikhachev:

> During the night on this date in 1829, I had a terrible dream that in some town all the houses, stone and wooden, were destroyed, as if by an earthquake, and a dark haze was in the air. Maybe that dream was an omen of the unpleasantnesses that I had with my household serfs that summer.[94]

In this dream Andrei associated an earthquake, a proverbial act of God, with serf unrest, suggesting that he did not understand such incidents as willful acts by individuals unhappy about their circumstances, but rather as random destructive forces that injured everything involved, as an earthquake destroys a whole town.

The incident with Chernavin's Afanasevo peasants as well as the trouble with household serfs on the Chikhachev estate—whether the latter was a mere provocation or something more serious—and Andrei's interpretation of his prophetic dream all illustrate the ever-present nature of the threat posed by serf unrest even on small, well-run, and reasonably prosperous estates, with the constant presence of well-intentioned landlords. These two documented incidents may not be generalizable, although it does also seem significant that in both cases peace was apparently restored after the removal of a few ringleaders. Finally, the serfs involved appear to have been discontented in a general way, without specific demands (unless these were simply ignored in the documents).

Natalia mentioned one other kind of incident, which may be more typical of their (or perhaps her) daily relations with serfs. Significantly, Natalia concluded this dispute through negotiation. This episode was recorded undramatically, amid a long list of household matters, in a letter to her brother written into the notebook correspondence on November 6, 1834:

> [T]he peasant women are not even thinking of giving me canvas cloth for three years (and they are supposed to pay me 10 *arshin* per year); I offered that if they are not going to give it to me, then they are welcome to come and spin for me for three days at home and three days for me; and they asked for time to think until the 9th. I don't know what they'll decide; but I want them to [illeg.] to come and spin[.][95]

Even though these peasant women appear to have been deliberately breaking agreed-upon conditions, Natalia was left waiting to find out "what they'll decide," after already offering a concession. Negotiation was at least as necessary a tool as discipline in the Chikhachevs' relations with their serfs, and probably a much more commonly used one.[96]

All these incidents together give an impression of landowners who were far from the unquestioned masters or "ruling class" that has been posited of Russian serf owners in their villages.[97] Indeed, in different ways in all three incidents, the Chikhachevs seem to have felt themselves to be at the mercy of their "property." However, these incidents were exceptions to the rule; generally the Chikhachevs appear to have been respected or appreciated by their serfs, and business on their estates usually ran smoothly, as attested by the dozens of reports received by Andrei and Natalia from serf elders over the years conveying the welcome news that "all was well" on their various outlying estates. While such reports cannot be considered candid accounts of these peasants' real views, given their intended audience, they do indicate that the recorded incidents of open unrest were isolated.[98]

External sources of instability, however, were frequent and had the potential to be so devastating that it was perhaps the sense of common vulnerability to fire, crime, isolation, and a precarious seasonal economy that most accounts for the relative stability and longevity of the provincial noble-owned village.[99] Wilson Augustine noted a concern about the "lack of security of property in general" in the countryside as very high in the priorities of the eighteenth-century landlords participating in Catherine the Great's Legislative Commission of 1767, a sort of survey of the state of the empire.[100] This same concern is also heavily present in the Chikhachev-Chernavin papers, despite the fact that in 1852 Vladimir province was described in a military-statistical atlas as "one of the most calm and peaceful" in the empire. According to this atlas, in 1849, 1,409 persons were on trial for various crimes, of whom 346 were acquitted and 157 not convicted but left "under suspicion" (a kind of suspended sentence). One of the most common crimes was illicit logging, for which ninety-one persons were convicted in 1849. Twenty-six people (seven of them women) were convicted for murder, seventy-three for theft, six for fraud, and one for robbery. Arson was apparently a female crime, with twelve women and only one man convicted for it. Vagrancy, arguably an indicator of poverty more than crime, accounted for eighty-three convictions.[101]

A prominent external threat in the Chikhachev papers was theft. A letter from the adult Aleksei (written *after* emancipation—which took some time to take effect throughout Russia) referred to "household servants [who] are helping splendidly in all the work, and for that I am feeding them millet kasha," and then complained that one serf's savings of forty rubles in assignats (which he was saving for his funeral) was taken by thieves. Since no one else had anything stolen, Aleksei and unnamed others—presumably his elders or other trusted serfs—concluded that the thief was one of their own. They suspected Maksimka or someone from his family. Maksimka had been caught stealing boots recently, and another time stealing a coat.[102]

Much earlier, in 1836, Yakov reported a similar "small incident": "Yesterday my people saw that the lock in the smithy is torn off and the mechanism is pulled out. [U]pon examination it turned out that some strange man had the need of the bolt from the tongs attached to the anvil and some other insignificant tongs—everything else is intact! [W]hat an odd fellow! Was it worthwhile to risk being beaten up for such things[?]" Andrei replied that "you should have conducted an investigation. It's winter time now: are there any footprints: if so, what kind? From boots or from woven slippers? And where are their toes directed? And where are the heels directed? [I]f no clear evidence is found, at least it would be possible to leave [the culprit] under suspicion. . . . Otherwise, if not for the fast, would [it] be possible to try to lay a trap?"[103]

Troublemakers in the village, including those involved in the Afansevo affair, were portrayed as isolated figures whose behavior put all the other peasants' well-being at risk, as well as the landowners'. Fears of thievery and the destruction of important resources at the hands of a few malcontents was discussed in much the same spirit as an even more common fear shared by all rural residents—that of fire.[104] Invariably, a fire occurring anywhere in the province was news worthy of mentions in diaries and much discussion, and when fires occurred nearby, everyone was called out to help extinguish it, in precisely the same way that incidents of thievery were reported and everyone called upon to help identify the culprit. In this case at least, peasant disobedience was one of several factors that threatened village security and stability—for all its residents—as much as it was an issue of authority between serf and master.

Of course, the issue of authority was never absent, even when noble family and peasants all shared a sense of external threat. A fire in Dorozhaevo in March 1835 led to an investigation. A peasant deputy was appointed by a judge "to ensure justice because he was not a nobleman and thus he would not favor either side," suggesting that Andrei suspected arson on the part of a peasant, seemingly one belonging to a neighbor. Rachok assured Andrei that the investigation was "conducted absolutely fairly." The "harm" that resulted came, according to Andrei, "from the peasants themselves, who during the questioning about the arsonist's behavior stood there like idols, even our [peasants]." Andrei could not account for the behavior, wondering "[w]hether it was some magnetism or some galvanism at work, the devil knows." More likely the peasants were suspicious of the investigative process, fair as it seemed to Andrei and Rachok, and perhaps preferred to deal with the matter on their own. From Andrei's perspective, the unsuccessful investigation was the final outcome, as he concluded in bewildered frustration, "[o]ne must think they are wary of his revenge in the event he will go on living in the village."[105] Generalizing about a system in which this could be allowed to happen, Andrei wrote somewhat cryptically, "Here is for you a small sample of human relations and of the intricacies of elected service. What a farsighted intricacy to guess that the judge may dislike the unmasked criminal."[106]

On March 31, 1837, Yakov's village, Berezovik, also suffered a fire. It began around midnight in the home of a peasant nicknamed Kon. Eight houses burned, but it was Kon's family who suffered injuries. According to Yakov, the "old man" got "painful burns," "his old woman [was] also strongly burnt," but the "most terribly" affected was their son Nikolai, burned "from the shoulders to the fingers." Yakov's response to the fire was to drag his dresser, a chest of papers, and some books out into his entryway, and to take pictures down from his walls, in case the fire spread to his own home. He then sent his men out to fight the fire. By dawn the affected buildings collapsed, which extinguished the fire—"everything then calmed down." Yakov's final line was, "Thank God everything was quiet and the folks were all home [to fight the fire]; if this happened a few hours later— . . . all the people would be at the bazaar in Teikovo" leaving the fire to spread unchecked.[107]

And in 1861 there was a fire at the Ikonnikovs' estate, Gubachevo. Five houses burned down, but "Thank God that Nik. Sergeich [Ikonnikov] at the time was staying with me," wrote Andrei. This fire was started by a soldier's wife, Anna Petrova, who when quarreling with her husband "wanted to burn him and started the fire, as she herself admitted, having added that about a year ago she committed another crime, having strangled her own infant."[108] Andrei then described another fire in the village of Gridkino caused by boys "fooling around while the grownups were away cutting hay." The result of "these pranks" was that only two houses still stood, leaving thirteen houses as "victims of the flame."[109] As in the other incidents, isolated troublemakers put everyone at risk.

Beyond theft and fire was the equally devastating threat from the weather, which could drastically affect everyone's livelihoods overnight. In 1834 Natalia wrote sadly to Yakov about the estate: "it seems I can't say anything good about it. Cucumbers also disappeared, potatoes we barely gathered as much as we planted, rutabaga we gathered only a trifle of. Beets are lousy and carrots are even worse. All of this is very bad." The family was more insulated from these ill effects than the peasants were, though. For Natalia "what is worst of all is the fever that has been torturing me."[110] But from year to year most landowners faced the possibility of failure. Statistics published in the *Agricultural Gazette* show amounts of land used for various grains seeded, harvested, and sold from 1821 to 1835, contributed by one landowner. The chart demonstrates enormous variability from year to year, with the total profit earned on all crops ranging from 229.40 rubles to almost ten times that number. There were multiple sources of variability: some years more cultivated land yielded higher crop yields, but not in other years. Sometimes higher amounts of grain being seeded raised the yields, sometimes it did not. And some very high yields earned only small profits, depending presumably on variations in market prices.[111]

The Russian provincial village existed in precarious economic circumstances, remote from neighbors and from the political center of the country. Its residents, regardless of social estate, depended for every practical need on the precisely prescribed roles defined by their social order. Thus, in Andrei's eyes this was not a society defined by the oppression of women or by the enslavement of peasants but by the interdependence of every member, even though the distribution of power remained decidedly unequal. In the Chikhachevs' world, men had better educations and greater opportunities to see the outside world, while all the nobility had vastly greater mobility and freedom of choice in their everyday lives (females less so than males), compared to their serfs. But, at the same time, everyone in this system was confined to his or her prescribed duty, seen as divinely ordained, and to a specific rank in the hierarchy. Stepping outside that duty or role was more likely to result in ruin than freedom. The prescribed duty for the wife and mother was in part determined by the fact that the Chikhachevs owned serfs. It was Natalia's duty to oversee and negotiate their daily labor, as it was her job to manage the material welfare of her husband, children, and household servants; in this paternalistic world where land-lords viewed serfs as children, Natalia's dependents extended beyond the nursery to in-clude dozens of serf villages.

4

Estate Management

SEVERAL ICONIC IMAGES of womanhood that derive from nineteenth-century European literature were as familiar to the Chikhachevs as they were to any other European reader of the period: the lady of fashion, frivolous and useless; the ingénue, a young lady whose fate awaits her in marriage; the mother, warm, nurturing, and preoccupied with her children to the exclusion of all else. Like most other real-world readers, the Chikhachevs would have found such images far removed from mundane, idiosyncratic, and complicated reality. For people like the Chikhachevs who owned serfs and lived on scattered, minimally profitable estates, another image of womanhood was much more relevant; this image is best described by the Russian word *khoziaika,* the word most often used by the Chikhachevs to describe Natalia's role in the family.

Khoziaika is not quite translatable in English, any more than the concept this word describes can be removed from the context of serf-owning estates in which it originated. Variously translated as "mistress," "landlady," "housewife," or "hostess," the Russian word encompasses all four English terms and conveys an additional connection between the mistress/landlady/hostess and the economics of agriculture, since it derives from the same root as the word for "economics."[1] Given that the Russian provincial estate was a varied, extensive, and nearly self-sufficient economic realm that depended on unpaid serf labor, it contained a "household" that extended into fields, mills, weaving workshops, peasant households, and a complex, seasonal financial system. As *khoziaika,* Natalia Chikhacheva ruled over a domain that encompassed both household and agricultural "economics." Her domain, to be sure, did not extend beyond the borders of the family's estates, since she participated neither in state service nor in literary or intellectual discourse or organizations, as her husband did.[2] However, within the estate Natalia's authority and responsibility—over serfs, over family members, and over a huge variety of economic activities—was vast.

Russian law and customs of female property ownership differed significantly from the Western model. In the early nineteenth century in England, the United States, and in the large swathes of Europe that were dominated by the Napoleonic law codes, any property owned by a woman became her husband's when she married, and married women were largely unable to represent themselves legally in property transactions.[3] Even widows and unmarried women, who retained their property, were usually constrained by social and cultural prejudice from acting on their own behalf with regard to their property.[4] In Russia, however, married noblewomen retained the legal right to own property throughout the eighteenth and nineteenth centuries. Until recently, this legal right was considered largely a fiction with little significant impact on women, since church and family law dictated that married women were virtually property themselves, given that they could not relocate without a passport granted to them by their husbands (in certain extreme cases, it could be granted by state authorities), and divorce was extremely difficult. However, it has been demonstrated that the combination of Russian landholding patterns, ubiquitous state service careers for men, and the nobility's desire to defend their private property rights against the claims of the state caused Russian noblemen to accept and even applaud female ownership and control of property.[5]

Thus over the course of the eighteenth and early nineteenth centuries, it became increasingly common for significant numbers of women to maintain both ownership and control of their property.[6] Ownership and control of property afforded these women a measure of security and, perhaps, leverage in face of the much more restrictive family laws governing marriage and divorce. Most significantly, women not only were able to run their estates but, according to extensive memoir accounts, doing so was neither unusual nor understood as undermining their status or femininity. It was seen as a practical and obvious part of their other management duties, effectively defining the "home" as multiple estates with serfs.[7]

Many of the women who managed their estates—and especially those who also managed their husband's property—did so in their husband's absence, in default of the husband's ability to manage, or in some cases as a matter of self- and family preservation in light of a husband's destructive behavior (these latter cases may of course be disproportionately represented, since key sources for this data are legal records).[8] The Chikhachevs are an example of a family in which the husband was a strong daily presence on the estate and, in his own mind at least, deeply committed to what he perceived as his responsibilities to his family. He was neither abusive nor tempted by gambling, drink, or extravagance into jeopardizing the stability of his family or household. On the contrary, he was devoted to what he understood as his role as father and husband. Thus, the Chikhachevs provide a doubly interesting case study in the significance for family life of married women's control of property. Their marriage was based not on an assumption that a woman might control property in the absence of her husband, but instead that it was her rightful and appropriate role, while his was, or at least could be, something quite other. This chapter uncovers what Natalia's activities as estate manager actually involved, and subsequent chapters explore what this division of labor meant for her marriage and family—how the respective roles assumed by Natalia and Andrei informed their understanding of parenting, of the family and community, and of the ideology of domesticity with which they were familiar but which derived from a gender order and socio-economic circumstances very different from theirs.

Natalia Chikhacheva owned her own dower property; her property was actually more valuable than her husband's while his remained encumbered by debt, and of nearly equal value after his debts were paid off due to her careful management.[9] She also managed both her estates and his during at least the period when their children were young, and probably from the beginning of their marriage until a point sometime in the 1850s when her health permanently deteriorated. While her husband oversaw the education of their children and pursued intellectual projects, Natalia oversaw serf labor in the house and fields, managed the finances, and ensured the material security of both her family and the hundreds of serfs they owned. Agricultural work on this scale, especially in a comparatively infertile region, involved constant attention and intervention in serf labor, obsessive record keeping, and even under the best management was subject to sudden disaster in the form of famine, disease, or fire. The majority of the Russian gentry at all income levels were indebted in part because the agricultural economy was dependent on poor soil, an inefficient labor system, the seasons, and the weather, so that cash was available only for short periods of each year. The fact that the Chikhachevs' only significant debts were inherited, and that they were eventually able to repay even these debts is a testament to the extraordinary talent and drive of Natalia's management.

In Britain, the birthplace of the rhetoric about domesticity that was being promoted in prescriptive literature and fiction throughout Europe at this time, gentlewomen did sometimes manage money, but they did so in more limited and exceptional circumstances than Natalia. According to M. Jeanne Peterson's influential study, English gentlewomen participated in decisions about money, without independently controlling finances, and were often in charge only of pin money and children's expenses. Single women or widows enjoyed greater control, but even this was dependent on the goodwill of husbands or fathers who granted control to individual women through wills, marriage settlements, and trusts. Married Victorian women did, however, have more financial control than had long been assumed, especially as executors and trustees.[10] And Joyce Warren's study based in the United States found that many nineteenth-century American women were true "players in a money economy," although this required going against "the behavior that their culture had defined as natural to them as women." Some of these American women advocated female economic independence and, in other instances, female control of family finances, but they had to do so through a "new discourse" that directly challenged the dominant one.[11] These women's activities are indeed significant but represent a different case from Russian gentry women like Natalia who enjoyed a direct form of economic power protected by both law and custom.[12]

Even exceptional cases from the British context are still limited in comparison to Natalia's situation. For example, Peterson recounts the story of Catharine Spooner Tait, who was described as a financial manager for her family and was "not only the record-keeper but an active participant in decisions about spending."[13] Natalia, in contrast, did not "participate" but solely controlled day-to-day financial matters. Exceptions were situations such as legal disputes and submitting taxes, in which both Andrei and Natalia together made decisions and kept records; Andrei was the legal owner of half their collective property, so his participation was necessary, and more importantly legal matters were best resolved with the help of patronage connections, and that was Andrei's domain. Another exceptional example from the Victorian context is one Mary Smith who called herself the "Domestic Bursar." Her husband deferred to her on all spending, but—significantly—they publicly pretended otherwise.[14] Natalia was a "bursar" in this sense, but in addition she was a chief financial officer: she not only disbursed funds, but also managed the source of the family's income, and did so openly with no sense of transgression.

Natalia kept three volumes of diaries between 1835 and 1837; the first began on January 1, 1835, and was continued faithfully, every day, until the end of the year. She wrote on small sets of paper folded into quarters, leaving pages of about four by eight inches, with a title page for each bundle that reads "Daily notes of Natalia Chikha-chova, Borduki [or Dorozhaevo]," followed by the date in large, carefully formed letters. Several such sets of paper were later bound together and covered with green paper to complete the diary volume for the whole year. Her second diary was made in a similar way, but records only September 24, 1836, through March 2, 1837. A third volume is shorter still—from July 13 to October 12, 1837. It too is simply bound, this time with cardboard preprinted with a floral pattern in green, orange, and lilac on a black ground. In addition to these three volumes, Natalia kept an account book—containing only simple lists of credits and debits—from 1831 to 1834, and a six-page diary for the month of January 1842, when she and her husband were in Moscow. Also significant are her laconic but frequent entries in the notebook correspondence kept primarily by her husband and brother from February 1834 to April 1837. Finally, there are a few lines in her hand in various notes and drafts relating to the estate and its finances, and a single postscript, added to a copy of a letter written by Andrei and addressed to their son Aleksei and his wife, Anna, in 1859.[15] It is from these documents that the following account of Natalia's activities is reconstructed, both her work as estate manager or *khoziaika* and her life beyond the duties of the estate.

The diaries recording Natalia's work and other daily activities from 1835 to 1837 are, at first glance, merely repetitive prose lists of goods, transactions, prices, illnesses, and the comings and goings of family members and visitors. Yet patterns emerge over the course of the diaries that demonstrate the intense, almost obsessive meticulousness with which

Natalia approached her work, the complex and seasonal nature of the agricultural cycle, the large number of people who depended on Natalia for their material needs and whom she was expected to command in order to keep the estates functioning prosperously, and also the interconnectedness of her work within the family home and out in the fields, with textiles and with finances, in the barns as well as in the kitchens. Natalia's work included that which was typically understood as a feminine realm anywhere at that time—needle arts, supervising the kitchen and the indoor servants—as well as work that in other contexts fell well outside the female realm, such as financial and agricultural record keeping, day-to-day negotiations with and overseeing of serfs working in fields and outbuildings, and the collection of serf dues. Although Natalia's duties encompassed what may be seen as contrary realms, these realms did not conflict in her mind or in her daily life or those of her family. Her duties consisted of interrelated aspects of one general purpose, which they gendered as feminine: managing the material welfare of the (larger) family (including all the dependents of the estate). Seen in this light, there is nothing contradictory about a day spent knitting children's stockings while overseeing serf labor in the fields, preparatory to planning a menu with the cook for the next day's guests, and wrapping up the day with a careful accounting of the estate's credits and debits, according to information received from those individuals who ran errands on Natalia's behalf and at her command—a group including not only serfs but the master of the house as well.

Natalia's diaries show that the nature of her work on any given day was dependent on the seasonal agricultural cycle. By far her most active season, during which her movements were greatly restricted due to the intensity of work, was the autumn when she oversaw the harvest and calculated in her diary the intensified labor and produce of this season. These written records were vital to making future decisions, such as how much to plant or how to schedule the labor, and these concerns are reflected in Natalia's diaries by dozens of entries filled with the state of the rye, the cucumbers and the cabbages, the prices received for different grains, how much of bread, clothing, or fabric and other goods was given out to serf laborers, and how much the serfs brought in as quitrent payments, in cash or kind ("They threshed oats today, 4 barns' worth, and the lord gave 12 *chetverts* and 5 *chetveriks* of rye.").[16] In these autumn months she had little time for needlework, reading, or visiting.

At other times of year, when agricultural work was less onerous, Natalia supervised the spinning of flax into fabric for the estate's use and for sale; she made her well-loved preserves; she supervised "the women" who worked in the house and garden (she used the slightly rough Russian word for peasant women, *baby*); and she had more time for leisure activities and socialization. A typical entry on a slow summer day reads: "Having prayed to god, I made jam—raspberries in honey. The day today was hot. Sold in Shuia 1 *pud* 26 pounds of Isaac's oil with the barrel [footnote: "in the barrel 15 pounds"]. Money received: 21 rubles. Went to the banya. Gave out for bread 1 and one-half *pud*. Went for a walk in the field."[17]

In the 1830s the Chikhachev family moved to their secondary residential estate, Borduki, neighboring the Chernavin estate at Berezovik, just before the New Year holiday. At Borduki, Natalia's work continued: she made sure that order was maintained on this estate and on their other properties in the area, which had been relatively neglected while they were living at Dorozhaevo. But this was also a time of increased socialization, as roads were easily traveled by sleigh, so visits with neighbors and friends became more frequent. The Chikhachevs enjoyed the company of Yakov Chernavin and Timofei Krylov almost every day until spring, when they returned to Dorozhaevo and Natalia again dove into estate matters there, supervising the planting and the processing of textiles that continued through the summer. Throughout the year, Natalia supervised the sale of estate goods and the family's supplies of purchased goods, frequently making purchases from traveling peddlers and commissioning others to make purchases for her in Shuia, Kovrov, and Suzdal.[18]

Examining her work seasonally reveals the intensity of Natalia's labors. Her regular tasks can also be categorized by type, a process that reveals their broad range, including into realms that in other contexts were understood as feminine and into others usually considered masculine: needlework; kitchen tasks; provisioning the estate; supervising and recording the sale of the produce of the estate; contributing the family's small-scale charity to the church and the local poor; overseeing serf labor in the house, garden, mill, barns, or fields; and finally, keeping the accounts, which included daily credits and debits, harvest and planting records, records of supplies given to serfs and quitrent payments received, and serf work schedules (such as the watch kept over harvested goods, or the duties given to different weavers).

Natalia's needlework included work she did herself and work she oversaw. The products clothed not only herself and her family but also serfs ("[c]ut out [fabric for] a sarafan in printed cotton from my house robe for Akulina's daughter Aksiushka. And a cotton shirt. I sewed her an apron myself, and the sarafan out of printed fabric, and gave a scarf").[19] These activities stand in stark contrast to contemporary norms in early Victorian England, where women of the upper middle class were expected only to issue orders, apparently often remaining unaware of how most domestic work tasks were actually accomplished.[20] Similarly, by this period among property-owning families in England, gentlewomen were usually confined to decorative needlework, not the creation of necessities for their families, let alone for servants; such needlework might have been given away for charity, but was not sold for profit. For many women who did not have Natalia's responsibilities, life was often painfully boring; needlework and other domestic crafts served as an innocuous way to fill the void.[21] In Natalia's household, surplus fabric or finished pieces were usually sold, and thus Natalia's textile work was a matter of business as well as of family necessity.

Much of Natalia's needlework was accomplished during stolen moments, often in the evening while listening to Andrei read aloud to the family, but it cannot be described as a leisure pursuit since it was never merely decorative work.[22] Her handwork consisted chiefly of sewing, lace-making, and knitting. In addition, she oversaw the processing of flax into woven linen fabrics of various weights every year, and the spinning and weaving of wool. She occasionally spun herself, but more often oversaw serf spinning and weaving. While she sewed many items of the family's clothing and occasionally some scarves or shirts for serfs, she was more likely only to cut out the fabric herself, ensuring that none was wasted, and then assign the simpler task of sewing up to the "women" or "girls" who worked inside the house. Weaving was done in an outbuilding, where there was a chief weaver assisted by various others, both male and female. Cotton fabrics, as well as the occasional fancier material or a finished garment, were purchased—sometimes in Moscow in the case of very special articles.[23] One diary entry indicates that knitting stockings kept Natalia occupied when she was supervising labor for long periods of time in the fields or barns; this necessary but dull supervision of labor gave her the time to complete many much-needed pairs of stockings each year ("I spent all day in the field. The women reaped 2,000 sheaves. I started a little stocking and got to the toe. They gathered more than the second *chetverik* of the heads [of the stalks]").[24]

Given the frequency of entries in which Natalia was "knitting a stocking," it seems that she kept the family well provided in these essential everyday articles. The lace she worked herself adorned her own and her daughter's clothing, while the surplus was given away to friends. Once in 1835 she mentioned selling stockings at a market: "The coppersmith sold in Shuia 3 pairs of small stockings of my work for 2 rubles 60 kopeks."[25] The phrase "of my work" was used sparingly and pointedly about her needlework, and demonstrates a sense of pride in the salable quality of her handiwork. By contrast, when Natalia recorded transactions of lesser note she generally omitted pronouns and used a passive verb with a neuter ending, noting simply that something "was done"—who did it was irrelevant. On other occasions when she mentioned doing work that was not normally hers to do, she again emphasized the fact, saying, "I sewed [a peasant girl] an apron *myself*."[26] On another occasion she wrote, "I made lace, [I] read a book, [I] pickled cucumbers, [I] wrote to the young Ikonnikov ladies," atypically using the first person pronoun at the beginning of the sentence and the singular feminine ending on the verb for "pickled"—as well as embedding the pickling of cucumbers within a list of her more usual activities—to emphasize that she did this menial task with her own hands.[27] That she took such pains to make this clear (when the chief purpose of the diary was to keep a record only for herself) demonstrates that she took a measure of pride in the work performed, and pleasure in recording it. In an English context, documentation made in cases of property theft show that the phrase "my own work" was commonly used by gentlewomen there, too. Handwork done personally by the woman of the house was a source of pride and independence: "even among the highest nobility women's craft helped to define and defend personal property against the devouring maw of the estate."[28] The difference between this example and Natalia's case is that the British noblewoman would not have sold her handwork for personal profit; Natalia was pleased when her work did well at the market.

Natalia also sometimes used the first person—usually plural—when describing agricultural work, which she almost certainly did not actually participate in with her own hands. The pronoun must be taken, however, to indicate a personal sense of accomplishment in this kind of work:

> Today we sowed 1 *chetvert* of flax, and 6 *chetveriks,* and we'll sow another *chetvert,* but today it's very windy: the same strips are planted with potatoes as last year; but we used up twice as many potatoes for it as last year. We suppose it's because they are larger than last year's. . . . I am going to finish planting potatoes in the garden on the left side.[29]

The phrase "we suppose" in this entry implies that Natalia discussed the state of the harvest with her serfs as they were doing the work, and her diaries show that serfs reported to her daily on all manner of activities. In other words, Natalia worked closely with nearly everyone resident at Dorozhaevo and Borduki, as much with men working in the fields as with the "girls" sewing in the house. Natalia's final sentence from the quoted passage, employing the first-person singular pronoun, refers not to her plan to literally plant potatoes with her own hands but rather her ownership of her responsibility for planning future planting—though the serfs would do the digging, the decisions (which would affect how many potatoes were available for everyone to eat the next year) were ultimately hers, and hers alone. This may be contrasted to elite English homes, where even male house servants were considered too difficult to be properly managed by a woman, leading to a preference for all-female house staff.[30]

Noblewomen's control over the larder, or kitchen and food supplies, goes back at least to the early modern period in Russia and in western Europe, so it is not surprising to find Natalia in regular conference with her serf cooks and even more often counting the level of various supplies remaining in storage.[31] The preparation of meals was generally left to the cook, although Natalia firmly closeted herself, with several women helpers, in the kitchen every summer for the annual production of her special preserves (probably made of raspberries in honey, as she specified on July 24, 1837).[32] During other parts of the year she only occasionally wrote, "[I] occupied myself with the cook," presumably meaning that she gave orders for meals, which would have been especially important when guests were expected.[33]

Like many other mistresses of a home, Natalia concerned herself with keeping her family well fed partly as a material expression of love. Concern for well-being as expressed through food is most often evident in the documents when Natalia sent her brother Yakov treats from her kitchen ("I am glad, my dear little brother, that you liked the sugar pretzel. I am sending you another big one that was not ready earlier").[34] The kitchen being only a small part of her realm, however, she was just as likely to send her brother home remedies for headache or digestive trouble, advice about his harvest, seeds, or the fruits of her harvest for his own cook to deal with at his discretion. On such occasions, Yakov acknowledged her care packages in the notebook correspondence:

> Thank you my sweet, dear sister for the food you sent—I ate it at once and for that reason, I think, will not eat again for a while. . . . Thank you my sweet little sister for

the offer to send me food; I have had something cooked. I think some peas and cutlets will be plenty for me—I took two glasses of brine yesterday—it worked but not as well as one could expect.[35]

As a bachelor Yakov managed his own estates, and he often reciprocated in the exchange of foodstuffs, remedies, or advice. He did so with the same connotations of love expressed through concern for material welfare that Natalia employed, as when he wrote, "I am sending you everything that is left of the 'greedy weed'; I wish it will be just as good for you as it was for me. And I think to me specifically it was very helpful!" Or as in this even more enthusiastic instance: "I am rejoicing, very much rejoicing, that is, rejoicing, very much rejoicing [sic] because you, my sweet little sister, want to try my cutlets with peas; and I will rejoice even more if you'll like them."[36] Natalia replied, "I very much thank you for the cutlets [you] sent yesterday, which I very-very much liked."[37] On another occasion when Natalia complained that her digestion was troubling her, Yakov loaned her his cooks:

I don't feel well today, my dear brother; it seems something like spasms in my stomach. It's evident that yesterday I ate a lot at your place: I need you to teach me how you observe your diet. I beg you, my dear . . . send [Dorofei] to us, for which we'll be very much in your debt.

Votre Soeure [sic; "Your Sister"] N. Chikhachov

My cooks I send to you, and I hope that you will be pleased with them.

—Chernavin[38]

On the whole, the kitchen held little more than the minimum required interest for Natalia as one of the means through which she carried out her duties, but far from an exclusive one. That the kitchen and larder were not an exclusively feminine domain is demonstrated by her brother's more enthusiastic devotion to culinary questions. Yakov might just as well have left these matters to his female serf housekeeper, or male cooks, had he been so inclined.[39] This is far from an unprecedented observation: Sergei Aksakov's semi-autobiographical novel features a male landowner who "reigned over the table" as well as the fields.[40] Like that male landowner, Natalia's concerns in the kitchen, as every-where else, extended beyond the satisfaction of her immediately family and guests: she was sometimes occupied with providing for servants from her own larder, as when she sent Yakov some malt for making beer, enough to make four or five "good" buckets for him and "about ten buckets for the servants."[41]

The business of managing the whole estate's consumption of various goods and the selling of its produce takes up more space in Natalia's diaries than any other single ac-tivity. Traveling peddlers—a few who came regularly were known to the Chikhachevs by name—stopped by the estate as often as once a week. Each time, Natalia would purchase cloth, ribbon, paper, candles, sometimes a book, or other small everyday articles. More significant purchases were made in market towns, most often Shuia, where the Chikhachevs purchased, for example, vodka and table wine.[42] In the complicated management of material goods, Natalia and her diary played a crucial role in recording not only every kopek spent, received, loaned, or owed but also the type and location of each purchase and the price and the quality of each item. She wrote some transactions into the diary with blank spaces reserved for prices or amounts to be filled in later (occasionally she forgot to complete the entry). Similarly, she often added footnotes to her entries, which without exception related to accounts, work, or weather (the latter being important for agricultural planning); usually the footnote reference was placed in a seemingly random location in the main part of the entry, although probably they followed the chronology of the day, as did her footnote to the entry for March 2, 1835:

> After dinner [my] brother [Yakov] came and 4 young Cherepanov ladies and [servants] brought them . . . coffee, and served them jam.* The young ladies left . . . at 5 o'clock, and [my] brother drank tea, and Cherepanov, and left at 7 o'clock.
> *Started a head of sugar.[43]

In this case a head of sugar "started" during a seemingly unrelated visit from the Cherepanov ladies shows that while the visit was uppermost in Natalia's mind as she wrote out her narrative of the day, some time later when she went over the entry, she was careful to account for the sugar consumption entailed by the visit.

When it came to dealing with serfs, Andrei remained a final authority in any serious matters, but it was Natalia who had the daily duty of giving most orders and taking reports. She regularly walked out to the fields, the mill, or the barns to oversee the work and confer with her laborers. That this was primarily her duty is clear from the reference in her diary to one occasion when Andrei filled in for her only because she was too ill to take charge herself: "Prickling pain in my belly. I didn't go to the threshing in the morning; Andrei Ivanovich went instead."[44] She also received the serfs' quitrent payments, remonstrated when the payments were late, and negotiated new deadlines when payments could not be made (e.g., "Received the remaining half of the quitrent payment for 1836, 105 rubles 11 kopeks in coin, whereas it should have been in notes"[45] and "[t]he women brought thread—129 *taliks*; they still owe 7 more").[46] In contrast to Andrei's handling of the few incidents of serious serf unrest with which they were faced, Natalia's daily dealings with the serfs were informal and based loosely on a negotiation of duties and obligations.

In short, Natalia's duties encompassed all the work done exclusively within the extended boundaries of the Chikhachevs' joint estates, and all of it, from maintaining the larder to making the lace to counting the rye was "women's work"—the duty of the "mistress of the house" or *khoziaika*. A record of work such as Natalia's diaries is only a very partial portrait of the writer, but they may be put in some perspective by comparing them to the formal account book she kept before the first diary (1831–34), to the six-page daily diary kept in 1842 on her trip to Moscow (away from home and duties), and, most important, to her entries in the notebook correspondence, which represent the only significant surviving writing meant for others to read. In addition to the comparison of Natalia's own papers, her writings can be contextualized with those written by her husband, brother, and son.

Although Natalia's diaries can be best described as a form of work record, as opposed to a repository for introspection or any other form of personal narrative, they are nevertheless quite different in form and content from the account book that she kept earlier. There is some evidence that the diaries were not simply an outgrowth or elaboration of the earlier account lists: the occasional credit-debit list found on loose sheets or on the last few pages in the back of diary volumes suggests that after the surviving account book ended in 1834 she kept both kinds of documents simultaneously. Thus, the diaries' first purpose was probably as a less formal rough draft type of record, tracking every transaction more or less as it happened on the estate each day. Natalia then went over her diary occasionally, so that key data could be converted into formal tables of credits and debits. Several other documents survive where annual income, costs, and debts were computed, both in Natalia's hand and Andrei's, and these computations must have been based on analyses of her diary records.[47]

Natalia was surrounded by diary keepers, all of them obsessed with writing down what they did each day, seemingly for its own sake. Her father, brother, husband, and son, like Natalia, systematically recorded repetitive data. Andrei, for example, recorded the time the sun and moon rose and set each day in his 1831 diary, and in that year and his later diaries he named all religious holidays and every notable date relating to the imperial family. In his parallel diary he also wrote in a homily or proverb for each day, presumably copying them from some book or periodical.[48] For her part, Natalia recorded the time she rose and dined (almost exactly the same every day), and the weather, which was significant to the agricultural rhythm of estate life but of little interest for posterity. Unlike the other diary-keepers, however, Natalia also kept vigilant daily records of the "loaves of bread remaining" at the end of every day and how much bread was "given out," presumably to household serfs,[49] showing that her diary (unlike those of her male relatives) served as a record as much of the state of affairs for the household as of her own activities (the data Andrei recorded, significantly, related more to the outside world beyond their estates).

How and why other kinds of notations did sometimes creep into Natalia's diaries—such as what the other members of the family were doing, when she read a book or newspaper, or recitations of who visited and when they left—is impossible to establish for certain, but what is certain is that she could, as easily, have simply recorded the necessary estate-related data in a notebook, like those kept by her brother in his estate notebooks, separate from his diaries and lacking any personal information. It seems that for Natalia, the line between estate work and personal matters was simply less clear.

Natalia's entries in the notebook correspondence read much like her diaries. She was affectionate but laconic and business-like, usually sticking strictly to her areas of responsibility, which she called her "department," as in the following longer excerpt from the same, typical entry first quoted earlier. Natalia wrote the initial entry, and then Yakov added his comments in the margins around her writing. Natalia began, "We finished picking the flax on the third. We picked 3,400 *sk*[*amei*, an unclear unit of measure] from 12 *chetvertik*." Next to this Yakov scribbled, "we have 430 *skamei* from 2 *chetverti*." Natalia's original entry continued, "on the thirteenth or fourteenth we'll start beating the flax," and Yakov noted next to it, "we are already beating it." Beside Natalia's "but we don't even know what to do with the oats," Yakov wrote: "same here." To Natalia's "can't cut it either with a sickle nor with a scythe; the village Elder advises to pull it like flax. The cucumbers are no good at all," Yakov again wrote: "same here." And then Natalia finished, "the frost killed them—we got only 2 *chetveriks* of really bad ones; our apples are being stolen quite a lot; they are being guarded day and night: during the day one guard and during the night three; and the Elder [illeg.] sleeps in the garden."

Natalia then asked Yakov, "How is everything at your place my dear?" (to which Yakov replied, "God is merciful, it seems,") before she turned back again to specifics: "[w]e have no beets or carrots; cabbage is very bad." Again, Yakov morosely replied "same here." But on the bright side, "[t]he potatoes which we planted in your presence are good," and Yakov admitted, "we did not look [at ours]," before Natalia summed up depressingly, "the rest of it is very bad." In closing Natalia tellingly wrote, "Well, it seems I described to you everything that belongs to my 'department.' At this, having kissed you in my mind [Yakov added, "and I you"] and wished you heartily all the best [Yakov: "and I"], and most of all good health [Yakov: "complete well-being"], I remain very much loving you and always ready to serve you, Natalia Chikhacheva." Natalia paints here a grim picture of the harvest; her resigned pessimism contrasts markedly with her husband's typical state of dreamy abstraction (while Yakov, a good friend to both, was uniformly sympathetic to both spouses' preoccupations).

Natalia's entries in the notebook correspondence were not only always business-like, they were also much briefer than the other contributors' entries and much less regular. Once, Natalia explained why she was not more prolific, writing to her brother: "I apologize for not writing more. First, because I get up early, there is no time to sleep late these days—and second, because everything is already written by Andrei Ivanovich."[50] This comment suggests that Natalia did not lack for other things to say, but in addition to being genuinely busy with her estate work, she felt that her husband's many densely filled pages were quite enough, or at least covered most topics of interest. Natalia wrote less in part because Andrei wrote so much, but she also may not have valued the written word for its own sake as her husband did. In any case, her entries in the notebook correspondence are—just like her diary—lists of harvest reports and illnesses, along with vaguely phrased but probably sincere platitudes about her affection for her brother.[51] In a handful of instances, Andrei wrote to Yakov on Natalia's behalf because she was too busy to write:

> I beg you to excuse my wife, and your dear sister, for not writing, she is on her feet all day until she gets tired, having gotten up early; moreover, she was taking care of the guests. She humbly thanks you for the information about the soul-tax money. . . . N. I. wishes to know whether you have . . . the barley, and how much of it came out?[52]

This excerpt vividly demonstrates that Natalia worked first, kept work-related records second, and only indulged in personal correspondence with her brother when time permitted. That Andrei entered Natalia's domain (and she his, given that casual or personal writing can be considered part of his domain) only in cases of extreme necessity is demonstrated by the fact that, in this case, Natalia was "on her feet all day" having "gotten up early" to see to her responsibilities, while Andrei was apparently left in peace to write in his notebook.

Not only was Natalia too busy with estate work to record the kind of ruminations or playful verbal games that her husband so loved to indulge in, but in the following entry Natalia explicitly claimed not to know what to write "about herself," falling back as usual on agricultural matters. After greeting her brother affectionately, she wrote: "and what shall I tell you about myself? I don't know; but it seems like, thank God, little by little we [illeg.]: today we brought in [illeg.] four hundred cucumbers; paid 3 rubles, minus 10 kopeks."[53] This incoherent passage, with its hurried handwriting also pointing to her discomfort, was followed by nearly a dozen orderly lines about vegetables, beef, and fruit. When Natalia was at a loss for what to say about "herself," she switched to the plural— "we"—and to the matters of interest to this "we"—the household, in the largest sense—the quality and quantity of provisions. While Natalia demonstrated her concern for the family's food supplies over herself (or, more accurately, equated them), her husband equally typically spoke for the children, adding the following postscript in the margin of Natalia's note to Yakov: "Both children, Alesha and Sasha, kiss your dear hands and convey their respect for you, my dear brother, as well as to our Respected uncle Timofei Ivanovich."[54]

In short, both spouses represented themselves in these intimately private documents according to their prescribed parental roles; Natalia concerned herself with maintaining the material well-being of the estate and all its inhabitants. Andrei was, on the other hand, the intellectual, the abstract thinker, and the nurturing educator-parent—in this case like many others instructing his children in manners and engaging the whole family in his educational projects (in which the notebook correspondence was a vital part).

Significantly, motherhood (in the sense expected according to contemporary domestic ideology) and "female" sensibility are largely absent from Natalia's papers. Yet, estate management was in a sense another way of being a mother—a way that emphasized the providing of material needs over affect and teaching. It was also different from Western definitions of motherhood at this time in the crucial sense that Natalia was providing for her husband and serf dependents as well as her children. If the purpose of the diary was to record this work, it is only natural that the other parts of her life were subordinated on its pages (though not necessarily in life). When she sat down to write it was not her purpose to record that part of her life, which she considered personal, or apart from her duty as *khoziaika*—her feelings for her children and husband, her thoughts and values. She may also have shared Andrei's opinion that personal, intellectual or whimsical writing was his domain and thus closed to her.

In 1831, Natalia traveled to Moscow with the Ikonnikovs, leaving Andrei behind with her responsibilities. He recorded in his diary evidence of his uncertainty in such matters:

> Fedosia Aleksandr[ova] asked whether the calico should be woven two threads thick—saying that the lady [Natalia] wants it thicker—and into this reed [of the loom] one thread does not quite do it. I said this is not my business—but resolved her difficulty by ordering [her] to weave two threads thick in [those] cases [where] Nat. Iv. wanted it thicker: because the samples are all different.[55]

Andrei was under normal circumstances oblivious to this vital part of estate work, and when pressed deferred to Natalia's judgment and disclaimed any interest in her "business." Like his wife Andrei seems to have had an everyday rapport with his serfs at their home estate at Dorozhaevo, but his familiarity with the peasants took different forms than Natalia's: he stopped to chat with the men, and in projects that seized his imagination— such as any kind of building project or his "inventions"—he took charge.[56] But it is clear that there were only a few areas of estate work that he considered his own; his contribution was sporadic and at his own discretion. It was Natalia's daily supervision that kept the estates running smoothly. When she did ask her husband to step into her shoes, it was only in cases of absolute necessity. (The case quoted earlier when Andrei "went to the threshing" because Natalia had a pain in her belly is a singular one. That incident occurred during the busy fall season when Natalia was working from dawn to late in the evening, possibly to the point of making herself ill, while Andrei's usual activities were little affected by the harvest).

That these work roles were well-defined and accepted within the Chikhachev household and referred to in explicit terms by both parties is evident in the notebook correspondence for 1834, when Natalia wrote her description of the harvest in meticulous detail and concluded, "Well, it seems I described to you everything that belongs to my department."[57] Andrei confirmed his identical understanding of Natalia's "department" in another letter to Yakov, written two years later, saying: "Nat. Iv. does not add anything to the letter because time is short and because she is busy with her estate management, which, I must say, she does in general superbly, well, excellently, commendably, in a model fashion, etc., etc."[58] In the same vein, Andrei observed to his wife that he himself "keeps grabbing the poetic matters, and to you, madam, is left the extensive field of economics."[59]

Andrei's activities were not exclusively confined to "poetic matters" though. His diaries show that besides tinkering with his "inventions" he oversaw the training and exercise of horses, acted on the family's behalf in property disputes, planned and oversaw the almost continual building and re-building that occurs on a large country estate, and was peripherally involved in local gentry politics. A large folder of records he kept while serving as local health inspector during the 1831 cholera epidemic testifies to the thoroughness and competence with which he handled this duty.[60] In addition, serious disputes with or among the serfs were dealt with by Andrei. He also enjoyed gardening, although his interest was limited to the flower garden and nurturing exotic seedlings in the greenhouse he called his "orangerie," as opposed to the outdoor vegetable garden over which Natalia had responsibility.[61] And, finally, of greatest importance, Andrei spent much of his time tutoring his children and in correspondence and writing, activities that he saw as his vocation. All this Andrei considered his "work," which in his eyes was comparable and complementary to the estate work done by his wife. He regarded his work as "outside the home," even though most of it was conducted in his study, because it dealt chiefly with ideas. He considered her work, by contrast, as "within the home," thus implicitly defining the "home" as, in fact, the limits of their many scattered properties and the hundreds of serfs who lived on them.[62] Natalia's notes refer most often to the *produce* of the estate and to serf labor (organization, results, small disputes). Aleksei once briefly mentioned Natalia giving the children white plums from the orangerie, a singular instance that highlights Natalia's interest only in that which nourishes the body; Andrei's endless writing about his orangerie emphasizes the blooms, and by extension, their nourishment of the soul.[63]

A sense of Andrei and Natalia's differences in personality and style of thinking can be gleaned from such extensive samples of their personal writings, and these differences suggest that, if they did not choose their roles or were not lucky enough to find them a natural fit, they had been shaped by them over the years. Andrei's papers reflect a man who was imaginative, verbose, playful, and impatient of anything that distracted him from the life of ideas and dreams. His vocabulary was extravagant, and he reveled in synonyms (often stringing together three or four), in foreign and invented words, and in colorful nicknames. Natalia, by contrast, was meticulous, somewhat humorless (though capable of the occasional tolerantly bemused remark about her impractical husband), orderly in all things, and anxious for her own physical and material comfort as well as that of the people who depended on her.[64] Her vocabulary was utilitarian, her syntax economical. Even her handwriting was plain, while her husband often filled half a page with extravagant curlicues. Natalia expressed her affection by taking care of a person's material comfort, and eschewed the encomiums and confidences that her husband gleefully disposed as expressions of his own affection.

While Natalia was patently more comfortable working with numbers, and actions, than with words, Andrei confessed to less than perfect competence in practical matters, as in the following entry in his 1831 diary, in which he bemoaned his mishandling of the lawsuits that settled the debts incurred by his "wastrel" older brother in such a way that his inheritance was left seriously encumbered: "But who then is to blame that the estate is in disarray and tangled up? The lawsuit opened my eyes to everything: what people are and what I am myself. It opened up my character, which even frightens me."[65] Andrei blamed himself, in other words, for mishandling perhaps the most important practical task given to him. While he capably handled other matters—his inspectorship during the cholera epidemic, other legal affairs, and the troubles they had encountered earlier with rebellious serfs—he constructed his self-perception in these papers as a man incompetent to handle the estate management his wife performed (and therefore conveniently unable to assist her in any but the most dire necessity).[66] Apparently Andrei considered lawsuits *merely* a practical matter because they involved interactions with an impersonal bureaucracy for which he had no respect. His task as health inspector for his county during an epidemic and as head of his village in time of crisis can be looked on as parental (and paternalistic) rather than "practical" tasks, and therefore within his usual sphere. It is impossible to know whether Natalia resented her husband's immersion in ideas while she shouldered so much practical responsibility by herself. Natalia once wrote to her brother: "How about my And. Iv., he wants to out-do Bulgarin [his favorite writer]. That's our people: but let him write." This passage could represent her (reluctant?) acknowledgment of his vocation—"let him write"—although it could equally simply be a result of her knowledge that he would read her note.[67]

In all Andrei's writing there is only one pair of clear complaints directed at Natalia, and this in the first surviving diary, kept in 1830–31, beginning with a single sentence written in French (a language he used as code for off-color remarks), saying: "This day will remain all my life as a bad memory: because I have been so irritated by my wife that I didn't know where I was and what I said."[68] A short while later he wrote: "The day was awful, to an even higher degree than January 19. After <u>18 days</u> of time, a terrible repetition drives me to madness!!!—A day which kills me, which I would wish to exterminate from my memory." Andrei gave no indication of the cause of his extreme "irritation," though it must be significant that it did not recur after this pair of entries, at least in his written accounts.

Other, less serious entries indicate that while he benefited enormously from Natalia's talent for estate work and demonstrated his appreciation of it in writing, Andrei occasionally chafed at the way her relentless focus on mundane or practical matters could intrude on his "dreams," literal or figurative. In 1835 he jokingly described having been broken out of his literal dream in the middle of the night by Natalia's complaint of pain in her ear. After describing the dream, he wrote, as if it were a line from a play: "<u>Wife</u>: I have something in my ear!" and complained, "And for this reason the dreams stopped, and instead I have got myself busy with Faddei Venediktovich [Bulgarin]," whose work he read by candlelight.[69] Later the same day he added, "[The female sex] is not too eager for Bulgarin's little articles."[70] It seems that Andrei had tried during the day to interest

Natalia in the ideas that were so occupying his mind, and she was no more sympathetic than she had been in the middle of the night.

Another of Andrei's anecdotes involving his wife suggests that he was bemused by her way of ordering him about: "I was coming back from the funeral last night, having spent two days in Shuia; just passing Zimenki I hear someone say, 'Lord is with you! Natalia Ivanovna is WAITING FOR YOU!'"[71] Along similar lines, Andrei recorded another dialog in the form of a script, prefacing each line with "I" or "Wife." Here he brought to life what must have been a typical interaction between "sense" and "sensibility," with Natalia as the representative of "reason" and pragmatism, and Andrei as the embodiment of imagination and sentimentality. It begins with Andrei "walking in the hall and fantasizing" about "the first six times I [would] tour Europe, Asia, Africa, America, and just as I gotten to Australia—" his thoughts were interrupted. Natalia's entrance line as he recorded it was, "Andrei Ivanovich, we don't have any chopped sugar. Perhaps you should do it." To which Andrei responded unhelpfully, "Pray, dear *matushka,* what would Bulgarin say if he found me in this situation?" but Natalia was not interested: "Truly, there is no sugar chopped." Andrei persisted: "I believe you, but Bulgarin . . ." and Natalia became more insistent: "You keep joking, but please, break some up." Then, invoking characters from a Bulgarin work to make his point for him, Andrei suggested, "why not the kamer-junkers, Henrietta, Amand-Louisa, Dorothea, Rosa, Eleonora?" But Natalia resisted the bait. "You know that I like tidiness." Finally Andrei recognized defeat: "Ah! *Reason*! Alright!" but bemoaned what his fictional friends would make of him: "and if Vas. Evd. would catch me so, it would be a sufficient reason to consider me ridiculous." Concluding the dialog, Andrei finally admitted to Yakov, "And so at 6:40 I started battling boiled-down cane juice, and exactly 50 minutes later washed my hands for the second time." Only after the task was done did Andrei "retire to [his] boudoir" where he realized that "the smell seemed funny [so] I smoked two pipes quickly, for Faddei Venediktovich [Bulgarin]."[72]

Joking aside, it is clear that while Natalia took on the habits and modes of speech suited to practical, highly organized work (whether these came naturally to her or not), Andrei pointedly represented himself as less than adept in such matters. He called himself a dreamer who spent his time fantasizing, who claimed "poetic matters" as his sphere and accused himself of having acquired huge debts due to his own carelessness. While Andrei relied on Natalia's competence, Natalia's bachelor brother deferred to her for advice on estate matters, and her son, on the rare occasions when he wrote of her at all amid many entries about the studies and pastimes he shared with his father, wrote of the things she bought for him, or of the packages she sent him. For example, as a schoolboy in 1838 Aleksei wrote, "[y]esterday's studies continued still today. Maminka bought me material for a tie and vest from a peddler"[73] and, when the whole family "rode to the fair in the village of Voskresenskoe," his "Maminka" bought the boy "a little ring and for dear sister, earrings." Ten years later, as a young man living with the army in Vilno, his reports were similar: "Received a package from Dorozhaevo with preserves and various sundries."[74]

Here he did not even specify "Maminka" as the sender of the package, though it must have been Natalia, because these were her famous preserves. Later in the same diary, Aleksei added, "After dinner a few [of us] played cards and treated ourselves to the preserves, which everyone quite liked."[75] Natalia's sending the preserves seemed to have been rather taken for granted, at least compared to the attention, criticisms, or treats bestowed by Aleksei's father. Natalia was thus defined by the rest of her family, as much as by her own writing, according to her work as estate manager.

It is impossible to say how typical the content and style of Natalia's diaries might have been; diaries of any kind kept by obscure women were too rarely preserved to know how often they were kept. Further, one must assume that diaries recording daily household accounts would be considered particularly ephemeral and therefore even less likely to be kept than other kinds of diaries by women. How then to explain the existence and preservation of Natalia's diaries when others like her either did not write, or if they did, their diaries were not kept by their descendants? The obvious reason that Natalia's diaries were preserved is that they were one part of a much bigger family archive; her papers may have been kept for no other reason than that they accompanied Andrei's, and Andrei achieved local fame in his time. It is another task to explain why Natalia's diaries existed in the first place. In an introduction to the American Anna Quincy's 1833 diary, Beverly Wilson Palmer identifies a variety of motives that pushed some women to write diaries in the earlier decades of the nineteenth century. Noting that such journals "reflect the constricted worlds [most women] inhabited," Palmer lists motivations ranging from the simple recording of daily events, large and small, to journals kept only for special events like journeys, or for self-reflection, as a means of sorting out one's feelings.[76] Anna Quincy's diary began as letters to her sisters while they were away, then took on a life of its own, but only for one year. Natalia's diary was not motivated by any of these purposes. Though other women of her time kept account books or filled out preprinted ladies' daybooks, Natalia's diary seems to be unusual for the period and her position in the extent to which she devoted space to work, exclusive of other subjects.[77] Of published diaries by women, it is most comparable to the early nineteenth-century Maine midwife Martha Ballard's—another quasi-professional woman before her time—but it is important to note that Natalia's social position was much higher (Martha Ballard had no claim to elite or privileged status beyond that she was a free white woman).[78]

Natalia's diary seems even more unusual when placed within the context of known Russian women's diaries or letters. Natalia did not write in order to justify choices that broke the rules of her society, as Catherine the Great did, or her confidant Catherine Dashkova (the first woman head of an Academy of Sciences), or Nadezhda Durova (a soldier's daughter who fought against Napoleon while dressed as a man), because Natalia made no such rebellious choices, and her diary was not intended as a public document.[79] She did not write in order to have her posthumous revenge, as Anna Labzina probably did in her memoir about her marriage to an abusive man whose reputation while he was alive was unassailable. Natalia was not nearly so discontented with her role in life or her marriage.[80] She also did not put pen to paper to express her own ideas because writing was her vocation, as it was for Karolina Pavlova, Elena Gan, Evdokiia Rostopchina, and other women writers of the period; nor did Natalia write because she had copious leisure time, an advanced education, and the encouragement of a literary social circle, as aristocrats like the Elagin sisters, Elizaveta Ushakova, Zinaida Volkonskaia, Anna Kern, and Anna Olenina did.

So why did Natalia write a diary at all? One reason must have been the influence of the other diary writers in her family, although it is significant that the other surviving diaries were all written by boys or men. Since Natalia probably began her first diary as an extended, more detailed version of the account books she had kept before, it seems that she began writing for practical reasons.[81] She used the diaries most of all to record and refer back to a dizzying variety of financial transactions and work activities, but she also chose to include precise records of the comings and goings of family and visitors (though rarely mentioning what activities or conversation passed during these visits). She mentioned her children (though rarely and with little description of their activities). She kept a daily record of her uneven health—which may have related to her scrupulous notations of what time she rose and what time she supped—and she also noted when she prayed, and when she read, and occasionally what she read, less often whether she liked it, and never what she thought about her reading. It is not possible to know whether she expected other members of her family to read the diaries (as they did read other family documents). Either way, Natalia's family affirmed the value of these records by preserving them. In this environment, her "daily notes" were a tangible testament to what she accomplished.

The third volume of Natalia's diary ends abruptly after a unique series of entries in October 1837, in which she wrote of becoming nearly unhinged by grief when Andrei announced that Aleksei must go to Moscow for school. The timing is certainly suggestive that Natalia's diary writing did not end randomly, but rather that this moment represented an important break in Natalia's life. A lasting change in her behavior seems especially likely given that the second known infant death in the family, that of her daughter Varvara, followed eight months later in June 1838.

In addition to other troubles, Natalia's illnesses increased over the course of the 1830s, and her work on the estate may have come to seem less important after her children left the nest, since her estate work seems to have been directed primarily toward the material well-being of her family. The Chikhachevs finished paying off their debts in the late 1830s, so they would have been in a significantly better financial position than at any time previously in their marriage. This too may have made Natalia less invested in her work, and therefore in her diary, as the challenge and urgency of her personal management lessened. The last entry in Natalia's final diary, for October 12, 1837, reads:

> Got up at 9 o'clock. All night I couldn't sleep, I have become very ill. The day today was warm and it rained all day. Paid oats, 1 *chetvert*. The women trampled the flax, 4 stacks 9 bundles and altogether 21 stacks 7 bundles.[82]

There is nothing in this entry to explain why it was the last. In the fall of 1837, instead of picking up the diary again a few months later, as she had done the year before, Natalia ceased keeping estate records in diary form. Later, in 1842, when she and her husband joined their children in Moscow for six months and then traveled as a family on a pilgrimage to the monasteries of Kiev, she again took up the pen but only for the month of January. There is nothing special in her final entry in this diary, either, and Andrei's parallel diary continues regularly from that time through the following five years. That Natalia began a diary again at all, especially while in Moscow and away from her work on the estate, suggests that she had come to value her record of her life as well as her work. But habits (and long-defined roles) are difficult to break—this diary, like the earlier ones, was written in a terse and business-like style, occupied mainly with purchases and the naming of visitors. She was often ill at this time and stayed at home almost exclusively while her husband traveled through the city nearly every day, visiting their children's schools, shopping, running errands, sightseeing, and attending church services. In the preface to Anna Quincy's diary, Laurel Thatcher Ulrich observes that "with all the unrealized plots, dead ends, and confusions of ordinary life" diaries "more often . . . sputter to an end in half-finished sentences on a still empty page."[83] There were probably many reasons why Natalia stopped keeping diaries. Yet, much of the impetus for her diary was clearly its purpose as a work record (and as a testament to the value of that work), and Natalia's work either changed or became less important to her after 1838.

That the record of Natalia's work is rare does not imply that the nature of her work itself was unusual; on the contrary, the way the Chikhachevs discussed Natalia's role in the family implies that they understood this arrangement of roles as natural, and it is surely difficult to maintain an impression of a behavior as natural if it is not reasonably commonplace. Both Natalia and Andrei spoke explicitly of Natalia's realm of responsibility as estate management, and equally clearly they saw Andrei's realm as an intellectual one that included primary responsibility for the upbringing of their children. While it is unclear to what degree both spouses were content with this arrangement, neither questioned its necessity or efficacy, and both were either naturally inclined toward their own "departments" or deliberately chose to behave as if each was unable or unwilling to encroach on the other's sphere.

Natalia may have initially taken on the job of estate manager out of simple financial necessity: she had married a man with large debts and no practical inclinations. And, certainly, she must have had few choices about her life's direction in a more general sense. In her culture, time, social estate, and financial position, she was obliged to marry; she would have children to the extent that she was physically capable; and she would have to live in the country on an estate where cash was scarce and income seasonal. Within these constraints, it seems Natalia either followed her inclinations or developed them to find a way to do well for herself and for her family. Certainly she must have been far from the only woman of her circumstances to derive some satisfaction and relative independence from her duty as *khoziaika*. Her satisfaction in her own handiwork, in a good harvest or a healthy calf "granted by the Lord" demonstrates frequent moments of content in work well done and duty fulfilled. The significance of Natalia's work and her acceptance of that work as her "department" is not that other women all did the same, but that other women *could* do the same. The model of mother and wife as *khoziaika* was not universal for all gentry women. But Natalia's unquestioning adoption of this role and the ringing silence left in place of justifications or criticisms of that role demonstrate that it was available to gentry women as much as other models were (such as the nurturing mother or the lady of fashion), and like the other models was similarly understood as a properly feminine role.

5

Sociability, Charity, and Leisure

THE DIFFERENT WAYS in which Natalia and Andrei engaged in sociability, charity, and leisure pursuits—their main areas of activity outside of their respective duties as manager and educator—reflect the limits by which they defined their gendered domains as much as their work activities did. Natalia socialized and participated in charity on a scale and by means suitable to her position as mistress of significant properties, yet neither activity ever extended beyond the bounds of her estates and those of her friends and neighbors. Her engagement with the world of literature and journalism was entirely personal: she consumed it with avid pleasure but never recorded her thoughts about it even privately. Much of the family's leisure time was enjoyed in the background of Natalia's work, as illustrated by the October 1836 notation in her diary, "in the evening the children danced and I looked through last year's notes."[1] By contrast, Andrei's engagement in all three pursuits was concentrated specifically in the realm beyond their estates. Andrei maintained correspondence with far-flung acquaintances—many of whom he had never met beyond the pages of journals—his charity was on an extraordinarily large and public scale, and he participated in the increasingly active print culture of his province. Natalia's engagement in nonwork pursuits was, like her estate work, pragmatic, rational, serious, and emotionally restrained. In these same spheres Andrei embodied many of the attributes of nineteenth-century Western femininity: he was sentimental, often frivolous, voluble, inclined toward leisure, and deeply affected by his emotions. The definitions of "her" domain versus "his" extended beyond work to every aspect of the Chikhachevs' lives.

If there is a sense of dissatisfaction in Natalia's writings, it comes in the occasional impression she gives of social isolation. She was disappointed when weather or roads put a stop to visits, and she once complained feelingly that life in the country was stifling: "we have no news, neither a bird nor a man go by or fly by [here], we live in the most god-forsaken place."[2] When Andrei was absent, she confessed to missing him: "And. Iv. with Aleshenka [Aleksei] went to Vladimir on Monday at 5 o'clock after dinner, and we are rather bored; we are waiting impatiently for their return."[3] Natalia prized her social life highly and was more frustrated by its occasional loss than her husband was. No com-plaint of isolation was ever expressed by Andrei, who on the contrary filled pages with paeans to country life, writing that local society was "one home-like family" and boasting how "the Shrovetide week just past was all taken up" by social invitations.[4] Andrei spent more time visiting others and was more likely to travel far from home, and therefore was not actually as isolated as his wife. But their differences were mostly a matter of percep-tion: diary accounts make clear that they both enjoyed regular social visits, sometimes two or more separate occasions on the same day.[5]

During a bleak February week in 1835, Natalia asked her brother Yakov in the note-book correspondence, "How are you feeling, my dear little brother! Did you sleep well," but without even finishing the final query with a question mark, she rushed on to complain, "I had such frightening dreams, the Lord save me from such things, that I cried terribly in my sleep, and Andrei Ivanovich woke me, thanks to Him." Whether the nightmares affected her mood, or loneliness brought to the fore the complaint about nightmares, her next thought was, "Our guests have been led [away], and so it's a little boring. Having dined at home early, I feel like going to see you." With a greater effu-sion of affection than she was wont to indulge in, she concluded, "I kiss you tenderly my dear: *pour toujours votre soeur* [always your sister] loving you very much, Natasha Chikhacheva."[6]

Andrei then added his note, beginning with an apparent complaint that his wife was always pining to go to Berezovik, "I can't stop being amazed by your dear sister: it's always about seeing you, always about seeing you—this can get tiresome." But he was exaggerat-ing playfully, pretending that Yakov must be tired of seeing the Chikhachevs when he knew this was not the case:

And in my opinion, once a week, on Sundays, is entirely sufficient. No! To tell the truth, this also is too often: seven days pass like nothing. Once in every two weeks, that's about right! It's not too often, not to seldom; not tiresome, or boring. But this every day—every day. What is it, for you to not see us, or us not to see you? I think that this is why you're always wanting to tweak my nose, because you're so tired of seeing it.
Stop!
Chikhachev[7]

Chernavin responded to both notes in kind, saying to Natalia, "Thank you, my dear, dear sister for your intention to come to me today. I beg you to bring it to fruition!" But to

Andrei (addressing him with the playful diminutive for "brother" that they used for each other, "*bratikos*") Yakov wrote, "As for my dear brother, I see that it's necessary to tweak his nose again!"[8]

We know that Natalia was close to her brother and cannot be surprised by her desire to see him frequently, nor by the typically teasing tone adopted by Andrei and Yakov, who knew full well that they shared Natalia's desire for frequent meetings. What is most striking in this exchange is Natalia's confession of boredom caused by the departure of her guests. The occupation that takes second place to work in her diaries is her social life, and during those periods when her estate work took less of her time, she was anxious to fill the void with the responsibilities, and the pleasures, of hosting guests. In addition to the fact that hosting visits required extra work and preparation, accounted for accordingly in the diaries, it is clear that Natalia took sincere joy in the frequent visits that she and her friends exchanged. Sadly for Natalia, her illnesses often curtailed social occasions, although sometimes her closest friends were able to lighten the load of her bad days and enrich her time spent as an invalid, as when Andrei wrote: "*Ma femme* is lying on the bed; and around her are her nieces and companions."[9]

Because of the impassability of the roads for much of spring and fall and the intense nature of agricultural work in summer, winter was the season for visiting, and the entire Chikhachev family frequently traveled even in bitterly cold weather. For Natalia, visiting probably held special appeal precisely because it was restricted to those periods when her estate work was at a minimum, while Andrei traveled year-round. However, the calendar of provincial life was filled with special occasions, including religious holidays, name days and birthdays, and, less often, weddings. Each village celebrated its own saint's day, with the patronage of the nobles who owned it, and the Chikhachevs were usually invited to celebrate the annual saint's day at Berezovik (Yakov once calculated the exact date on which the holiday—the tenth Sunday after the Peter fast—would fall up to 1986).[10] Every year after the threshing Natalia hosted an entertainment for the serfs of Dorozhaevo, which was hardly mentioned in her own diaries but was described by Aleksei in 1848. The main event was a dinner for the serf men in the hall, with music. Later in the same evening, Aleksei reported that they "sent to Zimenki for Maksim Ilich, the Gusli player, who amused us all evening with his music," but it is not clear from this notation if the evening festivities included the serfs, or why the women were not present for the dinner.[11]

Easter and the New Year were the most significant general holidays. Easter was mainly a religious celebration, and part of the series of holy days including Shrovetide and Good Friday, which were observed by attendance at church and special foods, but were not occasions for visiting (though sometimes a guest happened to be present). The Chikhachevs spent the New Year with Yakov and Timofei Krylov in the 1830s, but this holiday too was usually celebrated modestly (though in 1834 Yakov recorded dancing and singing).[12] Andrei described one of the first of such occasions in his 1831 diary (two years before Yakov's retirement from the navy and thus in his absence from Berezovik):

I gave Natasha and the children teacups; and Natasha bought me a green silk neck scarf. I rode to midday service alone. Sufficiently cold. Returning from the service, I went to greet the Ikonnikovs. They had only just returned from [visiting] [Maria Petrovna] Izmailova, and drove up at the same time as Timofei Ivanovich [Krylov] and myself. Then we had a celebratory shot or two [probably vodka]; then I headed home—and immediately [went off] to dine in [Teikovo]. Maria Petrovna, Dmitrii Vasilevich and Natalia Ivanovna were already seated at the table. 23 degrees below freezing, and windy. After dinner everyone played cards. At supper the conversation was about estate managers and [paid ladies'] companions.[13]

Andrei paints a picture of a relaxed holiday with few special rituals: other than the small gifts exchanged, he went to services alone, and entertainment after dinner was only the usual card-playing and chat. It is notable that the New Year was not an exclusively family-oriented occasion, nor particularly child-oriented. Rather, friends and neighbors went only slightly farther out of their way than usual to pass on everyone's "greetings" and exchange the "celebratory shot."

Other holidays were more raucous; Yakov wrote on a feast day in August 1835 that "the holy day continues and there are plenty of drunk people." Weddings, especially, were a major event. In Andrei's words, "how can you have a modest wedding?" He described his own as "a world-class feast."[14] On such occasions friends traveled from many *versts* around to attend, staying for sometimes several nights in a row, and passing the time with cards, talk, dancing, and musical recitals. When a family was unable to attend, they quizzed their more fortunate friends for all the details, as the Chikhachevs did when Yakov attended a wedding without them. An exception that proved the rule was when a neighbor, A. A. Kashcheev, married "his beloved." The Chikhachevs and Yakov had rather awkward relations with this man, and Yakov wrote to Andrei about the wedding that "I was not at home at that time, I was in Suzdal; they say that there were a lot of people in the church, but no one from the nobility!" Using the words "his beloved," as opposed to a named person the Chikhachevs ought to have been acquainted with, suggests that Kashcheev may have married beneath himself.[15]

At large events, serf orchestras or smaller groups of musicians played for the dancers, and when a landowner could boast a particularly talented serf musician, he might be called upon to loan out his services for gatherings throughout the area. But the noble young men and ladies of these houses also performed, as Aleksei did on the violin and Aleksandra on the fortepiano ("we danced a lot, the music was our own").[16] When the Chikhachevs hosted a large party, their main room was cleared for dancing in the evening and then made over into a dormitory for guests during the night; sometimes the parties Natalia hosted were so large they necessitated that some of the male visitors sleep in a barn (recalling Pushkin's *Eugene Onegin,* where guests at a ball also spent the night on the floor of the drawing room).

Less formally, the Chikhachevs and their friends gathered for small parties whenever weather permitted. Picnics were a frequent enough occurrence to warrant two separate phrases with specific code numbers in Andrei and Yakov's telegraph signal book, under the heading "pic-nic": "When will we have the picnic?" and "Where will the picnic be?" In addition—demonstrating the central importance of weather to all their social activities—under "Road" the signals listed were: "How is the road?" "The road is good," "The road is ruined," and "the road is muddy."[17] On another occasion Andrei complained of the muddy roads: "[O]ur journey more resembled a sea voyage."[18]

Natalia enjoyed the challenge of these informal parties, frequently welcoming friends with evident enthusiasm even when she was ill or busy and often doing so without prior notice, even though providing large quantities of food and beverages must have been a complex task. The Chikhachevs all enjoyed the relaxation of ceremony on informal occasions, demonstrated by Andrei's mockery of Yakov's manners when receiving his in-laws: "[P]lease do not receive us while still in bed: this is not smooth for my person, who is used to proper greetings, not farther than the second threshold. On the contrary—you stretch out our hand while lying down, and even wearing your sleeping cap. Come on! What is this?"[19]

Private indoor parties consisted of, in addition to music and dancing, a great deal of card-playing. While card-playing for significant cash stakes was considered a masculine pursuit, and certainly the very high-stakes games pursued by true gamblers in urban locales were closed to ladies, in the privacy of the family circle it was Natalia who enjoyed the thrill of playing cards for money while Andrei preferred chess, checkers, or billiards (though he played them "poorly").[20] Natalia dutifully recorded the small amounts she won or lost at whist, *preferance,* Boston, lottery, speculation, "Stukolka" (a popular Russian card game), or "idiot" in her diaries, and in 1831, Andrei described a typical marathon: "Chernev, Nikolaev, Izmailova and Nat. Iva. played Boston all day. In the evening the game was Neighbors, and then *Secretaire,* which went very well."[21] Despite his reluctance, Andrei played billiards with Yakov often, conveying invitations for a game via their telegraph system. In their notebooks they teased each other about games ("Judging by our last battle, you did not remain victorious: you must straighten yourself up")[22] and exchanged advice ("when you sit down to play with Andrei Nikolaevich, never let him have the first and the last game: your entire winnings will depend on this").[23] The pages of the notebook correspondence include several scorecards, though it was not noted to which game they referred. Later in life, card-playing became a pastime Natalia shared with her children, seemingly together only with reading aloud and visiting. Card-playing was thus perhaps the only strong interest that Natalia shared exclusively with her children and may have taken on particular significance in this light: Aleksei wrote, "Had tea with Papinka in his study. Then after having tea Maminka, Sasha, Evgenii and I sat down to play *Preferance,* and played right up until supper."[24] Since Aleksei often played billiards or rode with his father when guests were not present, but usually joined his mother in games when guests were there to make up the requisite numbers, another reason for Natalia to look forward to visits may have been the opportunity to enjoy more of her children's company.

The most frequent visitors with whom Natalia talked, played games, and exchanged gifts and favors were her cousins by marriage, the Ikonnikovs and the Yazykovs (the former family were often referred to in her diaries as "our Ikonnikovs"). Judging by the language of her diaries, Natalia's greatest joy outside of a job well done, a day of good health, or perhaps a few hours free with a good book came from visits with these and other ladies from neighboring estates, perhaps because some of them may have shared similar estate responsibilities (no correspondence between Natalia and her female land-owning friends or relatives survives). Several of the "young ladies" in nearby families were her goddaughters, and she was especially attentive to them, sending them small gifts and inquiring after their welfare; godchildren, too, were among her dependents.

The Chikhachevs' children participated in this social life, accompanying their parents on visits from a young age. Aleksei and Aleksandra were well acquainted with neighboring families, and a smattering of diary entries by Aleksei suggests that these neighbors could act as fond extended relations even in cases where no blood relationship existed. He described how his father escorted him on visits to all their close neighbors before they departed to Moscow for Aleksei's return to school in August 1838, so that these neighbors could congratulate the boy on his progress in the past year and wish him well for the next. One such entry reads: "Because of my journey to Moscow, Papinka brought me to the neighbors to say goodbye, first to the Ikonnikovs', then from there to the Kultashevs'. Vasilii Mikhailovich gave me a little book as a keepsake."[25]

As they grew up, Aleksei and Aleksandra increasingly joined in dancing, music, and card-playing with their parents and guests. A series of entries from Aleksei's 1847 diary covering Aleksandra's name day provides the most complete available narrative of this kind of sociability, and also demonstrates that Aleksei and his sister enjoyed a wide circle of friends, comprised of young men and ladies from families much like their own, whom they had probably known all their lives. Aleksei's narrative begins on the sixth of November, in his words "[t]he name day of my sweet, dear sister Sasha." Aleksei began the day by sleeping through the midday service, but his sister and her friend, a "Elena Alekseevna," attended, apparently without their parents. "At 1 o'clock, they returned and were met with music." The guest list was impressively long: "dear Uncle Nikolai Ivanovich [Zamytskii], Ivan Mikhalych Kultashev, Vasilii Mikhalych Kultashev with Agrafena Vasilevna and her children and their governess, Evgenii Vasilevich Pozharskii with his dear mother Avdotia Nikolaevna and dear sister Maria Vasilevna, Olga Petrovna, Natalia Petrovna Nelidova with Anna Ivanovna and Filip Aleksandrych with Elena Alekseevna." All the guests stayed for dinner, tea, and supper, and Aleksei "couldn't have spent a better time, danced away." They danced until "2 or 3 o'clock" in the morning, and as an after-thought Aleksei mentioned one further guest, Aleksandr Krasovskii, who arrived in the middle of the festivities. The next day Aleksei played billiards with his Uncle Zamytskii, but before the morning passed the young people were dancing again, "in two pairs, me with El[ena] Al[ekseevna] and Evgenii with Sasha." After dinner, four guests departed, and the evening was spent more quietly, merely "sitting" in the drawing room.

On the third day, Saturday, Aleksei took Krasovskii to "look at the horses in the corral, and . . . [for] a walk in the garden," but after dinner they regressed from such adult pursuits, playing like children "on the swings" and "with a ball and ring." The evening brought card-playing while at the same time, Aleksei reports, "Papasha read through my diary and expenses," presumably bringing a bit of a damper to the festivities. On Sunday, Aleksei went to the midday service with Krasovskii, then they stopped by Zimenki to have breakfast with Vasilii Mikhailovich Kultashev. "Returning home we found at our place dear Uncle Nikolai Ivanovich [Zamytskii]. After dinner we sat in the living room and chatted. Played billiards with Papinka and dear Uncle."²⁶

This circle of friends, relatives, and neighbors constituted for practical purposes the extent of the young Chikhachevs' world: Aleksei and Aleksandra, like most young people of the provincial gentry, eventually married into local families.²⁷ The Chikhachev children both chose families whose names had appeared in their parents' writings decades earlier—Aleksei married into the Boshniak clan from Yaroslavl province, and Aleksandra into the Rogozin (or Ragozin) family, several of whom were friendly with the Chikhachevs. Though neither courtship was recorded in the diaries, Aleksei wrote of his satisfaction with his sister's match in one of the final entries of his Vilno diary ("Was completely delighted with a letter from Papinka and Maminka, in which they write that Sister Sasha got engaged to Vasilii Ivanych Ragozin"), and it can probably be assumed that both marriages were pleasing to their parents, even though Aleksandra's first child arrived less than nine months after her wedding.²⁸

Another side to the lively social life the Chikhachevs enjoyed, however, was that gossip festered in such circles, in which everyone knew everyone and many of them were related to each other. Andrei alluded to this phenomenon when he wrote "[a] conversation in Maria Petrovna's bedroom was about those women about whom a multitude of black praise has been said from all sides."²⁹ They also gossiped about local events, spreading news from village to village: "Father Ivan, arriving from Kovrov, told us about a female thief of silver spoons and forks in Redikuno."³⁰ In 1860, rumors were flying among Andrei's correspondents because the marshal of the nobility for Tver province was removed from office.³¹ National and international events were also discussed among neighbors, as when Andrei reported to Yakov that his doctor, Vorobievskii, had informed him that "Paskevich [the field marshal who suppressed the Polish revolt of 1830-31] did not lose his mind as some are starting to say . . . he is in love with a Pole, wanted to divorce his wife, but the Sovereign having found out about it, said 'Has he gone crazy?'" Andrei continued on the topic of the imperial family by noting that "the heir" was expected to visit Shuia a month later.³²

In one case, gossip implicated Natalia in some sort of social tangle, recorded cryptically by Andrei in his parallel diary: "Filip Aleksandrovich Pozharskii came to explain, claiming that Natalia Ivanovna gossiped that Pozharskii's mother The Princess was trying to ensnare Young Chikhachev in her Net."[33] The Pozharskiis were neighbors, and, as the title suggests, some degree of social superiors to the Chikhachevs. Presumably, "Young Chikhachev" refers to Aleksei, who was twenty-two at the time, but it is hard to imagine what kind of "net" the princess could have ensnared him in—perhaps she was trying to make a match between Aleksei and a Pozharskii daughter? More likely, the princess had a string of young admirers, and the Chikhachevs balked at the notion of Aleksei engaging in a worldly, casual flirtation.

Rumors could be terrifying also. In 1866 Aleksei heard that his wife, Anna, traveling for her health, was in a "hopeless" state: "the rumor even passed around in Vladimir about her end. I don't believe it and trust in God. Could it be possible that you [Andrei and Natalia] and I would not be notified about it?"[34] On the whole, however, references to gossip warrant comparatively brief mention in the diaries; Natalia generally did not bother to write about it, and Andrei referred to it scornfully. More often, the opportunity to chat with their friends and equals (living as they did in a village of their own, with no adult social equals within its limits) provided a gratifying outlet, as Andrei assumed it did for Natalia during her 1831 trip to Moscow with the Ikonnikovs. He noted in his diary that the trip would give her an opportunity to discuss topics of such enormous emotional weight as the loss of children and the then-virulent cholera epidemic. After wondering to himself if Natalia could have made it to Moscow already despite a blizzard, he wrote, "If at Nesterova's, then [she] probably found there a bunch of 'brunettes,' and some of the fashionable visitors, for example Mrs. Sleptsova. How much conversation! . . . Surprises . . . Regrets . . . the matter of cholera . . . of the daughter's death."[35]

Sociability had to have been a comfort and source of stimulation to any resident of the countryside. But Natalia's complaints of isolation, and the enthusiasm she showed for visits, demonstrate that the lessened mobility her estate work entailed took its toll in greater loneliness and boredom. At the same time, the social life offered in this provincial setting appears to have been sufficiently lively and diverse—more so, at least, than Russian novels of the mid- to late nineteenth century would suggest. This provincial society enjoyed a wide range of social events, from serf entertainments and village holy days to private weddings for hundreds of guests to impromptu picnics to the semi-social visits of local clerks, doctors, merchants, and others of middling ranks. Although the national statistical reference book compiled by the military in 1852 claimed that landowners in Vladimir province were privileged in living relatively close to Moscow because they could "leave their villages in winter or move" to the capital, where life was "more varied, more cheerful, and [only] a little more expensive than life in Vladimir," in fact the Chikhachevs and their friends were usually content with winters in the country.[36]

Outside of visiting and her estate work, Natalia's chief occupations revolved around religious observance and charity (which was almost always connected with her religious observance). Historical work on gender in a variety of nineteenth-century contexts has suggested that religious faith sometimes offered privileged women alternative avenues for personal fulfillment and cultural influence. In western Europe, philanthropic women were in the vanguard of coping with major nineteenth-century social dilemmas, constituting a separate but parallel "public sphere" to the wage-earning sphere of men. Russian women, too, used their moral authority as women to create a meaningful place for themselves in the larger world via charitable organizations. Ranging from the activities of Romanov empresses and grand duchesses to those of the earliest proto-feminists, Russian women's charity in this period was a way in which women used assumptions about female virtue to expand their sphere, as well as simply an expression of sincere religiosity.[37]

While Orthodox faith and the charity this faith demanded were important to both Chikhachevs, Natalia's benevolence was distinctly that of the landowner, and as such strikingly different from the "female" charity documented by historians in Russia and in western Europe and the United States.[38] Natalia recorded in her diaries the exact amounts of the small change she gave daily to the village church for candles, and to the local poor living in or passing through her villages (both peasant and noble: "The poor nobles Bolot[?]ovy came from Kostroma with the little orphan, the secretary's daughter. Gave them 12 *arshins* of canvas; 10 *arshins* of printed cotton; my light-blue canvas house-robe; a handkerchief, a skein of [white?] and 3 rubles 20 kopeks of money").[39] She also participated in needlework done for the church (such as helping to decorate priests' vestments), she handed out "sweets" to "the little children,"[40] and she taught her own children and grandchildren to do the same by giving them money with instructions to donate it (writing once to Aleksei and his wife that the five-kopek coins she sent for their son, and described as a "present," were to be "used for the church, not for something else").[41] Her charity was on a small scale, of an almost daily regularity, and entirely local. It was directed exclusively toward the needy of her immediate community, most of whom constituted her dependents in any case. In this sense, her charity can be seen as an extension of a management role that revolved around the feeding and clothing of all the peasants and the clerical family in her domain.

By contrast, a great part of Andrei's later years were devoted to his work as a lay church elder (*ktitor*), which would provide the impetus for much of his charity. Having experienced a religious epiphany in 1848–50, faith became one of his most passionate interests, a subject to which he devoted a short memoir. Natalia is scarcely mentioned in this memoir; a rare exception, significantly, explains that it was she and Aleksei who convinced Andrei not to become a monk on the grounds that his first duty was to his family. Andrei later built a brick church in Zimenki, which involved collecting donations for the construction, for the famous icon they placed there, and for the restoration of a nearby monastery. Natalia may have helped in this endeavor, but neither spouse left a record to say how, or to what extent.

Natalia once mentioned her joy upon receiving an icon, delivered to the Chikhachevs in Moscow from Dorozhaevo, and this, along with the daily prayers mentioned in her diaries, suggests that she, too, had a strong personal faith. She described the event of the icon's delivery in her 1842 diary: "A picture of the Vladimir Mother of God was brought

from Dorozhaevo and she, the Little Mother, made me very happy."[42] This entry is notable because Natalia so rarely referred to her feelings, remarking only very occasionally on
a book that she "enjoyed it" but otherwise speaking only of objective facts. In contrast, on
the same day Andrei merely wrote, "From Dorozhaevo they brought the icon of the
Vladimir Virgin"; this icon did not carry the same significance for Andrei as it did for
Natalia.[43] When Natalia was not able to attend daily church services, she recorded in her
diary that she performed her own prayers at home. Occasionally, on a religious holiday, if
Natalia was unable to attend the village church, their priest would perform a special service in the Chikhachevs' home. She read the same religious works as her husband, and
when he befriended the cleric Father Sila, from Kovrov, she participated in their talks
when they visited each other.[44] Despite the common cultural assumption (perhaps limited to the capitals) that village priests were uncouth and semi-literate, both Chikhachevs'
references to local priests, in their own village and others, are almost invariably respectful,
and they spent a great deal of time with the Dorozhaevo and Zimenki clerics. (One possible exception was when Andrei met two priests while traveling and described one as
"feeble-minded"—the other was one-eyed.)[45]

Natalia may have reinforced, though not driven, Andrei's religious fervor in his later
years. In a singular incident from his memoir, "Notes from a Monk's Cell," Natalia, specifically, prompted one of their religious excursions. It was around 1850, while they were
visiting their relative General Pavel Kupreianov in Moscow to thank him for his patronage during their son's military service, that "on [Natalia's] suggestion" they went to pray
to the miraculous icon of the Mother of God, named Defender of Sinners, at the St.
Nicholas Church in Khamovniki (on the outskirts of Moscow at that time).[46] Beyond
these few references, Natalia's faith, unlike her husband's, continued to be expressed privately and thus little more can be known about it. Perhaps her interest in icons of the
Virgin indicates a link with Marianism, a movement venerating Mary, but there is not
sufficient evidence in the archive to substantiate this.[47] It may only be said that Yakov
shared Natalia's attention to icons and other religious tokens. In 1837 Yakov mentioned
to the Chikhachevs in the notebook correspondence that he had commissioned a painting of St. Barbara the Martyr with a cypress frame, for two rubles. At the same time he
ordered twelve little glasses from the same craftsman, who would not be able to deliver
them or the portrait of the martyr until after Holy Week, because "he is in a hurry with
his decoration of the *kiota* [a box for icons with a glass door] for the image of Nicholas
the Miraclemaker."[48] This attention to the outward signs of faith is both characteristic of
Yakov and Natalia's more practical and less philosophical outlook on life (as compared to
Andrei's) and perhaps a tendency they shared from their common upbringing.

Andrei's faith was made a public matter when he wrote his memoir about his religious
experiences (unpublished, but addressed to posterity and written in a formal manner
appropriate for a public work), and by the hundreds of letters he sent to friends and
strangers alike describing his religious epiphany and asking for donations to his charitable
projects. His charity could not have been more public, in the sense of having to do with the

world beyond their estates and people he did not actually know. The opposite of Natalia, Andrei was philanthropic only on a grand scale, building the church and library, and restoring the monastery all in a single decade of flurried activity. The fact that Natalia's presence in these endeavors, if any, was not visible shows that her expressions of faith and charity remained of a personal, local nature, as in her diaries of the 1830s. Perhaps, already being responsible for the well-being of several hundred people through her position as manager of the family estates, she lacked some of the motivations that pushed other women of her time into public philanthropy.

When they were not praying, working, or visiting, all the Chikhachevs spent copious time reading, and like all their other activities, reading was gendered. A beloved activity for both spouses, reading occupied the whole family nearly every evening and often at other times of the day. Reading was also interlaced with their social lives, since they shared books and journals with their friends and read aloud during visits. While the access to worlds beyond their own that books and newspapers offered was highly valued by all, the significance of reading differed for each spouse.[49] What was livelihood to the husband was respite and recreation for the wife.

In her diaries Natalia recorded that she read something—"a book" or "the newspapers"—in nearly every entry, with the exception of some periods during the harvest season when it is apparent from her handwriting and the content of the entries that she was too exhausted even to be coherent in writing, and thus was unable to devote time to leisure. But on a normal day, she either read or knitted in the mornings after her prayers, or read in the evening instead. On many evenings Andrei read aloud while Natalia knitted, presenting an image of patriarchal domestic bliss undermined only by the knowledge that Andrei understood his reading as an act of pedagogy aimed primarily at himself and his children (not his wife), and Natalia was not knitting the decorative purses or doilies called for in the new Victorian knitting manuals. She was, like Andrei, engaged in *her* work: knitting stockings for her dependents.[50]

Tastes in reading were necessarily eclectic in an environment where there was never enough new material to satisfy avid readers. Journals, newspapers, and books were devoured with equal enthusiasm by Andrei, Natalia, Yakov, Timofei Krylov, and their friends and neighbors. When new material was in short supply, Yakov once resorted to re-reading newspapers from the entire year of 1814. He enjoyed himself thoroughly and shared with Andrei a fascinating anecdote about the financial scandals of Lord Cochrane (the real English lord who inspired the fictional characters Horatio Hornblower and Jack Aubrey).[51] Andrei referred to books as if they were candy: "I have literary treats for you in sufficient amounts."[52] And Natalia teased her brother with the possibility that an issue of the literary journal *Library for Reading* "which is so famous" (having already been mentioned several times by Andrei) could soon be his: "Wouldn't you like, dear brother, to read [it]. . . . If you do, let me know, and I'll send it to you."[53]

Exchanging reading materials only after everyone had had a chance to peruse them could get complicated, as when Andrei wrote: "Enclosed is an issue of newspaper so that

I might, in exchange, borrow another issue, and if Uncle has read this one as well, please loan me both: because N[atalia] I[vanovna] has read it but I have not even touched it."[54] The most enjoyable texts were read multiple times, especially out loud: "I have read with special pleasure the necrology [by?] the Saratov [archpriest?] Skopin in the newspapers. I have read it twice in a row, the first time for myself and the second time aloud for Nat. Iv. Quite a little priest!"[55] Impatience crept in when reading matter was held up: "The newspapers are still being read by N.I. (at least this is what she is saying),"[56] and "I am not sending it to you because Nat. Iv. has not even finished the first parts yet, which are both, God be with them, so thick!"[57]

Written mentions of their reading are the pale reflection of more frequent discussions that took place in person: "I have quite liked this book [about Napoleon by Zilov], and I hope that when we meet, my dear brother, we'll chat about it for a good while."[58] Andrei was draconian about how reading aloud in the family should proceed, including that it be followed always by discussion. He declared to his brother-in-law that the hours for reading aloud should be "appointed" (Yakov understandably protested that it was unpleasant to be forced to read when you "don't want to"), but Andrei averred that nothing else "creates a more fruitful conversation," nor could reading by oneself "give so many occasions for judgment, contemplating [and] reasoning." He declared that reading and discussing with others even "familiarizes a man . . . with himself" better than reading alone. Concluding, Andrei asked Yakov to "dedicate" to reading aloud with him "if not . . . every meeting, even if not every week, at least two hours per month." Yakov could but reply, "I agree completely."[59]

Reading aloud was clearly on Andrei's mind that spring of 1835. A short while earlier he had similarly lectured Yakov on precisely how a session of reading aloud must proceed (using a numbered list of rules, no less): "there must not be any interference, and no getting up from one's seat," the session must begin immediately at the appointed time, with any other issues for discussion put off for a later time, "[i]t is only permitted to interrupt the reader for an explanation that concerns the subject being read," and finally, after the session was complete, "it is permitted to talk, even if the piece being read is still not done," so long as the allotted reading time of one hour was fulfilled. Andrei claimed that according to his plan the reading "would be both pleasant and useful," as opposed to a more loosely organized evening during which "we just purr on to ourselves." Rather ominously, Andrei also alluded to his temper and its unpleasant consequences for listeners who did not obey his rules: "[o]therwise what we have is going in, going out, knocking, noise, talk—and I am throwing the book to the floor and am most terribly annoyed."[60]

The Chikhachevs had their own subscription to the *Agricultural Gazette* and several other periodicals.[61] They all regularly mentioned reading "the newspapers," which included the *Vladimir Provincial News* and sometimes issues of the *Moscow Provincial News*, probably brought along occasionally by a traveling friend, as well as the large-format daily national newspaper the *Northern Bee*, Andrei's favorite, which devoted itself to both political and literary topics: covering domestic and foreign news, and containing a *feuilleton*, book reviews, and announcements in every issue. Foreign news was particularly hard to come by. Andrei reported with frustration that "[i]n the newspapers and the *Northern Bee* they printed that [Field Marshal] Dibich has been summoned to Poland. There's no further word about military affairs."[62] Another newspaper called *Russian Invalid, or Military News* catered in part to retired nobles like Andrei, who retained a lifelong interest in military matters. It consisted of only a few pages of domestic military news, announcements, and the text of decrees issued by the emperor. *Invalid* also included a literary supplement, but Andrei despised its "uneven style," declaring one day that "everything there is apathetic and rotten."[63] Some of the periodicals they read were less for aesthetic enjoyment and more for reference, such as the *Moscow Medical Newspaper* or the *Library of Medical Sciences*. Others were mentioned in passing, probably borrowed from friends, like the *Odessa Herald* or the *Journal of People's Enlightenment*.[64]

In addition to newspapers and technical works, the Chikhachevs enjoyed a relatively new component of the Russian print market: journals. Thicker and less frequently published than newspapers, these contained both Russian and translated works of literature and poetry, essays, and miscellaneous features of general interest. The Chikhachevs read most of the popular journals of the day: *Son of the Fatherland*, which included fashion notes, sometimes in French; the *Muscovite*, covering news and literature; the *Russian Herald*; the *Dawn;* and the *Library for Reading*, which Natalia claimed as her favorite. This latter journal was described on its title page as "a journal of language arts, science, art, criticism of industry, news and fashion," and contained poetry, plays, prose fiction, and history written by many of the major writers of the time, as well as essays and "mixed" pieces. Notoriously middlebrow, the *Library for Reading* was the most successful periodical of the time, possibly the only one to be truly profitable and popular, judging by its impressive circulation numbers.[65]

Between new issues of periodicals, Natalia and her husband and brother frequently shared books, which they ordered from booksellers in the capitals, or had fetched by friends.[66] Conflicting accounts list Yakov's library as containing either 245 volumes, or 600, and Andrei's collection must have been at least comparable.[67] Although Natalia does not seem to have shared Andrei and Yakov's predilection for military memoirs or reference books (especially the *Encyclopedic Lexicon,* much admired by both men throughout the notebook correspondence), they otherwise shared equal interest in novels, plays, poetry, histories, and religious works.[68] They mentioned religious texts regularly, but Andrei admitted that these were not always as beguiling as the other literature they consumed: after reading the Gospels and catechism Andrei wrote that while this had been good for the soul, it was a shame that "we like this reading less than the vain, lay reading."[69]

In her diary, Natalia mentioned Fanny Burney's *Camilla,* and the whole family read Jane Austen's *Emma*.[70] Andrei admired *Emma*, saying "the style is smooth, the characters are picturesque, the reasoning is convincing," in contrast to another translated novel, called *The Cuckold,* which he disapproved of without quite knowing why ("The end is pathetic, and also there is just something there that I did not like.")[71] The family also read Sir Walter Scott's *Rob Roy* (Yakov complaining that it was difficult going at the beginning, but the worn condition of the book—indicating it had passed through many hands—attested to its quality), Byron's "Bride of Abydos," an unnamed work by Balzac (which also did not meet with Yakov's approval—"too fashionable"), as well as much older foreign fiction like the seventeenth-century novel *Hao qiu zhuan,* the first Chinese literary work to become famous in Europe, translated into Russian from English (as *The Fortunate Union* or *The Good Match*) in 1832.[72]

Of contemporary Russian authors, Bulgarin and Pushkin were Andrei's favorites. Their latest works were read quickly (often aloud, for the whole family), re-read, and then discussed by Yakov and Andrei, partly on the pages of the notebook correspondence. Andrei even listed the year of Pushkin's death in his chronology of major dates in his family's life.[73] Another favorite Russian writer was the historian and sentimentalist Nikolai Karamzin, whose popular *History of the Russian State* Yakov called "the key to history."[74] Karamzin's story "Poor Liza" was listed by Yakov as among the books in his possession in 1843, and he mentioned "works" by the eighteenth-century poet Gavrila Derzhavin in a notebook along with Karamzin's history.[75]

Military history and the history of the Romanovs were especially popular topics in the Chikhachev household. Yakov and Andrei mentioned books regarding Russian wars or military campaigns from the years 1808–09 (Finland), 1812, 1813, 1814–15 (France), and 1828–29 (Turkey). While reading Danilevskii's notes about the campaign of 1812, Andrei wrote: "the imagination is so occupied by the occurrences of that time, and especially by the descriptions of the properties of the Meek and Blessed [Emperor] Alexander [I], that I did not want to lay down the book even for a minute." Andrei read these histories for entertainment as well as edification, since he noted that "at the first reading I wanted to know quickly what happens next and much escapes the attention," so that he had to read the book again.[76] Other nonfiction ranged from a book about how to keep nightingales and canaries to "The Art of Writing As Quickly As One Speaks" to a handbook for the "home healer," a genealogical table of Russian princely families, a book on mediating land disputes, Polevoi's popular history of Russia, "Conversations with Children about Astronomy and the Sky," a "Memorial Book of the Postal Service," and a "Repertoire of Russian Theater and a Pantheon of all European Theaters."

Natalia mentioned reading *The House of Romanov* in her diary, and when on another occasion Andrei read aloud to her a history of Catherine the Great, she commented, "the *tsaritsa* was wonderful!"[77] It is tempting to imagine that she admired the empress specifically as a female manager (on a very large scale), but if she did, she did not put it writing. Most often, Natalia simply wrote, "I read a book," or "I read the newspapers," only occasionally adding after finishing a book, "I enjoyed it."[78] While there is a record of Natalia reading at least a few titles that related specifically to women (in addition to the history of Catherine II, there was a work called *Transformation of the Beauty,* which may have been a translation of *Pygmalion,* and another book titled *God's Amazons*)[79] or written by women (*Emma, Camilla*), these texts were also read by the rest of her family, and neither Natalia nor anyone else mentioned these titles in such a way as to identify them as "female" texts. There is no indication that novels, or French novels, or novels containing romantic plots were feminized or in any way distinguished from other works of fiction enjoyed by the whole family.[80] The only definite reading preference noted as Natalia's alone was her penchant for the journal *A Library for Reading*, which can only be distinguished from other journals by its relatively broader coverage of many subjects, from the arts to news to "industrial" topics.

In short, neither the daily context of reading nor particular texts were gendered by the Chikhachevs. Rather it was the purposes that reading served that differed for each spouse. Reading helped Natalia to get through difficult periods of forced inactivity brought on by illness. The following conversation from the notebook correspondence in 1835 demonstrates that reading as a source of comfort was encouraged by the men in her life, as they sought to obtain books to her taste (in lieu of a visit from "the Cherepanov girls"). Yakov wrote, "Dear sister is asking for something else. The Cherepanov girls have just left Gubachevo, I think to go home. For my dear sister I am sending you *The Anecdotes of Peter the Great*; and if [she?] wills, will also send you to read the History of Napoleon and Karamzin's *Spirit*." Andrei replied with specifics of Natalia's continued illness ("Natalia Ivanovna's side keeps getting sometimes better sometimes worse. [T]his is no joke: ear ache creates pain in the entire head, and the slightest movement again creates pain.") and said he was returning *Anecdotes of Peter the Great* with a request for another title "to exercise the eyes." Ending on a lighter note, he indicated that Natalia was sleeping by punning on the verb for "to snore," *khrapet,* saying that she was "in dialog with Khrapovitskii," Andrei having "put her to sleep with Napoleon," referring to the history that Chernavin had passed along to them.[81]

Although Natalia did not share her husband's compulsion to write down her responses, reading clearly comprised a highly valued form of leisure and stimulation for her. The nightly readings aloud within the family circle made it a social activity as well (despite Andrei's draconian rules), bringing the family together, along with the nanny, governess, or tutor who may have been living with them at any given time in the 1830s, and the relatives, friends, and local clerics who were also frequently present during their evening activities. Perhaps the fact that participants discussed their reactions in person accounts for why Natalia wrote so little about her responses in the diaries; the pleasure she took from reading along with her family was sufficient.

This could not be the case for her husband, because reading was at the center of his responsibilities to his family. Andrei considered reading important to his self-education, which in turn was vital to his project of educating his children. Thus, when he read Karamzin's history, he did not merely "enjoy it" like Natalia, he attempted to memorize the content, saying, "after the end of the entire story I will start from the beginning, so that the matters that have entered my memory would not pop out again, and then I will write down on a sheet of paper all the 'chi': Iziaslavichi, Vseslavichi, Vladimirovichi,

Olgovichi." For Natalia, reading was personal, involved only the private circle of their household, and was appreciated as a respite from estate work. But for Andrei, reading was his entrée into the greater world beyond the estate, in which he could engage with other men who shared with him only their common interest in ideas. This prepared him to be a better moral and intellectual guide to his children.

The opportunities afforded to the Chikhachevs by reading were a relatively recent phenomenon for provincial Russians. The exact nature and depth of the rising reading culture in Russia in the second quarter of the nineteenth century is debated, but it is apparent that significantly more books and periodicals were printed at this time than previously. The degree to which they were read and by whom is more contested, and on these issues the Chikhachevs shed some light.[82]

Print culture in Russia began to expand gradually in the mid-eighteenth century, and there was a contemporary perception of a vast explosion in the 1820s and '30s. This development is so closely comparable to the canonical expansion of print culture in England at the same time as to give rise to speculation that there was in fact little or no explosion in Russia, merely a perception of one brought about by excessive copying from the British periodical press.[83] Judging the existence of an explosion depends on whether one measures the number of books and periodicals being printed, the number of readers, the type of readers, the nature and quality of the texts published, or the means by which printed materials were produced, distributed, and sold.[84] At one extreme, scholars argue that at least in Britain technological innovations led to an explosion in the number of books and periodicals, along with the number of readers, and that the nature of readership expanded to include middle-class and perhaps even lower-class readers; the type of printed materials also changed rapidly with a shift from poetry to prose, the emergence of novels, especially gothic novels, and a proliferation of new periodicals, especially satirical journals, which offered a wide variety of reading material including criticism and the juxtaposition of fiction and nonfiction. Much is also made of the emergence of lending libraries, which made available by subscription books that may not have been otherwise affordable. Scholars have questioned or qualified all these facets of the print culture explosion in Britain, but the general conclusion remains that more middle-class readers were reading more novels and periodicals, often borrowing them. However, an important caveat is that books remained expensive, restricting access to the latest Romantic literature to the wealthier strata of society.[85]

In Russia there is a roughly comparable story on a smaller scale. Under Catherine the Great in the late eighteenth century several new periodicals emerged, including the first without government sponsorship, sounding the opening salvos in the process of expansion. The mechanization of printing continued to lag well behind Britain (as it did in most countries in Europe), but despite these obstacles there was growth in the Russian print industry, especially in the 1830s. Even so, editors and publishers lamented the difficulty of reaching subscribers, and a seeming glut was reached by the early 1840s that forced publishers to cut back, many finding themselves in financial difficulties from overinvestment.[86] At the same time, scholars have observed a preoccupation in advice literature and even artistic literature with instructing readers in how to read: articles addressed how cheap and superficial French fiction adversely affected readers; literary critics battled each other over whose motives toward readers were pure (as opposed to those whose motives were profit-driven); and in a remarkably widespread phenomenon, writers and editors posed as imaginary provincial readers, modeling the kind of contribution from readers that they hoped to inspire. All these phenomena have forced some scholars to conclude that provincial readership was limited in quantity and social composition. At least in the eyes of urban writers, provincial readers were also naive and uncritical.[87]

Arbiters of print culture in this period were also preoccupied with the nature of the provincial estate, the role of the provincial landowner, and the technical and scientific minutiae of estate management, agriculture, and domestic culture—an interest that seems to have arisen in response to the 1762 emancipation of the nobility from mandatory state service, which left nobles newly able to spend significant time in the country. Scholars surveying the vast literature on these topics observe a pattern: enthusiastic self-styled experts printed thousands of pages in the hopes of transforming the Russian countryside for the better, only to meet (or feel they met) with failure in their own experiments and ringing silence from the public.[88]

Yet, the Chikhachev family and—significantly—their neighbors were enthusiastic provincial readers who not only subscribed to periodicals, bought books, and absorbed nearly every printed word they could access (and they had surprisingly easy access to a surprising amount), but were also moved to act on what they read (at least sometimes), were critical readers (though their assessments often did not align with those of the Petersburg literati), and, at least in Andrei's case, began to contribute to ongoing printed discourse. Were provincial readers myth or reality? Clearly, real readers did exist, and they were happy to consume more printed material as it became available and affordable. Recent studies focusing on Tver and Tula provinces have demonstrated the existence of a provincial reading public from which it can be extrapolated that the much-discussed, improbably high circulation numbers of the *Library for Reading* were not invented.[89] The Chikhachevs' responses to their reading reveals, in addition, something about the reason for urban perceptions of an inert or unenthusiastic, or even nonexistent, provincial reading public, as well as something about the likely nature of real provincial reading habits.

What is perhaps most peculiar about Andrei's, and by extension his family's, reading habits from the point of view of canonical Russian literary history is that their favorite Russian writers were Faddei Bulgarin and Alexander Pushkin.[90] Pushkin can boast the rare achievement of great fame and admiration in his lifetime along with a lasting place among an internationally recognized pantheon of great national writers. Pushkin is credited with inventing the Russian literary language as well as writing several of the greatest works in the Russian canon, from the novel in verse *Eugene Onegin* to the narrative poem "The Bronze Horseman" to the historical novel *The Captain's Daughter* (although he is not as well known abroad as Tolstoy or Dostoevsky, due in large part to the difficulty of translating his inventive way with language). In his lifetime Pushkin managed both to be associated with the liberal Decembrist rebels and to enjoy the sometime patronage of the arch-conservative Tsar Nicholas I. Moreover, he came by both reputations honestly. The Decembrists were friends of Pushkin who deliberately kept him out of their conspiracy to protect him. Pushkin's relationship with Nicholas was fraught, but it appears that Nicholas, while fearing Pushkin's liberal sympathies, respected his enormous talent, not to mention his cultural influence.

Faddei Bulgarin, on the other hand, was Pushkin's opposite in almost every respect. His writing and publishing projects did well financially, but in his time he was reviled by his fellow writers as a hack, a plagiarist, and most devastatingly, an informant for the Third Section, Nicholas's secret police. His long-term legacy is nearly nonexistent, and certainly his works are rarely read and even more rarely admired.[91] Along with his fellow editors and writers Nikolai Grech and Osip Senkovskii, Bulgarin was part of the "unholy triumvirate," responsible, in the account of other writers, for either debasing the public taste or at least catering to it out of base motives. Between the lines, these men were reviled for popularizing Official Nationality. The Polish-born Bulgarin was also the opposite of a national writer; he was criticized for mangling the Russian language, overusing cloying words, and making grammatical mistakes.

How could the same reader who considered Pushkin almost a member of the family regard Faddei Bulgarin as equally beloved, like a personal friend? Andrei left little explanation of his love for Pushkin, though perhaps this, at least, is unnecessary. Pushkin is an icon because the aesthetic quality and timeless appeal of his writing are difficult to deny. The urban literati who criticized Bulgarin may have harped on Bulgarin's style and content in large part because they could not write openly about his work as an informant for the Third Section, but Andrei could not have been aware of his hero's involvement, and if he had been, he may have admired it. If he had known of Pushkin's connections and sympathy with the Decembrists, he may have disapproved. It should not be surprising that provincial readers, had they been aware of these political undercurrents, may have interpreted them through a more conservative and unquestioningly patriotic lens.

A good part of the public campaign against Bulgarin consisted of a series of devastating critical reviews of Bulgarin's journal *Ekonom* in the competing *Notes of the Fatherland*. Interestingly, Andrei did not subscribe to *Ekonom,* and apparently not to *Notes of the Fatherland,* though the latter did occasionally get mentioned by the Chikhachevs.[92] So Andrei may not have been aware of the vitriol against Bulgarin. It is also possible that effusive as Andrei's praise of Bulgarin was, he did not necessarily approve of every one of Bulgarin's ventures, such as *Ekonom*, which concerned itself with domestic and agricultural matters, and was notoriously inaccurate in its advice. It is easy to assume that Andrei simply preferred the news and literary content of Bulgarin's *Northern Bee*, while Natalia, who was more likely to be interested in domestic and agricultural content, may not have been satisfied by the offerings in *Ekonom*. Of course, it is also possible that Andrei did not subscribe to *Ekonom* because it was one of the more expensive journals.

One of the most cutting charges lobbed at Bulgarin by *Notes of the Fatherland*—that Bulgarin's journal was full of material plagiarized from his competitors—would probably not have tarnished the hero's reputation in Andrei's eyes. In the 1820s Pushkin led the way in establishing writers' rights over their intellectual property, so the concept of plagiarism as stealing was still relatively new.[93] Since Andrei did not make his living by writing, and his society still generally considered writing a hobby of gentlemen whose incomes were supposed to come from land ownership or government service, it is not hard to suppose that the plagiarism charge would not have seemed serious to many contemporary readers. Moreover, Andrei and Yakov made daily practice of collecting excerpts from novels, instructional and religious literature that they found useful or interesting, and putting all these excerpts together into their notebooks. They may have viewed Bulgarin's role as journal editor in a similar light, as a collector of interesting pieces.

In addition, Bulgarin's florid and repetitive style was probably not offensive to Andrei, since it is remarkably like Andrei's own writing style. Andrei also overused sentimental terms and belabored his prose with excessive adjectives.[94] That said, Yakov enjoyed Bulgarin nearly as much as Andrei did, and Yakov's own writing style was much more restrained, not qualifying as "Bulgarinese." Yet, even Yakov rhetorically asked, "can Bulgarin write badly[?]" in unabashed approval of the historical novel *Ivan Mazepa*.[95]

Andrei did criticize style in the works he read: he admired the "smooth" quality of Jane Austen's prose and disliked the "uneven" style of the *Invalid* literary supplement. But he was never more specific about how or why particular styles did or did not appeal to him. Most of his critical remarks are, at bottom, statements of differing taste rather than substantive critiques, such as his colorful comment that "the creation of Mr. Svinin seemed like the sounds of the animals that are cognate with his name [swine]" or "Natiazhka! . . . A tiring story, whose every line weighs 100 *puds*. I hardly have the patience to finish off part three, and I still have one more left!!!!!!"[96] Criticizing *Invalid's* editor Pliushar, Andrei sounded like one of Bulgarin's critics when he wrote, "[Pliushar] either must have failed to read it himself or otherwise does not know how to value literature."[97] Crucially, though, unlike Bulgarin's professional critics Andrei did not specify how he himself valued literature.

Andrei noticed that his criticism was not like that of professionals: "to critique [literature] in a true manner is the affair of a strong scholar-wizard. But as to ourselves—it's a so-so, domestic [kind of criticism]!"[98] Putting Andrei and Yakov's various comments together, their reading of literature seems largely moral rather than aesthetic. When they approved of a work, they approved of the behavior of characters, or they agreed with the reasoning of the author or characters. When they disliked a work, they disliked it for being "fashionable"—that is, urban, secular, Western—or for otherwise not ringing true to their own values and experiences (as Andrei wrote, "[I r]ead in bed from Karamzin's Anecdote by the title *Jealousy* but it didn't please me: for too much was made up").[99] Finally, when Andrei complained about the literary supplement of *Invalid* he added that his complaint was not merely that his time was wasted by reading something that did not please him, but that he was actually harmed by reading bad writing, such that it could even impede his own ability to write:

> It's not enough to beat up the time in an empty way, without any benefit. No! There is also the greatest harm for me. Because the uneven style weighs on me with all of its burden in a murderous way. Having forced myself to read more of this rubbish I might lose my last ability to drive the inked pen around on paper.[100]

After finishing another work Andrei vowed, "I give myself my word not to read these Messrs dime-a-dozen writers. It only bangs away the time for nothing."[101] Wasted time was time not spent in worthwhile pursuits, and that was a form of moral failure.

One of the central matters of confusion between the perception of the reading public given in the periodical press and the evidence of the Chikhachevs is what seems to be a simple matter: How much reading material was actually available to provincial readers? Only the *Library for Reading* had steady and profitable subscription rates in this period, according to the complaints of its competitors.[102] Yet historian Gary Marker has found that even in the eighteenth century the book trade was already reaching out into the provinces (though at a financial loss).[103] In 1802 Nikolai Karamzin claimed "that most readers [were] merchants and townspeople."[104] Extrapolating from the British model, it seems reasonable to suppose that even in an environment of increasing publication, many readers of middling or modest wealth would not have been able to maintain expensive subscriptions.[105] Yet, in contrast to all this, Andrei once complained that "[d]ue to lack of books published by contemporary authors, I am reading Buffon's [eighteenth-century] *Natural History* translated into Russian." He then mentioned reading the *Moscow News* and *Northern Bee*, which "once a week remind us that something is still being published in our Rus." If not for these newspapers, wrote Andrei, "the literary world would be completely alien to us," since without new infusions of reading material "our region" had only "things printed in the 18th century . . . to read."[106] In specifying "our region," Andrei was arguing contrary to the conventional wisdom of the capitals, saying that the provinces were in fact filled with readers hungry for new material that was *not* necessarily forthcoming.

Aside from the availability of affordable reading material, there was the matter of taste. Literature scholar Melissa Frazier has noted that "the new readers of an apparently burgeoning literary marketplace in Russia, Great Britain, and elsewhere have generally been credited with a good deal less sophistication than the smaller and more elite reading publics of earlier eras,"[107] but a growing reading public will, by being larger, also become more diverse. Provincial readers like the Chikhachevs and their friends simply did not always share the tastes of the literati (which is not the same as being uncritical readers). Seeming to recognize the underlying purpose of many Russian periodicals to encourage provincial reading habits, Andrei ranted about the literary supplement to *Invalid* that "[t]his is no way to lure someone in but to repel them; devil take these supplements; there is nothing useful in them except for the paper on which they are printed."[108]

The relationship between reader and writer was conceived by Romantic writers as analogous to an ideal marriage, according to Frazier: "[T]his apparently intimate sharing of interpretive control ironically devolves into the concentration of power in one side of the relationship alone," the powerful side being that of the writer.[109] The tension of this unequal relationship was felt by readers like the Chikhachevs, as when Andrei railed against the editor of the *Invalid* supplement. The consciousness of any given text being directed at a particular kind of reader was not lost on these provincial readers (to give a simple example, Yakov once wrote that "[t]o read Polevoi's history is quite curious and engaging—even though it is composed for <u>elementary reading</u>").[110] There is also a suggestion that reading quality literature could intimidate Andrei, who dabbled in writing a novel in the 1830s but never completed it. He wrote to Yakov in 1836, "You see what it means to read [Griboedov's] *Woe from Wit* for the fourth time; verse sticks to my pen by itself so that I can't tear it off."[111] In contrast, Bulgarin's less impressive output directly inspired Andrei to contribute nonfiction pieces to journals and newspapers, which he ultimately did with considerable success.

To what extent is it possible to assess what kind of tastes provincial readers may have shared? Prefacing his remarks as "the kind of criticism of one who has not finished reading," Andrei wrote a detailed critique of a work by "Mr. Lutkovskii," which illuminates what Andrei was looking for in his reading.[112] Describing the author as "more of a dreamer than an experienced man" based on his descriptions ("basically sketches without shadows"), Andrei was disappointed that "[t]he author's thoughts that peek through in some places show that he observes the human heart, but these places are not many." Andrei found fault in the writer's relative lack of soul or heart, which quixotically marked Lutkovskii as *less* experienced and *more* of a dreamer—in other words, to Andrei an experienced man acquired heart or soul, while a superficially polished mere "dreamer" lacked depth of feeling:

> I don't know why I think that Mr. L-kii could be a man who did well in school, who knows a good deal, has read a lot, possesses polite manners, is efficient in the written aspect of any kind of service, a kind fellow, a nice chap, the soul of any company, and a writer—just not a Romantic writer.

It is not surprising for a man of Andrei's personality to come down on the side of sensibility over sense, but he claimed at least that he spoke for the tastes of his generation: "We are not living in the age when Lolotte and Fanfan were printed," he wrote, referring to Francois Guillaume Ducray-Duminil's *Fanfan and Lolotte, the Story of Two Children Abandoned on a Desert Island,* originally published in Paris in 1787 and printed in several Russian editions. "No," he said of his own day, "the author must seduce, delight, charm, engage us. Otherwise [we] will hardly buy even half the print run of the edition."

Romantic readers, according to Andrei, could not be satisfied by characters that "are understated, underdrawn."[113] He seems to attest to the worst assumptions of the condescending literati that provincial readers craved broad emotionalism over artistic subtlety.

Details of the "Chinese novel" (*Hao qiu zhuan*) enjoyed by Andrei and Yakov offer some compelling suggestions as to why it would please a provincial readership: it features an idealized emperor who punishes evil courtiers and officials.[114] Similarly, the other works marked out by the Chikhachevs' circle for approval seem to speak to their own experiences, and often in terms that, as Andrei put it, "seduce, delight, charm, engage us." Perhaps it was precisely because urban periodicals attempted to "provide models of the capable reader in an attempt to build an audience," that so many of them failed, and perhaps the *Library for Reading* succeeded because it did find real-life readers, rather than merely wait for readers to conform to an imagined ideal.[115] In her study of *Library for Reading*, Melissa Frazier found "Romantic reader-personae who have . . . been largely cut loose from what we might call the 'real world' and turned into something of a joke."[116] Being turned into a joke on the pages of journals no doubt turned off some readers, but in middlebrow literature that reflected middlebrow worlds, it was probably also easy to assume the joke was on one's neighbor, not oneself.

Analyzing the *Library for Reading* as a Romantic text, Frazier emphasizes the Romantic preoccupation with reading and writing as a conversation, initially conceived as occurring in real life, through journals written by and for very small circles, as in Russian salons of the 1810s and 1820s. As publications reached wider circles of readers, people whom the writers would never meet, the relationship between writer and reader necessarily became metaphorical. Working against a world that Romantic writers perceived as increasingly commercial and anonymous, for them "audience creation operates by convincing the reader that he or she is already part of an intimate, special set."[117]

While writers in the capitals may have been feeling increasingly disconnected and remote from their readers, readers in the provinces in many ways retained more of the salon type of reading than has been recognized. When the Chikhachevs and their circle read aloud in a group and discussed reading in person and later on paper, they were enjoying a Romantic type of social reading, but with the notable absence of the writer. Moreover, Andrei continually referred to fictional characters as if they were real friends, most notably in the instance when he referred to characters from a Bulgarin story as excuses to put off breaking up the sugar at his wife's request, as if the characters were real companions who waited for him impatiently.[118] It is hard to imagine that Andrei and his friends were consciously re-creating a Romantic conceit modeled on the earliest Romantic journals and writers, of most of whom the Chikhachevs must have been unaware. It is more likely that for provincial readers, reading had been a social activity for a long time or, in this period, was an extension of actual social clubs or organizations, such as the Free Economic Society or Moscow Agricultural Society (Andrei belonged to the latter).

The prolific eighteenth-century writer and diarist Andrei Bolotov read the journal of the Free Economic Society because, according to literature scholar Thomas Newlin, it gave him the "real-life correspondent he had heretofore lacked."[119] A different study of eighteenth-century gentry correspondence shows a common longing for this kind of intellectual interaction.[120] By the 1830s Tver gentry enjoyed a lively culture of provincial gentry organizations and socialization.[121] For provincial readers in the mid-nineteenth century, reading was a social activity but one that did not require the presence of the writer. Naturally, this may have been a source of aggravation to Romantic writers seeking to create an intimate dialog under their own control.

Ultimately, provincial readers—by definition not literary professionals—simply did not necessarily take reading and writing as seriously as the writers and editors who worked so hard to shape their reading habits. This fact is aptly illustrated by a satire of Russian reading culture penned by Yakov Chernavin in the notebook correspondence:

> [S]ociety, limiting itself to literature only, wishes to know for its economic considerations: how much and of what kind of wine, vodka . . . is needed for the production, for example, of a poem, a verse, a novel in verse, or a prose work of a certain kind. In this respect, it should be researched: what kind of beverages are more appropriate for Romanticism and which ones for Classicism; also, what influence the drinks of different countries have upon local color. That is, does one need to drink champagne for notes about France, porter to express the English humor, Alicante for Spanish jealousy, and our dear mead and rye milk [vodka?] in order to animate ourselves in Russian novels? Likewise to conduct an archeological study: which wine is the closest to that which Homer's heroes drank, so as while producing tragedies not to treat the viewers to French cider, which has been our custom until now. For the middle ages to compose an approximate Gothic drink, and for our modern age some strong cosmopolitan herbal drink.[122]

In sum, there was a real unevenness in the quality and range of topics in Russian print culture in the 1830s and 1840s, and a real difficulty in maintaining a steady market of subscribers and book buyers, but there was also a real middling reading public (not necessarily a large one, but certainly larger than it had been in the eighteenth century), and there was a real disconnect between the way writers and editors imagined "the provincial reader" and actual provincial readers. Real readers, of course, varied, but one thing they had in common was having tastes that were not obedient to the dictates of urban critics. Provincial readers like the Chikhachevs liked to read about people like themselves, yet no doubt disliked being talked down to about their lives by urban "experts." They wanted a steady supply of reading matter, but probably could not always afford the prices set in St. Petersburg and Moscow, and they certainly shared each copy of a book or journal with many friends, keeping subscription rates low even while readership was proportionately higher.

In 1836 the literary critic Vissarion Belinsky imagined a provincial gentry family reading an issue of *Library for Reading*:

Imagine the family of the steppe landowner, a family reading everything that it comes upon from cover to cover. The daughter reads Ershov, Gogniev, and Strugov-shchikov's poetry and Zagoskin, Ushakov, Panaev, Kalashnikov, and Masalskii's stories; the son, as the member of a new generation, reads Timofeev's poetry and Baron Brambeus's stories; the papa reads articles about the two- and three-field systems and about various means of improving the land, while the mama—about a new means of curing tuberculosis and dyeing thread.[123]

Belinsky's imagination reflects the stereotypes urban intellectuals maintained about provincials, probably gleaned from Western stereotypes, since people like Belinsky were often more familiar with European literature than with provincial Russian realities.[124] The Chikhachevs offer a counterpoint to these stereotypes, filling out an image that is richer and more complicated than the family of Belinsky's imagination. The Chikhachevs gendered their roles in all aspects of their lives—including leisure, faith, charity, and sociability—in parallel to their gendered work roles, which in many particulars ran contrary to the models formulated in western Europe. The same pattern continues in the darker side of the Chikhachevs' non-work life: their experiences of illness and loss.

6

Illness, Grief, and Death

THE FIRST ENTRY in Natalia's first diary, written on January 1, 1835, revolves around illness, and depicts a writer who is, physically, barely holding herself together. This telling entry reflects the fact that the chief obstacle limiting Natalia's ability to perform estate work, according to her diaries, was not any sense of constraint or conflict in her role as wife, mother, and estate manager but rather her physical ability to carry on with demanding daily duties:

> [We] got up at 7 o'clock. I very much feel a severe pain in my chest, and a shooting in my ear—my brother and Uncle came for dinner. Received a letter from Vera Nikiforovna . . . from Yaroslavl; and presents for the children <u>candy</u> and <u>chocolate.</u> In the evening I dragged myself out of bed but [feel] altogether very ill. Paid for 1 ½ [*puds* of] bread. In the evening my brother left.[1]

Natalia often complained in the notebook correspondence, as in her diaries, of illness, and sometimes she did not manage to write at all, leaving Andrei to explain that she was unwell. Natalia made some mention of her health nearly every day, if only to say on some days that she was feeling better than usual ("thanks be to God"). When Andrei and Yakov mentioned Natalia in the notebooks, it was most often in order to inquire or pass on news about her health (because when her health was good she would write herself).

Natalia may, like many undervalued women before her, have complained of illness as a means of attracting attention and sympathy, but it is notable that her complaints in documents read by others were no more frequent than her brother's or Timofei Krylov's (and it was the latter who was teased by Andrei as a hypochondriac, compared in jest to Mr. Woodhouse in Jane Austen's *Emma*),[2] and Natalia's complaints were less plaintive than those of her brother or Krylov. It seems rather that Natalia genuinely suffered from a variety of chronic illnesses.

Natalia complained of regular migraines, and Andrei mentioned them as well ("My *baba* [woman] has been lounging in bed all day long and does not get up: she says it's migraine").[3] She also mentioned pains in her side, in her ear, in her leg, and complained of generally feeling poorly. She was often unable to sleep due to severe coughing, or "spasms," and sometimes was unable to get out of bed the next day, either from exhaustion, or because pain affected her mobility ("poor thing, [Nat. Iv.] stayed in bed all day: no pain anywhere but great weakness").[4] On all the occasions when she did not rise from her bed, she still managed to record all the usual data about work or errands performed on the estate that day.

Natalia's health was always a cause of concern for her husband and brother. When Natalia returned from her journey to Moscow in 1831, Andrei worried about her decline while she was away: "Ach! how my traveler has become thin! Ach, how she wheezes! Ach, how she coughs."[5] The course of each of Natalia's illnesses was discussed by them in greater detail than the illnesses of anyone else (although health was always a popular topic). One typical period of illness was recorded in the notebook correspondence with alternating entries by Andrei and Yakov until Natalia was able to contribute a note announcing her return to health. Andrei began, explaining to Yakov that "our intention to visit the Ikonnikovs' didn't work out; N.I. took ill. Her head and chest hurt."[6] Yakov responded with concern, saying "I am extremely sorry that my sister is not well. I would certainly expect a visit" but added lightly, "I ask you to inform me about my sister's health, and what are you doing yourself, and whether you washed your face today?"[7] Andrei responded that while Natalia's illness continued ("Natalia Ivan. didn't get up from her bed all day"), it did not prevent her from keeping up with most of her usual activities, including both receiving guests ("Today we expect a visit from the inhabitants of Gubachevo [the Ikonnikovs]")[8] and estate matters ("Natasha is occupied with the most thorough examination of the financial spending for the entire past year, after which the results, which are pretty curious, will be divided into classes and sent to you as well").[9] Finally, Natalia wrote, thanking her brother for thinking of her but going on to complain of how poorly she felt, "[a]fter yesterday's trip I feel not too well. I think also because of the weather my head and my back are aching a lot, and my eyes most of all," and the fact that she was missing the opportunity to visit her friends ("I keep wanting to visit the Ikonnikovs after dinner because they asked me to very, very much [*sic*]").[10]

Unable to travel, and then bound to her bed by illness, Natalia still received visitors; three days after retreating to her bed and *before* she made the effort to write to her brother to tell him of her recovery, she took on the "examination of the financial spending for the entire past year." It is also illustrative of how Natalia behaved during her bouts of poor health that, a few days later when she feeling well and Andrei was uncharacteristically struck down, it was he, not his wife, who was put "in a bad humor" by illness: "Andrei Ivanovich thank God seems to be better today, but yesterday it was no good; all day [he] was in bad humor."[11]

While Andrei suffered only the occasional health scare, and apparently not always with good grace, Natalia several times caused a stir of concern with periods of serious debilitation, beyond her chronic complaints. One such period began mildly with Andrei writing to Yakov: "Natalia Ivanovna is in bed with fever from the day of my leaving home to visit you. She is really craving some of your good *kvas* [a light beverage made from fermented black bread], for which I am sending my coachman in a sleigh."[12] Later the same day Natalia took a turn for the worse and Andrei added: "The patient spent the night very badly: her entire body is aching and she does not get out of bed. I would visit you, but for this reason [am] staying at home. Must meet the New Year in an extremely unhappy fashion."[13] Yakov wrote back with the hope that his sister would be well enough to read the notebook herself: "Sweet little sister—how is your health?—god grant that I would hear from Grigorii [a serf messenger] that you, thank god, already are doing better!" but it was Andrei who scrawled only, "somewhat better."[14] By two weeks later, Natalia was sufficiently well to write but still in pain ("I am kissing you in my mind, my leg pains me very much, swollen at the ankle").[15] The next update was again written by Andrei:

> Natalia Ivanovna's heels are swollen, and the swelling is getting bigger even on her feet at the ankle. And I, ascribing all of this to the illness which the doctor [diagnosed], would suggest disregarding the Shrovetide, or the first week of Lent, to start the treatment right away. But everyone has one's own disposition of spirit, will, expectations, hopes, and so on.[16]

While giving us little clue as to the nature of Natalia's illness, this note does show that Natalia took charge of her own medical decisions. Although Andrei disagreed as to the course of her treatment, the decision was made by the sufferer herself.

In sum, although illness could be a debilitating obstacle to Natalia's work, it was neither an excuse to avoid work (since, rather, she seems to have felt driven to work despite even serious illness), nor did her illnesses detract from her status as a responsible decision-maker in matters of finance or her own health. Her chronic illnesses eventually led her to retire from estate work, but she notably did not do so until after her children were grown and the debts were repaid.

Andrei regularly referred to his wife's episodes of ill-health as "spasms and hysteria." Both terms were common ones in the early nineteenth century, and it is difficult to say now what precise symptoms they may have referred to. In a diary entry from 1842 during their stay in Moscow, Natalia wrote, "I am entirely ill and cannot get up from bed," in the course of an entry that also mentioned a visit from her friend Praskovia Melnikova, and purchases made from a peddler of fabric and firewood.[17] On the same day, Andrei's entire diary entry reads: "Praskovia Ivanovna Melnikova was with us all day, and stayed the night. My wife had hysterics. O! Hysterics!"[18] Andrei's more melodramatic version of what Natalia painted simply as one of her bad days suggests a complaint on his part, as though her illness were something she had control over in the sense of nervous "hysteria" as an excessive emotional display. But even this sense of the word "hysteria" was often understood in the nineteenth century as having a physical cause. In any case, Andrei mentioned the same "spasms and hysterics" in a way certainly referring to a real physical malady in his article about building a stone house, saying that he wanted the snug new house in part to prevent his wife's ill-health, implying that her illness was a result of an unhealthy environment and therefore physical in nature.[19] And in 1843, Andrei wrote with concern in his parallel diary that "during the night . . . my wife experienced such spasms as it seems I have never before seen happen to her,"[20] certainly implying that the "spasms" that in other contexts could have referred to a vague generalization about "female" behavior referred in this case at least to spontaneous physical symptoms.

It is possible that these mysterious spells of "spasms and hysterics" related to another, almost unspoken but inescapable part of Natalia's position as a married woman: childbirth and the physical toll multiple pregnancies took on her body. "Hysteria" was sometimes used as a euphemism for problems of the reproductive system—the word (borrowed as *"isterika"* in Russian) derives from the Greek for uterus, *hystera*.[21] It seems clear at least that part of Natalia's chronically poor health was attributable to "women's illnesses." The experience of pregnancy and birth was unromantic and often awkward, embarrassing, invasive, and painful. These experiences could easily be more prominent for mothers in their child-bearing years than time spent doting over infants and toddlers, especially when the woman in question occupied a position that took most of her time away from her children, while a wet nurse and a nanny actually watched the children in their earliest years.[22] Though Natalia almost never depicted herself in her diaries as mothering her children, the constant mentions of illness may have been an oblique reference to the more literal and physical task of bearing children.

Natalia had at least four pregnancies that resulted in live births; the infants born in the first and last of these did not survive. Her uncomfortable fourth pregnancy and birth was mentioned several times in the notebook correspondence. On January 24, 1837, Natalia "felt herself ill," after going visiting twenty days earlier despite being heavily pregnant.[23] In late March, Natalia thanked Yakov for being her soon-to-be-born daughter's godfather but, in the same breath, told him she was not feeling well:

Thank you my sweet Friend and dear, beloved brother for your promise to be godfather to our future little one; also for all your fulfilling of the favors I've requested of you; I mindfully kiss you and wish you from my soul all boons from the Lord; my sincere regards to Dear Uncle; and the children, both Alesha and Sasha, kiss your and his hands. Forgive me that I write little, and so by God it is difficult for me; I feel very, very bad. With this I am and will be your much-loving Sister and always ready at your service, Natalia Chikhachova.[24]

In the next entry, Andrei wrote that "NI's health is still not improving: she is weak, pale, and extraordinarily emaciated, and refuses to send for Mr. Vorobievskii [the doctor]." On March 23, the baby was born, and on April 1, after the baptism, Yakov replied, "I forgot to tell you last time that all of my 'court personnel' [household serfs] convey to you their most diligent congratulations on your newly born daughter." Timofei Krylov added a line to wish a speedy recovery from her illness. Two days later Andrei sent an update indicating that Natalia's recovery was still not what it should be, "Nat. Iv. feels herself very weak: yesterday (2 o'clock) she was only with difficulty able to brush her hair—her hair was very matted up." Yakov began to show more concern, saying, "You, my little sister, I request to get better soon—it's time to recover." By April 8, Yakov added, "it is extremely bitter to hear, my dear sister, that you are still weak in health." Natalia finally allowed Dr. Vorobievskii to be called in; he left a prescription, and "by the evening the medicine's effect was clear and the patient spent the night much better than all the preceding nights." As Andrei reported this on April 10, he hovered near his "patient," reading to her.[25] In this correspondence childbirth was treated principally as an illness, and talked of in much the same way as Natalia's other illnesses. Although Yakov conveyed his congratulations "on [their] newly born daughter," the focus of everyone's attention was on the health of the mother.

Natalia had mentioned the pregnancy in only one other entry in the notebook correspondence, at about four months along, when she matter-of-factly complained that her condition was inhibiting her ability to get to the fair to purchase supplies (though the road was a worse obstacle):

> [A]s to myself, I'll tell you that I am wandering around with my belly, and it's becoming quite heavy already: but it is becoming quite necessary to go to the fair: we have very little sugar, tea, coffee, and "wooden" oil [cheap olive oil used for lamps], but because the road now is not very good and we have no winter carriage and so can't go.[26]

Although the second volume of Natalia's diaries stopped during the third trimester of this fourth pregnancy, she never mentioned her condition there, nor did she mention the infant Varvara in the third, subsequent diary. Aleksei once mentioned visiting his former wet nurse, and so one can assume that Natalia employed one for Varvara as well, which accounts for her ability to resume her usual activities during Varvara's infancy, though not for the absence of mention of the baby in the diary altogether.[27] Our account of Varvara's death comes from Yakov's diary: on June 14, 1838 he wrote, "Terentii brought from brother the letter that Varenka passed away." Yakov left immediately for Dorozhaevo. Arriving there the next day, "[n]ext to the little grave [he] saw brother with his men. The departed Varinma [Varvara] had just been lowered into the grave."[28]

In short, Natalia's account of childbirth in the notebook correspondence conveys only the physical toll it took, while pregnancy is almost absent from her diaries (except perhaps obliquely through the mentions of poor health). All the writers employed euphemisms for pregnancy ("heaviness," "my belly"), and they wrote of her condition in much the same tone and language that they employed with her other illnesses. Given that couples in this time and these circumstances were unlikely to have practiced birth control, Natalia probably also suffered one or more miscarriages, in the four-year gap between the birth of Aleksei (in 1825) and Aleksandra (in 1829), and in the nine-year gap between Aleksandra's birth and Varvara's in 1837. Miscarriage may thus account for one or more of Natalia's serious illnesses in this period, and the pain in her "side" may have been a euphemism for this or for menstrual cramping.

In 1853 Andrei wrote in his religious memoir of "the most tormenting of female illnesses," suggesting that by the end of her childbearing years at least, Natalia suffered some more debilitating consequence of motherhood.[29] Although Natalia eventually died of an unspecified "illness" in 1866, this does not seem necessarily to have been connected to the chronic symptoms that troubled her throughout her life, since she continued to travel and work on the estate even after her children's marriages, in the 1850s and early 1860s (albeit not as actively as before), and did reach a fairly advanced age for the time (she was sixty-seven). However, the undoubtedly serious and prolonged nature of the complications she experienced in childbirth must have colored her understanding of this biological aspect of motherhood, perhaps to the point of overshadowing the less tangible, more affective sides; at any rate, that was the effect on the pages of her "daily notes." The legacy left by Natalia is reinforced by fleeting references to other mothers in the archive. Natalia's daughter-in-law, Anna Boshniak, suffered ill health in consequence of childbirth for several years, including what she described as "paroxysms"; the illness was serious enough for her to travel great distances seeking relief.[30] A generation later still, little had changed except that it was possible to be more direct about these matters in writing. Aleksei and Anna's son Konstantin ("Kostya") wrote in his diary about his wife's reluctance to endure too many pregnancies: "I started to look at someone else's baby, which really got at me. I am wary to disturb my wife too often, she is nursing a baby, while also always complaining that she has to give birth often, [and] is afraid that she is pregnant again."[31]

If there was such a thing as a "male illness," it may have been depression. At any rate, among Victorian men recurrent depression was a common complaint. Often blamed on previous illnesses or injuries, George Gissing called depression the "intellectual disease of the time." Historian M. Jeanne Peterson found that the Victorian women in her study suffered from melancholy only in reaction to specific instances of grief over the loss of a loved one. In contrast, men frequently suffered recurrent depressions with no obvious circumstantial cause, and their symptoms were those "usually attributed to Victorian women."[32] Strikingly, both Aleksei and Andrei mentioned periods of depression, while Natalia did not, despite her heavy responsibilities and frequent physical illnesses. In early 1834, responding to a complaint from Yakov about a fever, Andrei wrote:

I also have been feeling very poorly from that time onward—but my poorness comes more from myself: I take in too much crap into my head. At the same time

This is a section title page from the notebook correspondence that passed between the Chikhachev and Chernavin families in the mid-1830s. The page shows Andrei Chikhachev's playful French title (*"Cahier de Poste parmi les deux freres"* [Notebook correspondence between two brothers]), inscribed on January 18, 1835. The facing page exhibits a typical effusion of flourishes with which Andrei had completed his previous entry. *Photo by the author with permission from the State Historical Archive of Ivanovo Region*

This page from the notebook correspondence features the handwriting of Aleksei, Aleksandra, and Andrei Chikhachev. At the top of the page is the end of a note signed by Aleksei Chikhachev, eleven years old, to his uncle Yakov Chernavin. It is followed by a note from seven-year-old Aleksandra Chikhacheva; the short, formulaic missive is one of only two documents written by her that have survived. She writes that she "kisses the hands" of her uncle Yakov Chernavin and her "grandfather" Timofei Krylov. The bottom third of the page was filled in by Andrei Chikhachev. *Photo by the author with permission from the State Historical Archive of Ivanovo Region*

This title page from one of Natalia Chikhacheva's diaries reads, "Daily notes of Natalia Chikhachova, begun in Borduki, 1 January 1835." The diary was constructed from stacks of paper folded into quarters, each with its own title page, and later bound together into a book. The carefully inscribed title pages and binding used for a notebook, which mostly contained Natalia's records of estate work, testify to her own sense of the importance of her work. *Photo by the author with permission from the State Historical Archive of Ivanovo Region*

These pages from one of Natalia Chikhacheva's diaries, in contrast to Andrei's entries in the notebook correspondence, are orderly, simple, and efficient, consisting largely of data related to the estate, including a footnote about 50 *arshins* (39 yards) of woolens given out for dyeing. *Photo by the author with permission from the State Historical Archive of Ivanovo Region*

The Chikhachevs built their house between 1835 and 1843, of brick covered by plaster. This photograph shows the front façade of the Chikhachevs' house in Dorozhaevo as it stands today. The original entrance was in the half-circle portion of this façade. Since the 1917 Revolution, the house has been used as the village school. *Photo by the author, 2005*

This photograph shows the village church of Zimenki, neighboring the Chikhachevs' home village of Dorozhaevo. Andrei Chikhachev founded his public library next to the Zimenki church in 1854 and also raised funds for a second church building (not pictured), which was supplied with valuable donated icons. The public library building was destroyed, but both church buildings still stand and are being put back into use after decades of neglect. *Photo by the author, 2005*

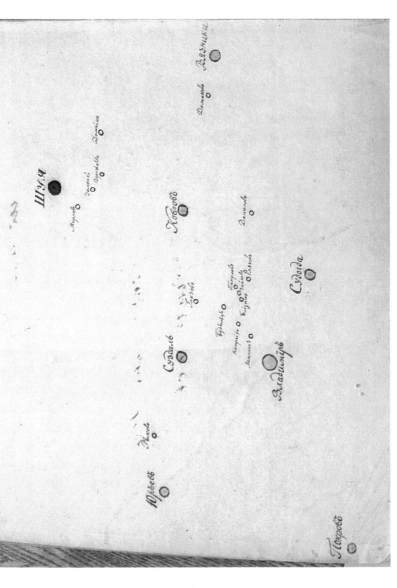

This map of Vladimir province was hand-drawn by Andrei Chikhachev, to be used for a geographical game he devised for his children. It features the major towns of their province (Vladimir, Shuia, Kovrov, Suzdal, Sudogda, and Yuriev) and also the villages the children encountered in their daily lives: villages owned by their parents, and villages they visited or passed through on their regular journeys through the province. These include Dorozhaevo, Zimenki, Domnino, Mirkovo, Rykovo, Budyltsy, and Glazovo. *Photo by the author with permission from the State Historical Archive of Ivanovo Region*

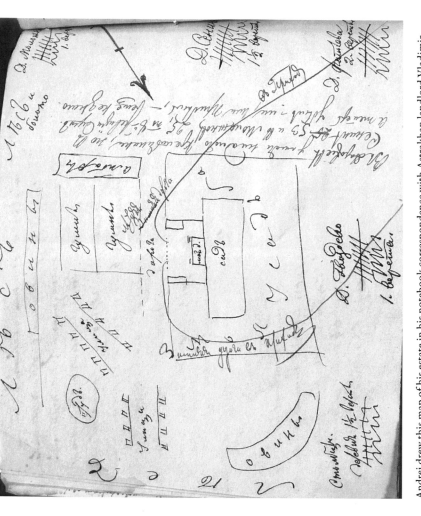

Andrei drew this map of his estate in his notebook correspondence with Astrakhan landlord Vladimir Kopytovskii. It indicated "my house" in the center, surrounded by a garden, and then roads, outbuildings, and the "limewood allée" leading to a pond. *Photo by the author with permission from the State Historical Archive of Ivanovo Region*

This floor plan of Yakov Chernavin's house in Berezovik was drawn for Yakov and Natalia Chikhacheva's father, who built the house in 1809–10. This was the house where Natalia grew up, where the Chikhachevs visited Yakov, and which Aleksei Chikhachev eventually inherited. The entire building measured about 50 x 50 feet. The rooms are described as a nursery, a "sofa room," parlor, ballroom, a work room for female servants, a dining room, study, a small bedroom with a wardrobe-sized space for the "library," a billiard room, a manservants' room (at the opposite end of the building from the room for female servants), and a foyer and "corner room." The floor plan also indicates an unheated mezzanine with two rooms and a foyer, and dotted lines indicate a "former orangerie." *Photo by the author, 2005, with permission from the State Historical Archive of Ivanovo Region*

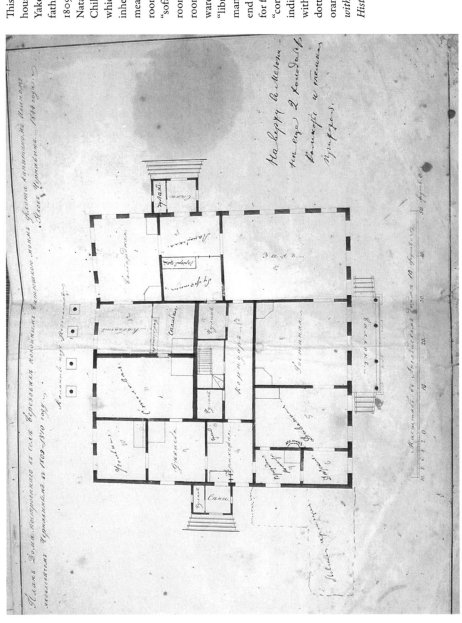

This watercolor of the Chikhachev family coat of arms was apparently commissioned by Andrei Chikhachev from the Heraldry Office in 1841. It was without a motto and came with the following official description: "Within the escutcheon with an azure field, there is one small silver shield, within which is depicted a black bison head with horns. The shield is crowned with a helm and coronet, on whose crest is indicated an exiting lion [*lion issuant*] wearing a crown, which is holding in its right paw a saber, and on its sides there are two standards, blue and red in color. The mantle [*lambrequin*] on the shield is blue, underlain in silver." *Photo by the author with permission from the State Historical Archive of Ivanovo Region*

This 1823 painting depicts a "landlady's morning," during which a provincial mistress of the house much like Natalia Chikhacheva hears morning reports from her serf girls, or gives instructions for the day. The mistress sits with a pen poised to record their information into the estate accounts. *Alexey Venetsianov,* Morning of the Landlady *(1823), oil on wood. The Russian Museum, St. Petersburg, Russia*

I feel all the insignificance of my dreary thoughts, but do not have the power to correct myself. For this I am punishing myself: not sharing my feelings with anyone.[33]

Andrei is clear that his problem is a mental one—"in my head"—not a physical one; his feelings were the product of "dreary thoughts" in someone who considered thinking to be his calling. This is a remarkable parallel to the all-too-physical and practical obstacles caused by Natalia's illnesses, reflecting her practical definition of herself.

Nearly thirty years later, Aleksei also suffered an episode of depression. In a letter home written in 1861, Aleksei responded to a query about his "morning pains," probably a physical complaint, saying they had stopped only to be replaced by something more difficult to endure:

[I]t seems that because of my pitiful condition I will not for a long time regain my normal state. I have become so used to solitude that with all the wishing to go somewhere I can't go even to Andreevskoe. And god knows what happened to me, I can't recognize myself looking in the mirror, I am as if made of wax and don't have the slightest appetite for anything. Please do pray for me to God so that he would relieve my mental sufferings.[34]

Aleksei exhibited classic signs of depression in his inability to face a social visit, to "recognize myself looking in the mirror," and his sense of being "made of wax." At this time, Aleksei was coping with his wife's illness, separation from her and from his family, and the stress of imminent serf emancipation, so his depression is understandable, but the openness with which he describes it seems, perhaps, surprising. On the other hand, to a man who understood masculinity as distinguished above all by intellectualism and the shouldering of a greater moral burden, depression may in that light be logically seen as a men's disease.[35]

Naturally not every illness was gendered. Probably the most common complaint mentioned in these documents was stomach upset, suffered equally by all. In April 1835 Yakov experienced "the same thing that had happened to Varvara," speaking of an acquaintance, after he ate a goose leg at supper.[36] Timofei Krylov regularly overindulged and suffered the consequences, as when he "disrupted his stomach to the extreme" on New Year's Day,[37] or when he went "all the time out onto the porch; and judging by his grimace it is clear that poor uncle feels horrible!"[38] On another occasion Natalia became ill "from Izmailova's salted pork" to the degree that the poor woman "walk[ed] around all twisted."[39]

The next most common complaints were colds and fevers, which were often recurring. At least in some cases the fevers were quite severe, as when Yakov wrote:

[T]oday after 4 p.m. I felt the usual fits of the fever that seem to have returned. In order to entertain—no, to occupy myself I wanted to continue writing, but rising fever, especially in my head, forced me to stop <u>here</u> . . . the fever kept increasing in my entire body except for the legs which were cold for a long time. At last I fell asleep; while asleep I was all heated up.[40]

Timofei Krylov suffered from a chronic problem with his legs, causing swelling and dizziness, which he considered some sort of punishment for his "sins," probably overindulgence, suggesting the condition was gout: "I spend every day in sickness for my sin and walk as if my legs were made of crystal, plus there is a noise in my head . . . and I hear the bells ringing . . . [I] must put up [with this as a punishment] for my sins."[41] Punishment for overindulgence was a theme: one night after dancing with visitors until three in the morning, Natalia "became very sick, the constriction in my chest was terrible and blood went from my throat; but thank god in the morning I felt better."[42]

Andrei also complained of being nearsighted, and although he wore spectacles, they apparently did not completely correct his vision. Listing the places to which he had traveled, Andrei complained that he had to do his traveling in a closed carriage, and with his sight this meant it was "as if I had not traveled at all." However, as soon as he reached a provincial capital, he immediately hired a fiacre (a small carriage with a folding roof) and "[got] to observing the city."[43] Aleksei inherited the problem. In 1867 at the age of forty-two he apologized that his quill was "writing thick" because his "poor eyesight does not permit [him] to sharpen it."[44]

Everyone also suffered from what Andrei called "half-issues," which he specified as "little bumps, boils, and thingies."[45] While Aleksei was in service in Vilno, he developed on his back "a huge boil" as well as stomach problems, headaches, chills, and fevers.[46] The timing of other mentions of his boils suggest they may have resulted from unhygienic travel conditions on his long journey.[47] Years later Aleksei visited a friend with an advanced illness who had grown "a pig's teat" in his armpit, as well as losing all his strength.[48]

Minor matters could quickly become more serious. Nikolai Zamytskii had a harrowing experience that began with simple constipation, apparently brought on by the chilly temperatures in the "toilet in his house," and diagnosed as "intestinal rheumatism" by the doctor. Laxatives were ineffective, and two enemas "remained in his stomach," preventing the doctor from trying any more. Dr. Vorobievskii happened to come to see another patient but was unable to get medicine for Nikolai because the apothecary in Shuia was closed. Instead he tried an "Alexander's Leaf" and a hot tub, with "no result!" (The next day on his way to Shuia, the same doctor stopped to bleed Natalia, apparently also not feeling well, and achieved "a full deep dish" of her blood "exceedingly quickly.") By night the Shuia apothecary sent "one powder and a jar of laxative oil" for Zamytskii, and they also applied "a tobacco enema," "tobacco vapors," and another bath. Zamytskii was at this point—unsurprisingly—in considerable pain, and unable to stand, sit, walk, or lie down, so that he could find ease only in kneeling. As Andrei wrote, "A terrible picture!"

On the third day Dr. Vorobievskii came again (he was paid fifty paper rubles per visit), applied leeches, and put the patient in a tub again with "a large dose of stinky drops." The next morning the doctor left, frighteningly declaring that "the patient is unlikely to get up again," but promising to send other medicines. Zamytskii was ominously advised to "use a spiritual medicine, to take part in Holy Mysteries." A letter was received from the doctor that night saying that the Shuia apothecary was again closed, so that help would have to be sought in Vladimir. "Imagine," Andrei wrote, "how it felt for the patient to hear these lines."

As it turned out, all was not lost. At the "end of the extensive letter" a "tiniest bit of white powder" was included, folded into paper. The doctor advised taking the powder in honey while waiting for further medicines from Vladimir. The patient prayed, and after the fourth dose of powder, "because of God's will—the power worked in a most beneficial way; and Mr. Zamytskii (speaking without the slightest exaggeration) is resurrected!"[49]

Infectious illnesses were also a constant fear. In 1836 "the servants of Andrei Petrovich" were ill, and Andrei warned Yakov not to allow "his people" to "mingle" with them. "They say they have sickness both here and in Vladimir and Nikandrushka [a serf] is already dead. We 'smoke' vinegar in the rooms every day, and you should order the same."[50] Most traumatic was the cholera epidemic of 1831, though the Chikhachev family was spared. In 1837 an acquaintance, Maksim Mitrofanovich, lost his daughter to scarlet fever and gangrene, as Yakov sadly reported.[51] In 1859 Aleksei's brother-in-law Nikolai Boshniak was diagnosed with consumption.[52] Closer to home, in childhood Aleksei mentioned in the notebook correspondence that his sister Aleksandra had "scrofula in her head."[53] Scrofula was a serious bacterial infection that could cause sores; a statistic from 1847 claimed 90 percent of children in St. Petersburg suffered from it.[54]

The military-statistical review of Vladimir province in 1852 listed causes for mortality in the region as various kinds of fevers, eye inflammations, feverous rashes, nervous and wasting illnesses, edema, bleeding, "bloodless outflows," chronic cathexis, and local illnesses (bumps, broken bones, and so on). Diseases were dependent on the season as well as other factors, with winter noted as a dangerous time for catarrhal fever, rheumatism and rheumatoid fever, throat inflammations, gastric fevers, diarrhea, and eye inflammations. There was a scurvy epidemic in the province in 1840, cholera returned in 1848, and *febris intermittis* (intermittent fever) reigned in 1842–43.[55]

It is no surprise in these conditions that the Chikhachevs and their friends spilled a great deal of ink discussing remedies. Home remedies for every conceivable ailment were passed along and their efficacy discussed, and recipes were copied out of newspapers (later, Andrei contributed "a treatment for toothache" to the *Agricultural Gazette*).[56] Common remedies ranged from cod oil (in this case prescribed by a doctor; Andrei's correspondent Aleksandr Makaveev wrote: "despite all of my disgust for its unpleasant taste and smell, I am starting to get used to [it]—only I don't know if there will be any benefit from it") to plasters given for toothache, mint drops and Harlem drops (either of which may be the same "drops" Natalia took for her "spasms"), "Spanish Fly" and camphor for migraines, burnt sugar with water, cranberry (probably infused in tea), and

various herbs, also usually infused in tea, wine, or vodka.[57] The Chikhachevs' friend
Father Sila sent fifteen kopeks one day to cover some "Hoffman's drops" they had given
him.[58] Mint in wine was mentioned for headache. An herb called "toad grass," generally
used as an antiseptic and for diabetes and high blood pressure, was mentioned as readily
on hand.[59] A different "mouth-rinsing herb" was recommended with "that liquid that
Hippocrates prescribed to add to it"—presumably referring to alcohol.[60] Vodka infused
with artemisia was for rheumatism or stomachache.[61] And St. John's Wort was used by
Timofei Krylov for a pain in his side, but it did not work.[62] When Natalia was ill after
Varvara's birth, Yakov sent her cigarillos, saying, "[k]eep smoking them for good health—
when you run out tell me and I'll send more."[63] When a plasterer was brought to Andrei
with a painful skin condition, Andrei dosed him with a teacup of wine with a spoonful of
olive oil in it, which made the man sleepy (despite this, the man went back to work).
Andrei also ordered him to rub the affected areas with wine and vinegar, and "put horse-
radish against the back of his head."[64]

A letter written by Andrei to his doctor in 1835 provides a remarkably detailed account of Andrei's thinking with regard to healing. Andrei wrote on the fourth day of
an illness that began with "a small chill, and then a fever" as well as a sore throat. The
fever had abated, but he still felt a chill on his "back" and the sore throat persisted. He
began his analysis with the conventional wisdom that he caught a cold from being in
literally cold air: "I was careless enough to often sit near a window open in its lower
part when it was windy." He believed that he was especially susceptible to catching
cold because he "had to lie down continuously for over a week because of the boils that
I had then and in part continue to have; therefore, I could become unfamiliar with
outside air." He dosed himself at first with "a rinse made of vinegar with honey and
sage that was lukewarm and boiled," but then became concerned that "acid might
cause harm," so he replaced the vinegar with milk. When he did not improve the next
day, he decided to consult the doctor, to "ask your advice, and for whatever medicine
you will think it useful to give." He complained then of a swelling on the right side of
his throat, a "considerable cough, during which thick bluish liquid comes out." His
throat continued to be sore, and he had a pain in his chest, which he believed
"stemm[ed] from the cough," and his face was "almost always sweaty," as well as his
body to a lesser degree.[65]

This illness sounds remarkably serious at a time when Andrei was generally regarded as
a picture of health compared to Natalia, Yakov, or Timofei Krylov. A passage that Andrei
copied into his diary from a book titled *Nature* suggests something further of his understanding of the bases of health (assuming Andrei copied it because he agreed with it). The
passage begins, "[w]hat could be more harmful for human life and health than . . . the
passions of our soul? What kind of terrible actions are not committed by anger? Does
not passionate love, secret unquenchable longing, eat up the root of life?" It continued to
meditate on a connection between body and mind. The text was not religious, though
Andrei also quoted a psalm immediately before it.[66]

On a more practical level, the Chikhachevs understood that moderation in diet and regular exercise were important to both good health and mental and emotional well-being. In 1835 Andrei wrote, "It seems to me that having a lighter stomach I will be fresher, smarter, kinder, healthier, and more active, and more caring, and more foresightful, and more neat, and more attentive, etc. etc." This came after describing a fasting dinner of "mushrooms instead of soup, fried potatoes, pea jelly—No one wanted any kasha," so Andrei's sense of well-being may have been related to the religious observance.[67] Yakov countered, though, that exercise was more important: "You, brother, have been sitting down for too long—it's not healthy; I would advise you to make a promenade around the billiard for an hour and a half—two hours; this would be more beneficial in any event."[68] Trips to the banya (a sauna, where oak or eucalyptus branches were used to exfoliate the skin) were also frequently recommended for maintaining health, along with large amounts of tea and cranberry juice.[69] But the banya could be a source of illness as well as its cure: Aleksei reported that the saunas in Vilno were "very untidy," which may have had something to do with his several illnesses there.[70]

In 1836 Andrei offered as remedies for wet, cold weather "[a] cup of coffee with a pipe" and when these failed he resorted to "the drops of Neptune, Bacchus, Minerva, Apollo, Erofei, Universal," by which he must have meant literature and/or alcohol.[71] More esoterically, on another occasion he theorized that fright could induce a "rapid recovery" from "heavy illness," supposedly evidenced by "incidents that are recounted by our history." He offered this to Yakov to comfort him after he was frightened by a fire at Berezovik, and further explained the physiological effect: "The blood changes in its movement, fibers and muscles are strengthened, and a desperately ill person—there supposedly has been such a case—was nine days later dancing a mazurka. Believe me this is not my invention, but something I read myself with my own eyes."[72] This superstitious theory was not out of place at the time; a survey of the province boasted the presence of a holy well for curing disease, for example, located outside Vladimir.[73] Much stranger was another quasi-medical theory of Andrei's, which was probably less than totally serious. He wrote to Yakov that he had "guests: maid Kuhlman and a couple of pancakes with smelt," then asked, "[d]o you know why she caught a cold? Not at all because her coat was too cold for October. Not at all because she was waiting for her carriage for a long time—no! I think she acquired her illness because of her virginity, which became agitated while contemplating the newlyweds—and demanded its destruction. Yes!"[74]

In times of serious illness the Chikhachevs consulted with doctors and sometimes with less formally trained and cheaper medical consultants (feldshers). Considering that the professionalization of medicine was still in its early stages even in western Europe at this time, it is remarkable that the Chikhachevs were able to regularly consult a university-trained doctor. In fact, the Ivanovo merchantry was even reported to hire doctors for their workers.[75] Mikhail Petrovich Vorobievskii, sometimes nicknamed "Little Cossack" and usually addressed as "Dr. Vorobievskii," was also described as a *lekar*, a term which literally translates as "healer" or "medic" and is equivalent to doctor or physician.[76]

A doctor's role, besides diagnosing an illness, was sometimes to bleed and sometimes to prescribe medicine, which had to be prepared by an apothecary.[77] On one visit Dr. Vorobievskii stayed three hours with Natalia and then was given a ride "on fresh horses" by the coachman Terekha, who returned late the next morning with medicine, which Andrei described as "the Latin kitchen." By evening, though, Natalia was much improved.[78] Other doctors were occasionally mentioned, as when Andrei wrote to Yakov of some mutual acquaintance, "[l]ast night sent for a physician from Kovrov—it seems that the affair is becoming serious." However, he went on to say that he and Natalia would go to visit the invalid to give their own advice, because "[d]uring illness it is necessary to visit, to visit, and to think 'how should this be done better?' Maybe even my input will be useful here."[79]

In 1861 the Chikhachevs received a letter from a Klavdia Glazyrina about her daughter Elena, who was seriously unwell. The "Doctor Johanson" (clearly a foreigner) who treated the girl said "that this happened from constant occupation and a sedentary life, and therefore prohibited all work," and even reading and going outside, because the weather had turned to fall and the girl was coughing. "[I]n order to strengthen her he prescribes her . . . powders and orders her to take fresh milk, wine, cocoa, rare meat; she has become so thin and changed that it's a pity to look at her, poor thing!" Finally, Klavdia wrote that she put on her daughter a cross sent by Natalia, saying, "this is the best kind of doctor."[80]

Despite their frequent consultations with "the little Cossack," the Chikhachevs and their other friends often expressed skepticism of medical remedies, preferring simple home cures, and once Yakov recommended an uneducated peasant healer, one "Peasant Nikolai Vasiliev Bolshoi in Moscow on Tverskaia," who was "famous for healing."[81] A letter from Anna Boshniak's brother in 1860 is the most detailed example of medical skepticism. He explained to Andrei and Natalia that Anna was not recovering from her illness, and that the "apothecary's kitchen clearly showed its helplessness for such a complex illness," therefore Anna's friends were "left with the remedy that is very simple and that should have been used a long time ago—it's cold water." He does not "soothe [himself] with hope that it will be of big benefit," but he claimed that it was "more harmless than all the vegetable and mineral poisons that are sold in drugstores, such as mixtures, tinctures, pills and powders, [which] only disrupt the organism and deceive the ill with their short-lived effects." Concluding with emphasis: "Everything shows how shaky medicine is!"[82]

Closely related to illness in the mid-nineteenth century was its sometime sequel, death. Natalia's two lost infants (Anna in 1821, and Varvara in 1838) were part of a long series of family deaths. In addition to Natalia's parents' deaths in the early years of her marriage, she had lost her two oldest brothers in the boating accident in 1825, and in 1845 Yakov died. With his death Natalia lost her last surviving brother, and Andrei lost his best friend. This loss was made even more tragic because of the shocking and gruesome circumstances. On May 26, Yakov accidentally swept a lit pipe off his desk with the sleeve of his dressing gown. It fell onto fireworks that had been laid out on a couch next to the desk, and sparked an explosion. Servants found him quickly enough to put out the fire before it spread to the rest of the house, but Yakov's injuries were severe, and he died at 9:00 a.m. the next day, after unimaginable suffering. Andrei and Natalia were summoned by "Ilia Kirilov," a serf, but were unable to get from Dorozhaevo to Berezovik with a doctor in time to help the sufferer or say their goodbyes.[83]

Poignantly, Yakov's death came just as he and the Chikhachevs were mending their relationship after a serious rift that must have caused great grief in the years preceding Yakov's accident. The circumstances of the quarrel are not clear, but it occurred sometime between August 1838, when Aleksei mentioned visiting his uncle as usual,[84] and the morning of the gunpowder explosion, when Andrei recorded having received a typical "congratulatory letter" from Yakov.[85] Mention of the quarrel survives only in a pair of letters to his brother-in-law that Andrei copied into his parallel diary. In these letters, Andrei took responsibility for their rift, citing his "pride" and "self-love," but begged Yakov to "extend his hand" to him, to renew the "closeness" they once shared. Andrei declared his intention to continue writing such letters as long as it took for Yakov to respond. The letters copied into the diary are dated April 15 and 22, probably 1842 (when the Chikhachevs were in Moscow visiting their children, and three months after Natalia's last diary ends).[86] Andrei recorded writing another letter to his brother-in-law a few weeks before his death, and this combined with the "congratulatory letter" from Yakov received the morning of his death shows that the men had begun corresponding again at least by May 1845, if not much earlier.[87] Though in his first pair of pleading letters Andrei invoked the memory of Chernavin's dead parents and brothers to provoke him to mend their relationship, it is notable that he did not mention Natalia, Yakov's own sister, or her view of the quarrel. Surely, she must have suffered most in a quarrel involving her husband and her beloved brother.[88]

Three years after Yakov's shocking death, Natalia must have felt more than usual trepidation as she sent her son into military service in Poland at a time when the Russian army was engaged in that region.[89] But before the Chikhachevs could rejoice in his safe return, another shock struck them: they lost their twenty-one-year-old daughter Aleksandra to complications from childbirth. The details of her illness are unknown, but having married in 1848 and died in August 1850 after the birth of her third son (on July 30), her pregnancies had come in dangerously quick succession.[90]

Aleksei retired from the army the year that his sister died, and returned home to Dorozhaevo. In the early 1850s, he married Anna Konstantinovna Boshniak. Their first son, Konstantin ("Kostya"), was born in 1854, and another son, Andrei ("Andryosha"), in 1860, but again a "difficult" birth resulted in a long illness for Anna, eventually leading her to travel abroad with Kostya and some of her Boshniak relations, leaving Andryosha with Andrei and Natalia, while Aleksei lived alone in Vladimir. The extreme anxiety felt by the Chikhachevs at this time was vividly conveyed in Andrei's letters.[91] Although anxiety would always be natural in such a situation, for Andrei and Natalia it must have been intensified almost unbearably by their previous experiences. The tally of family tragedies eventually also included two of the Chikhachevs' grandsons, both named after Andrei and known as "Andryosha" (one the son of Aleksei, the other of Aleksandra), who both died in or around 1861.

Natalia, especially, experienced an excessive share of grief, a significant portion of it related to pregnancy and childbirth. Yet death, too, is absent from her diaries. Where Andrei marked the death dates of loved ones and friends in each of his diaries and composed small written memorials to mark the most significant losses in his life, Natalia was silent (on paper) through the losses of two infants, her dearest brother, her grown daughter, and two grandchildren. Characteristically, Andrei left behind a record of deep emotionalism and sensibility, while Natalia refrained from emotional display and simply continued (in her writing) with business as usual.

In fact, by the time her grandsons died Natalia had apparently long since ceased to write at all, but her husband left the following touchingly incoherent list of memories of Aleksei's Andryosha, whom he and Natalia had helped to raise for a few of his toddler years. Andrei's record of his namesake conveys much of what the child must have meant to his grandparents but, typically, mentions Natalia directly only as providing the child with material goods—in this case, "little shirts":

1. In my study: [illeg.], and in the [illeg.], [he] taught Sergei the red letters. 2. In the [illeg.] around the rooms; —asked me to pick him up in my arms and walk with him through all the rooms. 3. A—a—a!!!— — — where!!!—4. On the windowsill of the billiard room, looking at the model mill. 5. In the hall on the carpet with lots of toys. 6. Loved to imitate the priests. Burned incense. Drew the Zimenki church from a picture. Bowed to the ground when he prayed. Kissed the icon. 7. In the little red jacket and little white hat in the garden, with a flower in his little hand. 8. Loved to look at the [illeg.]—at the steam coming from the samovar. 9. In his walker quickly got around all the rooms. 10. Showed [off] the new little shirts made by his grandma.—Loved to sort out the tiny candies. 11. Came to watch while I broke up sugar. 12. Not long before his passing, held in his hands [by] himself the little book about monasteries. 13. Riding about the rooms, and sitting on my bed, let us know that by this he would be remembered.[92]

Andrei ceased to keep his parallel diaries after the death of Aleksandra in 1850; he noted her death, in his packet of letters received in that year, with only a few words and the date, surrounded by a thick border of black ink.[93] Later, after re-reading his son's diary from 1847 to 1848, he wrote passionately: "Reading Sashonochka's name, already a ½ year since her death, it is as if my heart and soul are burned by boiling water. Lord! Forgive my grief!—Forgive my sins!" And after Yakov's death in 1845 Andrei wrote the following on the first page of a bound volume of the notebook correspondence he had shared with his brother-in-law a decade earlier:

Look, it's already been 65 days since my brother Yakov Ivanovich is not on this earth! Lord, my dear God! How time passes, and how one after another people leave this life for the other. It grieves [me] to think of this, but we all take part. And who knows whether the Lord has appointed me to live long? And with what kind of death will I expire? If the Lord would only lead [us] with [illeg.]. Yakov Ivanovich is not on this earth! Ach, my God, my God! But this is our earthly life[.]⁹⁴

As it turned out, Andrei would live a very long life, even outliving his son by a short time, in the process mourning the passing of many friends and family members.

Death was no stranger to anyone in the mid-nineteenth century. In 1850, when Andrei was still immersed in grief over Aleksandra, he received a letter from a childhood friend, who wrote sympathetically that he had lost a sister in August, and that cholera had killed his father, son, sister, brother-in-law, and a sister-in-law all in one week. "Who would not be horrified by such a number of deaths in a family[?]" he asked, describing how he "became gray in a week" and did not know how he "stayed alive given my weak health." His solace and "the only joy in [his] life" was his "good wife," but she—much like Natalia—was "constantly ill after three unfortunate births."⁹⁵

One of the passages from his reading that Andrei copied into his diary in 1831 stated that "[t]he alleviation of all sufferings—even the most inexcusable ones—should be sought only in the Christian Religion, which so strongly fortifies and delights during misfortune."⁹⁶ Nearly twenty years later when Andrei faced his greatest challenge, in Aleksandra's death, his response was to retreat to a monastery, devoting himself to religion as a means of making sense of his loss. His friends and neighbors understood his response but begged him to come back to the earthly sphere for the sake of his remaining family. Aleksandr Kupreianov, a family member of General Pavel Kupreianov, Aleksei's sponsor in the army, wrote to Andrei in November 1850. First he expressed his condolences and his respect for Andrei's "pious and soul-saving exercises and activities," but then he changed his tone, gently questioning Andrei's decision to become a monk: "But as for you to condemn and dedicate yourself forever to solitude, for this I can't and don't dare to give you advice—and this because you still have sacred and necessary duties in the world and can be quite useful both to your esteemed spouse and to your dear son." After this reminder that his earthly duties might be as "sacred" as a more direct dedication of his life to God, Kupreianov concluded with a seemingly objective admonition to leave the matter in the Lord's hands—although with another reference to the well-being of Andrei's family to emphasize where Kupreianov really stood: "Let the Lord order all your affairs to further the salvation of your soul and the well-being of your family." Kupreianov's closing line again emphasized how Andrei's family needed him, and he needed his family: "Let the Lord's holy will be done, and let the Lord order the fate of your dear son for your joy and consolation."⁹⁷

A letter Andrei received from his friend and neighbor Mikhail Kultashev ran on the same themes, this time emphasizing Andrei's duties to his wife in particular (Kultashev, as a neighbor, must have seen firsthand how Natalia was coping with both the loss of her daughter and her husband's absence at the monastery). Kultashev lectured Andrei that God does not want such excessive grief: "I wish from all my heart and pray to God that the New Year brings you to the thought that 'everything is from God,' and to express regret, to grieve, and to torture oneself means to be discontented." Not mincing words, he told Andrei outright that "you have become an egoist." He took his friend to task for abandoning Natalia in her hour of greatest need: "your joy you divided equally with your best friend [Natalia]; why then, in the days of trials, do you abandon her; when precisely now this weak woman needs all of your firmness, manliness and will power." Kultashev was not without sympathy for Andrei's attempt to find solace, but he firmly denied Andrei's interpretation of God's will, positing his own in its place:

> [H]aving diligently prayed to God, seek solitude for a minute, only to resolve the question posed to yourself: "do you have the right, being married, to acquire solitude, and do you act <u>decently</u> leaving your God-given best friend and mother of your children without consolation and without strengthening her with God's word?["] Think well, and don't leave the path shown you by the Lord.[98]

Kultashev was convincing where Kupreianov had not been: after six weeks in seclusion at the monastery in Suzdal, Andrei returned home (in his own account, he would say it was the pleadings of his wife and son, directly, that changed his mind).[99] Thereafter, Andrei poured his energies into religious philanthropy, but he never again removed himself from his family.

Even before losing Aleksandra, death was a subject often on Andrei's mind. After a day of reading Bible commentaries, Andrei wrote in his diary, "[w]e know our end—we know that the subject of our brief life is salvation, but we forget about it constantly."[100] However, Andrei himself rarely forgot. Like a mantra, he added a caveat to nearly every plan he ever made in writing to the effect that he would carry through if he lived long enough. Such comments are ubiquitous from his young days in the 1820s and '30s through his advanced age, when he took to referring to himself as an "old man" in his newspaper column. A typical example is Andrei's response to a simple recommendation from Yakov to read Polevoi's history of Russia: Andrei replied, "Polevoi's history I will read in the winter if still alive."[101] When in his later years he worked on an encyclopedic reference book of the county, he made plans that one copy of his work would be given to the provincial marshal of the nobility in the event of his death, and made sure that plans for future work on the book were detailed enough for others to carry on without him. Recounting this to his friend Kopytovskii, he jokingly admitted he had not yet actually sent on the extra copy because he was, of course, not yet dead.[102] Andrei's compulsive thoughts about his own death read as an entertaining quirk because he made the references so frequently, in every possible context, and because he lived a very long life. But death was always a realistic possibility; he had seen his loved ones taken from him too soon and with no warning, from his earliest parentless childhood. Death was all too real. As Andrei morbidly imagined it in another of his many ruminations on the subject, the slightest step in any direction was fraught with danger: "Chunks of ice that fell down [from the roof] showed me how close one is to one's death. I was without a hat: the sharp end of the ice chunk could fall onto my head, through the skull into my brain, and given their heavy weight, I would likely have been killed. The saying is right: our thoughts and intentions are far beyond the mountains, but our death is right here just over our shoulder."[103]

The losses the Chikhachevs endured did seem to come "one after another," as Andrei had put it, and perhaps even more so to Natalia, lacking as she did Andrei's outlet for his grief in writing and in work that reached beyond their own estates. Although her contributions to the notebook correspondence were brief and more formal than the others', Natalia's notes there do demonstrate her sincere attachment to her brother, while indirect evidence attests equally to her strong feelings for her children. That is to say, Natalia did not feel less than her husband; rather, her expression of grief was unwritten. Thus even in the extremities of life, both Chikhachevs continued to enact their established roles: Andrei was sentimental and nurturing, spilling his affections onto paper, while Natalia refrained from written effusions, instead focusing on keeping the household running through every crisis.

Andrei's diary-cum-work record served not only as an outlet for his hopes, fears, and grief but also eventually as a stepping-stone to a modest publicistic career; it served him beyond the legacy of the diaries themselves. Natalia's work as estate manager did not carry with it the potential for this kind of public outlet (at least during her lifetime). Natalia's diary almost certainly began simply as a work record, and although other parts of her life were occasionally recorded there, the persistence over time of her writing about estate work despite the importance in her lived experience of sociability, reading, faith, motherhood, and the memory of those she lost suggests that the material that appears most in her diary was what she *chose* to preserve: her work as estate manager.

The image that emerges from these papers, then, is of a woman who completely identified herself with her role as *khoziaika* both in work and in leisure. Within her own domain, Natalia was talented, forceful, successful—and exhausted to the point of serious illness. Outside of her domain, she was virtually invisible. This distinction between that which happened "within the home"—meaning the estate or *pomestie*—and beyond it determined the extent of all her activities, from estate work to sociability to charity and leisure pursuits, and even to how she and Andrei handled illness and grief.

7

Domesticity and Motherhood

IN 1883 ANDREI and Natalia's grandson Kostya inscribed a warning at beginning of his diary: "Dear young ladies! I beg of You, do not read this diary, as you may meet here such things, which to know and to read would be improper for those who are tender and modest."[1] Kostya's words are immediately recognizable as a concise formulation of classic nineteenth-century domestic ideology, which defined women's sphere as the home and men's as the public world. Identifying tenderness and modesty as exclusively female virtues and females as exclusively virtuous, Kostya begged his female readers to retain their virtue by ignoring the impure masculine world represented by his diary. Some time earlier (though it is not clear precisely when), Andrei inscribed the inside cover of one of his notebooks with the words, "Children! Children!/Live in amity/Honor your mother."[2] The message behind Andrei's inscription is less obvious and less easy to label or fully understand. Why did he specify the female parent (*roditel'nitsa*) in his plea to his grandchildren? He may have written this note after his wife's death and so intended it as a kind of memorial. A wife might have written the same about a male parent, if he had predeceased her, whereas it is impossible to imagine Kostya's words addressed to any male reader. Yet there is something paternalistic in an order to children to honor their mother—it is still the father who gives the order, implying that the mother's authority alone may be insufficient to elicit the "honor."

The Anglo-French model of domestic ideology was widely propagated in the Russian periodical press and advice books of the middle decades of the nineteenth century. These sources disseminated images of family closeness and happiness, and recommended piety, purity, and submissiveness to girls and women.[3] At the same time, the Russian monarchy was disseminating a similar, borrowed model of domesticity as embodied in the (German-born) Empress Alexandra, as model to all mothers of the empire. This notion was again that of the close-knit, emotionally tied family ideal, but with particular attention paid to the mother's role, which in this case "embod[ied] the purity, wisdom, and selflessness associated with child-rearing," and thus guaranteed "the sound moral development of her children."[4] The Chikhachevs' diaries show that they were avid consumers of this print culture. Andrei, especially, was receptive to imported ideas of domesticity; his writings about women at first seem contradictory because he used this imported imagery while also applauding a broader sphere for his own wife, but he was not himself aware of inconsistency. He drew his ideas from the intersections of his own life and his reading by disregarding those aspects that did not fit his particular needs and the older models of the family with which his family was operating, while adopting some of the rhetoric to soften his depictions of his life. By these means, rhetoric about domesticated motherhood and separate spheres rested alongside his private understanding of a mother's role as material provider and a father's ideal role as paternalistic moral guide.[5] The aggregate of ideas that Andrei developed emerges clearly only in the context of the private writings of both husband and wife. It is only because we know the nature, extent, and genuine importance of Natalia's work as estate manager through her diaries that we may understand the full complexity of Andrei's published work on the subjects of the *khoziaika* and domestic order.

In his journalistic career Andrei was a participant in the production of domestic ideology—albeit adapting the ideology in his own way—through his three-part article published in 1847–48 under the single title "The Importance of the *Khoziaika* in the Home." In his private writings Andrei also spoke the rhetoric of domesticity when, for example, he described loving scenes in which Natalia was lying with a sick child, yet in his article on her "importance" he never mentioned motherhood as any part of a woman's role as *khoziaika*. Andrei exhibited no self-consciousness in his several published articles about the upbringing of children in which he assumed that raising children must be the primary concern of a father; it was perhaps a situation so normal as to be taken for granted. Female control of property was common enough in imperial Russia that the Chikhachevs' arrangement of marriage roles was also, if not typical, at least normal enough to be invisible.

Natalia and Andrei give an impression in their diaries that he was the thinker and dreamer of their partnership, while she was the practical one, occupied almost exclusively with household management. For most of the time they lived together, Andrei had no actual responsibilities to speak of in the "outside" world. Natalia made sure the estate prospered and the family was comfortable, managing her dreaming husband when necessary to ensure that household affairs continued to run smoothly. In his *khoziaika* article, Andrei delineated the ideal roles of husband and wife as he saw them, and presumably much as he understood them to actually be in his own marriage:

The man has a purpose for the most part to direct affairs outside the home. Often, he will not know whether he will spend all day tomorrow at home, or perhaps this very day some happenstance . . . will demand his departure for an indefinite period; who then would preserve concord if not for the mistress of the home, whose title is not less respectable, and whose activity is not less laborious, than that of the head of the family himself[?] Take the queen out of the beehive, and not a single one of the 20,000 bees will stay in the hive or, indeed, alive.[6]

In part Andrei simply reiterated the central claim of the Western model of domesticity—that of "separate spheres" for male and female work. He explained away his physical presence at home by suggesting that he could be called away at any moment for some "outside" purpose, unlike his wife. But then he departed from the Western model when he emphasized that women's work was "not less laborious" and that the life of all others in the *khoziaika's* orbit—which explicitly included the field and household serfs—depended on the work of the "queen bee."[7]

In the second part of the same article, Andrei invoked a comparison between a gentry man's service "to the tsar and fatherland" and his service "to benefit [his] family," calling the latter a "calling" that ends only with a "coffin." His private documents and other articles show that the chief calling of a father in Andrei's mind was as *vospitatel* or moral educator. Andrei further adjured his readers to treat "family services just as regularly and carefully as our service to the fatherland."[8] When a man's public duty was technically done at the moment he retired from his service career, Andrei wanted him to consider himself as beginning another service, of at least equal importance and of much longer duration: rearing his children to be faithful, moral, educated people. In a provincial world where many women controlled property, and where most men, after their short and often perfunctory service terms, had few opportunities in political or commercial affairs, Andrei suggested that men might find a meaningful sphere of public importance by devoting themselves to educating the empire's future subjects.

Andrei then extended the military analogy by asking his (male) reader to think of his wife as his "permanent chief of staff." That is, the wife was the second-in-command, a "queen" to a king and a "chief of staff" to a commanding officer. Here Andrei was mixing his metaphors: a queen bee is a ruling queen, who does not herself work—and there is no king bee—while a chief of staff may easily be said to actually "command," while his "commanding officer" often serves merely as figurehead and ultimate bearer of responsibility (and credit). Andrei knew that some husbands of the Russian nobility remained in state service for longer periods, living far from home semi-permanently. In such cases as these his analogy of chief of staff and commanding officer would be apt in the sense that the "commanding officer," as figurehead, maintains ultimate authority but operates above and beyond mundane or everyday tasks, while the "chief of staff" performs the lower but highly responsible task of commanding daily operations, in this case by supervising estate labor and accounts.[9]

Perhaps Andrei assumed that an absent father-figurehead would be the typical situation for many of his readers. But he himself retired from service before his marriage, as indeed did many others, increasingly over the first half of the nineteenth century, and he never left his wife's side for longer than a few days, except for the one notable instance of six weeks spent in the monastery. Moreover, he published this article in the *Agricultural Gazette,* a periodical explicitly aimed at a resident provincial readership. Andrei thus explained his own constant presence in the home by declaring that even a man who lives principally on his estate may, according to "happenstance," be called away at any time to deal with matters of importance beyond estate boundaries.[10] Andrei's definition of his intellectual role as "outside the home" offered his readers a tantalizing image of themselves as playing an important part in some public project, if only metaphorically.

Approached from this angle, Andrei's analogy of the absent commanding officer and his chief of staff was not inappropriate even to his own situation. Although he actually conducted his "work" in the family home, it existed metaphorically "outside the home" in that his definition of his work comprised thinking and writing, and these activities necessarily concerned abstract ideas—that is, "affairs outside the home." Though most of his published writings—and by far the most original of them—actually concern exclusively domestic matters (child-rearing, cleanliness, and order in the home), Andrei saw these writings as an important public contribution because they were part of an over-arching effort to stem the tide of what he saw as the destructive urbanization and secular-ization of Russian gentry culture.[11] Thus he argued that "the plough, the spade, the axe, as well as the quill, thinking and contemplation cause sweat. Everything that strains our powers, whether physical or moral, is work," in a context in which "we are all sentenced to permanent labor, without any exception. Isn't it therefore a serious error to suppose that one might enjoy life without work?"[12] Work was central to life, Andrei's thinking and writing were his work, and since his thinking and writing concerned matters of public importance, he therefore considered them a public act.

Thus, Andrei saw himself as the figurehead, the ultimate commander, and the intel-lectual superior of his family. His wife's work came second, but was nevertheless vital to the lives of all, and to the "concord" of the home. Her responsibilities were "very diffi-cult": "They should be studied in advance, both theoretically and practically."[13] Her work was not abstract or intellectual, but she was or was meant to be a *skilled* commander—not, in other words, either a drudge or a "lady of leisure." Both his role and hers required the use of reason, but man's reasoning was abstract or theoretical, and therefore of a higher order, while women's reasoning was meant to be applied only in practical matters.

Andrei also stated in his article that though what he described there was the ideal, gentry women who were willing and able to do this kind of work were rare (he hoped they would become less so); but, of course, Andrei's understanding of this "ideal" was based on Natalia's reality. While her activities may not have been common, they did not transgress accepted norms in their social circle. A telling passage from a diary demon-strates, rather, that Andrei assumed in life as well as rhetoric that running the estate was primarily a *khoziaika's* job, that could become a man's job only in the event of the *khoziaika's* absence or incapacity. In 1831 Andrei went to visit his neighbors the Merkulovs at their village of Medvedkovo. Andrei was horrified by what he saw there: "My God! What have I seen! The house in its exterior and in its interior is bad, ancient, disorderly, untidy; the cold is extraordinary; the doors open up from the bottom—carelessness everywhere." His next thought, after expostulating, "God thine is the will!" was that "[t]he lady should not be blamed, because her son is lying in sickbed for the fourth year. But Ivan Stepanovich needs to be given a good whipping." In other words, in seeking the responsible party for property in a state of gross disorder, Andrei's mind leaped first to the *khoziaika*—yet, in this case, "the lady should not be blamed" because other duties had a prior claim over her time, namely the probably life-threatening illness of her son (in other words, she was required to provide first for her son in the most elemental way). Only in her absence did Andrei then turn to the man of the estate to take responsibility for its condition. In concluding his visit, Andrei "sat with the *khoziaika* for ¾ of an hour," before he "became completely frozen and went home."[14] Apparently the man of the Merkulov house could not be bothered to host visitors, either, but his lady could, despite her nursing duties.

The role of estate manager was gendered female in Andrei's mind but not according to any biological or "natural" claim exclusive to women. Estate management was simply the lesser of two roles (because it was practical rather than abstract, and because it was within the home instead of beyond) and therefore was appropriate to women, while in extreme situations it was equally natural for Andrei to assume that the man of the house would take over these tasks temporarily (as Andrei occasionally did when his wife was very ill).

Natalia's diaries support Andrei's view of their marriage to an extraordinary degree. Both of their work records—Natalia's recording of agricultural statistics, expenses, and serf work rotations, and Andrei's working out of his ideas before eventually writing many of them up for publication—bear out the distinct and separate domains described by Andrei as his ideal in his article. Andrei was of course as much a daily fixture inside his home as his wife, and his wife was in effect the recognized commander of this household in all but a few matters. Andrei was interested—to a point nearing obsession—in domestic order and the upbringing of children, while Natalia's "professional" interests focused more often on the space outside her immediate family but still under her purview—that is, the estate and all its inhabitants in her charge.

Yet by considering his domestic interests in an abstract light, Andrei defined them as "outside the home" and of public importance. Similarly, if "home" includes the outer limits of their estates, the *khoziaika's* domain was "within the home" and therefore he could maintain much of the rhetoric of separate spheres even in this very different context than the one in which that ideology originated.[15] Andrei's intellectual work gave the family prestige and was valuable in cultural terms, contributing in this way to the maintenance of the family's status. Educating children was vital to their future prosperity, even more so in these years when educational opportunities were expanding and serf emancipation was on the horizon. Upbringing was serious and responsible work, which Andrei was well qualified to do. The fact that it was usually considered women's work in the western European fiction and advice literature they read went unremarked because Andrei emphasized the intellectual over the nurturing aspects of this work. Relieving Natalia of this part of mothering (while serfs relieved her of some physical and practical aspects of it) made it possible for her to oversee the material welfare of a huge number of dependents.

Andrei began the last part of his article by darkly warning readers that insidious influences were encroaching from the capital cities into the villages and degrading the morals of young people. He blamed these bad influences on parents raising their children according to worldly rather than moral and religious values. These children, he noted, failed to cross themselves when they passed a church, and by implication, were equally oblivious to their other duties toward God and their communities. Andrei then asked rhetorically whether this reasoning that worldly values degrade morals can "apply to economics and estate management." It does, he asserted, in "the same way that food is necessary to life, that lumber is necessary to building, that the present is necessary for the future." As a solution he argued that "only a thorough . . . moral-religious upbringing from the earliest days to the departure of the fledglings from the nest can . . . implant . . . from generation to generation a direct love for the affairs appropriate to our position." And from the idea of upbringing in general he jumped to the upbringing of young ladies, the future mistresses of gentry homes, saying: "a young wife, having turned first to her duty rather than to the amusements of village life, will not fear or be bored by it, but will remember and be convinced that here is the true arena of her glory; her temple is the family, her servants are the priests, the idol is the common good, and the incense is mutual love."[16]

There are, again, several familiar elements of Western domesticity here. The world outside is a source of degradation, particularly to women. A young lady, singled out by her sex as having a particular role or sphere, must be morally and religiously educated to inculcate in her a sense of piety, duty and love for family. The family, indeed, is her "temple." Yet, again, motherhood is not mentioned. Andrei feared not only that young ladies would be corrupted away from morality and religion by an outside world, but also that they would be idle, fearful of their duties, or seduced away from duty by amusements. The abstract young lady he envisioned is one who could not afford to be decorative or even particularly maternal; a more vital duty came first. The angel of this house found her "glory" by playing her part in *khoziaistvo,* in the village economy and management of the estate. Though her temple was the family, she was a *khoziaika*—a landlady, hostess, estate manager and mistress of the house—before she was a mother or wife.

The argument Andrei made about the "importance" of the *khoziaika* in 1847 grew out of many years' experience and thinking. Fifteen years before he wrote this article, when his own daughter was two years old, Andrei stated in his diary that "It is necessary to drum into a girl ['s head] how she should always [behave], i.e., both when single and when married: meekness, submissiveness, kindness, justice, sensitivity and compassion to subordinates and to everyone: these are her virtues. And shrewdness, trickiness, the wish to lord it over her husband, falsity and other such [qualities] constitute a misfortune to her, to her husband, and to the entire family."[17] Again, this list of virtues is familiar to students of Western domestic ideology, as is his list of "misfortunes" for a young lady and her family. But as his article made clear, in Andrei's mind the purpose of these virtues and the cost of such "misfortunes" was different. Because the "young wife" of Andrei's article would grow up to be a *khoziaika* first, her virtues or lack thereof were indeed closely, materially, tied to the economy of the community. Unlike the Western model, the mother's work outside the family—in the economy of the community—took precedence over any private role she played as mother, wife, or nurturer.[18]

In another entirely private document written on a loose sheet of paper shortly after Natalia's death in 1866, Andrei recorded an astonishingly short list of memories of his wife, with whom he had shared forty-six years of marriage. Heading the list, "So many remembrances of my unforgettable little dove, my assiduous little old care-taker,"[19] he listed the following memories:

–How hard it was for her when our little son went abroad.
–How she examined the glass-pictures in his letters from Marienbad.
–[When] they cut out and sewed for the children, she sorted the gold trim, little crosses and stars for the priests' vestments.
–The departure and return from Shuia of Antonin.—Glazyrina's medicine [*illeg.*]
–Various instructions for Anton—funeral pancakes.
–In the summer, berries, apples and mushrooms.
–For name days—she loved to send a bit of sugar by post.
–She gave out various sweets to the little kids.[20]

With this list, Andrei domesticated Natalia's memory, subsuming her estate work beneath her love for her children and her care of others. While the list may also have been an accurate, if selective, reflection of Natalia's actual activities, it is totally unlike the version of her life that she wrote herself in her diaries. Here Andrei stressed her love for her son in the first two, possibly three, memories, while also mentioning her charity work for the church and stressing her involvement in food preparation rather than in finances. Yet, even here the means through which Natalia is depicted as expressing her love and caring for others is actually the providing of material comforts, not emotional display or any more directly personal nurturing act.

Andrei mentioned his wife in several other published articles about domestic matters besides the three-part piece chiefly occupied with her "importance." In these other articles Natalia played the role of a highly competent, discerning lady of the house, who required protection in illness—in the form of a healthier stone house—but who also demanded a standard of cleanliness and order that must be met for the greater good of all concerned.[21] One notable exception is an article "on clean air" in which Andrei depicted Natalia, along with all her countrywomen, as less knowledgeable or resourceful about cleanliness than the family's German governess, who was also mentioned several times in his articles as a representative of higher, Western standards.[22] This may be read as an attempt on Andrei's part to put in her place a wife who was so much more competent than he in most practical matters. However, he was usually anxious to portray himself as inept—or rather *above*—practical concerns. He took a measure of pride in being impractical; it affirmed his sense of masculinity as an educated thinker, not a manager. Significantly, then, in the article in which the German governess taught the Chikhachevs the benefits of fresh air in the home, Andrei depicted himself and all the remainder of their household (that is, the Russians) as equally nonplussed by the German woman's peculiar habits. He then entreated his Russian readers to learn from the Germans, as his family had, a way of living better than their ancestors had known. In other words, while Andrei claimed that a Russian *khoziaika* like Natalia may have had a few things to learn from an outsider, he blamed the problem on national development (or relative lack thereof) rather than on female action or inaction.

An anecdote that Andrei narrated in an article "on debt" in 1848 suggests that, according to Andrei at least, Natalia took on her role as practical manager as the result of a "mutual agreement" they achieved through "conference." While Natalia's (unrecorded) view of this "mutual" agreement might have differed from Andrei's, it is nevertheless significant that Andrei chose these words in which to couch his account of their early relationship: "Having moved to live in the village, my wife and I had a conference to determine how things were to be in our everyday life, and we promised to each other never to change the plan sketched out through our mutual agreement."[23] Where Andrei might have announced how he (alone) had arranged his marriage, or even employed the language of separate spheres (as he did in the "Importance of the *khoziaika*" article) to portray the arrangement as natural or inevitable, instead Andrei imagined it here as a "mutual agreement" achieved through "conference." The considerable distance between his language and the conventions of the time suggests that he may have been accurately reporting his own understanding of the case.

Andrei then explained how he and Natalia worked together to address the problem of their enormous debts (which he took pains to point out "were not created by us"): they explained their income and expenses in some detail to their serfs and begged them to understand that "their diligence and prudence can help in this situation." Andrei and Natalia promised not to increase the serfs' obligations but would instead "monitor constantly and attentively" whether the work was adding up to their "periodic expectancies," on the grounds that there was "an unbreakable chain" from lowliest serf to master and if everyone did their duty to their utmost ability, all would be well.[24] Significantly, Andrei described this first part of the Chikhachevs' speech to their dependents as both his *and* his wife's, yet he introduced the next part of the speech—directed to a "specially invited" priest and clearly of a moral nature—with the words, "then it was my turn":

Then it was my turn, to speak about *all our responsibilities to them as their landlords*, and that in the activities that we expect of them, we will try to constantly set them an example. And you, Holy Father, I said to the Priest who was specially invited for this purpose, you, who must without any pretension [constantly] remind, educate, teach, reason, forbid, you will be the witness of everything said here, and, because without asking for God's blessing no affair should be consummated, we beg you to conduct a mass this very moment.[25]

It seems safe to assume that the details of expenses and the patterns their finances were expected to follow given in the first part of the speech were actually provided by Natalia, while Andrei depicted himself, as usual, as in charge of moral and spiritual matters. Natalia assumed the role of manager not only of the family's finances but of the fates of all the members of the village. Likewise, Andrei considered himself a father to them all, which in his terms meant that his chief role in the village was as spiritual or moral leader, educator, and guide.

In the early and mid-nineteenth century, western European and American homes were changing enormously due to industrialization, above all in Britain, where the process began. For the British middle class, the home was ceasing to be a productive unit, becoming separate from the (increasingly male-only) workplace.[26] As the middle class prospered, servants became a marker of status, and their presence freed women from household labor, while participation in the family business was also being removed from her sphere. This left little for women to do other than entertain and decorate, and be a mother, and it simultaneously reduced the father's role to providing.[27] The family as an economic unit was gradually supplanted by the family as, in historian John Tosh's words, a "sentimental and emotional" unit.[28] Tosh also describes how the new home brought with it new rituals that reinforced the new understanding of the family, focusing on "standards of comfort, privacy and routine." The space in middle-class homes was often arranged around these rituals, which included lessons for children, reading aloud by the fire, playing the piano, and entertaining a small circle of friends or relatives.[29]

The Chikhachevs engaged in many of these same rituals; the music, social life, and reading aloud were all familiar activities, as were the lessons for children (though they were usually led by the father, with tutors and governesses only secondarily). Yet for the Chikhachevs the home was still a productive unit, indeed the same form of productive unit it had been for centuries for people of their social estate. Servants were present, but they were far more occupied with estate production (textiles, animal husbandry, agriculture) than with easing life for the family. Natalia's management was essential to the running of this family enterprise, and it left her very minimal time for leisure activities.

In elite homes of late eighteenth-century Britain, taste in decoration, socializing, and material consumption became increasingly feminized realms, and many women used this power over the management of space to assert themselves and their families socially.[30] All this was unnecessary for the Chikhachevs. Natalia could not spare the time for such pursuits even if she had been willing to allow the expense. It was Andrei who dreamed about remodeling their home, and his dreams were modest. Looking at house plans, Andrei once declared practically that a separate bathroom was "not expensive and very useful," and "better than boudoirs and flower galleries."[31] Socialization and leisure for the Chikhachevs was less formal, more familial, and apparently uncompetitive.

The arrangement of space within the Chikhachev home similarly reflects much earlier models of domestic life than the contemporary fashion in Britain. The Chikhachev home was divided into rooms for female work (a sewing room for women servants in addition to the kitchen and larder) and rooms for male work (one for serfs and also Andrei's study), as well as a room for male play (the billiard room). Andrei sometimes referred to a "hermitage," variously as his own or his wife's, but it seems this was his way of describing whatever room he or his wife sought out to get some peace, rather than a designation for a specific physical space. The house revolved around the drawing room (*gostinnaia*), in which the whole family gathered for the sort of "rituals" that a Victorian family also enjoyed. Sleeping spaces seem to have been flexible, probably depending on weather— Andrei mentioned waking up near both his wife and children on occasion, and other indications suggest that Natalia sometimes slept separately (probably when ill). The "nursery" was in fact the whole house, as the children were to be found variously in any of the rooms, though one room was designated "the children's" on one of his drawings. Specialized indoor servants were limited to cook and nanny; others were "women" who worked as needed on spinning, weaving, and sewing projects, in a room labeled by Andrei as the "estate room" (*khoziaistvennaia*).[32] Undoubtedly these women also did the heavy cleaning in the house, but there was no equivalent to the British hierarchy of parlor maids, kitchen maids, footmen, or butler.

Largely because of the textile industry then establishing itself, Vladimir province had the third largest number of female-owned enterprises in the empire in 1832, even though it was the eighteenth largest province by total population. A sample of twenty-six noble female owners of enterprises shows that they often came from well-known, sometimes titled families.[33] These data, together with Michelle Marrese's extensive research in legal records and memoirs from across the empire over a very long period, suggest, first, that Natalia was unexceptional as a female manager of a large enterprise, and second, that compared to titled women factory owners, Natalia's activities were far more readily reconciled with Western gender norms.[34]

As late as 1901, there is evidence of a Russian merchant family who understood gender roles precisely as the Chikhachevs did, despite an ultimately unsuccessful marriage and their different social estate (although, crucially, this family shared middling wealth and education with provincial nobles). In a divorce petition, Varvara Kupriianova, who referred to herself as a *khoziaika*, complained that her husband had failed to provide their children with a proper "upbringing or instruction," and that he had undermined her authority "over her own domain, the household," by "demeaning her before the servants and the children."[35] Kupriianova's "domain" was smaller than Natalia's, but she conceived of its borders in a similar way. The wives of several of Russia's greatest writers also operated as *khoziaiki* in much the same way Natalia understood that role; their husbands were absorbed in "labor" understood as having intellectual and moral significance, while wives facilitated the financial and material aspects of the family livelihood. For example, Dostoevsky's wife, Anna, was his publisher, overseeing typeface, illustrations, and bindings for his books.[36] Elite women of the Bakunin family also played key roles in the background of male intellectual labors, even intellectual and creative roles (this was probably not something a family like the Chikhachevs could afford, even had Natalia been so inclined).[37]

The image of the Russian woman as *khoziaika* appeared in the press only rarely, however, and as an exception to the rule. In 1835 the *Northern Bee* listed under the topic "economics," a piece on the forest management of Countess Sofia Vladimirovna Stroganova.[38] Another woman contributor to print culture about agriculture was Elisaveta Gotovtseva, who wrote about her experiments in the *Agricultural Journal.* Some of her experiments appeared in the *Agricultural Gazette,* but significantly, her work was merely summarized by a male author. She was treated as an oddity in the newspapers, on par with the occasional peasant contributor.[39]

Natalia's example may shed some light on the seemingly strange fact that women frequently managed property yet appeared in provincial journals about agriculture only as oddities. While neither Natalia nor her family questioned that agricultural management was her sphere, *writing* was decidedly Andrei's sphere and considered a specifically masculine task. Perhaps women appeared and were addressed only rarely in the periodical press about agriculture not because they were uninterested in or not respected authorities on agriculture, but because the acts of reading and writing and educating the mind through print culture were all very much male spheres. The first significant Russian women writers did begin to publish in this period—from creative writers like Karolina Pavlova and Elena Gan to advice writers like Avdeeva. Their appearance was, at first, a curiosity that paved the way (slowly) for more female participation in print culture.

Separate spheres in the West were defined according to rapid economic and social changes. In the English middle class, nineteenth-century women were concerned with educating their children and supervising servants, but were largely exempt from heavier tasks.[40] English noble mothers were effectively confined to the home while their children were young, when men were expected to engage widely with the outside world.[41] Natalia was not immobilized by the nursery, but by her fields and laborers. According to historian Amanda Vickery, the rule for English gentry women was that "[if] you did not provide the shirts [for your men] you were hardly a wife," and the provision of shirts from thread and cloth—and then laundering and repairing them—was a complicated task.[42] How much more complicated was it for Natalia, for whom the phrase "your men" included serfs, and who oversaw the production of cloth itself, from the growing of the flax to its spinning and weaving, before shirts could even begin to be sewn?

The British shifted away from self-sufficiency and toward consumerism over the course of the eighteenth century, although even toward the end of the century wealthier households continued to engage in some aspects of domestic production (such as beer) while also becoming increasingly active consumers of imported luxury goods.[43] For much of the English landed nobility, the reality—despite the rhetoric of domesticity—was that household management was often a woman's sphere; it is important to note, however, that in the English context women rarely exerted financial or managerial authority beyond their children and household servants (that is, unlike Natalia they did not oversee field labor or collect rents, for example).[44] Even in this English context, according to Vickery, "[t]he pride that women took in their status [as housekeepers] is obvious in the frequency with which they claimed the label 'housekeeper' in court, and the regret with which widows deposed that while once housekeepers, they were now only lodgers."[45] In England married women juggled being both "deferential wives" and "powerful mistresses" of their homes, which was, Vickery argues, "a conceptual inconsistency that women often manipulated to their advantage and a contradiction from which men often profited."[46] Victorian women who stood out for their times as managers often concentrated their skills in projects that were at least partly, if not wholly, charitable, reinforcing rather than belying the image of women as nurturers first, managers only exceptionally.[47] For example, a British curate's wife who earned money independently because her husband was unable to provide was crossing a boundary.[48] But Natalia operated well within the boundaries of everyday expectations for women in her circle. Where the curate's wife could provide for her family *only* when her husband failed, Natalia and the large numbers of women like her identified in Michelle Marrese's study provided for their families for a variety of reasons, sometimes unrelated to a previous failure of a male provider. These women managed and provided because the expectation that a man must do so if he possibly could simply was not universal in the Russian provinces. Instead, men focused their self-identities on entirely other goals, chiefly service (whether to the state directly or in a more metaphorical sense as moral-intellectual leaders and writers, like Andrei). This left the more mundane matter of providing for a family financially and administratively open to some women, *without* transgressing boundaries.

A more fruitful comparison to this Russian model of marriage can be found by looking to Jewish cultures in eastern Europe and the Western diaspora. Speaking of the "daughters of the shtetl" around the turn of the twentieth century, historian Susan Glenn writes that "Jews considered it something of a religious obligation for the wife of a Torah scholar to work while her husband devoted most of his time to study and prayer."[49] The Chikhachevs' marital arrangements did not derive from their religious practice (although a convincing argument has been made by Nadieszda Kizenko that there was a "liberal variant" of Russian Orthodox thinking that "regarded women as autonomous beings" and insisted on "fundamental equality . . . in marriage"[50]). But there are other key elements of the Chikhachev model that mirror the Jewish one. Though the women Glenn describes were "viewed as inferior beings," they like Natalia were recognized for their material contributions to family well-being, and were less restricted by cultural expectations of purity.[51] The common element to both cultures was the importance of intellectual activity in defining masculinity. This is the same element that contrasts most starkly with studies of British and American men. For the latter there was a tension between dedication to the home and family (which domestic ideology encouraged in men as well as women) and the demands of commercial or professional careers.[52] No such contradiction existed for the father-educator.

Fundamentally the Chikhachevs' arrangement of roles derived from financial and practical necessity, and is also recognizable as an echo of the influential sixteenth-century guidebook, the *Domostroi* (literally, "house order"), calling for the mistress of a noble home to act as "keeper of the larder."[53] The *Domostroi* described an ideal household as self-sufficient and hierarchical, with the wife as second in command, controlling several levels of dependents, from children to household serfs. When the *Domostroi* was written, women could control the household budget but were physically confined within certain private sections of the home, while men operated mostly outside it, in the tsar's service. Women's roles as bearers of children and markers of social success—through their piety, chastity, and family connections—were also emphasized.

But social expectations for women changed rapidly in the eighteenth century when Peter the Great ordered noblewomen to come out of their homes, discard their traditional dress, and take part in *Assemblées* on the French model. After Peter's death, continuing Western influences and a string of powerful empresses continued to raise the importance of fashion, Western manners, and sociability in gentry culture. By the 1830s Russian gentry wives and mothers had been exhorted to follow western European models of womanhood for more than a century, yet the material conditions of life on the provincial estate that prompted the *Domostroi* model of wife as both keeper of the larder and second in command of estate and serfs—and that had ceased to obtain for the gentry of most of western Europe by that time—were, in the Russian provinces, no less pertinent than they had been in the sixteenth century. It is clear from Andrei's writing that the Enlightenment and sentimental literature had done much to soften the hard edges of early modern gender roles in the household, but the fundamental division of labor remained the same.

Finally, early importations of Western domestic ideology were filtered through to Russia in a relatively limited way in the 1820s and 1830s, making it easier, perhaps, to ignore or reinterpret its tenets. Print culture in those decades was so disproportionately occupied with defining the role of the nobleman newly freed from state service that the female half of domesticity may have simply been neglected. In the late eighteenth century, Andrei Bolotov's journal *Economic Store* made occasional reference to topics "for the ladies," but they were extremely limited in scope and entirely restricted to categories that were feminized in Western literature propagating domesticity, such as cosmetics.[54] Other printed depictions of provincial life in the late eighteenth and early nineteenth centuries similarly seem to have borrowed from the foreign press without much reference to Russian reality: the assumption was made in print that peasant women worked only in the house and garden, not the fields, in a nation where terms for field labor were calculated according to husband and wife labor teams.[55]

Similarly, the early nineteenth-century Russian press depicted women as helpmeets to their husbands—who were at least sometimes depicted as hard-working—and the nature of women's work was sharply restricted to the home and garden, despite an often contrary reality.[56] Besides an excessive dependence on the direct translation of foreign articles, it has been argued that another reason for the awkward unreality of much of the Russian press in this period is that many of these writers adhered to a late-Enlightenment, universalist philosophy that national boundaries were irrelevant to the rational and scientific spread of knowledge.[57] Only as the nineteenth century progressed did notions of female work in the kitchen gradually become less about attempting to cover, in an encyclopedic fashion, every form of labor, and more about redefining the kitchen as the rightful domain of the "dear ladies," as part of the main message to be propagated. Cookery became separated from agriculture, and as it developed the separation fell along gendered lines (whereas in the initial formulation, both cookery and agriculture were presented as masculine interests).[58]

For much of the first few decades of the nineteenth century, it was assumed that ordering meals and taking interest in culinary arts were open to both men and women, although generally among those wealthy enough to depend on servants for actual cooking, the former was presumed to pertain more to women and the latter more to men. Then, the publications of a merchant's daughter named Ekaterina Avdeeva, beginning in the early 1840s, changed the landscape of advice literature. She found an audience that was not previously believed to exist; when spoken to directly, it turned out this audience was present and eager. According to the historian Alison Smith, Avdeeva formulated "the idea of the experienced, Russian, middle-class housewife, who herself gave advice and actively sought to educate younger women."[59] Or perhaps Avdeeva simply reflected a reality of many real Russian women who were, before Avdeeva's appearance, finding their voices ignored.

Avdeeva spoke for women of modest wealth and large responsibilities, who craved information that spoke to their specific situations. She reflects the beginning of two different categories of new writers: women, and people of the merchant or *meshanskii* classes. The emergence of both groups at the same time and, in Avdeeva, even in the same person, may be a factor in the shift in advice literature in these decades increasingly toward the explicit promotion of a housewife who was the unquestioned mistress of her domain, but a much smaller domain than had previously been possible. Real Russian women of the middling classes did not, of course, live up to the ideal of the Western middle-class housewife (even *they* did not). But it was seemingly this gap between rhetoric and reality that pushed writers, male and female, to "educate" Russian women about the parameters of their role (understood as part of the larger project of modernization through westernization). Avdeeva was explicit about addressing middling Russian readers, and about the importance of texts in teaching younger generations of women how to perform their roles scientifically, marking Avdeeva's project as a modernization project. In her later books, Avdeeva hoped to move beyond the home into "farms," orchards, and animal husbandry. This project, however, was unsuccessful. It seems strange that a merchant's daughter could have been as "experienced" in these matters as her middling gentry readers, but the real problem with her ambition to move out into the fields was probably that as emancipation neared, the role of the *khoziaika* who inspects field labor and the state of the pigs was approaching extinction.[60]

In 1859, in a letter from Andrei to his grandson Kostya, Andrei wrote that "grandmother sends some presents to her dear grandson, while grandfather only sends air-kisses and advice, which he always dispenses so generously."[61] And so into the second generation Andrei and Natalia maintained their roles: Natalia sent things, and Andrei sent only "air-kisses"—affection—and "advice"—moral instruction. These roles were about more than which parent did which work; they were fundamental to the ways parents related to children, and defined the channels through which parents expressed their attachment to their children. According to the dominant rhetoric at the time the Chikhachevs were writing, motherhood was supposed to be central to womanhood, defining the most important part of a woman's life, her most important contribution to society, and her primary motivation for all that she did.[62]

The centrality of motherhood in nineteenth-century domestic ideology derived from the idea of "Republican motherhood" that followed the French Revolution: the Revolution defined citizenship as a set of obligations and a growing sphere of public activity, and the "citizen" at that time was gendered male. As spheres of activity and rights for men expanded, the space left to women contracted and became increasingly centered on the duty to raise future citizens of the Republic. By the 1830s, Republican motherhood had become a ful-fledged and powerful conventional wisdom across much of Europe that judged women's value, success, and femininity against that one yardstick more than any other. Although the Russian empire was no kind of republic, this aspect of domestic ideology was also present in the Chikhachevs' daily lives through the prescriptive literature they read. Even the Russian monarchy was anxious to endorse the notion of domestic motherhood (though they naturally disassociated it from notions of citizenship and other republican and middle-class ideals).[63] Just as the prominence and nature of estate work in Natalia's diaries emphasized the preeminence of this duty to her role as *khoziaika,* so too does the near absence in these documents of idealized motherhood reveal that in this family model, motherhood was subsumed under the umbrella of household and estate management. Motherhood in this sense was understood first as the duty to provide for one's children's material welfare, in marked contrast to the sentimental, nurturing, and morally guiding role reserved for mothers in the domestic ideology that was being propagated by the monarchy and the (hardly independent) Russian press.[64]

The explanation for the absence of certain forms of motherhood in Natalia's diaries cannot be that she was uninterested in or resentful of motherhood, because indirect evidence suggests that she was strongly attached to her children: she dropped other duties to attend to them when they were ill, she opposed Andrei's decision to send them away for school on emotional grounds, and she followed her son's later travels with avidity. Whatever were her feelings and experiences of being a mother, these were not included in her written record of herself, and thus appear to have been considered by her as lying outside of and separate from her primary duties as an estate manager. Thus, where ideal, nurturing motherhood was the defining duty of womanhood in Western rhetoric, Natalia recognized her own duty otherwise and confined motherhood to the purely personal or private part of her existence that went largely unrecorded. Her children's well-being might have been a prominent or even the first goal of Natalia's work, but she (and her husband) included in it the care of serfs and other dependents as well as children. Parenting was a task Natalia divided with Andrei, and the nurturing and guiding aspects of parenting were decidedly in his domain.

In Natalia's diaries, it has been shown, motherhood is indirectly present through the physical toll childbirth and miscarriages took on her, and through the work and planning she devoted to her children's material well-being. In one of the very few instances where Natalia mentioned engaging in an activity with one of her children, she also offered to feed her brother (that is, to attend to his material comfort) in the same entry: "Will our dear brother [*bratikosochka*] decide to eat with us a very good *solianka* [soup]: this would be very good. Alesha is excited by the book "Golden Mirror"—he sits with me and reads."[65] In almost every case in which Natalia mentioned the care of the children she included her husband, phrasing her concern as affecting "us," meaning husband and wife (emphasis added):

> Thank you, my dear little brother Yakov Ivanovich for remembering *us* and for your congratulations, and for the treat for *our* birthday-boy [Aleksei]; he himself wants to write and to thank you; and on his birthday he frightened *us* quite a lot, he became very, very sick—shooting pain in the ear, strong headache and toothache, today thank god he is better.[66]

When Natalia mentioned her children, she did so in a matter-of-fact fashion, and worries were expressed as affecting "us." In contrast, when Andrei remarked on his wife's ministrations to the children when they were ill, he employed diminutives and other rhetorical devices to paint an endearing, domestic scene:

> Sashinka's tooth is hurting, she is crying a lot! Mother put rum on cotton cloth— she cries even more. . . . Yesterday I came back home and found a tall, fat creature with shining eyes and steam splashing off it. In other words, the samovar was on the table. My wife was lying with Sashonochka, who was crying because her teethies were hurting.[67]

And while Natalia usually failed to note incidents like these in her diary, Andrei was frequently inclined to make sentimental notations about his offspring's illnesses in his diaries, as in the following entries from 1831: "Alesha vomited 6 times and the poor little guy is very wan."[68] Later that day Andrei tried to go visiting "with a weak Alesha," but the boy worsened and they cut their visit short. Then a cleric, Father Kiprian from Suzdal, came and "suggested a raspberry infusion for Alesha."[69] Andrei not only recorded more detail about his children in his diaries, but he did so in sentimental terms ("poor little guy"), and not only in regard to his son. On the day following Alesha's bellyache he added a fond notation about his young daughter, whose growth and progress he was evidently watching closely: "Sashinka was inoculated for smallpox in the morning. It is one year, 14 weeks and 3 days from her birth."[70] (Meanwhile, Natalia apparently was the one who dealt with some of the less romantic aspects of childrearing: Andrei once wrote that when two-year-old Aleksandra vomited, "Natalia pumped her stomach.")[71]

Andrei also spent a great deal of time with the children, almost certainly more than Natalia did. He traveled more, often taking one or both children with him (the inverse occurred only rarely; Aleksei once noted: "Maminka and my dear sister went to Shuia, while Papinka and I stayed home").[72] Throughout the 1830s he either led or oversaw their lessons, and as Aleksei's diary demonstrates, he kept an extremely watchful eye on their intellectual progress. On the extended visit to Moscow in January 1842 that the Chikhachevs took to be with their children, Natalia recorded little more than her almost constant illnesses, which kept her at home much of the time, away from the children who lived at their respective schools. Andrei spent this time visiting the children at their schools almost daily, quizzing Aleksei's unfortunate tutors and fellow pupils. Natalia visited Aleksandra's *pansion* only once, to speak with the headmistress, stopping also at Aleksei's institute on the way back, and chatting with some women she met there.[73] She also faithfully recorded the occasion whenever her children visited their parents at their lodgings and for how long. However, while the children were with their parents Natalia was almost always talking, playing cards, or knitting with some visitor or friend. Other than helping Aleksandra with her needlework for the headmistress of her *pansion*, which may be seen in the same light as the tasks Natalia performed at home to ensure the material well-being of those around her, she did not once mention sharing any activity directly with her children.

Instead Natalia wrote continually about what Andrei did with them. In Natalia's own words Andrei's peripatetic day revolved around the children ("Andrei Ivanovich brought Sasha to the *Pansion,* and stopped by with her in town. He bought me 4 tiny snuffboxes, drank tea with the landlord, and in the evening went to the children, and stayed with them until 9 o'clock"), while Natalia's life was stationary ("I knitted the stocking. Kater[ina] Bogdano[vna] sat with me"). Each day was nearly the same, at least from Natalia's point of view—"Andrei Ivanovich went to [see] the children in the morning and evening" though occasionally the children came to her: "Alesha asked of the Inspector if he may spend the night at home, and came at 1 o'clock, and played with the rubber ball" (on this day, all she recorded of her own activities was, "Bought 64 puds of hay for 45 kopeks"). Another day, Andrei "brought" the children, then "went to evening service at the university"; the syntax makes it unclear whether Natalia went along, but her final words "I finished knitting the stockings" imply that she was, again, left home alone.[74]

In every one of these and other similar entries, Natalia was an observer of her children's lives while Andrei was an involved, even an interfering parent. Natalia certainly acted in the background to ensure the family's comfort, but in all the conventional aspects of parenting she portrayed Andrei as the sole actor. For his part Aleksei, in his diaries, always referred to letters from "Papinka and Maminka" but went on to explain at length only what Papinka said, what he advised, and what he criticized. When Aleksei went home on visits, he talked, played billiards, rode horses, and read with his father, and his father quizzed him on his studies, appearing in nearly every sentence of the boy's diaries. The number of times that Aleksei mentioned his mother over the course of the same set of diaries can be counted on one hand, and in two of only a handful of cases, "Papinka" was mentioned alongside "Maminka."[75] Children have a tendency to take mothers for granted when so many of a mother's tasks (including Natalia's), such as cleaning, providing, and nursing through illness, tend to be "invisible," while fathers (including Andrei) are more likely to reward and to punish and therefore to loom disproportionately large in a child's mind. Aleksei's diaries show that Andrei was also simply a more constant literal presence in his life, while Natalia was more likely to be occupied with estate work.

This is not to say the boy was not emotionally close to his mother; his affection was recorded in Andrei's diary: "Alesha asks incessantly: will Papinka soon go to meet Maminka [on her return from Moscow], is it time to lay the table, and so on. . . . Alesha and I got dressed and in that manner were completely ready to go meet *Mamasha*!!!!"[76] In a much later period, an adult Aleksei wrote about his mother as an expert on how best to find a nanny: "my *Mamasha* knows everything better than all of us and about her little grandson as well and as to who will be his nanny will think about it carefully."[77] If a diary by Aleksandra had survived, she may well have been able to attest to a difference in how the Chikhachevs parented their daughter as opposed to their son, but unfortunately no such account exists.

There was one exception to the rule that Natalia kept her feelings for her children separate from her estate work and therefore her diaries. The occasion of Aleksei's departure for school marks the one episode in the diaries in which Natalia opened a window into the strength and nature of her feelings about her children (or about anything else), yet even this one incidence of deepest misery was embedded in notations about the barley and the flax. And she closed the window just as suddenly: the diary ends eleven days later.

Natalia began her entry for September 6, 1837, in the usual way: "Got up at 7 o'clock. The day today was warm and pretty but toward evening it became very cold. They threshed 4 barn-fuls of flax." She continued for a half-page more, listing how much of various kinds of grains "the lord gave," and then concluded: "Andrei Ivanovich thinks to send Alesha to a *pansion* in Moscow; I spent all day crying and feel very bad. I cut out [fabric for] pantaloons for Alesha and knitted Alesha 2 cotton stockings." Andrei had decided that Aleksei was old enough to be sent to Moscow for the formal schooling and social contacts necessary to his future (his sister would follow him two years later).

Throughout the following three weeks, Natalia added to the usual list of harvest-related accounts a running tally of the clothing she was preparing for Aleksei. By September 27, the time for Aleksei's departure was drawing near, and she interspersed lists of clothing prepared with phrases like, "we were all very miserable to be sending Alesha away," and "I sobbed all day and was miserable; very sick about Andrei and Alesha leaving."

The day after they finally left, she wrote: "I prayed to God, and knitted a stocking a little bit, but I'm very miserable, and don't feel well and don't feel like doing anything." On the following day her last entry referring to the incident reads: "Got up at 8 o'clock. I prayed to God, and all morning I sat with my brother [Yakov] in our common room and talked about Alesha, and about Andrei Ivanovich, and he advised me not to be miserable about their leaving. But I can't overcome myself and am suffering terribly from sadness. My brother left soon after dinner. The day today was warm; at night and in the morning it rained. Last year's barley was harvested for grain, 4 chetveriks."[78] Yakov's diary mentioned only that "Sister is grieving!"[79]

This episode, in which Natalia apparently could not help but pour her "misery" onto the page, suggests that she might have chosen to write much more about her feelings for her children and the losses she suffered. But apparently she usually chose not to, and therefore this one incident must have marked a moment of deepest significance for her, breaking the rules that normally guided what she wrote. It was perhaps the only moment in their lives in which Andrei's and Natalia's roles came into direct conflict. Andrei was in charge of the children's upbringing, so how and where they would be educated was his decision alone. It does not appear that Natalia questioned his right to make this decision. Rather, her "misery" derived from the fact that Andrei's irrevocable decision took her son out of her sphere of influence. While Aleksei was at school Natalia would no longer be responsible for his material needs and would likewise lose both this means of control over her son's life and her primary means of expressing her love for him. She coped with the loss according to the means she had to command: she devoted herself to preparing Aleksei's clothing, to ensure his comfort while in Moscow and also, perhaps, to make sure that he remembered her through the material goods she provided him.

If Natalia saw the purpose of her diaries (without necessarily articulating it to herself or anyone else) as recording the work she accomplished for her family, then her distancing of her children in her diaries may have been simply because that part of motherhood was not her duty. Her duty was of necessity a rational and unemotional one. If she used her diary, beyond its obvious practical uses, to define her role in the family as a khoziaika rather than as a mother, this does not imply or require that motherhood was less important to her personally. The diary implies only that motherhood was not how she understood her duty: as she said herself—she simply considered "economics" to be her "department"; rearing the future generation was Andrei's job, in an almost direct reversal of the Western model.

To summarize Andrei's position, the role of a wife on a provincial Russian estate in this period did require that she represent the family socially, bear and raise children, and make the home into a "nest" (the Russian word for "nest," *gnezdo,* is a term traditionally applied to gentry estates). In addition, however, on relatively small provincial estates like the Chikhachevs', isolated from the central government, with poor soil and primitive roads, the secure maintenance of the gentry lifestyle depended on wives as well as husbands taking an active role in managing the serfs and controlling the finances. In Andrei's language, a wife was expected to be "meek," "submissive," and "kind," but she also—in all practicality—needed to know how to supervise the threshing, balance the budget, discipline the servants, and order supplies from the nearest town with enough sense and foresight to keep the family comfortable. The "family" in this case meant not only the nuclear family and sometimes extended relations but anywhere from a dozen to a few hundred households of serfs, each comprised of children, the elderly, and the sick as well as the workers who brought in income. When a *khoziaika* mismanaged her estate, not only did her family suffer directly but they would face the likely threat of serf unrest as well.

Was this marriage as radically different as it seems from the patterns called for in the Western literature Andrei and Natalia were reading? Andrei deferred to his wife in matters of finance. Yet, what power accrued to the manager of the finances, when finances were so tight that managing them was a matter mostly of careful accounting and difficult choices—in other words, of hard work? Natalia's management allowed Andrei to spend much of his time as an amateur scholar and writer (an endeavor that brought some social status and pleasure for the whole family) as well as allowing him to devote himself to the education of their children. Natalia was without question the junior partner in the family business of maintaining the provincial gentry lifestyle. She did the majority of the work of management, and made the smaller decisions, while Andrei made the major ones. The episode in which Natalia described her "misery" in the face of Andrei's announcement that he would send Aleksei away for school may perhaps illustrate her only means of protesting, or at least registering her unhappiness, when a decision of Andrei's conflicted with her own sphere of interests or desires. But, if so, her protest was ineffective: Aleksei left anyway, and the matter ended with Natalia's brother Yakov unhelpfully advising her "not to be miserable." She then insisted that she could not "overcome herself," and ceased to keep her diary, but other family documents show that, despite her persistent misery of that autumn, life continued as usual, and Andrei's decision was final.

Although Andrei was inspired by the ideals of Western-style domestic bliss he saw in their reading, for the Chikhachevs the borrowed images of ideal motherhood that lay at the core of domesticity were still subsumed beneath the need to manage the greater "family"—including the serfs on whom their incomes and even personal safety depended. Andrei and Natalia's roles were not balanced or equal and were decidedly separate, but their relationship was stable and effective in achieving their goals. The masculine and feminine spheres seen here encompassed different activities in response to the different needs of an elite society that was more dispersed, less wealthy, and less powerful than their social counterparts in western Europe and America. Andrei neither rejected, nor fully accepted, either Western-style domesticity or the model represented by the

Domostroi. He combined elements of each with his own circumstances, and each of these elements was important to the whole. While the difficult economic conditions of Russian provincial landownership had to be the most fundamental factor in determining the division of labor within the Chikhachev marriage, the particular way Andrei and Natalia understood their respective duties in life—motherhood as the provision of material goods, fatherhood as moral and intellectual leadership—did more than protect their family. It was also a way of making sense of serf ownership, and of a man's role in an empire with no vote and few commercial or professional opportunities at this time.

When Andrei wrote his article about "the importance of the *khoziaika* in the home," he was not only explaining and elevating Natalia's role but doing the same for his own role at the same time: by publishing an article about his ideas, Andrei was participating in an intellectual sphere beyond the home. This, however, was a culmination of many years' development of his role. Initially, he defined his role more narrowly (though still "beyond the home" in the metaphorical sense) as the intellectual and moral leader of his family and village. For many years, the enormous task of bringing up his children to be virtuous and well-educated adults was enough by itself to consume nearly all his time.

8

The Education of Aleksei

ANDREI CHIKHACHEV DEFINED his sphere as the realm of intellectual thought, writing, and teaching. The way Andrei's abstract "work" most palpably contributed to his family was in how he carried out *vospitanie,* or the moral education of his children. Andrei treated *vospitanie* as a serious intellectual undertaking of enormous personal and moral significance. And although Andrei was literally present in the home, he considered his efforts to educate his children—and abstract thought more generally—as an "outside," or public, domain, which he claimed as a masculine sphere. Andrei devoted most of his energy in the 1830s to either the direct supervision and training of his children, or to furthering his own studies in order to make himself a better *vospitatel,* or moral educator.[1] He believed that study improved one's "soul and heart" as well as one's mind, and was necessary "so as to leave a good memory of oneself."[2] And so he devoted himself to his own lifelong studies and those of his children.

The Russian word *vospitanie* that Andrei exclusively employed to describe this aspect of his duties is without an exact equivalent in English. Its literal meaning is "nurturing" but it also encompasses what is meant by the English "education" in addition to the instilling of morals and manners. A proper *vospitanie* molds a young person, imbuing him or her with moral fiber, and with the knowledge and manners considered appropriate to the individual's social position and sex. In mid-nineteenth-century Europe, under the influence of the French Enlightenment, *vospitanie* was considered a subject of great social and civic importance. The Enlightenment-based idea that, first, reason and knowledge were the underpinning of an advanced society and, second, that reason and knowledge could be acquired (as opposed to virtues and behaviors that were merely "bred") led educated Europeans to place enormous significance on child-rearing. They believed that the values, habits, manners and knowledge that they considered essential to human progress could be implanted, if the process began in a child's earliest years, before the child could be corrupted by irrationality, laziness, or immorality. From this point of view children were seen as essentially unformed beings, molded by time and experience. With care the child's character, habits, and modes of behavior as an adult could be molded into the desired form. Progressive thinkers of the period therefore sought to establish programs of moral, rational upbringing as a direct means of changing the world.[3]

Seeing *vospitanie* as a specifically masculine calling, as Andrei did, may initially seem quixotic from the perspective of western European domestic ideology, with its images of the male leaving home each day for work in the great world of commerce, law, medicine, or politics. But of course that ideology was born among middle-class British men, and many of their activities in these professional realms were alien and inaccessible to Andrei. Yet, despite these differences, on closer inspection even the most stereotypical Victorian men ascribed to many of the same core values that motivated Andrei (as Queen Victoria herself put it, "Dear Papa always directed our nursery and I believe that none was ever better"[4]). For Englishmen domesticity provided a refuge from the tensions and contradictions of commercial and industrial life, and offered an alternative to an older model of masculinity based on personal heroism and adventure, which was no longer applicable to British middle-class life.[5] But masculine status in Victorian Britain was also "the gift of one's peers"; fatherhood was a prominent means by which Victorian men established their place in posterity, by providing for and protecting their sons' inheritance. Training a son to eventually take on one's own role, even where it was rarely done through one-on-one daily tutoring in the home, was an integral aspect of mid-nineteenth-century European masculinity.[6] Andrei's methods were unusually intense, but much of the difference probably lies in the fact that Andrei had no need to work outside the home. In addition, of course, it is unsurprising to see the patrimonial inheritance aspect of masculinity take first place in Andrei's ambitions and in the sentimental vision of "home" to which he was so attached, since his status derived from his inheritance of a patrimony that originated as a gift from the tsar in return for service to the state.

What is known of Andrei's early ideas about education and upbringing comes mainly from his 1830–31 diary and from the notebook correspondence covering the mid-1830s. In the diaries Andrei blocked out a relatively small space for each day's entry and often wrote in incomplete sentences, abbreviated notes, or lists. Like his wife's diaries, Andrei's served primarily as a work record, consisting of elaborated lists of events, activities, or transactions related to what they each considered their duties. While the purpose of their respective diaries was similar, the content—the specific items listed or described—differed greatly. Where Natalia listed grains, Andrei listed correspondents and visits. Where Natalia gave an impression of productivity and industriousness broken only occasionally by well-deserved respites of reading and visiting or bouts of illness, Andrei gave an impression of copious time devoted to books, thought, and talk, all of which were thoroughly integrated into his upbringing of the children and thus were part of his "work" and the counterpart to Natalia's estate management.[7]

The content of Andrei's diaries is so different from Natalia's that, at first glance, they may seem to fall into the "modern" type of diary defined by literary historians as reflective, personal, exploratory, and representing an expression of selfhood.[8] Andrei Bolotov's elaborate late-eighteenth-century diaries have been described as containing "self-revelation [that] is unwilling, an analysis that probes only to a certain level of uneasiness." Bolotov's diaries are not, in this sense, examples of "modern" diary writing.[9] Andrei never went far enough into reflection even to become uneasy. He wrote continually about ideas, his own and others', but he speculated without reflecting or probing. His ideas flowed outward, first toward the education of his children, and eventually evolving into a vision for the future of his community and for Russia. Defining, as Andrei did, his "work" as ideas, correspondence, and the upbringing of children, then in fact both husband and wife were writing in similar ways and to similar purposes: they were both recording their work, and at the same time building a testament to its value.[10] It was in both cases a process of self-creation but not self-exploration.

Because none of Aleksandra's papers have survived, and the coincidence that she was too young for lessons in the years when Andrei wrote almost daily in the notebook correspondence and in his first diary, the study of Andrei's ideas about upbringing necessarily revolves around Aleksei. Three of Aleksei's diaries survive. The first, begun on his tenth birthday (1835) and kept only very inconsistently for a few months, was heavily damaged by water so that only small parts of it are legible today. The second and third diaries survive in their entirety. The second diary was labeled by Aleksei a "diary of a *vospitanik*"—a *vospitanik* is a student, the object of moral education. It was written, like his first diary, on small, narrow sheets of paper sewn together into book form and kept during his first summer holiday at home after he had begun attending the Noble Institute in Moscow. He recorded every day of this 1838 holiday, beginning with his journey from Moscow in June and ending with his return there in August. The third diary was kept in a pre-bound orange leather blank book, originally used as a diary by Natalia in January 1842 (covering only the first six pages). Aleksei then used the rest of the book for almost a full year in 1847–48. Like his second diary, this one, too, marked a major milestone in Aleksei's life: it begins with his journey to Vilno at the start of his army service, covers his entire initial period of training with meticulous daily entries, and ends at the moment he set off for his first campaign on active duty. Like his "diary of a *vospitanik*," the Vilno diary is notable for the regimented neatness of the handwriting and the formulaic nature of its contents (in stark contrast to the surviving letters Aleksei wrote as an adult, in which his handwriting and sometimes syntax disintegrated into near unintelligibility, due to his failing eyesight).

Aleksei began the first boyhood diary in 1835 with the words, "Papinka gave me this little book as a commemoration of this day of my birth, so that I will write my journal in it every day."[11] The second and third diaries, also, were kept in obedience to Andrei, and for his fatherly perusal. The "diary of a *vospitanik*" contains the note "feeling tired from the road, I took a nap after dinner. Papinka looked through my grade-sheet and school-books."[12] In 1850 Andrei "re-read" Aleksei's Vilno diary, leaving a note in the back of the book to mark the occasion.[13] There is further evidence that Aleksei wrote them with his parents in mind, beyond the dutiful nature of their contents. In the Vilno diary Aleksei made an error, first addressing his readers directly with the word "you" (in plural form) and then crossing it out and replacing it with the third-person "Papinka and Maminka."[14] Like the diaries, the few other extant papers in Aleksei's hand dated before 1850 are obviously the written remnants of an educational program: a notebook of French language exercises, and a smattering of formal notes written to Yakov Chernavin and Timofei Krylov in the notebook correspondence, each strictly following the forms of polite letter writing.[15]

In every document written by Aleksei, Andrei's voice is omnipresent. In his schoolboy diaries, Aleksei was anxious to please his father and chastened by his criticism. Aleksei's diligent studying and Andrei's reaction to the boy's every deed dominates the content of the first diary especially, as the following selection of entries shows:

> *Learned from Papinka* how to make envelopes. *Papinka praised me* for my good handwriting. . . . *Papinka examined me* on the [catechism] and French, and *was quite pleased with me*, after this *we* inspected the stable and threshing barn. . . . *Papinka examined me* on German and Latin, and again *praised me*, with the prayer that I will also study as diligently in the second class as in the first. . . . After dinner *Papinka made me copy* a list of students from the Institute and *was very pleased* with my handwriting, for which *he gave me* a picture. . . . *Papinka and I* were occupied with French reading, and he was very much satisfied. . . . After dinner *Papinka took me with him* on a visit to the village of Zimenki to the misters Kultashev, where they praised me very much. . . . In the morning *Papinka made me read* the first chapter of the French *Telemachus,* and *much praised me* for good reading.[16]

Notations like these about lessons or activities engaged in with "Papinka" were accompanied by little else but the briefest remarks about visitors and occasional details about horses. The overwhelming impression is that Aleksei's life in these years revolved around "Papinka." To a less marked degree, the reverse was also true.

In his diaries and notes Andrei was specific about how he intended to act on his hopes and questions in regard to Aleksei's education, as when he recorded having a literal dream about his son's future. After waking up from the dream in the middle of the night, he wrote that he looked immediately for his wife and "Alesha," who were both sleeping nearby:

> I kissed one, caressed the other, looked at my little <u>Dibich</u> [Aleksei] and thought: what is awaiting this dear son of mine in the world?—will he really become a Dibich

[a successful general], or simply a [middling]-private person; rich or poor? Is he destined for success, happiness, or obstacles, failure, disturbances of the heart and of the soul??—He is a person.—Therefore one cannot [exempt him] from the common human destiny to slide, stumble, fall, be deceived, to wish, to receive, to expect, to worry, to roll in the whirlwind of vanity . . . and so on. Having kissed [them] again, having caressed [them] again, I glanced around me, wishing to grab something printed and to read.[17]

After contemplating all the possible fates time might bring, Andrei's next impulse after kissing and caressing his wife and child was to reach for something to read. His response, in other words, to the fears any parent confronts about their children's future was to turn to books for wisdom and guidance.

Farther into the same entry, Andrei became more specific about what kind of future he wanted for his son. Though dreaming of him as a future general, Andrei also wanted more than military success for Aleksei. In fact, he claimed that "scholarship" and "authorship" were not only a kind of "service to the fatherland," but were even "privileged in comparison to all the other duties." His reasoning was that knowledge was lifelong, while other forms of service were temporary:

At 25 years of age, a military man, even if he is a colonel, has all his importance limited to his uniform if his knowledge is limited. Once he takes it off and retires, he will become a nobody. A scholarly man, an author, will everywhere be the same person—engaging, wealthy, and happy. . . . I wish (God willing) that my son turns out to be educated. . . . [T]hat he will all of his life be tied to the most noble [of] occupations.[18]

Andrei saw military success (the most likely worldly occupation for a provincial nobleman) as transitory and unfulfilling, and attributed true lasting "nobility" and success— even wealth—to scholarship instead. The Enlightenment-based reasoning that education had tremendous power to mold the future of the young and to provide them—and the state—with benefits beyond but also including material success unquestionably lay behind Andrei's intense interest in upbringing, and the intrusive, all-encompassing way in which he personally undertook the raising of his children in their youngest years and beyond.

The intensity of Andrei's educational program also grew out of a sense of urgency, as he noted in his diary when both children were very young and he confronted the very short time given to him: "But time is dear—it's irretrievable—in the *vospitanie* of children it's even more incomparably dear. One ought to treasure it as much as possible, so as not to lose anything regarding the sciences and education."[19] In these years, Andrei occupied himself even when he was not actually with his children in improving reading, to help him to better guide their lessons ("Started to read 'A Natural History' for the use of the children").[20] One notable work among these informing texts was an unnamed "book about *vospitanie,*" which Andrei mentioned repeatedly and discussed with his neighbors. First he mentioned picking it up from a peddler along with a primer for Aleksei,[21] then he wrote that he was taking notes while reading it, then copying useful excerpts from it, then he sent it to his friend Cherepanov, along with a letter and a copy of the journal *Russian Invalid.* A few pages later, he noted that Cherepanov had sent the book back, but "without [his] notes, about which I was going to ask him."[22] It is significant that Andrei's (male) neighbor was also interested in reading the book, though apparently not with the same enthusiasm that Andrei did, judging by his failure to pass on his notes, if he made any.

Although it is not possible to reconstruct all the sources of Andrei's educational program, a scan of the periodical literature Andrei was reading in the early and middle 1830s—especially his favorites, the *Northern Bee* and the *Agricultural Gazette*—shows that *vospitanie* was a subject on many minds. In January 1835, the *Northern Bee* reviewed a pedagogical journal that aimed, in addition to guiding young persons heading for a pedagogical career, to "deliver to parents the knowledge necessary to allow them to act thoughtfully in the *vospitanie* of their children." Though one of the highlighted works was a description of the Lancastrian educational method, native Russian ideas were also represented, such as "lessons in reading and writing, arranged as conversations" by a Mr. Guriev, and a piece "on the higher and lower views on teaching" by a Mr. Gugel. The review also highlighted one German article as having been "highly praised by the *Journal of the Ministry of Education.*" Finally, the review concluded that this "area" was "still poorly defined, especially here [in Russia]" but *vospitanie* was nevertheless "so important" that the editors of the *Northern Bee* urged that parents and educators had "much, very much" to gain by a periodical that was really more of a "book of materials . . . because its articles have a value that is permanent and not temporary."[23]

Another article in the same *Northern Bee*, a month later, highlighted the importance of exercise in children's education, much as Andrei had already done in his diaries. The journal, however, emphasized the value of calisthenics and gymnastics especially for girls (as well as "for persons of middle age"), in the process arguing against much of what the authors assumed was the conventional wisdom of their time about female education, including corsets, which the authors deemed unhealthy, and excessive "rest" time wasted on embroidery, which only weakened a system already exhausted from "lengthy mental labors."[24]

Similarly, the *Agricultural Gazette* featured regular reports on various examples of agricultural schools in Russia and abroad, and general educational topics such as "The Benefit of Public Readings," or "Public Readings in the Countryside."[25] In one case, the *Gazette* described an experiment in children's education embarked on by an English landowner, in which children of "poor but industrious persons" were given garden plots to tend "only in free time," which brought "double benefit: the children learn gardening and . . . forgetting idleness, [they] avoid the personal flaws it brings about."[26] Andrei would heartily agree on the benefits of outdoor labor as part of any well-rounded educational program, and not just for children of the poor. The educational program Andrei

developed stressed subjects, skills, and methods that were being discussed more widely by
his peers, all of whom were animated by decades of Enlightenment thought. These ideas
originally reached Russia through such organizations as the Free Economic Society and
the provincial Agricultural Societies, but were disseminated widely by the middle decades of the nineteenth century through the periodical press and cheap educational
books such as the one Andrei purchased from a peddler in 1831.

Beyond the bare recording of visitors, his studies and the horses, all of them infused
with the presence of "Papinka," Aleksei provided outlines in his diaries of frequent journeys, including his long journey from and to his school in Moscow, and also frequent
trips with his father to Vladimir or with the whole family to visit Yakov at Berezovik. On
these occasions Aleksei described very little beyond his destination and the villages where
they stopped to rest and feed the horses or stay the night ("Dear Uncle Yakov Ivanovich
went as far as Voskresenskoe to see us off. We had an overnight in Malygino, and because
of the immeasurable heat in the [peasant] hut, we slept in the carriage").[27] These frequent
journeys, recorded systematically by Aleksei with emphasis on the names of villages and
the time taken to reach them, reinforced Andrei's geography lessons, in which he emphasized an encyclopedic knowledge of the local, combining both the early Enlightenment's
obsession with encyclopedias and the late Enlightenment's focus away from universalism
and toward the study of distinctions between places.

In an article written many years later, Andrei described in detail a game, "a journey
around the county," which he had invented for his children in their early childhood, to
teach them the names and locations of every populated area of their county. First Andrei
prepared a simplified map by placing a real county map over a blank sheet of paper and
punching through the two sheets with a pin to mark notable parishes or townships.
Then he drew straight lines between townships to connect them. According to Andrei,
"[t]he purpose of the game is to travel around the entire county, and whoever does that
first, wins." Dice were used, and "raspberry-colored sticks like in Lotto" marked one's
place, as one traveled from any chosen starting point. Accuracy was stressed ("[t]he
names of parishes and townships should be indicated clearly and correctly") as was the
independent nature of the child's play, which would result in their learning the place
names and locations incidentally to the game ("[e]ach of them, trying to get the largest
number from the throw of the dice, in order to travel around the county, will appear as
an independent actor, and, visiting the townships, will memorize their names and the
region itself").[28]

Two simple maps drawn by Andrei in his 1830s notebooks were made according to the
method described here, so it is certain that Andrei's children indeed played this game as
he described it later.[29] Elsewhere, Andrei mentioned more formal lessons on local geography. In his 1831 diary, for example, he mentioned whiling away time with a study of the
location of Vladimir province and its neighbors: "Natalia Ivanovna went to Cherntsy;
and I with the children stayed home. Geographic location of Vladimir province and of
those [provinces] that border it."[30]

The emphasis on knowing one's native, local environment was also not unique to Andrei. A heightened "territorial consciousness" has been recognized as developing in eighteenth-century Russia as a result of the importation of scientific principles.[31] Enlightenment-based impulses popularized geography as a subject of study (which was understood broadly as not only the physical characteristics of a region but also the manners and customs of its people). The fashion for geography was closely linked to notions of patriotism: as Andrei put it, "[t]his game, there is no doubt, will please the children and will serve as the very first and true foundation for the study, and therefore to *the affection for* one's county."[32] Writers like Radischev, Derzhavin, and Karamzin shared Andrei's devotion to geography, likewise associating it closely with notions of selfhood and civic responsibility.[33] Andrei's source for his geography game may actually have been a 1785 story by Nikolai Novikov, which described children playing "cards" with local maps and other county information.[34] And in 1850 Andrei referred to an "old book" called the *Geographical Dictionary of the Russian State,* by L. M. Maksimovich, a six-volume reference work published in Moscow in the late eighteenth century and again in 1809.[35]

The fashion for geography among the Russian gentry was expressed not only in enthusiasm for general reference works but also provincial atlases, a trend which Andrei would take up later on. In his campaign for the publication of a reference book about his own Kovrov county, he was to include, in part, data that he had collected in his private notebooks over the years.[36] Though this book project fell through, Andrei received considerable moral support from his readers. Like the provincial atlases of the previous generation, Andrei's project was based on what historian Willard Sunderland calls a "three-way love of province [or in this case, county], accuracy, and utility."[37] Andrei saw geography both as a useful prism through which to instill in his children feelings of patriotism and sentimental attachment to place, and as a means of teaching the basic scientific principles of factual accuracy and organization. That both these principles were dear to Andrei's heart is abundantly evident in his diaries and notebooks full of sentimental appreciations of Russian country life, on the one hand, and on the other his highly organized notebooks recording everything from the ratio of absentee to resident landlords in Kovrov county to the number of steps from his garden gate to his well.[38] Andrei and Yakov's shared passion for Enlightenment-style information gathering went well beyond geography. Yakov's notebooks, especially, were usually arranged as reference books, with alphabetical tabs cut into the page edges. He titled one of these notebooks "Agenda, or My Berezovik Encyclopedia," and listed in them everything from his properties, peasants, and books to temperature conversion charts, the French Revolutionary calendar, the roman numerals up to one million, the latitude and longitude of all the villages and towns they knew, and the distances from Berezovik to all the major cities of the world (thus conceptualizing his village as the center of his world).[39]

In addition to geography and a more general exposure to Enlightenment-style encyclopedism, Aleksei's formal studies before and after leaving home emphasized foreign languages ("I occupied myself with the tutor reading French, German and Latin from the book *The Instruction of Empress Catherine II* ").[40] Andrei was Aleksei's first tutor in French ("I sat on a sofa in the drawing room having given Alesha his lesson from the French conversations"[41]) and the practice sentences in Aleksei's French exercise book were composed by his father.[42] Andrei's French was imperfect, but he read French texts, was able to express himself in short passages in the notebook correspondence, and he always made a point of studying any new words he encountered.[43]

Andrei demonstrated only superficial knowledge of foreign languages other than French, and the documents indicate the on-and-off presence of paid tutors for German and Latin. Judging from their names, most if not all of these tutors were Russians, and at least one was a seminarian from Vladimir.[44] Foreign tutors would have been expensive; even the cost of local seminary students was a significant portion of the Chikhachevs' budget. The fact that these financial sacrifices were made and the tutors were found for both the children, male and female—and that Andrei later expected readers of his articles to do the same—suggests that the children of the provincial gentry perhaps had greater access to a wider variety of subjects than might be expected so far from major cities. It also emphasizes the financial struggle required for families like the Chikhachevs to pursue a broad education outside of the capitals and, therefore, the significant value they placed on knowledge of languages as an essential component of a superior education.

The Chikhachevs also pooled what resources they had at home: in addition to tutoring French, Andrei oversaw the children's writing, although his instruction seems to have been limited to a strict oversight of handwriting and the forms of polite correspondence ("Papinka occupied me with model letters.")[45] Yakov was put in charge of Aleksei's earliest efforts in mathematics. Yakov Chernavin had a sophisticated understanding of his subject, especially geometry, which he acquired in the navy, so Aleksei entered the Noble Institute well prepared in this area as well.[46]

The notebook correspondence contains a detailed record of exactly how the mathematics lessons began, which attests to Andrei and Yakov's genuine enthusiasm for these lessons, and the playful atmosphere surrounding them, in which games of written "charades" were integrated into lessons. Andrei began by thanking his brother-in-law: "For accepting [your] nephew under your patronage I bring you my extreme gratitude." He hoped that Chernavin would "not be bored, and have enough time," because as long as Chernavin was willing, Andrei promised not to keep Aleksei away "because of wind, or because of snow; if one binds him in a sheepskin coat like a little beastie, he is not going to sense any change in atmosphere, given the close distance." Yakov protested that he "enjoy[ed] spending time with [Aleksei]," but added a caveat suggesting that he did not have the most enthusiastic pupil: "I truly wish that Alesha spent more time on mathematics." But Yakov continued, with a passion for innovative, Enlightenment-style education and its power to transform young minds:

I sincerely think that it will greatly aid the development of his abilities; because mathematics, even in its most elementary principles, requires some reasoning; and to memorize the rules I think there is yet no need because at this time this can tire him out; he needs to understand the rules of any problem with his little brainie; and this is what needs to be explained to him—in any event, if you wish him to memorize the rules by heart, then we should order the newest arithmetic book for him, because the language of this one is too old and uptight.[47]

In his response Andrei turned to their ongoing game of charades, providing answers that suggest the two men's minds had not strayed far from the subject of Aleksei's education: "Two of your first charades I have solved: 'field' and 'papa'; [for] the third one I suggested *'dolg'* ['duty' or 'debt'], and I have not dealt with the rest because I became interested in Alesha."[48] Yakov replied with more charades answers ("'field'; 'papa'; 'Ya-kov'; 'old woman'; 'Tri-fon'; 'Sim-on'; 'blue'; 'rad-i-us'.") then added: "[t]oday I had him study very well and I have been kissing him for [solving] numerous problems." He explained that he believed whatever difficulties Aleksei was encountering were not due to recalcitrance or lack of will: "It seems like he has a great desire to learn," but rather that "the elementary engagement with mathematics is completely new to him—and for that reason he sometimes forgets what I have told him; however, I am firmly convinced that he will make good and very good progress."[49]

Yakov shared with Andrei an assumption that the goal of Aleksei's lessons in mathematics was not to "memorize rules" but to "understand" them—that the practical applications of mathematics were less important than the skill of reasoning logically. Furthermore, Yakov was aware that his and Andrei's teaching goals were derived from the latest educational thought, for even if they decided that Aleksei was ready to memorize rules, they needed to be sure that he learned only from the "newest" book because the one they had was "too old and uptight." When Yakov rewarded Aleksei's progress with kisses and concerned himself not only with how well Aleksei performed but also with his "desire to learn," he suggests that physical discipline was eschewed in favor of rewards for good behavior, while attention to results was shifted to concern over motivation: unconsciously, Yakov recorded the differing principles that lay behind "old," pre- or early-Enlightenment ideas about learning and the newer models.

An account given once by Andrei about his own schooling suggests that the enthusiasm of his generation for the latest principles may have been a reaction to the way they had been brought up. Andrei's drawing teacher from 1805 to 1811, when Andrei was seven to thirteen years old, was one Ivan Ivanovich Yust. Looking back as an adult, Andrei described him as an old, impatient scoundrel, who would look at his pupil "like an old crow," and take the pen and paper out of his hands to draw a cartoon that mocked the boy for his efforts. Andrei's "soul would sink," at this treatment, so eventually he pestered his grandmother, Katerina Petrovna Kupreianova, whom he described as his patroness, about the problem. Kupreianova turned to the head of Andrei's school (the "Moscow Noble (Private) *Pansion*"). This man, a Dmitrii Filipovich Delsal, "sometimes followed my grandmother's will." Andrei concluded the story with an expressive, "Oy Yust, oy Delsal, and oy the Chikhachevs."[50]

Aleksei also participated in his family's rich reading culture; together the family read everything from Fenelon to Fanny Burney to Bulgarin, thus bringing the children's education up to date with some of the latest literary fashions. In addition, Andrei's educational program included extensive religious training. Both parents drilled the children in prayers and the catechism, and religion was ever present in the home through frequent church services, oral religious readings, and the parents' examples of daily prayers, charity, attention to clergy, and their private reading of religious texts. This example took root, yielding such precociously pious remarks from the young Aleksei as: "Tomorrow I must appear at the Institute for my lessons.—Lord, be to me a helper, and make me wise!" The children assiduously accompanied their father on the short daily trip to church services, and special services were noted by Aleksei in his diary ("Papinka and I walked to vigil service at the cathedral and kissed the relic").[51]

In the first few pages of his 1830–31 diary, when he first began to plan his educational program, Andrei wrote that he prayed that God would grant him "his great Grace so that I can nurture my children on this foundation to be firm in religion, devoted to the tsar, loving of their fatherland, and serving Him with benefit and honor throughout their lives—being virtuous and sensitive and compassionate to their close ones."[52] In this passage Andrei closely associated religion and virtue with a reverence for duty in general and for duty toward the Russian imperial family in particular. Thus patriotism, too, was a part of the educational program. In 1838 Aleksei recorded that Andrei had marked the birthday of the "SOVEREIGN EMPEROR" by explaining to his son that he "must someday be in the tsar's service, [a duty] which [he] must fulfill with the greatest zeal."[53] And when Aleksei and his father were in Moscow later that summer for the start of Aleksei's new school term, they took a walk in the Kremlin garden to enjoy a "magnificent firework display" in honor of some imperial occasion, which Aleksei also recorded in his diary with similar pomp and reverence.[54]

All the Chikhachevs used all-capital letters and, often, a different color of ink to refer to any member of the imperial family in their private diaries and notebooks. Name days and anniversaries associated with the Romanovs were always recorded in Andrei's diaries, and sometimes in his son's. Aleksei studied Catherine II's *Instruction,* and the whole family read histories of the Romanov family and of particular tsars.[55] Andrei began preparing Aleksei from an early age to think about his inevitable period in state service as a matter of reverence and duty, to be performed with "zeal." Andrei reinforced this message by escorting his son to the gala imperial occasion, instilling in him an awe for the monarchy and associating it directly with the rest of his education, thus communicating to Aleksei that part of becoming an educated person was having a sense of duty or loyalty specifically to the monarchy.

There was also a practical side to Andrei's educational program. Many of Andrei's "inventions"—including his telegraph and a "wall-clock" (a wall-mounted sundial)—were deliberately educational: "I am building a children's pump, which will at the same time serve as a gymnastic toy for them, and also as a useful water-system for watering remote parts of the kitchen-garden."[56] Other tools Andrei used in lessons were graphite and "self-teaching glass," put to use by a very young Aleksandra.[57] These tools and inventions were a direct application of the scientific principles Andrei worked to instill, serving as example to the children and sometimes improving the estate at the same time.

Another pursuit that had practical side benefits was music. Both children were taught to be competent pianists, and Aleksei also played the violin. These interests were supported at home: Timofei Krylov was commissioned by Yakov, on behalf of Andrei, to buy a violin for Aleksei on his trip to Yaroslavl and was given three rubles for it.[58] It is not clear whether he succeeded or even attempted the trip, since in the other notebook Yakov wrote of his own trip to Yaroslavl, where he could not find a violin, "not a single one of any kind!"[59] Eventually a violin was found, because by the time Aleksei was in the army in Vilno, he was finding time for private music lessons with a professional instructor.

Another practical realm into which Andrei deliberately introduced his son from a young age was the network of local gentry and officials. This was a second reason, besides the study of geography, for bringing Aleksei on journeys around the district: to make him known to the other landowners and gentry office-holders of their province, to prepare Aleksei to eventually take his place among them. As in Victorian Britain, as historian John Tosh put it, "[a] fine balance is struck between competition and comradeship as young men learn how to become part of the collective (male) voice of the community."[60] Through marriage and patronage networks, the ability to successfully navigate the larger male community of his province would have an enormous impact on Aleksei's future, for better or for worse.

Aleksei dutifully recorded the names of each of his new acquaintances in his diaries, cementing the occasions in his own memory and testifying to their importance: "Papinka and I went to visit dear Uncle Nikolai Ivanovich Zamytskii" . . . "[a]t Uncle's we found Mikhail Mikhailovich Orzhanskii and Aleksei Gavrilovich Vyrobov" . . . "we went to Maria Petrovna Izmailova's and dined with her, . . . [r]eturning home, we stopped by the Nikolaevs', and there were introduced to the family of Petr Ivanovich Gavrilov" . . . "[a]rriving in Suzdal, Papinka brought me with him to the County Judge Vasilii Andreevich Kablukov, where we found Petr Ivanovich Gavrilov and Aleksandr Dmitrievich Rogozin" . . . "[t]ogether with Papinka, dined with the Kupreianovs and in the evening went to see Anton Yakovlevich Savon."[61] When Andrei traveled to Vladimir, he made a point of bringing Aleksei along to introduce him to important men: "Papinka is getting ready to go to Vladimir tomorrow on business and wants to take me with him." . . . "Papinka and I were at an event at the Seminary, where the Archbishop and Governor were present."[62]

Once the boy found himself in the vastly more complex society of Moscow, Andrei worked hard to make sure that Aleksei would find his rightful place there, too, yet without taking on the secular ideas and dilettantish habits that Andrei associated with cities. Andrei achieved this by personally escorting Aleksei to some of the delights of the city (in Aleksei's words: "I showed myself at the Institute in the morning . . . [i]n the evening we [Papinka and I] went to the French Theater") and by ensuring that Aleksei was watched over by their trusted friends, many of whom Aleksei referred to in family terms ("Grandma" Nesterova) even though they were not related ("Heard afternoon service in the Institute—visited the Bogomolovs—dined with Grandma Nesterova, and from there drove through Petrovskii Park")[63]

While still in the country, Andrei did not limit his son's education to relations with members of their own social estate. Several times Aleksei mentioned family visits to local curiosities of Russia's emerging industrial zone, where the family socialized with minor industrialists and other town-dwellers. These visits were clearly educational for Aleksei; he recorded "look[ing] at sluices" and a water mill, admired the layout of other people's gardens, and on another occasion the family visited a cotton mill "run by steam engine."[64] Yakov mentioned taking a walk with Aleksei and Andrei to see a brick factory (where they "heard Rachok sing!").[65]

At the same time, Aleksei was carefully taught to maintain his superior and paternalistic social position in relation to the servant class, as when he was told to give a coin to a groom after a new colt was born,[66] or in the following anecdote from Andrei's diary, in which Andrei was concerned to prevent Aleksei's unsupervised association with servants. Their neighbor, Maria Petrovna Izmailova, invited Andrei, Yakov, and both children to visit, but Andrei ruminated, "I don't think I'll go, what for? [It would be like] exchanging one emptiness for another. . . . And Aleksei would wander about with the servants—it won't do. Better at home! Better at home!"[67] It "would not do" for Aleksei to associate too freely with servants on terms that did not maintain the observation of rank, but Aleksei necessarily spent a great deal of time with servants at home; it seems that as long as social distance was maintained this was acceptable, as when a serf (called Aleshka, the condescending diminutive for "Aleksei" as opposed to "Alesha," used for Aleksei Chikhachev) made snow pies with buckets for Aleksei's pleasure: the boy then "broke them up with his little spade and very much enjoyed himself."[68] Or on another occasion, when Andrei "rode with Alesha to Gubachevo. We stopped by the housekeeper's rooms and she treated him to soaked apples."[69] In the first instance, Aleksei was allowed to play with a serf as long as this serf "played" a position of servitude: the servant made the snow pies for Aleksei to smash. And when Andrei rode with Aleksei to the Ikonnikovs' estate at Gubachevo, the housekeeper (a relatively privileged serf) could "treat" the boy, but only in a controlled setting where Andrei was present.

A final type of practical education to which Aleksei was carefully exposed, according to the boy's diaries, involved his apprenticeship in the inner workings of the estate. While Aleksei did not mention his mother in his entries relating to what was unquestionably her realm, it is notable that these entries do *not* mention "Papinka." The diaries show that Aleksei was taught to understand and appreciate the rhythms of the agricultural cycle and the interdependent life of a country estate, integrating this easily into the pattern of his other, more formal lessons: "The sowing of rye began. I threw the first handful. During the rest of the day it rained a few times, and near the end [of the day] very strongly, so that sowing wasn't possible.[70]

Much of Aleksei's attention was devoted to horses and riding. Horses appear to have been one of the boy's few discernible independent interests, albeit one strongly supported by Andrei: "In the morning occupied with French; after dinner went riding with Papinka on horseback and since my brown horse is unfortunately quite blind, Papinka gave me another, black one."[71] It seems that giving Aleksei access to horses was Andrei's best means to influence his behavior: "Papinka entirely delighted me by saying that if I study well then he will send a horse to get me at Christmas [vacation]."[72] At the same time, managing horses was also clearly part of estate management, and not incidentally one of the few aspects that Andrei concerned himself with personally and also one that Natalia was not involved in. It seems likely that horsemanship was a masculinized part of estate life (perhaps because it was physically dangerous); however this did not prevent Andrei from giving a newborn colt to each of his children in 1831: thereafter they would be referred to as "Sasha's colt" and "Alesha's colt." Andrei made it clear that this was a deliberate lesson in ownership and responsibility: "I consider that both these colts, and the future ones from these mares, must make up the children's property, no matter how many of them there will be. And that this appointment is not to be changed under any circumstances. Let this be their primary happiness."[73]

It was significant that Andrei chose to use colts to teach the children to take responsibility over property, as he taught them geography through a game. Games also played a prominent role in the only article of Andrei's large journalistic output solely addressing the issue of *vospitanie*. The main claim of this article, titled "On Children's Games," was that play had an important role in upbringing for its own sake. The value of play in a child's learning experience was then emerging among progressive educational thinkers.[74] In Andrei's interpretation, the advantages of play as a respite from study, and as a means of imparting important knowledge without the student realizing he was learning, were both emphasized:

> Anyone who loves children regrets to see that there is so little care about their amusement, which is so necessary after sitting down in the classroom. Of course there are many gymnastic games, but almost all of them require summertime in order to engage in them in the open air, and at the same time the inevitable fatigue afterwards still requires their replacement with such a game, that, in creating a relief from fatigue, would continue to engage them, and, if possible, to do so in a didactic manner.[75]

Other games mentioned in the documents clearly had a similar purpose. For Aleksei's eighth birthday Yakov sent him a "historical game," "to entertain you and also to benefit."[76] And in 1837 Yakov made a magic lantern, promising to provide "the little glass sheets" for it by the Easter holidays. Also mentioned was a homemade kaleidoscope; Aleksei wrote that Andrei had "not glued up" a covering for it even though Aleksei "bother[ed] him about it rather often." Yakov responded, "do ask your *papasha,* and he will glue it up, I give you my word he will glue it up."[77] Andrei was ahead of his time and most of his peers in educational thinking, and a close observer of his own children.

Andrei not only consciously intended Aleksei to be learning important geographical knowledge while roaming the countryside, but he also acknowledged (in a manner which likely owed much to Jean Jacques Rousseau) the importance of outdoor physical activity for its own sake—considering it sufficiently important to require a substitute outlet when weather made exercise in the "open air" impossible. To Andrei physical exercise was a necessary adjunct to intellectual pursuits for adults as well as children; he set an example himself with his almost daily recreational "motion." Andrei required Aleksei to practice comparable physical exercise and to do it out of doors whenever weather permitted: "[I took] a constitutional in the garden with Alesha—[I] had a little spade made for him and ordered woolen mittens knit for him."[78] The children often played active games—a shuttlecock was a gift from Yakov, which Andrei mentioned as specifically intended to inspire "bodily motion" as well as to "occupy" the children—"this would be good for them" as opposed to a ballgame they otherwise played, called "*chizhi*," which Andrei found too destructive.[79] Aleksei also recorded more vigorous exercise: "Papinka ordered a little ladder and pole made for my gymnastics, and I climbed up several times and [also] jumped rope." The next day, they started again early: "Before sunrise I took a walk with Papinka in the summer-wheat field; having rested from my gymnastics, I soon got calluses on my hands."[80] Dancing provided still another form of "motion," as well as teaching the children a skill that would be important to their social lives in later years. In October 1835, Natalia noted in her diary that "the children were dancing all day long and Grigorii [a serf] played violin."[81]

Andrei complemented his comprehensive educational program by joining his son in many of his leisure pursuits. The two played billiards together when Aleksei was older, while in his younger years they shared the seemingly masculine pursuits of driving and the casual inspection of horses and fields. These inspections were casual in the sense that they were engaged in as a leisure activity (they "walked around"), in contrast to the daily work of labor supervision that Natalia did (she "inspected" alone).[82] As Aleksei recorded, his uncle frequently joined them in these rides and walks, emphasizing the social and masculine nature of the excursions, which lacked any mention of a goal or the presence of laborers in the fields they walked through: "Rode with Papinka in the curricle and I drove myself" . . . "After dinner Papinka, dear Uncle and I in a trio walked around the fields for exactly an hour" . . . "After dinner Papinka, dear Uncle and I in a trio rode on horseback as far as the village of Burakova" . . . "Soon after the rain Papinka and I went for a ride on horseback, but returning from the walk Papinka took ill."[83]

Unlike the households of wealthier families where children led a separate existence in a nursery wing, the Chikhachevs lived in the same physical space with their children. Even though their house contained a separate schoolroom, Andrei at least spent time there outside of lessons ("Having had our tea, having sat for a while in the children's classroom"), and lessons sometimes occurred in the main family room.[84] When Natalia was in

Moscow in 1831, Andrei made more frequent than usual mentions of time spent with the children. These included running to comfort Aleksei at four o'clock in the morning (Andrei was awake, having stayed up reading and writing), going to bed early with the boy another night, skipping his supper, playing with "Alesha" on the bed and then falling asleep with him there, giving in to Alesha's "persistent request" to take him on a visit to "dear Uncle" Chernavin even though he had to wrap him in his own overcoat "because it was somewhat windy," and one evening while sorting old papers, he gave Alesha envelopes and unneeded old letters, with which the boy was "extraordinarily happy."[85]

Another entry recorded after Natalia's return from Moscow suggests that Andrei's day continued to be entwined with that of his son after her return. Andrei wrote: "I gave Aleshinka a lesson, but he started crying because he couldn't pronounce the word _nashim_ in the prayer The All-good Lord" then, "also went with my little son to the greenhouse and to the . . . stables, looked at the little colts, fed them bread," but later "Alesha had great tears because of his new pants, when mother ordered them to come off."[86] Natalia was present, but she was merely giving "orders" about his "new pants." Aleksei was sincerely attached to his parents and had a clear expectation of spending time with them, which a nanny could not replace: while Natalia was still in Moscow and Andrei took a long nap, Andrei wrote that six-year-old Aleksei cried to his nanny about their absence, saying, "Maminka is gone, and Papinka is asleep, it's so boring!"[87]

The children were a source of entertainment for their elders, as when Andrei colorfully described their excitement over their uncle's birthday, saying, "[t]he children, the kiddies, those little pigeons, buzz and mumble, trying to congratulate you more appropriately."[88] Another conversation from the notebook correspondence depicts a typical instance when the children prompted fond, knowing jokes between Andrei and their uncle, indicating that Andrei's closeness and sympathy with the children was shared by Chernavin. Andrei began: "The teacher could not stop admiring [the pupils]," to which Yakov fondly replied, "I am sure of that." Andrei added, "The children maintain that the evening telegraph is better than some of their lessons," and Yakov concluded, "In that I do not doubt, either."[89]

Many of Andrei's diary entries clearly place the children as important figures in his idealized image of the perfect village: "The air and the weather are so tempting that unwillingly I bring my steps to the balcony, go down to the clock without any purpose—here, there—breathe the first spring air, marvel at my tiny children in the open air, time flies by."[90] Idealized as such imagery is, in a private diary intended only for family use such scenes could not have been wholly invented. While they may have served to reinforce Andrei's image of idealized provincial life, they also imply that Andrei, at least, did enjoy a congenial home life very unlike that described in some of the more well-known memoirs written in post-Reform years by adults looking back on their childhoods in the 1830s and depicting fathers who were largely absent, and when present, tyrannical.[91]

This is not to say, however, that Aleksei was always a perfect or even particularly promising student, or that Andrei did not reserve a prominent place in his educational program for discipline and even physical punishment ("I was very displeased with Aleksei Andreevich, because he laughed in the classroom and did not obey the teacher, and so I was obliged to put together a bundle of lashes for him").[92] While Andrei occasionally reported Aleksei's strong performance in their lessons ("Alesha studied very well all day"), more often he merely noted "lessons with Alesha," and the most specific entries nearly always record lapses in obedience or studiousness, as in the following instances: "Alesha studied badly in the drawing room" . . . "Alesha studied more stupidly than yesterday" . . . "Alesha wears a cap [as a punishment] because of the grimaces he made against me." He wore the cap again when he refused to share his pastry with his sister.[93] In another, more serious, entry Andrei complained that "I have read more than a hundred pages [written] by the son of my wife, and I don't like any of it: a collection of nonsense without any reasoning."[94] Here, Aleksei became "the son of my wife," when the cause of Andrei's disappointment is a lack of "reasoning" in the boy's work. It was the abstract realm that Andrei had in mind when he referred to "reasoning," thus associating its lack with his wife. In failing to engage with abstract ideas, Aleksei not only disappointed his father directly, he also failed to fulfill the gender model his father expected of him.[95]

Despite many signs that Aleksei was not willing or able to follow in his father's footsteps as an abstract thinker or intellectual, Andrei's occasional dissatisfaction in the boy's progress seems merely to have reinvigorated his efforts on his son's behalf. After Aleksei was sent to school in Moscow in 1837, Andrei continued to track his son's progress with avidity, as was demonstrated in Natalia's 1842 diary, where she recorded how frequently Andrei visited his children's schools and even quizzed Aleksei's tutors and fellow students.[96]

Attesting to the specific nature of Andrei's fears for Aleksei once the boy left the family circle, Andrei recorded his "fatherly" advice for Aleksei's future reference on the eve of the boy's departure from home for the first time in 1837:[97]

Here you are, my sweet Aleshinka, my fatherly orders:
Always put your hope in God, and don't be [too] lazy to go to Church,
Listen to your tutors
In your studies be diligent and don't misbehave
Don't be friends with troublemakers
Treasure friendship with good comrades
                                                    —Your father, Andrei Chikhachev.[98]

The emphasis in this list of "fatherly orders" is, first, on obedience to religious values and, second, on keeping good company, presumably as a means of promoting the first goal. One of Andrei's biggest fears on the occasion of sending his son to Moscow was the secularizing or demoralizing influence life in that city might have on him. The moral aspect of *vospitanie* was always of at least equal value, for Andrei, to the academic aspect, and here it is clear that while Andrei sent his son away to school in the hopes that he would be exposed there to a broader and more complex education than Andrei could provide at home, as well as to important patronage connections, he also feared that in Moscow the worldly aspects of education might threaten the carefully instilled moral underpinning that Andrei considered essential to conscientious adulthood.

Aleksei kept his third diary during his first year of independent adulthood, but here, too, the expectations of his father—and the certain knowledge that Andrei would be reading this diary, as he had read and supervised all his son's previous writing—continued to define the content of Aleksei's entries, as the moral yardstick against which Aleksei measured all his actions. Although Aleksei was twenty-two when he wrote this diary, many of the entries reflect distinctly childish interests ("Vasilii Andreevich brought me a candy and a glass of wonderful ice cream" from a dinner at Aleksei's uncle's house; on another occasion Aleksei conducted his friend to a ball in his uncle's borrowed open carriage "so as to see the illumination").[99]

Knowing that this diary was a form of communication with his parents rather than a space for private reflection, Aleksei carefully recorded in it his modest expenses down to the last kopek. Hussar regiments were expensive, and Aleksei well knew that Andrei and Natalia were making sacrifices in order to pay for his uniforms and equipment, in the hopes that Aleksei would make better connections in this regiment (as Hussar regiments went, however, this one was not among the most prestigious).[100] Similarly, Aleksei was always careful to make a note of each dutiful attention he made to his relative and patron, "dear uncle" General Pavel Yakovlevich Kupreianov, as well as noting the general's approval of him, his attendance at church services every Sunday and on holidays, his routine of writing a letter home to Dorozhaevo every Monday, and even the fact that he either sat out card playing, which was always done for money on social occasions, or played for very low stakes among ladies ("We spent all evening at Vasilii Semenovich's. Ivan Ivanovich Sokolov was there and Vasilii Andreevich, they all played cards until 2 o'clock at night, while I watched," or "Four of us played *preferance* for kopeks. The lady and I won more than 35 silver kopeks").

Aleksei also recorded his joy at receiving a letter from home in precisely the same language nearly every week ("Was entirely delighted by a letter from Papinka and Maminka"), although some entries marking particularly rich letters or his re-reading of them do indicate that his "delight" was more than mere dutiful appreciation of what was due to his parents ("I received today a package from Dorozhaevo with enormous letters from my sweet parents and was entirely delighted by it," and "[I] re-read my sweet letter from Dorozhaevo and reading it I became sad. I crossed myself, kissed the parental letter and the sadness began to dissipate").[101]

In this diary, Aleksei listed each day his lessons in French or the violin, or drill, and his visits with his comrades, all of them fellow young officers of good family, several superior enough in military or social rank to impress Andrei with his son's ability to make useful connections (ranks and titles were always specified in Aleksei's diary when they were greater than his own). Aleksei made sure to emphasize how much he and his friends appreciated the jam his mother had sent, and he gave a general impression that sweets were his worst vice ("In the evening I went to a shop and bought myself some raisins and candies, and together with Egor Ivanovich we treated ourselves").[102] In a similar vein he recorded his first experiences with Polish food, and after a picnic reported that he and his friends enjoyed "sour milk with sugar and cinnamon" along with their tea and pipes, returning at the respectable hour of nine.[103]

Perhaps the one interest reflected in the diary that reveals something about Aleksei personally is the recurrent theme of music. In addition to his violin lessons with a tutor, Aleksei played either this instrument or the piano on social occasions and always made a note of any other musicians he encountered (often mentioning nothing else about an event: "I played the violin and fortepiano [at Grotedebukov's], then the German himself sat down to play a polka on the piano while I accompanied him on the violin. He asked me to visit him with my violin, so that we would play together.").[104] His notations about church services, too, when not simply marking his attendance, made enthusiastic mention of the quality of the singing ("I went to afternoon service at the Cathedral; Bishop [illeg.] conducted the service and His choir sang incomparably,"[105] and "[I] went to Budakovs' to the Polish cathedral church, where the Bishop himself was conducting services, and I was very curious to see how during the midday service the Bishop conducted an ordination into the priesthood—the ceremony was grand and an entire musical orchestra was playing up in the choir").[106]

The diary is limited in content to such an extreme degree that it reads more like a catalog of what Aleksei knew his father expected of him than an actual record of his daily life. As a young officer far from home, it is difficult to believe that even an obedient and pious young man like Aleksei never flirted with young Polish women or drank anything besides tea with his young officer friends, but any such incidents went unrecorded.[107] The few entries that include more than simple lists of the day's routine events mark precisely the sort of activities that Andrei no doubt hoped his son would engage in (they also reflect the seemingly sincere interests in agriculture and industry that Aleksei demonstrated in his earlier diaries). Once, he drove with his friend Vasilii Andreevich and his uncle's estate manager to visit "a rich Polish landowner, Sidarovich, to look at his flour mill, which is organized exceptionally well. He was very glad to see us." Another day, visiting Vasilii Andreevich, he "became acquainted with a young man, who is a local Vilno landowner." One fine morning he "rose at 4:30 and set off to walk in the Botanic garden and walked there until 6 o'clock. The garden is incomparable and there were quite a few flowers." And still another day he and Vasilii Andreevich drive "to Verki to the property of the Prince Vingtenshtein. The estate is lavish; the garden the most charming, and its placement simply marvelous; such that I have not seen [anything] more comfortable."[108]

Aleksei's character and thoughts remain a mystery; his diaries serve, instead, as a record of Andrei's expectations for a young Russian gentleman. He expected piety, thrift, devotion to family and to public duty, as well as the sort of friendly curiosity about the world and his fellow man that prompted Aleksei to be continually cultivating new acquaintances and making excursions in and around the city, inspecting garden landscaping and flour mills. Andrei had also instructed Aleksei to be assiduous in making the right friends, by which Aleksei understood he meant sober, dutiful young men of good family. When he mentioned acquaintances, Aleksei made sure to assure his father that he was liked by the right people, as in this entry: "We went to [visit] Grotedebukov and stayed with him all evening; he was very happy with us; we had tea with him."[109] Reliable friends of superior rank were meant to serve as useful connections for many years to come, just as Andrei and Yakov stayed in contact with their own army or navy friends after their retirements. It was to some of these men that Andrei wrote letters about "Alesha" when he arranged his placement, first in his school and later in a regiment.

Further, Andrei expected his son to match himself in military zeal and patriotism. Thus Aleksei recorded reading *The Russian Invalid,* the journal for military men (he once mentioned reading his own father's article there), and demonstrated on the pages of his diary a genuine fondness for and pride in military pomp, mentioning that he enjoyed "listen[ing] to military stories" during one visit to a senior officer; he even became comparatively loquacious when he recorded that "[t]omorrow an inspection is scheduled by the Divisional General Baturin to all the officer candidates (junkers) of the Galitskii regiment, among them he will inspect me also." In his next entry he described a full day of basking in the approval of his military superiors: the inspection went very well, the general was happy with Alesha's musket drills and marching, and invited Alesha to his house, praised him, and congratulated him with his promotion to subaltern and gave him a silver officer's ribbon for his sword. Then Aleksei's friends congratulated him, and the company commander and three other junkers stayed at Alesha's quarters "the entire evening" and, apparently, drank only tea.[110]

Finally, Aleksei made sure to note it in his diary when an occasion occurred to show that his father's teaching had put him in good stead, as when he was asked to write out visiting cards for his friend Vasilii Andreevich—because of his meticulous handwriting—or when he was able to show off his extensive knowledge of local geography: "At Ivan Ivanovich Sokolov's, I had tea and stayed all evening. He asked me all about our native region, and then conducted me home and stayed with me until 12 o'clock."[111] It is a diary devoid of spontaneity, and equally devoid of the intellectual interests that Andrei had hoped to instill in his son, but it speaks poignantly of Aleksei's earnest efforts to be a dutiful son to the extent that he was able.

In his parallel diary for the late 1840s Andrei tracked Aleksei's movements from the moment in 1847 that he entered service in the King of Sardinia infantry regiment with which he traveled to Vilno, through his transfer to the Grand Duchess Olga Nikolaevna Hussar Regiment, from which he would retire, and throughout his travels in active service in Poland.[112] In this period of parental anxiety, Andrei recorded each day the exact number of days and weeks that had passed since Aleksei had left home, since he had been in Vilno, and since he had been promoted to junker (officer candidate).[113] The family was proud of Aleksei's status as a hussar (Natalia's friend Praskovia Melnikova affectionately referred to Aleksei as the "little hussar-dove"[114]), but they were deeply relieved when he completed his service. In January 1850 Andrei thanked God for "the fortunate and glorious end of the war," which would allow Aleksei to go on leave (this part was underlined).[115] And he noted in red ink Aleksei's official retirement from service on November 10, 1850, a few weeks after his sister's death.[116]

A letter to the Chikhachevs from their friend Aleksandr Merkulov, written that month, shows that Andrei had effectively pulled Aleksei out of the army early. Merkulov wrote to inform the Chikhachevs that Aleksei was discharged "by the Sovereign's order" from the army "due to illness." Merkulov, who worked for the War Ministry's Department of Inspection, attached the order to his letter, as it "would have taken much longer to reach him through usual channels." Merkulov then reassured Aleksei's parents that they had made the right decision for Aleksei to retire, not only because of "current disorders in the west," but also because "for a cavalry lieutenant it is difficult to find a military position outside the ranks; in order to become an aide-de-camp it is necessary to have served as an officer for at least 3 years." Aleksei had served only two, and was wanted at home.[117]

One of the central questions of the nature of *vospitanie* in this context of the father as *vospitatel* is whether and how upbringing may have differed according to the gendered expectations for male and female children. This important question is unfortunately impossible to answer definitively with these documents. It is clear, however, that Aleksandra's education was—perhaps surprisingly—similar to Aleksei's in at least one respect, because Andrei once mentioned her singing for him in German (in 1843),[118] and Aleksei mentioned sharing a tutor with his sister for lessons in German and Latin.[119] In addition, Aleksandra was probably also apprenticed to some degree to her mother. During the many hours that Aleksei spent riding horses with Andrei, or accompanying him to Vladimir to meet with local officials, Aleksandra was usually at home, and she must have been taught the various necessary forms of needlework and something about estate management, probably in increasing detail as she grew older.

In the final pages of the notebook correspondence a six-year-old Aleksandra began, like her brother, to contribute short, formulaic notes conveying her respects to her uncle, Yakov, and her "grandfather," Timofei Krylov, in a large, childish script carefully inscribed over pre-drawn guidelines: "And I sweet dear Uncle kiss your dear hands and also dear grandfather's, and wish you good health[.] [W]ith this I remain your niece Sasha Chikhachova."[120] Intriguingly, the second and only other such note written by Aleksandra contains a correction seemingly written by her mother. Although it is difficult to definitively identify the handwriting in this case from so little text, it appears that Natalia added the words "and goddaughter" after "niece" in the following note: "My sweet dear Uncle Yakov Ivanovich! I wish you good health and all well-being. To dear grandfather Timofei Ivanovich my regards. I remain your most obedient niece [and goddaughter] Sasha Chikhachova."[121] This note was followed immediately by another to Yakov that is certainly by Natalia, supporting the notion that she wrote the correction in

Sasha's note. It thus appears possible that Natalia may have—at least sometimes—taken on the task of reading and correcting Aleksandra's writings, where only Andrei had corrected her brother's diaries and exercise books.

In 1831, when Andrei repeatedly mentioned the "very useful" book "on *vospitanie*" that he had bought from a peddler, Aleksandra was at the time only a toddler. The book was probably one of many similar works disseminated in Russia at that time, translated or heavily based on Western works, especially those of François Fenelon, a favorite educational author of Andrei's ("Alesha and I are acting out the duet from [Fenelon's] Telemachus").[122] Catriona Kelly's study of Russian advice literature of the eighteenth and nineteenth centuries—based on works much like if not including Andrei's "little book on *vospitanie*"—demonstrates that these mass-produced works were themselves heavily influenced by Fenelon. Thus, Kelly's summary of Fenelon's views on female education might serve as a fair guide, for lack of more direct evidence, to Andrei's program for Aleksandra:

> Fenelon assumed that, from the age of three until adulthood, a daughter's education would be, directly or indirectly, the responsibility of her mother. Between three and seven (the "age of reason" in traditional theology), the mother would be responsible for teaching the daughter, or seeing that she was taught, her letters and also the fundamentals of religion. . . . Thereafter, she was either to engage a governess . . . or to continue instructing her daughter herself. Fenelon was insistent that a girl's education should be of the highest possible quality and that supervising it was an entirely appropriate task for the aristocratic women to whom he addressed himself. Though convinced of the innate difference of men and women (he thought women more inclined to "moral frailty", and in particular, to vices such as frivolity), he was an ardent supporter of women's education as a corrective to this, and not only for negative reasons (because it taught girls to avoid vice), but also for positive ones—because it provided women with interests other than pleasure and love, and gave them a sense of autonomy—a point that also applied to the mother (since spending time in the schoolroom was preferable to gallivanting in the *grand monde*).[123]

Andrei fervently believed in providing his daughter with more useful occupations than "gallivanting in the *grand monde*," and his equally strong feelings on "the importance of *khoziaika* in the home" also suggest that part of Aleksandra's education must have consisted of preparation for her future estate duties and that her natural teacher in this arena would have been her mother.

The only traditional young lady's "accomplishment" mentioned in the documents is that Aleksandra played the piano (as did Aleksei), but the Chikhachevs also employed a German governess, at considerable expense. The duties of a governess generally included teaching noble young ladies manners and "accomplishments," as called for by advice-givers like Fenelon. These ladies' arts were aimed at making young women more attractive on the marriage market, and no doubt the Chikhachevs were concerned that Aleksandra would be able to contract an eligible marriage when the time came.[124] Kelly's conclusion that "the overriding purpose of women's education was to prepare them for dynastic marriages where affect would play little, if any, part" is based largely on the values of higher-ranking nobles than the Chikhachevs, but in their less exalted world marriage was still enormously important for whole families. It was not a dynastic maneuver, but it was a necessary means of preserving the family's estate status and financial viability in an environment where partible inheritance was the norm, and eligible suitors were fairly scarce.[125] If landownership were not maintained, families like the Chikhachevs could quickly sink to the level of impoverishment at which they would live indistinguishably from prosperous peasants. Thus in his 1831 diary, Andrei described a set of virtues for females "both when single and when married," which would have served them much better on the marriage market than as *khoziaiki* on their own estates: "meekness, submissiveness, kindness, justice, sensitivity and compassion to subordinates and to everyone."[126]

However, Andrei's stated ideal for young ladies—articulated in similar terms in both his diary and his published articles—focused more than anything else on the preparation a young lady required for life after marriage, as a *khoziaika*. Thus while a German governess may have been employed to teach Aleksandra the latest "accomplishments" of the urban leisured classes (while tutors taught her academic subjects such as German and Latin), Natalia must have also taught her other necessary skills. Andrei Bolotov, writing of his sister in the late eighteenth century, described a young lady much desired on the marriage market despite a small dowry, because of her estate management skills. She was snapped up by a family burdened with a long-neglected estate.[127] While the degree to which Aleksandra's education was the responsibility of her mother cannot be known, it is certain that Andrei also took a role in it. Andrei's belief that broad education was a means of interesting young ladies in their future duties and keeping them from frivolity (stated in his 1847 article on the "importance of the *khoziaika* in the home") was probably not unusual; indeed, he would likely have found support in that "little book on *vospitanie*," if not the initial inspiration for this view. Moreover, in 1839 Andrei took the same step he had taken with Aleksei a few years earlier and sent Aleksandra to Moscow for formal schooling at a private school, a *pansion* (Natalia's reaction in this instance went unrecorded). The *pansion* was exclusively for young ladies, run by a Madame Shreier. Natalia visited with this headmistress as she did not do with Aleksei's headmaster, suggesting unsurprisingly that in Moscow schooling was more strictly gendered than Andrei's instruction had been at home.[128]

The Chikhachev children may be assumed to have had an education rather superior to other young people in provincial families with similarly straightened financial circumstances, due to the zealousness with which Andrei personally pursued their access to education. But in content Andrei's program was essentially an Enlightenment one, in accordance with the best principles of the time, which were widely disseminated in advice literature. Beyond this, Andrei contributed a rather extreme degree of his own attention, supervision, and authority; by far the most unusual aspect of his educational program was his own presence. Presumably, other fathers in his position (the intended audience for Andrei's articles and thus the people he hoped to convert to his way of thinking) may often have lacked his emotional and intellectual passion for the subject of education itself.

Andrei claimed to regret what he saw as his own limited education and especially regretted not having seen more of the world; these regrets prompted him to wish for his son to achieve what he had not been able to. Paradoxically, by raising him in an environment of constant scrutiny and criticism (benign and loving though that criticism might have been), Andrei's preoccupation with his son's development may have been a major factor in Aleksei's inability to live up to these dreams. Even in Aleksei's adulthood, Andrei continued to give his son lessons, though less formally and probably only in matters relating to Aleksei's maintenance of his estates. In the surviving account books that Aleksei kept in these years, his father's handwriting occasionally appears, just as it did in his first boyhood diary. In January 1843, when Aleksei was seventeen, Andrei confided in his diary that the boy had given him "great advice" about the stone house, "however, he disturbs me extremely by his studies: he does not exert the slightest care and in general does not have the slightest desire for study—What a pity!" A few days later, Andrei remonstrated, giving Aleksei "a big talking-to" for his "lack of dashing." His criticism became all-encompassing: "It's a pity to see how weakly and not enough he is working on himself not only in his studies even also around himself."[129] And in 1850, when Aleksei was twenty-five and retired from the army, Andrei made it clear that he continued to think about his son's education in the same way he had fifteen years earlier, seeking advice in books and wondering how to inspire his son's interest (in this case in household management, a subject perhaps neglected earlier in the expectation that Aleksei's wife would be his support in this endeavor; at this time, Aleksei had not yet married):

> Myself, not following absolutely any system in my estate management, I nonetheless would wish that my son would manage the household more effectively than I. Please tell me, for a brief introduction for novices, which books would be most useful in your view? And together with that, do describe your opinion as to how one can better interest a young man in household management upon his retirement from service: whether together or (if he gets married) to give him a little estate 50 *versts* from me, all ready, long since prepared.[130]

In the letters Aleksei wrote as an adult, after retirement from the army, marriage, and children, he showed both an unusual degree of affection for his parents and an unusual dependence on the advice of his father. In 1860, as a married man of thirty-five, Aleksei wrote asking for "parental advice." He was offered a "private position" with the railroad in

Vladimir, including an apartment there. He would be required to supervise workers and translate letters from French, as well as taking occasional journeys. The salary was forty silver rubles per month, a modest wage for someone with Aleksei's extensive education. "Everyone advises me not to miss this opportunity but I never resolve on anything without your advice and will wait for your opinion with great impatience. One must only have the consideration not that the position decorates the man but the man decorates the position. The work is not difficult and without responsibility, but they are inviting persons who are private and to some extent knowing the French language. I admit that Annochka [Anna, his wife] and I very much want to get this position but without you I waver[;] I will do as you will write me."[131] Despite having a very clear opinion of his own on the matter, Aleksei was unable to act on it without parental approval. Aleksei clearly grew up to be a responsible and amiable adult, but he remained semi-dependent on his father's advice throughout his life (pre-deceasing his father by one year).[132]

Nonetheless, a telling notation made by Andrei in his 1831 diary when he re-read it in 1850 suggests that overall the father was pleased with the results of his educational program: number six in a list of "laws" originally written in 1831 was: "[Conduct] Alesha's lessons more carefully." In 1850 Andrei added in the margin: "Thanks be to God,"[133] apparently in gratitude for the piety, duty, and general good humor demonstrated by his then-grown son. Though Aleksei was no intellectual and showed no sign of interest in abstract ideas, he had at least fulfilled the other, moral ambitions of Andrei's program, and the satisfaction Andrei expressed in this marginal note suggests that these moral aspects of the program were, in the end, the most important to him; in that respect he believed his program had succeeded.

9

Education for All

BY THE LATE 1830s, the Chikhachevs' debts were mostly paid, and in 1837 Aleksei was sent to school in Moscow. His sister followed two years later but "suffered a cruel illness" and may have been sent home again for a short time. In 1841 she entered Mme. Shreier's *pansion* in Moscow.[1] The following year Andrei and Natalia moved to Moscow briefly to be near their children, and then the entire family proceeded on a pilgrimage to Kiev. Soon after their return, in 1843, the brick house begun in 1835 was finally completed and they moved in. In the early 1840s Aleksei apparently attended Moscow University, and by 1847 he entered the army.[2] A year later, Aleksandra married. Starting in 1845, in these years when his children were both leaving the nest, Andrei began gradually to focus on applying his interest in "moral education" to a broader audience.

This impulse was intensified by his religious epiphanies of 1848–1850, which also inspired his audacious fund-raising campaigns to restore a monastery, build a brick church in nearby Zimenki (for which he also obtained donations of valuable icons), and found the first public library in the province open to serfs. Andrei's articles in these years described and promoted his religious projects ("A few words for those desiring to pray in Kiev") and educational theories ("Village education—on the upbringing of children"), but also considered such problems of everyday life for the provincial gentry as "How best to build an above-ground cellar," "On debt," "The Question of exterminating wolves," and "Relationships between landowners."[3] In these years Andrei bound and briefly annotated large sets of correspondence relating to his projects as well as family letters.[4] Taken together with his published articles, these documents reveal the development of Andrei's ideas as he applied them to the wider world beyond his own children and village.[5] This development demonstrates how Andrei's self-defined vocation of educating his children could be understood as an appropriate masculine role not only because it was an intellectual task but also because it allowed him to contribute intellectually to his society. He had come to understand his paternal role as a meaningful gift to the public sphere.

Andrei's education was objectively very good according to the standards of his time and rank, judging by the institutions he attended (a *pansion* in Moscow and the Noble Regiment military school in St. Petersburg). Yet after reading a book "on Rhetoric," Andrei wrote, "[o]n every page I regretted to the extreme that I was taught little in my young years."[6] And although he was a devoted reader, Andrei was constantly dissatisfied also with his self-directed study: "I always regret that despite my fondness for reading I have such a weak memory—even during the reading itself, having read a page I have forgotten it already. So what kind of use can I extract [from my reading]? None at all. And at the same time [I have] the bad habit of reading hurriedly as if being chased or urged forward?"[7] Andrei confided to Yakov that he felt driven to make a name for himself in the journals as early as the mid-1830s, but he hesitated to do so out of this sense of scholarly inadequacy: "It seems to me that if I had studied more diligently in my youth, or even if they simply whipped me seven or so times, I would sooner or later also publish [in] journals, even if [in] third-rate [ones]. 'What's the problem? Start now!' (you might say . . .)"[8] And again, on another day, he bemoaned how he had wasted his youth and was continuing to use his time (in his "old age" of thirty-seven years) less wisely than he might:

> Ach, my God, how fast is the time passing, and how little we see of it, and [how little] we know how to use it[.] I look back at what I have done in three years?— nothing.—If I were a good scientist, I could have made a useful discovery in that time, and gotten it printed. There is a usefulness, there is a living monument to oneself. Truly I often reason with myself: what a pity that I have studied only little and badly. I only now (in my old age) feel that learning is an inexhaustible treasure for a person. It engages and comforts him everywhere. And ever something new and pleasant! But enough philosophizing.[9]

While still bemoaning his inadequacy, Andrei began his first serious writing project, a novel manuscript, in 1835. It is clear from its subtitle that Andrei intended his "novella" to encompass his worldview and propagate it to a broader public: the book was titled *The Innovator* ("a true story of the 19th century").[10] The translation "Innovator" is imperfect— the original, *Prozhektior*, literally means someone who dreams up many projects. This, of course, precisely describes Andrei himself, so it seems that in his novel he meant to write about himself as model for the nineteenth century. His century was only finishing its first third as he was writing, so he was as much arguing for the path the future should take as describing the present. There are two passages from the manuscript recorded for Yakov in the notebook correspondence. The first is apparently the opening of the novel, which introduces a village feast: "In a village feast the guest who does not play cards is a pitiful person; the host who does not have a game is even more pitiful; and the hostess on any occasion when 25 people gather is a true martyr." This is followed by a disquisition on the onerous duties of the hostess: "If it is not interesting to sit quietly for several hours or to listen to prolonged vulgarities, then what must it be like being in continuous motion for 12 hours, to which a village feast condemns the hostess." To this line Andrei appended a footnote, probably prompted by Natalia: "during and after the guests." Andrei continued with a list of the hostess's tasks, concluding that woman's lot was a heavy one:

—An inquiry into the state of provisions of various kinds—a list of things to be purchased,—meetings with the kitchen master,—preparation of dessert,—care not only about the guests, but also about their servants—so that all are contented, calm and as merry as possible.—The hostess is the primary participant in all of this. Above that bring to light at least one failure, which can seldom be avoided,—and given a choice you would never want to be born not a man.

This passage exhausted Andrei's first effort; he then predicted Yakov's response: "So? Enough for the first time! Both well done and the introduction is as proper." Andrei replied to his own pleasantry with cheery confidence, "alright then. It's not for nothing that I am feeling Samson's strength in my right hand!" He became in fact rather giddy, proclaiming that he could "equally easily improvise in French"—followed indeed by a short monologue in that language—and then, "So what kind of doubt in my abilities can be possible?" However, he ended on a self-deprecating note, predicting that posterity would laugh at his "homegrown literature." Natalia's comment was: "How about my And. Iv., he wants to set out to outdo Bulgarin. That's our people: but let him write."[11]

Continuing his manuscript at a later date, Andrei's narrative reached the beginning of the village celebration: the clock had struck twelve, preparations were made, the "servants were uniformed in celebratory blue," and, with a singularly infelicitous simile, the "ball-like heads of all ages are nurtured by a glossy moisture." Two characters are finally introduced: "R. S.," the host, and Kuzma Ivanych (K. I.), a guest. R. S. had prepared for the celebration by wearing "a coat made of 16-ruble cloth" instead of one made from "6-ruble cloth," and was pacing his study with his pipe, glancing at the list of dishes and wines prepared for the party. A stultifying dialogue between R. S. and K. I. follows, which reads more like a transcript from an actual arrival at a village party than an opening scene in a novel. The only remark of any significance in the two-hundred-word dialog is when, in reply to R. S. asking how he is, K. I. asks: "Do you mean to discuss my service? Quite fine. Our Police chief is a wonderful man: he does not mistreat us deputies. He definitely wanted to be here today." By the end of the dialog the police chief does, in fact, arrive. Andrei's excerpt ends here, and the reader can only be relieved. Perhaps Andrei intended to explore relations between the gentry and officialdom; certainly the implied expectation that *most* police chiefs did mistreat their deputies (who were elected nobles) could do with greater explanation.

But instead Andrei's understandable dissatisfaction with his manuscript made him stop writing, for Yakov soon asked, "What about your literature, why has your novella [fallen silent;] it's time, it's time to get to continuing it; my sister and I in two persons represent the public—and this public is waiting impatiently for the continuation of our novel, whose beginning has interested it so much! *Courage jeune auteur—courage!*" Despite these best efforts from his audience, Andrei replied with one desultory word, "have no time" (*nedosug*), which in Russian usually implies, "don't feel like it."[12]

Besides the recognition that Andrei was quite right to turn from fiction to nonfiction, these novel excerpts reveal a few other aspects of Andrei's thinking. If his purpose was to describe—or guide—a nineteenth century centered around a man like himself, the inventor of projects, it is clear from his opening that this self-identity was intertwined with both the village and the vital supporting role of the wife. The setting of a village celebration tells the reader where Andrei's nineteenth-century is firmly situated: in the provinces. And despite conventional remarks about the "vulgarities" to be endured on such occasions, clearly this novel was meant to be peopled not only by members of Andrei's own class, and by representatives of a more middling group including police officials, but also by the serfs.

Even more significant is that the entire introductory passage focuses on, to borrow Andrei's title from his later article, "the importance of the *khoziaika*" (which meant hostess as well as estate manager). The hostess described here would not have been out of place in a gentry home in Georgian or early Victorian England[13]—hostessing was one aspect of Natalia's work that varied little from that of gentry women in Western agricultural contexts where large numbers of servants were present—but there are important differences here. First, the hostess in Andrei's novel could not be more prominently placed; she is the opposite of invisible. Second, Andrei's own wife was one of his first two readers for this text, and some if not all of the hostess's duties described were probably suggested or approved by her. Thus, even from so brief a glimpse into this unfinished project, it is obvious that Andrei's novel was meant to be prescriptive, and that his prescription for his times was based on an idealization of his own circumstances, specifically his and Natalia's gendered roles as mother-manager and father-educator.

As the years passed and with the encouragement of his family Andrei eventually found the courage to polish the ideas he had initially recorded privately and to reformulate them for a wider audience, this time in nonfiction form. The older, more mature and sobered Andrei of these later years—years that saw the death of his adult daughter, his religious reawakening, and his successful efforts at philanthropy—was a confident man, proudly referring to himself as a "*starets*," literally "old one," but suggestive of the wisdom that comes with age. The younger man who did not dare to submit his work "even . . . in third-rate" journals had given way to an experienced journalist with a regular column in one newspaper and dozens of articles in other publications, to whom strangers often wrote seeking advice. In the course of his adult life, Andrei had addressed his insecurities about his status as a writer and thinker by assiduously educating himself alongside his children.

As Andrei felt that he had grown, had improved his temper, and become authoritative (at least on certain subjects), he felt it was time for Russians, as a society, to mature. Moreover, he was optimistic that this was not only possible but was a relatively simple solution to the complex problems facing Russian society. Basing his ideas on his own experience of successful self-study, Andrei saw the task of becoming an enlightened parent through a lens colored by early Enlightenment thinking: it was a task that could be learned, by anyone, if only they could be made to see its importance and to read "two or three articles." Once fathers had learned these basic principles, life would simply and—it seems—almost automatically improve for everyone:

> *Vospitanie* gives us everything that makes us happy. Two or three articles [depicting the observations] of parents who follow impartially the characteristics of this age, which is [malleable] like wax, but which has a decisive influence on the whole life of a person, would be read with the greatest benefit.[14]

For Andrei, study, reading, and the gathering of factual knowledge served to bridge the gap between the practical limits of one person's reach and the wider world. In his article about his geographical game, Andrei had argued that children must be taught a thorough knowledge of their native region to inculcate in them "affection for one's county," and to teach them scientific-Enlightenment principles of gathering, recording, and organizing information. In another article written nearly at the same time as "On Children's Games," Andrei gave still another reason for his preoccupation with geography in particular and knowledge in general:

> How and where, if one was a not-so-wealthy private person could [one] satisfy one's sacred sense of curiosity about [one's] motherland? Is this condition not similar to that of a person who was orphaned in infancy and is now curious about the minutest details about one's parents?[15]

Andrei's comparison of a curious citizen to an orphan was a very personal way to explain a desire for knowledge about one's native environment. Andrei himself was an orphan, almost from the moment of his birth in the nineteenth-century sense of "orphan" as a child who has lost one parent (his mother). By adolescence he had lost his father as well, and since he was brought up away from home he had reason to have felt orphaned in every sense throughout his childhood. Thus, in Andrei's mind the connection between "motherland" and the literal mother was direct, and conscious. Just as he was curious about his own parents, he tells his readers, he was curious about his native land. A "not-so-wealthy private person," was at a disadvantage—just as an orphan is disadvantaged or helpless—because he could not afford to travel or study as the best means of fully understanding or "knowing" his native land (as an orphan can never directly know his parents). Other means needed to be found to pursue that curiosity about and love for one's home—analogous to one's natural love for one's parents and therefore requiring no explanation or justification—that did not depend on direct experience. Andrei found this means in books.

In this revealing comment, Andrei also made explicit the deep connection in his mind between the pure desire for knowledge and a sentimental and Romantic sense of the emotional importance of knowledge of and for the self. In comparing an orphan's lost parents to the unknown motherland, Andrei equated the local with the self, and the national with one's parents and forebears, that is, with the essential origins of one's self-hood. For him, the study of the local moved by natural stages to a study of and, finally, a sense of belonging to a greater whole. He did not reject the rational pursuit of knowledge and progress—valuable in its own right—that he had inherited from the European Enlightenment. Instead, he added to it other associations and values that were aimed inward, toward personal development or the fulfillment of personal duty first, and only secondly outward toward the betterment of society (understood as an extension of the self). This significant leap of understanding one's immediate environment and nation as an extension of the self that must be known and loved as one must know and love one's self (and analogous to a parent-child relationship) was an essential element in Andrei's worldview, and one of the main purposes of *vospitanie* in his mind.

Andrei's notion of *vospitanie* as it applied to his children was, in addition to a program of education quite broad for its time and place, also a mixture of love, positive attention, and warmth, but with an emphasis on supervision and discipline as well. Instructing his fellow parents years later, Andrei justified the intensity and discipline of his educational program as necessary to ensure that his values would withstand the onslaught of other, unpredictable influences after a child left home:

Don't look at [your children's] seeming inattention [or] lack of understanding[:] continue your didactic conversation in their presence [with] reading [and] prayer. This grain will not show growth for a long time, but the growth will inevitably be true. And if you hurry to move your son from under your own parental roof into a public institution, where your influence will be already limited, then do not hesitate to store him up with everything that is necessary, with such sturdiness which will not give in to any influence from his comrades—The method of some tutors, who allow slowness in obeying, is mistaken. Orders must never be repeated: "ordered—done" must be synonymous in *vospitanie*. [16]

But Andrei did not want other parents to neglect the emotional aspects of *vospitanie*: "Elevated sensibility should be the primary aspect of upbringing and education."[17] Andrei believed greater moral and practical education made people more useful, and less suscep-tible to outside influences, but he also indicated in this article that advanced, theoretical, or abstract education was specifically necessary for gentry men (the "sons" named above). Gentry men should be taught the theoretical principles of progressive management as

well as receiving a firm moral grounding, so that when a young man returned to his
estate after retiring from service "he will then become an excellent estate manager (*khoziain*) . . . because his main outlook will not be that which unfortunately places maximum
income as its primary goal."

Andrei's primary concern was the connection between moral education and good
management. It is still implicit here that he considered abstract, philosophical reasoning
a masculine realm while the applied, pragmatic rationality of daily estate management
was appropriate for a woman. His ideal of a *khoziain* was one who put the "greatest good"
of his dependents above "income"; this ideal describes a moral leader, not a practical one.
A few paragraphs earlier, he countered those "who speak against" him on the grounds
that he wanted "to make slaves out of ladies" with the reply that "absolutely necessarily,
order in the house must exist during every minute [of the day]," implying that only ladies
were capable of maintaining literal order (a practical task). Both parents, above all,
needed to put active effort into fulfilling their duties.

Andrei recognized that if country life was to prosper, the children who would be the
leaders of future village life had to be better prepared to understand their region, its
needs, and its way of life. For these reasons, Andrei was a strong advocate of regional
schools, even for gentry children, stressing the benefit of having one's children educated
nearby against the previously prevailing custom among the gentry of striving to send
one's offspring to the more prestigious educational institutions of the capital cities (as
Andrei had actually done): "I think that the time is near when the less prosperous nobility will be placing their children in county schools. . . . If parents will not be able to live in
the town themselves, they will be able to visit their children."[18] There was another reason
for young men to be taught about agriculture, specifically. In cases like Yakov Chernavin's
where there was no *khoziaika* available, the man of the house necessarily took on the tasks
defined by Andrei as ideally belonging to women.

Russian families were much less concerned with purported biological connections between sex and gendered roles in the family than their counterparts in western Europe and
America. While social and family roles themselves were rigidly defined, with a significantly unequal power differential between males and females, the individual who filled a
well-defined role—such as "mother," "father," "*khoziaika/khoziain*" or "*vospitatel*"—
could be flexible, as circumstances required.[19] In the Chikhachev household, it was expe-
dient for Natalia to act as *khoziaika*, and Andrei as *vospitatel*. Because this arrangement
worked well for him, Andrei wrote of it as an ideal arrangement, one which he assumed
his readers could find acceptable in their own families. However, he was also aware that
sometimes circumstances made this ideal situation impossible, as when Yakov managed
his own estates while also engaging in intellectual pursuits and the sort of provincial
public life that was appropriate for a male of his station. For this reason, men needed to
be at least generally knowledgeable about what was required in the normally feminine
realm of household management, just as female managers were universally instructed to
master the tasks they oversaw their serfs performing. Even a man like Andrei, who

deliberately stayed out of the "department" of estate management, believed he should understand the philosophical, social, and economic aspects of landownership. It was a necessary aspect of masculinity to command a sophisticated, quasi-scientific knowledge of such subjects, in order to successfully look after the "greater good."

In this view Yakov was in complete agreement. An article from the *Northern Bee* by one "Shelekhov" "about improvements in estate management" gave him "a rapid desire to have the entire book, and to become an estate manager." But when Andrei mentioned agricultural matters, he was interested in grand theories of improvement and new solutions to common problems—not, notably, in the day-to-day management of laborers, supplies, or produce.[20] Whether concerning matters elevated or mundane, and whatever the nature of a particular family's situation, the formal education of both sons and daughters in agricultural and management matters should not, according to Andrei, be ignored (as it no doubt was by many nobles who had or who aspired to the kind of wealth that allowed them to consign their dependents to the whims of hired intermediaries).

And so Andrei "was happy like an infant is glad to get a toy" about the establishment of a school of agriculture for hereditary nobles, even though by that time he "had no young children, nor any who are relatives."[21] Accordingly, his provincial public library was intended to benefit readers of the serf and middling classes.[22] He also wrote at length on the importance of educating young gentlemen about agriculture because this science was essential to their carrying out their proper roles as landlords in a future more complicated, yet with greater opportunities, than the world Andrei's generation had been born into. Andrei thus welcomed science and learning as a means for landlords to become ever better at fulfilling their eternal role. He blamed the failings of landlords on their lack of proper preparation (rather than blaming a social system that arbitrarily raised some individuals above others) and made the argument that readers, while adhering to the social order as ordained by God, nevertheless recognize that birth into an elite social estate was not in itself sufficient preparation for a nobleman to fulfill his duty, and to consider the costs to the individual and to his estate when he inherited land that he (or his wife, whose presence was assumed) could not competently administer.

Andrei's reasons were practical; he assumed that young gentry males had two careers available to them, military and civil, but the third, landownership, though "no less important, laborious and sacred," was unique in being considered something one did not require preparation or training for—"we reason about it something like this: 'well, God will let us eventually learn to manage estates and to administer; as long as the person is good, and has the inclination.'" But, Andrei argued, that "inclination" could not develop for "an activity to which I never prepared, which was never explained to me, which was not developed in me, in which I never perfected [my skills]." All activities, whether they were ordained as one's duty or not, required "special study": studying and preparing oneself was as much a part of duty as actually administering estates well, or rather, the latter could not be expected without the former: "do not expect any fine [accomplishments] in any [activity]: everything will be ordinary, mediocre" without preparation. Andrei then painted a picture of the nobleman who arrives to manage his estates only in middle age. This nobleman would have spent his formative years in military or civil service, "imbib[ing] all kinds of thoughts about free time . . . having taught oneself the activity and the outlook that are completely separate from and alien to agriculture." Andrei pictured such a person as not only lacking the proper skills and knowledge to run an estate, but "weakened" in "bodily constitution," and too used to urban life, this man would be "afraid of changes in the air" and "not . . . accustomed to the effects of mistakes, failures, losses, frauds, and all kinds of economic misfortunes." Andrei's final verdict was stark: such a person is "a useless, pathetic creature."[23] Andrei's usually ample imagination simply stopped short of accepting a life without purpose.

Andrei's strong awareness of duty, and specifically the sense of *noblesse oblige*—the idea that elite privileges were the result of and dependent on their duty to maintain order and justice for the people in their charge—caused him to be deeply offended, and to perceive a decline in values, when he witnessed his social peers' display of privileges with no corresponding effort to better the lives of their dependents. He wrote that when one looked into estates that were dirty or backward, absent landlords were to blame. In doing so he referred to the stereotype of the deeply indebted landlord (whose debts, it was presumed, were incurred through profligate city living), who considered it humiliating to enter into country matters out of "lordly hauteur."[24] For Andrei there was no excuse for such failures of duty: "[a landowner] will pursue as his primary goal the greatest good of those under his power, and the resultant income [he will only accept] as the result, caused by his primary goal."[25] The young people he saw around him seemed to be less pious or more rebellious than they used to be ("I am surprised at young men who never pray, neither in the morning, nor in the evening, nor at the table; can I ever trust in such a person?—Of course it's not good to be a <u>hypocrite</u>, but everyone should perform what is proper").[26] Andrei blamed this sad state of affairs not only the influences of the city but more pointedly on parents' lazy refusal to invest themselves in the vital task of *vospitanie*. He accused lazy parents of playing cards for hours on end instead of attending to the needs of children for whom they "care . . . but little."[27]

> We don't discuss serious subjects with children not because this would have been useless for them; but because it is a burden for ourselves. It is tiresome to many to wait for a long time before the planted seeds grow, and creates doubt that these seeds can even break the ground. However, he who knows well the character of the slowly growing grain, which grows slowly but surely, works reassured. [It is] the same with talking to children.[28]

Andrei was not the only Russian of his time, or indeed the only aging person of any time or place, to look with trepidation and disapproval on the changes wrought by a younger generation. "Imports" from western Europe of everything from literature to furniture to ideas about religion, society, and the state (directly undermining Russian

Orthodoxy, social hierarchy, and autocracy) were disturbing to many Russians at this time, even while a small, privileged, urbanized minority embraced these imports as a welcome redress of perceived inadequacies. Andrei's ideas stemmed at bottom from a complacent view that his own home, of which he was (within certain limits) lord and master, was self-sustaining, personally fulfilling, a healthy environment physically, spiritually and intellectually for himself and his family, and was essentially stable.

It might be tempting to attribute Andrei's deeply conservative and monarchical views—contradicting, as they sometimes do, his other equally strong beliefs in education and progress—to the strictures of censorship. His published writings stem, however, directly from private writings that were never intended to leave the hands of his family, in which the views expressed are entirely consistent with the published writing. He simply does not seem to have considered very deeply the significant objections to his view on which westernizing thinkers focused: that serfdom was morally unjustifiable, that Western-style industrialization was essential to future prosperity and security, or that the lack of democratic participation in government was stifling to the individual, as social estates were stifling to business and government.

Andrei's patriotism was in fact analogous to his faith; he derived inspiration and passion from his reading (catechisms and Bible commentaries on the one hand, histories of the Romanovs and the Russian state on the other), and he believed the Russian autocracy held earthly society together much as the Church held spiritual souls together. His sense of duty to the state and nation was spoken of in the same light as his sense of duty to God; one ruler for earthly life, the other for that which was immortal. Still, Andrei was not entirely uncritical of his country. He was quick to complain about the dilatory nature of the court system ("If the death that consumes humanity would employ our court institutions to notify people about its arrival—we would all live for hundreds of years!"), although of course complaints about bureaucracy might best be considered endemic to modern life and not indicative of a particular political view.[29]

Despite his recognition of flaws, Andrei was energized by what he saw as Russia's enormous potential, so he focused instead on contributing in his own ways, from joining his provincial branch of the Moscow Agricultural Society to his local philanthropy to public writing to his campaign to compile a reference book on Vladimir province.[30] In addition to his work as a cholera inspector in 1831, three years later Andrei received some sort of salary from the county—Natalia recorded twenty-three rubles "from Kovrov" in her account book.[31] Andrei encouraged others to be active: when Yakov mentioned reading "several articles from the civil laws," Andrei enthusiastically replied, "Do read Civil laws. In time, when you will be running for the Chairman of the Civil Chamber, [I] will solemnly and openly put my ballot to the right [to vote for you]."[32] Some of Yakov's activities reveal how these local occupations reinforced nobles' sense of patriotism: in Vladimir for the noble elections in January 1836 Yakov attended a dinner and supper "of all the nobles of the province" where an "anthem to the tsar" was sung, along with "verses" for the provincial marshal and civil governor.[33]

The day Andrei saw Emperor Alexander I in person was one of the great occasions of his life, and he was gratified to hear firsthand accounts of the imperial family, as when a member of his cousin's family, Petrusha Yazykov, told him "how the Tsar and Grand Duke Mikhail Pavlovich treat cadets graciously."[34] The Romanovs as hobby spread to Yakov: in 1834 he occupied himself by "composing the genealogy of Russian Princes and Tsars; it was rather difficult, but I finished it more or less." He commented that he was using Glinka's history, and it would have been "much easier" to use Karamzin's instead.[35] For these people, the imperial family appear to have carried primarily symbolic value as embodiments of the values of Orthodoxy and nationhood, and intimately connected with this was the notion of service to the state.

Andrei was also simply fascinated by the vast power of the Romanovs. On a trip to Vladimir one day Andrei was delighted to run across "a tall soldier in a uniform coat." The uniform featured five gold ribbons on the sleeve and two "little grenade symbols" on the collar. Andrei could not resist asking what all this represented; the man turned out to be a Palace Grenadier named Panteleimonov. Describing him as "a smart fellow," Andrei learned that all the officers of the Palace Company besides their colonel were promoted from the ranks (this merited two exclamation points), and that "only six persons" in the empire were allowed to see the tsar "without a report" (three field marshals, head of the Third Section Alexander Benckendorff, Minister of the Court Volkonskii, and Minister of War Chernyshev). When the tsar was in Vladimir, Panteleimonov was "posted in a rather important position next to the room of the Tsar himself." Now retired, and bored, the former Grenadier wanted to "personally ask the Tsar to accept him to the service, that is, he would be accepted in his former position into the Palace Company, where each private, that is, a sergeant, receives 320 rubles per year."[36]

Andrei's awe for the monarchy stopped short of paying from his own pocket to augment the tsar's retinue: twelve years after seeing Emperor Alexander I in Moscow, Andrei recorded hearing from the local police chief that Nicholas I would be passing through his region. For the occasion landowners were expected to supply either one horse per each 130 souls they owned, or pay seventy kopeks for every soul. Andrei was resigned: "Of course cash always ends up as a finale of any such oratory and so now I will have to send off 54.60 rubles when required." It appeared that this cash did not come from Andrei's own pocket—on the next page, Andrei reported talking to his peasants with the result that "everyone unanimously agreed to pay 70 kopeks, and of course this is how it was supposed to be. Everyone can figure out what is better for him."[37]

Andrei had served his country in the army from 1813 to 1818 (commissioned in 1816), and he continued to read avidly about the Russian military for the rest of his life. Military service even crept into his subconscious: Andrei once recounted a bizarre dream in which he was on a ship as an artillery officer, and witnessed a conflict between the naval captain and an army colonel whose regiment was being transported on that ship. The naval captain arrested an infantry sergeant, which irritated the army colonel, so that he "tr[ied] to injure" the naval captain, causing the dreaming Andrei to fear for the ship—and then he "decided to wake up."³⁸ It is tempting to read Andrei's dream as reflecting growing discord between himself (the army veteran) and Yakov (the navy veteran), but in any case the dream attests to the centrality of military service in Andrei's way of looking at the world, despite his scant five years of service, in which he did not see active duty.³⁹ Memories of service surfaced during unrelated activities of his later years, as when Andrei and Yakov found that their homemade telegraph was not quite working as they had planned it in their signal book, and Andrei reminisced about his experience in the Noble Regiment: "it happened that some Officers in the Duty Chamber were dashingly explaining all the formations of the battalion exercise; but once they went out into the exercise field and started to practice, one would lead his platoon to Jupiter, the other—to Uranus. Blinking the signals, sir, is not a difficult thing but we both make mistakes—frequently."⁴⁰

Beyond the notion of service—closely tied for Andrei to the management of serfs and agriculture as well as the army—Andrei's understanding of nationality was more or less limited to his devotion to his county and region, which he extrapolated metaphorically into a likewise devotion to nation: as he loved his county because it was his, he loved Russia because it, too, was his, though in a more remote way that seems not to have animated his feelings to the same degree. But the connection between himself and the empire was there, defined in part by his religion, and embodied in the imperial family. Ethnicity is not a concept that appears in Andrei's patriotism. Andrei's interests focused on such a narrowly defined locality that perhaps he had little reason to question the role of ethnicity in his understanding of nationality. In addition, though, Andrei's concept of nation was tied to a multiethnic empire, and the vast size and diversity of the empire contributed in obvious ways to its greatness. The 1830s was a period very early in the development of modern nationalisms, and in Russia there was often a tenuous connection between concepts of nationhood and ethnicity, probably because of Russia's status as a multiethnic empire.⁴¹

Andrei's relative disinterest in Russian ethnicity as nationality did not mean he was oblivious to ethnicity in general. He delighted in learning about the more diverse population of Astrakhan province through his correspondence with Kopytovskii. And he was not above making the occasional tasteless Polish joke: in 1834 Yakov recounted driving by his friend Cherepanov's estate and finding him not home; he was invited to stay anyway but declined, so instead he spent the night in "the wilderness" (probably sleeping in his carriage). Andrei responded, "I would have stayed. [A]s to you, you did not act Polish. [T]his means that I am a Pole."⁴² At the same time, Andrei was capable of making exceptions for Poles he respected. In 1834 Andrei mentioned his commander in the army, a "Mr. Shumskii," who happened to be a "well-born Pole."⁴³ But Polish jokes were almost certainly a popular pastime in these years surrounding the Polish rebellions of 1830–31, 1860–61, and the "springtime of nations" in 1848, in which Poles would no doubt have played a role if Nicholas I's gendarmes—assisted by an army officered in part by one Aleksei Andreevich Chikhachev—had not kept them in firm check.

Immediately after confessing that he spent too much money on a silk vest, Andrei wrote in his diary in 1831 that "there was an intense battle with the Poles, in which we suffered up to 8,000 killed and wounded."[44] Perhaps under the influence of this kind of news, Andrei repeated a rumor in his diary that he heard from his neighbor Maria Petrovna Izmailova: "among the Poles even women collect all of their treasures for the benefit of their fatherland against us," of which he apparently disapproved, even though if it were Russian women doing the same to fight a Polish occupation, Andrei would likely have cheered enthusiastically. Another rumor was that "outside Warsaw there was a bloody battle that lasted 44 hours and Warsaw is all ruined to the ground." Andrei apparently believed that this pointless destruction, though deplorable, could be safely blamed entirely on the Poles, since he added, "We must think that through God's will everything will turn to the better and when the violent rebels will be subdued, the government will be more careful and will not allow them to have their own army."[45]

Andrei's sense of nationality was bound up with his hopes for Russia's future. These hopes contrasted starkly with what he saw taking place in Western societies—a "false enlightenment," to be avoided at all costs: "Never has the question of enlightenment been as universal as at the present time, when poorly understood, poorly directed, completely false enlightenment has so fatally darkened the west of Europe." Andrei understood "true" enlightenment in a very simple way: "One should live according to one's experience and one's reason." In the West, reason had been misunderstood and misdirected. But he also insisted that reason and science were not sufficient in themselves, implying, first, that morality—intimately connected with religious faith—was also needed to complete man's existence and allow him to fulfill his duty, as "[t]he practical side alone is insufficient: with it alone a man can fulfill only half his predestination, [and] would be only half as happy."[46] That is, in addition to Enlightenment, Andrei required also morality, feeling, and emotionalism in a complete education and a complete life, even privileging the latter above other elements: "Elevation of *feeling* must be the principal article of *vospitanie* and education." This was then a rather curious admixture of Enlightenment rationality, Romantic emotionalism, and a religious or superstitious sense of predestination.[47]

Andrei's concern for the moral condition of his county and nation was heightened by a perception that the world was degrading into disorder, impiety, and irresponsibility brought on by secularism. Andrei resolved this dilemma—common to many conservative parents contemplating a post-Enlightenment education of their children—in the simple and trusting way of a man of faith: he believed that true religious spirit would act as an internal barometer of right and wrong and thereby prevent young people from becoming corrupted by the wrong ideas. No student of agricultural science or any other rational subject could fall into errors of wrong-thinking if his personal faith was firmly grounded from an early age. According to Andrei, with a religious *vospitanie* a young man might make many mistakes, but he "will never corrupt himself."[48] Parents had nothing to fear from enlightenment in such cases because "in every new science, in every new discovery, a young man will see only the utter Goodness of Almighty God towards weak humanity."[49]

Having steeped his children in the catechism and in the daily rituals of their faith from their earliest days, and having reserved for religion a firm place in the family circle, Andrei was able to confidently send his children to study in Moscow knowing that, as indeed turned out to be the case, they would return untainted by secular ideas. Andrei could be confident because he knew his values had become part of who they were through the process of *vospitanie*, and so he advised other fathers to do the same:

> Infancy is a period more important than many would think. A strict following of the fundamental rules of an honest citizen, a faithful servant of the Tsar, and a son of the Fatherland, which is absorbed during coming of age through one's own conviction, must be helped and eased even during childhood. Too early a study of the sciences is harmful, but early implantation of one's duties is salvation.[50]

Faith and duty must come first—if these were firmly implanted, then "study of sciences" could not be dangerous. This imperative was of course deeply conservative, even reactionary, yet it was also based in a firm belief that there was a kind of Enlightenment— "true" Enlightenment—that was as benign as "false" Enlightenment was dangerous.

Andrei's understanding of "false" versus "true" Enlightenment caused him to draw a sharp line within Russian society between urban and rural residents: the former had been seduced away from reason, duty, morality, and faith toward materialism and religious laziness or doubt, that is, toward "false enlightenment." The countryside lent itself more easily to a moral, dutiful, rational life. Andrei also claimed that the countryside held the advantages of "convenience"—the self-sufficiency of producing nearly everything necessary to life on one's own estates—and "freedom"—being the master of one's own domain (here of course he blithely ignored the fact that the vast majority of rural residents were enserfed). This view of the village was derived from Andrei's personal enjoyment of life there. In mid-April 1835 he recorded his raptures about "spring in the village," which characteristically expanded into a general speech on the advantages of country life over the city:

> Spring in the village—is for me an inexpressible pleasure: and if I were in command of entire millions of thalers, I would on the fourth week of the fast always leave the city. For what a huge difference it is to look at the dirty pavement, on the muddy carriages and pedestals of the buildings and dirty boots, galoshes and bottoms of clothes, nothing could be seen further than the house next door or to admire the gradually appearing extensive fields, the destruction of boundless masses of snow, to imbibe the poetic noise of spring waters, to see their large gathering, and the river returning through them into its banks. To spy through the looking glass the first ploughman—this is like your Venus de Milo, your Apollo Belvedere!! *C'est delicieux po[u]r moi!* ["I find it delightful!"] And the first unfurled green leaves? And the first thrill of a nightingale? Not in a cage in the Okhotnyi Riad [in central Moscow], no, there its song is that of a prisoner, but here in the bushes, in a forest, in a grove it is a most solemn ode to the entire Nature—the most magnificent

celebration of liberty. In the city the greatest of rich men has under his dwelling a *desiatina* of land, here we the men of rather medium means will become tired walking to the edges of our possessions. [I]n one word, to meet the spring in the village is <u>necessary</u>."[51]

People in the country, in Andrei's view, benefited from living close to nature, from having a recognized place in a hierarchical community, and from the strong influence of the church and priests within that community.

These benefits defined—or should have defined—the countryside versus the secular and cosmopolitan city. Andrei wrote that rural inhabitants—and he specified those who lived in the provinces year-round—could enjoy a completely different kind of life and "benefit from much greater advantages in the conveniences of everyday necessity" in comparison to town-dwellers, because country-dwellers enjoyed both a beautiful setting and "complete freedom."[52] In contrast, the city was enervating and spiritually empty, a place where, lacking the "freedom" and positive moral influence of health, work, and knowing one's place, and under the influence of urbanized Western societies, pure reason was misdirected into doubt, profligacy, and disrespect for the basic principles of an ordered society.

Andrei did not lack exposure to the temptations of city life. His well-connected friend Aleksandr Merkulov, who served in the War Ministry's Department of Inspection, wrote to Andrei of a more cosmopolitan lifestyle. Even Merkulov's child had a cosmopolitan name—he had an "Adelaida" in addition to his more traditional Leonid, Olga, and Maria. The Merkulovs also enjoyed a subscription to the Italian Opera "for the third year," and Merkulov spelled out for Andrei's benefit that they attended "every Friday from October to Great Fast (for 20 shows)." Adding details that could not have meant much to Andrei, Merkulov continued, "for music lovers it's impossible to find a better pleasure, especially given the singing genius Mario the tenor and Persiani the soprano."[53] What mattered more to Andrei than superficial pleasures was that the city could offer concrete threats: early in 1835, Yakov wrote to Andrei with disgust of a rumor that a tavern was to be established in the villages of Berezovik and Cherntsy. "Devil take it how nasty this will be!" he wrote, presumably expecting drunkenness and noise to increase as a result. Andrei responded in agreement, "it will be enough trouble if it will be a couple of *versts* away."[54] Although Andrei's disgust of urban values was a philosophical and moral position above all, it was grounded in the day-to-day unpleasantnesses of real encounters with city influences, and their impact on the countryside.

While idealizing country life, Andrei tempered his observations of the peasantry with a kind of balance—what he called "indifference"—born of real and complex interactions with the peasants who surrounded him all his life. In a telling conversation with Yakov, Andrei prodded, "You think that village celebrations are not interesting?" and Yakov replied, "Exactly." This gave Andrei his opening to half-jokingly speechify: "Ekh, brother, thus you are estranged from nationality." Yakov did not take the bait, writing "not at all," then a curious footnote, "bad nationality?" Andrei added, more seriously, "It's a shame! As to me, even if I am not admiring the [peasants], at least I am indifferent; you know that [Mikhail N.] Zagoskin would not have written so successfully *Yuri Miloslavskii* [, *Or, The Russians in 1612*], which I am finishing reading for the fourth time, if he did not attentively observe the construction of all ranks of our popular folk." Yakov responded, "in this respect, I agree with you," but added with less enthusiasm for the study of the lower ranks, "I also have observed, but only against my will."[55]

Andrei thus idealized the village and country life for its potential rather than its reality. He felt that this ideal had never been fully realized and was under serious threat in his time. His view rested on a notion of true order, but true order had not and to a degree could not be obtained.[56] In the real world he was conscious of room for improvement in village life in the realms of cleanliness, general order, economic efficiency, and the skill levels and education of people at every rank of the village hierarchy. He believed that time had already brought progress in these areas: "today is a different age, enlightenment, enlightenment everywhere,—if I say today, in the year 1847, we have very much that is dusty and covered in spider webs, what was there a hundred years ago?"[57] And there was much more change to come. He feared, however, that progress in the country was being derailed by that "false enlightenment that has so fatally darkened the west of Europe." In other words, improvements in cleanliness, literacy, and efficiency were welcome, but secularization, democratization, and industrialization were to be deplored.

Thus, Andrei richly praised a cheesecloth factory in Kovrov, calling it the "antithesis" of other factory situations, because it upheld the "morality" of its peasant workers—in direct contrast to urban industrialists. Small-scale peasant workshops located in agricultural regions where peasants could be employed when not needed in the fields and where they would grow up to their trade in an (implicitly) patriarchal village "family," could only be moral in Andrei's imagination. Anything else, for him, was inconceivable.[58]

Progress in the countryside was, instead of striving to be more like "advanced" Western societies, the ever greater fulfillment of the potential inherent in the individual and in his locality. As a faithful and moral individual, Andrei hoped to become a better, more dutiful person (working to curb his greatest fault, his temper). In the same way, he hoped that his peers and the Russian people as a whole would become more faithful followers of Orthodoxy, more literate readers, more knowledgeable tenders of their native land. This, in his view, would bring every other kind of social and economic progress that Russia needed:

I envision closely—very closely the time when even the remnants of false and real [legal] suits, pride, prejudices and all those companions of smoldering miserable obscurity which are still concealing themselves in some remote slums and tundras of our multi-climated, Great, boundless Mother Russia will be completely eliminated, and the very memory of them will disappear.[59]

His choice of words here is ambiguous—why does he specify legal suits, pride, and prejudice as the worst examples of "smoldering miserable obscurity"? His other writing shows that he associated legal suits with bureaucracy, which he hated for its pointless complexity and the way he perceived it to interfere in family affairs (given that he came out of two extensive legal battles over family inheritance burdened by heavy debts). In this case "pride" and "prejudices" probably refer to the "wrong-thinking" which he frequently referred to as a loose summation of everything wrong about urban, impious life. Therefore "miserable obscurity," to be found anywhere from "remote slums" to "tundras," must have referred to a general way of thinking to which he objected rather than any particular concepts or conditions. He associated this way of thinking with darkness and the past, while his own way of thinking was associated with Enlightenment and progress.

Andrei's view owes much to the irrationality of Romanticism and the counter-Enlightenment, and to basic conservatism in the sense of an idealization of traditional values. It is therefore difficult to consider his view progressive in any sense. Nineteenth-century thought has—since the ideological cataclysms of the late nineteenth and twentieth centuries defined "Right" and "Left" firmly on opposite ends of a linear spectrum—become boxed into a false dichotomy of the Enlightenment on one hand and Reaction to it on the other.[60] Andrei was a progressive thinker in the limited sense that he wanted forward change and development; specifically, he wanted more and better opportunities for education at all levels, but as a pious and sentimental man he wanted education to be steeped in Orthodoxy, and Enlightenment to be complemented by "elevation of feeling."

Again the elevated (and vague) quality of Andrei's philosophical statements can be qualified by his more mundane observations of everyday life. For example, Andrei's excitement over the progress of the telegraph he invented with Yakov, and even over such iconic westernization projects as the railroad, show that he delighted in advantages afforded by technological progress. He was not a Luddite, looking back to a romanticized pre-industrial past. He rejected the moral decadence of the West but not wholly its facility with technology: in 1836 he wrote of how he and Yakov could enjoy a conversation via telegraph on a rainy day with each man comfortably ensconced "in warm rooms a *versta* from each other." By association his thoughts leapt to "also railroads! 30 *versts* in 40 minutes." Such a rate of progress caused him to wonder "what will happen with our telegraph in two—three—four—ten years. I can tell you definitively, that it will suffice to use half, even a quarter of the paper we are now using on the notebook correspondence. And in quiet clear weather we'll only need 'heavy' mail with books and packages, and everything that fits in 25 lines, all will stay on the balcony."[61]

Considering the railroad again on another occasion, Andrei revealed his awareness of its military importance. In 1835, after reading an article advocating against railroads (they were thought by many conservatives to encourage popular unrest and damage the landscape), Andrei thought "[i]f England, France, and perhaps some other states eagerly spread them, and we eagerly resist them, could it be bad for us in times of war[?] There they will move troops and food in steam carriages by the seacoast as quickly as is done by water during the most favorable wind; whereas our communications will stay the same." He was prescient. The humiliating Russian defeat in the Crimean War twenty years later was largely due to Russia's technological backwardness in railroads and ships.

But Andrei added, "Or is it not our business to rack our noble head[s] about this?" perhaps sarcastically referring to the disinterest of the central government in provincial gentry opinion. Certainly Andrei did not really believe railroads were not his business, since he went on to tell Yakov to ask Timofei Krylov for his opinion, too. Then Andrei expanded his own ideas: "On the other hand, I also think that if some state establishes [itself] in large numbers and improves railroads, which cost millions of millions[; and] suddenly there appears a strong conqueror, [who] throws these roads apart and mutilates them with his mighty hand; [h]ow much will it cost to put them back in order again? Why would he [a conqueror] do it? So as to inflict losses and to undermine the prosperity of an entire Power." This remote prospect seems a weak objection, but Andrei was not finished: "I also imagine some other disadvantages of railroads, in valleys; but I will speak to you about it when I see you."[62]

Also commenting on public events, Andrei's friend and neighbor Mikhail Kultashev wrote to Andrei in 1850 with an account of how local factory owners sent a delegation to St. Petersburg to request a change in a disadvantageous new tariff on English goods. "[B]ut the deputies returned with nothing. [I]n order to enrich the fatherland, it is excusable to neglect the enrichment of several little beards [merchants]. The new arrangement will force them to be diligent factory owners, and not the scoundrels such as they are now."[63] So Kultashev, at least—a man intimately familiar with Andrei's outlook through many years of close association—spoke with approval of the form of capitalist competition that would "force" factory owners to not be "scoundrels." Whatever the nature of these factory-owners' "scoundrel"-like behavior, it could only have involved the quality of their product, its price, or their treatment of workers, and in any of those cases it is interesting that Kultashev cast his criticism in terms of moral judgment—they were scoundrels, bad men, rather than simply inept. In a similar vein, Andrei's friend Elisei Mochalin remarked in 1860, on the eve of serf emancipation:

> Strange is the life of the Russian people, we try everything, move forward, hurry to do everything, and for that reason we end up doing many things in a mediocre manner. Joint stock companies with their . . . directors and boards sunk in corruption. Nearly 60 journals discontinued due to lack of interest. The same fate is awaiting steam-powered agricultural machines and [illeg.]—does not this prove that progress must be carried out competently so as not to slip up in a dangerous place and not to fall into the abyss[?]"[64]

This statement provides a neat explanation for how one could, like Andrei, understand westernization as the enemy of progress, and how one could be both conservative and favor progress at the same time. The issue was of pace as well as direction; going too fast was perhaps worse than not moving at all. A year later, as emancipation was moving forward, Mochalin wrote again in the same vein, this time complaining that the pace of progress was too slow, because Mochalin's focus was on what he saw as the moral bankruptcy of court officials, who took two weeks to resolve land survey cases, all the while forcing peasants to keep watch outdoors in "brutal cold." Mochalin concluded: "God save us from such progress."[65] Pace was vital. These provincial men sought a middle ground between the too-fast of westernizers and the too-slow of corrupt officialdom.

Perhaps the most important conclusion to take from this one man's ideas is the intense and constant interplay between his theories and his life, his own ideas and those gleaned from his milieu, and between his personal perspective and what he learned from his loved ones. In studying Andrei's reading through his published articles and only a fraction of his unpublished private papers, it is too easy to fill the gaps with our own expectations, which are often drawn from creative literature rather than historical sources. Thus, at least one scholar has argued that Andrei was an example of the so-called "superfluous" nobility with which mid-nineteenth-century Russian literature was preoccupied: men who believed in progress but who lacked a sense of purpose or meaning.[66] Delving further into the sources, it is clearly inaccurate to describe Andrei as a man who lacked a sense of purpose or meaning, especially in his role as a Russian landowner. The case was quite the opposite.

Similarly, the assumption that Andrei's life was isolated simply because it was provincial is misleading. While isolation is obviously a relative quality—and it is true that Andrei did not personally participate in the intellectual discourse of the capitals—it is a significant context of his ideas that he believed his relative isolation was ideal, and that the putatively livelier city existence was actually corrosive. Without reading the diaries and notebook correspondence that reveal Andrei to have been traveling almost constantly within his province (and he was relatively uninterested in life beyond his province), it has been assumed that literature was for him an almost exclusive means to expand the boundaries of a narrow and detached world.[67] While certainly the Chikhachevs reveled in travel and historical literature as well as foreign fiction, this entertainment was not the pathetic sole connection to life that literary historians, following nineteenth-century novelists, have sometimes portrayed it to be. For Andrei at least, his world was in itself rich, fulfilling, and inspiring. It was the *outside* world that ought to strive to be part of the world of the village, not the other way around.[68]

Andrei's ideas about *vospitanie* grew in the years after his children were grown to inform his thoughts on almost every subject. These ideas together formed a program for the future progress of his society, which he attempted to disseminate through his published articles. Although Andrei did not personally interact with a larger sphere of intellectuals and was not a member of any defined intellectual movement, his ideas did develop within an intellectual landscape formed by the writers whom he most admired, and through his sometimes limited understanding of the major strains of conservative thought in the mid-nineteenth century. Exploring this landscape and Andrei's place in it can reveal the reasons that Andrei's program ultimately failed to be influential beyond his provincial circle, and what this intellectual isolation might have cost the provincial gentry.

10

The Landscape of Ideas

IN 1836 THE philosopher Petr Chaadaev published a series of explosive "Philosophical Letters" into a fraught intellectual climate dominated by Nicholas I's secret police. Chaadaev framed Russia's future as following one of two possible paths, one facing East, and the other facing West.[1] These letters inspired the formation of two self-identified groups: the Slavophiles and the Westernizers. The Slavophiles (led by Aleksei Khomiakov, Ivan Kireevskii, Konstantin Aksakov—who happened to be a distant relation of the Chikhachevs'—and Yurii Samarin) were deeply critical of many aspects of Western societies. They mourned the changes brought to Russia in the early eighteenth century by Peter the Great's westernizing reforms and sought a re-centering of Russian life along national lines, seeking inspiration for the "national" in peasant culture, rural life, and Russia's pre-Petrine past (much of which was imagined).[2] The Slavophile movement has been closely associated both with Romanticism and with so-called cultural nationalism, in which national identity is seen as an outgrowth of folk tradition and a unique, shared culture encompassing a common language and religion (and the state, by contrast, is seen as largely irrelevant).

The Westernizers, on the other hand, sought to catch up with perceived Western political and economic advancements; they fall into two camps based on how they envisioned the future progress of humanity. The "liberal" Westernizers (Timofei Granovsky, Vasilii Botkin, Pavel Annenkov) looked to industrialized capitalism and representative government for the solutions to Russia's pressing problems, while the "radicals" (Vissarion Belinsky, Aleksandr Herzen, Mikhail Bakunin) were more critical of capitalist development and over time found themselves an intellectual home within European socialism. Both groups of Westernizers were heirs of French Enlightenment philosophy and proponents of a "civic nationalism," based on the idea of the nation-state and the French model of citizenship-based national identity.

This dialog forms a backdrop to Andrei's ideas, although Andrei never explicitly positioned himself within the intellectual landscape of Russian letters, whether out of modesty or obliviousness. But doing so now can help determine the significance of Andrei's ideas for a broader understanding of Russian history. Knowing what Andrei was responding to (even if sometimes subconsciously) reveals what this provincial reader understood of the great ideas of his time, and how those ideas were adapted, altered, and sometimes misunderstood in the process of reaching this one member of the elusive "reading public." At the same time, situating Andrei's thought within the Russian intellectual landscape reveals how fatally out of step the intellectual sphere often was with the provincial sphere. While Andrei cannot be representative of all gentry landowners, he was an embodiment of a much-talked-about "type," which means his private papers provide unique insight into the flesh and bones behind the type. He was also one of many provincial landlords engaged in similar activities, which suggests that he may serve as a useful gauge of one of the available variations of provincial response to the "great ideas" propagated in St. Petersburg, Moscow, and western Europe.

Andrei was published only once in the *Moscow Provincial News,* and that article, "Two Words about Serfs' Work," is an undistinguished one in which he quoted other thinkers at length about the economics of serfdom, then moved on without transition to rehash an earlier article he had published in the *Agricultural Gazette* about cleanliness in the home. The juxtaposition seems bizarre, but the two themes were, in his mind, merely the reflection of one principle in two closely related realms: the house and the estate. Andrei began by quoting a like-minded, Slavophilistic landlowner, a Mr. Kozlov, on how the principles of order and reason should be applied to the estate:

> Basing economic relations on normal principles [i.e., paid labor rather than serfdom] will result not only in the profitability of agricultural work, but will lead further—to a change in economic habits, customs, which in their turn will have an irresistible influence on the moral and material being of all classes.[3]

Kozlov's claim that the rational arrangement of paid estate labor would improve not only profitability but also the "moral ... being of all classes" could be understood as an acknowledgement of the immorality of serfdom (which, by 1848, was generally accepted in most educated circles).

On the face of it, Kozlov was merely making the circular point that the abolition of serfdom would solve both moral and material problems, because serfdom caused both moral and material problems. But Andrei followed this quote with a harangue to fellow landlords to put aside their "lordly hauteur" and to inspect those dark corners of the home and estate that many apparently found "humiliating to enter" out of a false sense of their own status. He argued instead that the order and prosperity of everyone living on the estate—landlords, peasants, and those in-between—depended on the landlord's (and, implied, the landlady's) attention to every detail within and outside the home. Far from resenting the reach of the Russian monarchy into the daily lives of his aristocracy, Andrei proposed that each of the tsar's servitors should embody the same principle, to ensure order and thus most fully perform their duty: "But I say, and anyone who reasons . . . will also say, that necessarily and absolutely necessarily order in the house must exist during every minute [of the day], and so that any visitor could be asked to go anywhere [in the house] at any moment."[4]

Duty and order were moral terms to Andrei, so just as serfdom was both a moral and a material problem for landowners, lack of order in the home or anywhere else was a moral problem—a moral failing—of the landlord (or landlady) charged with ensuring the material comfort, health, and prosperity of all their dependents. Order "in the house" thus belonged unquestionably alongside the discussion of serfdom because they were based on the same idea: the moral obligations attached to the role of landlord. Andrei saw order as the sign and reward of morally correct behavior, which was in turn synonymous with the fulfillment of one's duty, as defined by social role. Whether order was achieved in the home, on the estate, or in society, order was always moral, and disorder was similarly a reflection of moral deficiency. Having already expanded the landlord's paternal role from his children to his serfs, it was a simple matter to consider the behavior and future success of the empire's landlords as a group as critical to the future of all. All this was the core of Andrei's thought, but this article was the first (and only) expression of his views on a national stage.[5]

The modest effort happened to stimulate a response from a prominent critic, Nikolai Ogarev.[6] Ogarev's response was widely discussed at the time (and since) as one of the notable articulations of the Westernizer point of view.[7] Andrei cannot properly be considered a Slavophile: he did not live in the capitals and did not participate in their salons or associate with any of the known figures of the movement. Andrei merely submitted an article relating a few of his ideas about serfdom and the Russian village to a newspaper. Ogarev, however, took the article as an opportunity to ridicule what he interpreted as a Slavophile point of view, while opposing it to his own. Andrei's article was only a moderate and moderating step toward the already well-established debate on serfdom, so it is difficult to guess why it caught Ogarev's attention. However, the nearly complete disconnect between Ogarev's response and Andrei's original testifies to the enormous gulf of misunderstanding that existed between the high-profile philosophical debates engaged in by the urban intelligentsia and the discourse of intelligent but fundamentally conservative readers and writers of provincial newspapers.

Ogarev began his response by quoting a closing line from Chikhachev's article. The line was typical for Andrei, modestly disclaiming scholarly pretensions: "if I have misspoken, gentlemen, please correct me and accept my deepest gratitude." Though not out of place in the pages of the *Agricultural Gazette,* this line was seized upon by Ogarev as a means of infantalizing both Andrei personally and his Slavophilistic point of view. Ogarev then used Chikhachev's name and patronymic disparagingly in nearly every paragraph of his article, as he ridiculed the principles Chikhachev had defended:

> You have misspoken, Andrei Ivanovich, very strongly misspoken!.... I am responding to you with full hope of your deepest gratitude.... This is where a misunderstanding of one single word can lure a young man!—I thought, having read your article. Likely, I will not be mistaken if I consider you to be a young man, and I am completely convinced, that given your abilities, after some years you will also acquire a more accurate knowledge of words that are used in scholarship, and a more positive outlook on things.[8]

Contrary to Ogarev's suppositions, Andrei was at this time a venerable man of forty-nine years, to Ogarev's thirty-four.

Moreover, Ogarev's article is full of empty rhetorical flourishes and circular logic that are every bit as amateurish and unscholarly as Chikhachev's more personal ramblings, as in the following passage, which responds to a call for landowners to fulfill their roles "conscientiously" as the means toward what Andrei called "normal" social and economic relations. Ogarev countered:

> The word normal by itself means popular [*narodnyi*], a model; but here, in my opinion, it also has the meaning of appropriate, suitable, positive, irreplaceable, corresponding to the spirit of the times, existing in the spirit of the people, undeviating from the root principles of any good advice, and heartfelt kindness.[9]

As Andrei had used the word (quoting Kozlov), "normal" relations simply indicated paid labor rather than "abnormal" enserfment. There were no objective grounds for Ogarev's "opinion" redefining a simple word to such an extreme, other than the consensus of Westernizers on what was "appropriate" or "positive" for society. Ogarev might seem personally vituperative toward Andrei, but this was not the case. Ogarev was using Andrei to stand in for anyone he saw as old-fashioned, as a pretext to publicize the Westernizer point of view.

Ogarev went on to say that conscientiousness could not be expected of "private persons," that such an expectation represented, or led to, "backwardness." He characterized the conscientious or moral individuals Andrei called for as "infantile," and Andrei's proposals as going "back to the time when a man has not yet tasted a fruit from the tree of knowledge of good and evil!" Instead, Ogarev insisted that "each of us demands from human society legality and justice to ensure that his interests are not infringed by the interests of someone else," and defined this "demand" as "manly," when it should more accurately be described as "Western." Andrei had written that "[o]ur late fathers and grandfathers would have done without the word *normality*, replacing it with the word *conscientiousness*," arguing that moral people had always wanted "normal," non-exploitative, relations with peasants. Ogarev was more cynical about human nature:

> I am quite in agreement with you, that conscientiousness is a very respectable thing; but please be so kind as to show me at least one state, one human society, which would base all of its labors, decrees, [and] relations, which make it into a complete whole, on the conscientiousness of private persons, of each of its members! Besides the fact that such a society does not exist and has never existed, even if it did exist, then you must agree that, besides an infantile conscientiousness, it would reveal to us a terrifying backwardness of the needs of industry, art, and knowledge.[10]

How is it possible to have legality without morality ("conscientiousness")? How is morality "infantile"? These points are not clear, leaving only the standard westernizing critique that only a good system can make good people, in opposition to Andrei's view that as long as people can be taught (through *vospitanie*) to be moral—("conscientious")—then the nature of the system is irrelevant.

Andrei was not left undefended in this feud. A Prince Didian wrote to the *Agricultural Gazette* in December 1847 in response to the exchange with Ogarev, and in support of Andrei's original article: "I cannot fail to join my opinion about this important subject, which concerns each of us so closely, to the opinion of Mr. Chikhachev." Andrei underlined this and several other passages in his copy of the article. Agreeing with Andrei that "experience and enlightenment are necessary," Didian added that "[w]hoever is a bad manager of serf labor will without a doubt be the same also in the management of hired labor, and vice versa." Andrei wrote a check in the margin on this passage, and added "yes! Yes!" beside Didian's concluding statement "to the opponents of the present order," that landowners should increase the peasants' "satisfaction" as their greatest duty, and this was "what makes us Russian." It was, Didian agreed with Chikhachev, "fatherly concern" rather than "constraining measures and calculations" that made men act with "generosity" toward others.[11]

This episode is indicative of the way in which Andrei's ideas do not easily fall into any school of thought of the period; instead, he—and other men like Prince Didian—adopted aspects of several strains of contemporary conservative thought and interpreted them all through their own lens. In Andrei's case at least, this lens was shaped by his devotion to the idea of *vospitanie*. If Ogarev was carrying the banner of revolution in the name of "correctness" or scientific rationality, Andrei and Didian were heirs to a variety of seemingly contradictory influences, from Catherine II's notions of Enlightened education to Slavophilistic or nationalist sentimental patriotism to Alexander I's sense that Russian society was "not ready" for representative government and his understanding of order as an absolute social good, exemplified in his military colonies (notoriously harsh civilian settlements governed by military order).[12]

The specific social and political changes Slavophiles hoped to achieve in Russia have recently been re-evaluated. Historian Susanna Rabow-Edling rejects the conventional definition of Slavophiles as Romantic utopians whose ideas were essentially negative or "introverted"—that is, focused on rejecting the rationalism and Western culture associated with the French Enlightenment. Instead, she argues that Slavophilism was a rational and critical "project for social change."[13] Romantics, like Slavophiles, "have been accused of retreating from an unattractive reality instead of trying to change it." In recent years, however, scholars have rejected these stark oppositions in favor of a strong continuity between the Enlightenment and Romantic thought. This continuity is seen as highly influential in the development both of progressive liberalism and "modern" authoritarianism.[14]

While Slavophiles criticized the exclusive rationalism and secularism of the Enlightenment, they also, like Andrei Chikhachev, embraced Enlightenment views on education, and the reverence for knowledge propagated initially by Diderot's Encyclopedia, especially knowledge of the local and of peoples of various regions. To this the Slavophiles added sentimental love of feeling (often religious feeling in particular) and reverence for sentimental attachment to one's own culture.[15] However, the Romantic emphasis on individuality did not find a prominent place in Slavophile ideology, since it challenged their allegiance to an imagined pre-Petrine past that was marked (in their view) by communality, a core religious concept referred to as *sobornost* (spiritual collectivity), developed by the philosopher Vladimir Soloviev and closely associated with Slavophile thinking.

The Slavophile Ivan Aksakov envisioned provincial life in terms that echo Andrei's worldview, "valuing domestic space as the precious vessel in which the essence of ideal patriarchy might be preserved."[16] This view encouraged even intellectuals to immerse themselves in the details of everyday domestic existence, as Andrei did. Andrei also shared with Slavophile thinkers the sense that the fate of western Europe after the French Revolution was a "false" or corrupted Enlightenment, and the hope that Russia could avoid what he, and they, interpreted as the extreme rationalism and social chaos of republican and egalitarian ideas.

Unlike the Slavophiles, however, Andrei had little interest in communality, perhaps because he was unable to romanticize the peasantry (choosing instead to idealize his own paternalistic leadership in the village). The founding Slavophiles were notorious for appearing at salons in "traditional" Muscovite garb. Andrei and his family wore European-style clothing, and Andrei's sense of conservative nationalism or patriotism was not an attitude for display—nor was it part of a larger Romantic project to imagine a national past—but simply a reflection of how he understood his immediate surroundings to actually be.[17] Andrei's frequent private effusions of devotion to the tsar and imperial family demonstrate that he differed from the Slavophiles in his entirely uncritical stance toward the monarchy and state, though he shared with them a disinterest in Western-style, political or civic-based nationalism that prescribed a large role for a representative state composed of "citizens" (as opposed to a benign monarchy that existed well above and apart from its "subjects").

Nevertheless, in several important ways Andrei's worldview and the intellectual work that he set himself to accomplish was in essential agreement with the Slavophile project as Rabow-Edling has defined it. But Andrei's view is closer in other ways to the conservative gentry-based national identity that formed the backbone of "healthy" nationalisms in western and central Europe. However, in Russia the landlord-led village life that formed the lifeblood of Andrei's understanding of national identity was destroyed in 1861 when the serf emancipation was carried out in such a way as to impoverish the landlords and alienate the peasantry. The survival of Andrei's peers and their view of national identity may, perhaps, be seen in late-nineteenth century *zemstvo* employees (*zemstva* were local self-government organizations, established in 1863, led by fairly wealthy landowning activists because of an election census but staffed by young professionals, many of them impoverished or of mixed ranks). But the toll taken by emancipation on the fragile economy and social relations of Russian country life prevented this group from growing, prospering, and professionalizing to the degree seen in western Europe.[18]

In this climate of cultural division, many intellectuals, both Westernizers and Slavophiles, articulated what they considered a central problem of Russia: that a cultural chasm between elites and "the people" (*narod*) had arisen since elite classes had begun to westernize in the early eighteenth century, while the majority of the population retained a largely traditional rural lifestyle.[19] These intellectuals inaccurately projected their own social and cultural isolation onto all educated elites, and this inaccurate projection has persisted in much of the historical literature about Russia until recently. The popular and state formulations of national identity are usually closely linked with a rejection of outside influences.[20] In addition, the official state nationalism of Nicholas I and his minister of education, Sergei Uvarov, was riddled with a deep eschatological pessimism about their ultimate ability to forestall modernity and political change.[21]

Yet Andrei firmly identified himself as the master of a cohesive community of interdependent subjects, and understood his own role as a nobleman with acuity. His rejection of westernized identity was not grounded in resentment but in the sentimental/Romantic (or perhaps merely commonsense) belief that one's identity must be grounded in one's own near circumstances. It can be assumed from the circumstances that formed Andrei's views on these issues—circumstances that were shared by the majority of the Russian noble estate—and from the reception of his articles and his popularity among his neighbors, that Andrei's worldview was more in tune with that of his peers than the views of prominent intellectuals in Moscow and Petersburg.

Perhaps it would be more accurate to speak of a "chasm" not between an educated, westernized, and "superfluous" elite and the "people" but rather between city and country (although this too is a simplification). Andrei was far from alone in focusing on those differences. Sergei Aksakov, the early nineteenth-century novelist, made a similar distinction between town and country life, "a distinction noticeable even when the town was a provincial place of no particular renown."[22] Going back still farther to the late eighteenth century, the poet Gavrila Derzhavin wrote of the country gentleman: "Blessed is he who is less dependent on others, Free from obligations and work-related troubles Who seeks neither gold, nor honors at the court, And is free from varied bustle!"²³ Of course, Derzhavin was himself a Petersburger, imagining country life from a considerable distance. Andrei would no doubt have retorted that country life, though independent, was actually full of "varied bustle" but of a kind that fed the soul rather than draining it. Over time Derzhavin's image of the countryside changed, coming closer to Andrei's, as he began to see the life of the rural landowner not as an escape from service to the state but as service in a different form.²⁴

Recent scholars have recognized a general trend mirroring Derzhavin's "increased appreciation for the role of the gentleman farmer modeled on idealized English practice."²⁵ But it was an appreciation based on an imaginary countryside created by the urban elite, comparable in its generalizations and inaccuracies to Andrei's demonization of the capitals based on his fear of secularization. It is no coincidence that attitudes toward rural life were in flux in the decades immediately following the emancipation of the nobility from service in 1762.²⁶ As nobles increasingly retired after only brief service and then lived out their lives in the countryside, both the country dwellers and the city dwellers were left to make sense of what it meant (or did not mean) to reject service for agricultural life. It was not long before urban intellectuals, officials, and Catherine the Great herself set about reframing rural life as this other type of service to the fatherland, based on maintaining the productivity of land and serfs.

In the new understanding cohering in St. Petersburg and Moscow in the first decades of the nineteenth century, there were at least two strains present in what was hoped for the countryside. One was that country life was associated with patriotism, "a patriotism rooted in an idealized, pastoral vision of the 'Holy Rus' of yore."²⁷ This was a view with which Andrei could entirely agree. In contrast was an English model emphasizing innovation, which Andrei could not so easily applaud. While progress and productivity were his goals, he saw little to gain and much to lose in turning to the secular, commercial, and impersonal English model to achieve these goals.

In 1765 Catherine the Great gave permission for the formation of the Free Economic Society, the first private organization in Russia (although it retained close ties to the throne). The Free Economic Society's main goal was to spread knowledge of Western-style rational agriculture in Russia. Over time, the FES was joined by the Moscow Agricultural Society, its provincial branches, and a host of writers and editors who conducted a campaign to enlighten a mass of provincials who were assumed to be resistant to change.²⁸ The writers behind this campaign varied from Nikolai Novikov, writing in the eighteenth century and often considered Russia's first journalist and a propagator of many Enlightenment ideas, to Andrei Bolotov, an eighteenth-century provincial nobleman who echoes Andrei Chikhachev in his graphomania and devotion to rural life, and who wrote from direct experience, to nineteenth-century journalist-editors like Faddei Bulgarin and Osip Senkovskii who rushed to fill their pages with the latest fad, agriculture, and famously profited from what often turned out to be inaccurate and useless advice.

In this literature, elevated language, often emphasizing "holy Rus and its agricultural destiny or referr[ing] to belief in the need to reform agriculture as a 'faith,'" in Alison Smith's words, "awkwardly combin[ed] the rational and irrational."²⁹ Such language was employed to counter accusations that agricultural reformers could not "speak for Russianness." In contrast, those who resisted reform claimed to be doing just that, attempting to "preserve Russian traditions in order to ensure a properly Russian future." Others felt change was "unnecessary or impossible, given the abundance of land and the institution of serfdom," and still another set of voices "thought the problem lay in the source of innovation: the West."³⁰ In this cacophony of voices there is no single "side" on which to place Andrei Chikhachev: deeply concerned with Russianness and suspicious of secularization, though not westernized per se (often a fine distinction), he favored both reform and tradition, progress within a stable moral framework.

Journal editors, especially the notorious Senkovsky and Bulgarin, invented imaginary landowners as contributors to their journals, presumably in place of actual contributions that never appeared or were not what the editors were looking for.³¹ At the same time, those like Bolotov who wrote in their own names about real agricultural experiments usually reported ultimate failure and disappointment. After a flurry of agricultural publications in the 1820s and 1830s, a depressed reaction set in in the early 1840s when many writers concluded that the entire campaign was a failure and laid the blame for this squarely on an inert, lazy, and unresponsive public (or lazy and unresponsive peasants, or both).³² Others have noted that in light of Michelle Marrese's findings about how many women were managing estates, part of the real reason for failure was probably that the entire campaign was directed toward the wrong audience (explicitly toward male readers), and framed in the wrong terms (with rational agriculture as a replacement for state service; women had of course never been in state service, and agriculture was not a new concern to them).³³

In her study of Russian agricultural literature from the late eighteenth century into the mid-nineteenth, Alison Smith has attested that, "[w]hatever their limits, these publishing efforts do demonstrate that Russia possessed a group of citizens committed to the idea of improving agriculture." Calling these people "true believers," Smith argues that they were devoted to saving Russia through agricultural development. Such voices, however, "were in danger of being drowned out by the explosion itself."³⁴ Thus readers like Andrei Chikhachev who annotated their copies of the *Agricultural Gazette* and contributed their own experiences were drowned among the many false experts, poorly chosen translations from the wrong contexts, and imaginary personages invented by editors.

If Natalia or her husband scoffed at inaccurate advice when they read this literature, they didn't do so in writing. Given that all their recorded comments and criticisms related to artistic, historical, or religious literature, it is tempting to believe they ignored much of the agricultural advice produced in the 1830s. But by the late 1840s—when most prominent thinkers and writers had given up on the idea of rational agriculture in disgust—Andrei had begun to publish in the *Agricultural Gazette,* which managed to survive throughout these years (founded in 1834 and published by a series of state ministries, it continued up to the Revolution of 1917), in part based on a growing body of real, named, provincial contributors like Andrei.[35] Even earlier Andrei responded with enthusiasm to the writers Faddei Bulgarin and Nikolai Karamzin. Karamzin was not as explicitly involved in campaigning for rational agriculture, although his ideas on landscape and geography were a clear influence on Andrei's understanding of the meaning of the countryside. Furthermore, Andrei was an active member of his provincial branch of the Moscow Agricultural Society, making him arguably a participant in the campaign as much as a part of the audience.

Bolotov, writing decades earlier, shared with Andrei an understanding that his service to his fatherland lay not in his extensive experiments in agriculture but in his role as an educator and propagator of new ideas.[36] This explains how Andrei, who did not personally take responsibility for agriculture on his estates, could be so active a participant in the campaign for rational agriculture—he understood his role as spreading the word about the possibilities inherent in the Russian village. Unlike Bolotov, Andrei refrained from giving advice on specifics of field and grain (these not being his "department") but instead focused on what he knew best, such as the role of the *khoziaika,* the importance of education, and how the Russian rural county might be studied so that knowledge could form the basis of future improvement. Andrei's participation was no doubt facilitated by earlier models of such contributions (real or invented). In education, for example, the *Northern Bee* published an announcement in 1835 about a new *Children's Journal,* which would direct the campaign for rational agriculture toward the next generation, no doubt gratifying and inspiring Andrei in the process. The journal would feature everything about the "fatherland," wrote its new publisher, A. Ochkin:

> Our extensive Russia, varying in its climate, the peoples inhabiting it, rich in products of all three kingdoms of Nature, will deliver me plentiful, even inexhaustible materials. History, old and new, geography, ethnography, even Russian statistics, Slavic mythology, biographies of famous compatriots, all this, adapted to children's understanding, may become the source of articles that are didactic and engaging.[37]

Andrei Chikhachev was both a participant in the creation of the model and a real embodiment of the ideal landlord early journalists tried to create.[38] Knowing so much more about Andrei's background and private life than about other provincial contributors, it is possible to pinpoint the ways in which the real man deviated from the "type," which suggests some further reasons for the ultimate failure of the entire project to rationalize the countryside. Most of all, the disconnect lay in the assumption on the part of urban writers that there was a prevalent sense of uselessness or meaninglessness among gentry landowners; while some individuals may no doubt have felt this, and the wealthiest elite, those secularized, westernized dwellers of the capitals, are documented as being greatly preoccupied with such feelings, Andrei's understanding was entirely different. He referred to the years before the 1762 emancipation of the nobility from service only as a time when his grandfather's estates were shamefully neglected. By contrast, Andrei's own day brought greater advantages of every kind and filled him with energy for the future. Unlike the older Bolotov, Andrei never became frustrated over failed projects. Andrei moved from one project to another with ever-greater ambition and no small amount of success. When an abrupt change came to Andrei's village, it was brought by the very outside world he feared, through a serf emancipation that left both landlords and serfs in an untenable situation and without the traditional modes of coping with which they were familiar.

In other words, in the earlier part of the nineteenth century there was a real need that Andrei recognized to reform the technology of Russian agriculture, but writers felt the need was for westernization, while readers, judging by Andrei, wanted to reform the moral and educational level of peasant workers. There was likewise a real question about the role of the noble "service class" after the service requirement was abolished, but while urban cultural critics seemed certain that estate management should be the new role, provincial landowners like Andrei and his neighbors took it for granted that there was no crisis in *who* managed estates, only in the financial and educational resources estate managers lacked or the recalcitrance or ignorance of the peasantry (and some landlords).[39] This problem, like virtually all others, Andrei felt could be solved through *vospitanie*.

The problem of authority in the provinces arguably dates much farther back than 1762. Part of the reason for the noble emancipation was that the countryside was being neglected, when it could have been producing much more for state coffers. Surveying the matter from the provinces looking toward the capital, however, it could appear that the state first impoverished the countryside by taking all noblemen into lifetime service, then turned around and sent these men (after generations of life in the capitals or abroad) back into the countryside to tell everyone how to reorganize work that had been done for centuries. In the late eighteenth century, in the midst of the transition period, Mikhail Lomonosov, a prototypical Enlightenment polymath, planned a newspaper to do exactly what the *Agricultural Gazette* would do a generation later, to solicit input from the provinces on how to organically improve production and quality of life. In the late eighteenth century, the project was a failure. A generation later when the central government's interest had flagged somewhat and that of intellectuals had flagged entirely, Andrei Chikhachev and others like him brought to fruition precisely what Lomonsov had envisioned. The difference was that Andrei's generation was the first to be raised with the expectation of remaining in the provinces for life after only a brief adventure in service.[40]

Another of Andrei's core ideas, his understanding of Russianness, exemplifies the process of selective borrowing from which his worldview was derived. For the sources of Andrei's understanding of Russianness, it is necessary to turn away from the intelligentsia and return to the middlebrow writers of advice literature. In her study of cookbooks and advice manuals in imperial Russia, Alison Smith traces to the end of the eighteenth century a challenge increasingly posed to writers of these manuals to "preserve Russianness," pushing writers to move past the direct translations from foreign sources that had hitherto sufficed, and instead define a Russian cuisine and Russian ways of dining (which, among other changes, had to take into account the Orthodox fasting calendar). Despite continued translations and other lapses into western European formulas, over the next fifty years the insistence on nationalizing advice and instructions for the primarily provincial readers of advice manuals would persist.[41] As cookbooks and household manuals became more "Russian," and especially as they incorporated more Orthodox influences, they began to resemble the encyclopedic character of the sixteenth-century *Domostroi*, which also featured instructions on household matters delivered in a male voice to a mostly male audience.[42] Certainly, this literature was part of the background that informed Andrei's interest in nationality.

In addition, Andrei enthusiastically adopted much of the official rendering of Russian nationality that was developed in 1832 by Sergei Uvarov, known as "Official Nationality" and encompassed in the slogan, "Orthodoxy, Autocracy, Nationality." Official Nationality was the autocracy's effort to put an end to dangerous intellectual discussions by providing an answer to the perceived identity crisis. Official Nationality was widely propagated by the academics Stepan Shevyrev and Mikhail Pogodin, men whom the principal Slavophiles respected (while they continued to disagree with them on several central issues, including the role of the state and their assessment of Peter the Great's reforms). The official slogan and the ideas it represented were also disseminated in the journalism of Nikolai Grech and Faddei Bulgarin, who shared unsavory reputations as pawns of Nicholas I's authoritarian regime while enjoying broad popularity with the non-intelligentsia public.[43] They were the editors of the *Northern Bee*, Andrei's favorite journal. Andrei's praise, always fulsome, reached heady heights when it came to Bulgarin, calling him "My Joy," declaring that he always read Bulgarin's articles before all others and instructing Yakov to give him a portrait of his favorite so that he might "look at him more often, in order to admire him more often."[44]

Andrei would return many times to the notion of acquiring a portrait of Bulgarin for his study, suggesting hero worship more than intellectual admiration.[45] Yet, Andrei felt that his readings of Bulgarin were deep, or at least ought to have been: he once complained to Yakov that they had "skimmed" Bulgarin's newspaper too quickly (in the throes of their rapturous enthusiasm) and were thereby robbing themselves of its nuances: "[our] understandings will also be slippery, centrifugal, like a veil, gaseous, gossamer."[46] Instead, Andrei suggested taking it slowly—"without haste, not on postal horses, not on the railroad by steam, no, but rather on one's own horses making two stations each day"—in order to appreciate its "tastiness." Andrei then raved specifically about the articles in issues ten to thirteen written by his favorite: "[M]y sweet, my kind, my clever, tactful, smart, varying, neat, sociable, deft, active, respectable, well-intentioned, exemplary Faddei Venediktovich Bulgarin—Akh, what a Bulgarin!" Going back to their discussion of obtaining a portrait of the hero, he added, "I am so stingy when it comes to money, and still, for a good likeness of him I would truly not spare the blue paper [assignat rubles]." As if all this were not sufficiently admiring, Andrei concluded the already ludicrously effusive passage with a final endearment, saying of Bulgarin, "Such a little berry!!"[47]

Without ever specifying particular tenets of Bulgarin's or which characteristics of his style appealed to him, Andrei made it clear that his sentiments were reflected more completely and accurately in Bulgarin's work than in that of any other author, and apparently this sympathy of sentiment was paramount in his judgment. Since this sympathy was so personal, Bulgarin's critics, of whom Andrei was only dimly aware, could not influence his own pleasure: "No matter what someone else might say, Faddei my Venediktovich writes sensibly, intelligently and from the soul. . . . This is a favorite writer of mine, and of [my favorites] the greatest."[48]

Before beginning his own journalistic career Andrei judged his potential efforts against a standard borne by Bulgarin, and at least in the mid-1830s he found himself wanting; he dramatized the scenario of his rejection by his idol for Yakov's benefit:

> If I had known an author's business a little better, then you would be encountering the letters "A" and "I" [for Andrei Ivanovich] in the Northern Bee for a long time now. . . . Perhaps I should just attack the matter directly . . . Bulgarin will put everything into a hole in the ground, everything into a hole—and in the end, if I continued to pester him, to be annoying, obnoxious—he would burn the entire hole-full and would shoot [a gun loaded with] the ashes on the way to Dorozhaevo and to Borduki.—And because he would possibly use too much gunpowder out of annoyance, then the neighbor from Zimenki having been treated undeservingly, would send a notice to the *zemskii* court; and the Berezovik neighbor, meaning you, would himself begin to ask me via telegraph, and through letters, and in person—"please, don't write! and if you do write, don't send it to St. Petersburg, but rather continue to send to me."[49]

The real Bulgarin, had Andrei known it, was far from living up to his admirer's ideals. As a young Pole during the Napoleonic wars, Bulgarin first joined the French army to fight against the Russians, only to switch sides shortly before the Russian victory.[50] Bulgarin had also been associated with several future Decembrists as a young man, which may in part have drawn him into his activities as an informant for the Third Section (he began in 1826, the year following the Decembrist Rebellion). But even his position as an informant was not as simple a story as it seems: Bulgarin was not fully trusted by the Third Section, and he actually abandoned it from 1831 to 1837 when he lived at his estate in Estonia. He subsequently returned but was never comfortable with his contact in the later period. Scholars have argued that his service to the Third Section, like his earlier service in the Russian army, was attributable to "expediency rather than conviction."

Summarizing Bulgarin's remarkable career, Melissa Frazier concluded that "Bulgarin's chief characteristic was his impressive ability to adapt to new circumstances. Never, though, was Bulgarin exactly at home."[51] Andrei in contrast—never challenged as Bulgarin was by a foreign background and unintentional involvement in politically dangerous circumstances—was a man eminently at home in every sense.

In 1831 in the journal *Telescope* Pushkin published two articles that constituted a now-famous personal attack on Faddei Bulgarin. Pushkin's unsigned review was based on the memoirs of a French "police spy, turncoat, and journalist," Vidocq, written with the expectation that "his fellow writers would recognize Bulgarin as his real subject, and those few who missed it were shortly enlightened by an epigram addressed to 'Vidocq Figliarin [Mountebank].'"[52] While other writers had no difficulty decoding the hidden layers embedded in this review, Andrei, if he saw it, could not have understood the subtext, since it is inconceivable that he would have continued to admire Bulgarin if he knew of his background as a turncoat, even if he had been able to approve the spying.

Though certainly closely connected to Nicholas's Third Section and the censorship regime, the statist vision of Russian national identity that Bulgarin propounded and disseminated did have some positive content, having been grounded originally in the ideas of Sergei Uvarov, a man of broad Enlightenment education and, at least in his earlier years, a sophisticated conservatism. Uvarov's notion of an ideally "Russian" education was one that nurtured sophisticated (and conservative) citizens who were exposed to all that was valuable in Western culture, but who judiciously used that knowledge only to enrich their own native identity.[53] This is a formulation that Andrei—consciously or unconsciously—echoed in his own formulation of an educational program.

Another part of Andrei's loyalty to the state and monarchy was a legacy from his military experience and subsequent fascination for military tales. But this legacy was a mixed one. He did accept uncritically the accounts of Russian military adventures abroad in the state-run journals, retaining his faith in the state even against evidence that these accounts were misleading. It seems, however, that Andrei's subconscious mind harbored some doubts and fears about the arbitrary power of the Russian state and army:

> At first I had a dream in which I was standing on my knees in front of some old fat General, whom I had intentionally insulted; and in his rage he threw a dinner knife at me, which flew next to my head, we were surrounded by a multitude of officers in some somber-looking room. I continued to beg for forgiveness but having not received it, I ended up in some city like Moscow.[54]

Andrei's subconscious thus saw military authority as harsh and without mercy, and his own position vis-à-vis military authority as deeply subservient, since he was on his knees before the general. And, almost comically, the ultimate punishment of Andrei's dream was of course being forced to live in a large city instead of the countryside.

Still another strand in Andrei's progressive conservatism came from the court historian and sentimental writer Nikolai Karamzin. Karamzin famously defined Russian nationality as the people's obedience and love for monarchy, portraying "the people" as the embodiment of Russianness. This quasi-populist notion, though perhaps familiar to Andrei, is not reflected in Andrei's own intellectual output. To Andrei obedience to duty and authority was essential to *any* society and not always a marked characteristic of the representatives of the Russian "people" with whom he had to deal every day.

Andrei's overwhelming emphasis on the importance of land, village, and local particularity in his understanding of and love for homeland probably has its roots in some of Karamzin's other writing. One aspect of Karamzin's writings that Andrei appreciated was his sentimental patriotism ("[I] lay in bed reading Karamzin's Panegyric to Empress Catherine II. Reading good authors. Beautiful food for human mind.").[55] Andrei found the style of Karamzin's writing a great comfort when his mind was disturbed. After he woke suddenly from an unsettling dream one night, Andrei looked around for a book to put his mind at rest and chose Karamzin: "Having opened it at random, I followed everywhere the 'Russian Traveler'—rejoiced together with him, and grieved together with him." Unlike the intelligentsia, Andrei did not automatically understand all literature as a species of political document; rather, he looked at literature as primarily moral in nature.[56] Continuing to describe his experience of reading Karamzin after his nightmare, he wrote: "His style I like so much, some very simple feeling is expressed so sweetly that I would have liked to be acquainted with him, to be his friend. It seems like his feelings are my own. In one word, I admire, am enchanted by his journey[.]"[57]

In the following instance, Andrei fixated further on his personal identification with the great author, imagining sentimental connections across time and space in a way that owes much to Romantic literature in general:

[H]ow did it happen that the book opened on [the description of] March. Eight years before my birth (1790) Karamzin was in Geneva, and 41 years later a creature similar to him in his sensitivity is admiring his pen.—No, I have not read another travel account with such pleasure! He says . . . that "A man's soul is a mirror of the objects surrounding him."[58]

Not surprisingly, Andrei appreciated the similar flights of sentimental fancy undertaken by Karamzin: "Not without pleasure I also read that on the bank of the Rhone in France the author collected several shining little rocks, and keeps them to remember a romantically spent night for the purpose of reminiscing."[59] However, at the same time that Andrei appreciated Karamzin's sentimental style and emotionalism, he grieved that Karamzin's greatest work, this *Notes of a Russian Traveler*, took Europe as its subject rather than Russia: "what's the good of looking at what is someone else's without knowing anything of one's own?"[60]

Andrei insisted that Karamzin's sentimental appreciations be applied to Russian circumstances and enrich Russian life. Happy to discover new ideas and inspiration from abroad, these ideas had value to Andrei only for what they might add to Russian life, not for their foreignness. Moreover, Andrei attempted to practice what he preached, as far as his means allowed him to do; thus he made his own sentimental journey to Kiev and back in 1842. He proudly drew a map of this journey and pasted it onto the cover of his "parallel diary," and in 1850 wrote the following loving description of each and every place he had been to in his life:

> My experience is only [of those provinces] traveled through from Shuia to Petersburg, Kostroma, and Yaroslavl; from Petersburg to Warsaw through Vilno and Grodno; from Moscow to Kiev through Tula and Orel, from Kiev to Kursk and Voronezh and from there to Tula and back to Dorozhaevo. . . . Kiev has excited me, and I keep it lively in my memory, especially on two occasions. There was a beautiful shady garden there, and a large pavilion in the highest, steepest bank of the Dnepr.[61]

One imaginary contributor to a journal edited by Karamzin expressed sentiments that could just as easily come from Andrei's pen, about "the inadvisability of entrusting the education of young noblemen to foreigners."[62] It is not difficult to see what Andrei loved in Karamzin when Karamzin writes what is virtually a portrait of Andrei Chikhachev. To Andrei, Russianness was equated most closely with landscape, literature, and religious traditions, and in Karamzin's sentimental stories "Poor Liza" (mentioned as in Yakov's possession) and "Natalia the Boyar's Daughter," the writer portrayed the Russian landscape as the source of beauty and virtue in his idealized heroines.[63] Karamzin's sense of geography, like Andrei's, rejected the "concentration on the accumulation of unstructured facts and its occasional insistence on formulating all-encompassing abstract theories" characteristic of the universalist early Enlightenment, according to analyst Mikhail Avrekh, in favor of "the newly developed method of topographic description with its continuous movement from the landscape to the object being described and back, as well as between the past and the present of the landscape, taken from the vantage point of a local oddity."[64] This, too, is an aspect of Karamzin's writing that must have attracted Andrei.

So far Romanticism has been conflated with sentimentalism, although Romantics generally defined themselves in contrast to sentimentalism. Romantic writers disclaimed such conventions of sentimentality as the "'powers of apprehension,' 'brilliancy of fancy,' and 'love of literature'" of Scott's Edward Waverley and so many other sentimental heroes. However, it has been persuasively argued that Romanticism was built on a sentimental foundation:

> Romantic writers continue to articulate their major concerns—whether subjectivity or history, social engagement or psychic retreat, domesticity or empire—within the discursive paradigms of sentimental culture, . . . well aware that theirs is a culture preoccupied with the workings of passion, the anatomy of feeling, and the communication of emotion.[65]

It was these latter characteristics that Andrei took from his reading, while apparently not noticing or rejecting the other, unique, tendencies in Romanticism—most crucially, the threads of rebellion and transcendence as well as the more sophisticated aesthetic goals of the movement.[66] Romanticism and sentimentalism are conflated here because Andrei conflated them himself.

Putting together Andrei's serious efforts to educate his own and others' peasants, his involvement with several peasants in his various "inventions" (especially his reliable bai-liff "Rachok" and his talented carpenter "M. Serge"), and his idealized notion of the village as the source of moral purity, industriousness, and progress, it must be noted that this was not the Slavophile romanticization of the village commune. Andrei evinced no interest in the supposedly communal nature of peasant decision-making. Rather, his ideal resembles a "village of letters" (analogous to the eighteenth-century "Republic of Letters") where an intellectual and moral community bound together members of, in this case, different social estates in a common project of enlightenment.[67] It is no coincidence that when he became the author of a regular column in the *Agricultural Gazette* in his late years that he titled it "The Correspondence of an Old Man" (*"Korrespondentsiia startsa"*). Although much of his writing is in the style of a rambling monologue, he conceived of what he was doing as engagement in a larger "correspondence."

Another, equally accurate way of looking at Andrei's ideal world is as a Romantic community of appreciative readers, bound together by ties of sympathy and shared experience. This may have been an unconscious extension of the community of readers Romantic writers envisioned, often as subscribers to the increasingly common lending libraries.[68] Recalling that Andrei himself founded the first public library for serfs in the province, this association of ideas is hard to avoid. Implicit in Andrei's worldview was that his community was a strictly hierarchical one, but Andrei viewed hierarchy as a means of keeping order to the benefit of all, and not as an impediment to community feeling, much less a source of oppression.

One of the most extended discussions of a literary work recorded in the notebook correspondence concerns a French novel titled *The Green Manuscript* by Gustave Drouin-eau. Drouineau wrote in a genre known at the time as the *"roman moral."* These novels emphasized discipline and conformity to family values, which were popular in the period of the French Restoration as a manifestation of the desire to restore order after the revolutionary years.[69] Andrei was not wholly pleased with the first volume, but after completing the second he changed his mind: "I must tell you that the second half of Part II delighted me so much, that I cannot say anything bad about the entire work."[70] Andrei took delight in many small aspects of the narrative, revealing nothing of his sense of the book's philosophical perspective: "The wedding and the description of the family life of Emmanuel and Lalageia—the insult of her at the ball is delightful—Louisa's letter is tragic—has its own physiognomy. Lalageia's visit in prison is touching."[71] Knowing his own ideas about education, however, it is likely that he did not object to the parts of Drouineau's work that uphold the value of discipline and the centrality of family.

Although the many translations from Western presses about agricultural and domestic life were notoriously inappropriate for Russian contexts, this was not always the case, and Andrei was often willing to learn from any useful source. One passage printed in the *Agricultural Gazette* in 1834 suggests that some of his enthusiasms, if not inspired by foreign sources, were reinforced by accounts like this from the West, which he almost certainly read. The piece described a small town called Bazungen in the Duchy of Meiningen, where inhabitants subscribed collectively to agricultural journals, read them at group meetings, and shared the results of their experiments. The piece ended with a statement from the Russian editor that this was "an example worthy of emulation!"[72]

Andrei was not opposed to emulating this example, foreign or not. The following passage from one of Andrei's articles may even seem like a statement of agreement with the myth of Russian "backwardness" compared to western Europe, at first surprising in a conservative patriot:

> Those who live in the houses of our Germans laugh loudly at our [version of] room cleaning, especially before the Holy holiday. They scrub, wash, clean, to the sweat of their brow, at Easter, Christmas, and I don't know when else. Whereas Germans have that 52 times each year, that is, every Saturday.... Having pulled away from the wall the cupboard, dresser, having turned a chair and an armchair upside down, with the force of a schoolteacher over a weak, helpless, young pupil, [Aleksandra's German governess] started to point with her long finger at the pretty spider web and layered dust, saying: what is this? and what is that? No, in all things we are still far from the Germans![73]

Andrei had acknowledged other deficiencies in Russia, and he wrote longingly about European travel in correspondence with his comparatively well-traveled brother-in-law. However, it would be too great a leap to assume that because he bemoaned old-fashioned ideas about hygiene that he considered Russia backward. It was an unfortunate oddity, not a sign of Russia's relative status or achievement overall. Andrei was insatiably curious about the world, including the parts of the world where some of his favorite writers and thinkers originated. And it is only natural that he enjoyed discussing foreign lands with a relative who had actually seen them; there is no such joking or serious discussion of foreign places in his surviving correspondence with anyone else. Thus, his playful game of writing from "Paris" to his brother-in-law must be seen as evidence of his powerful personal curiosity and imagination, not as evidence of dissatisfaction with his own place of origin. He was much too consistently proud and affectionate about the Russian village and country life to read his writings any other way.

A fascinating study of "thinking locally" in British Romantic fiction reveals multiple overlaps with Andrei's worldview. Martha Bohrer's study focuses on Maria Edgeworth's *Castle Rackrent* (1800), George Crabbe's *The Borough* (1810), and John Galt's *Annals of the Parish* (written 1813, published 1821); none of these works is mentioned directly in the

Chikhachev papers, but each is of a type and time period such that it is perfectly possible the Chikhachevs read them. Edgeworth was widely translated in Russia in the early nineteenth century, and *The Borough* was translated at least by the 1850s. Most strikingly, all three works "adopt the scholarly paradigm of the local parson-scholar and take a provincial locale as their main subject."[74] A "parson-scholar" is perhaps the best possible English translation of the terms Andrei used referred to himself: "*starets*" (wise elder) in his journalism and "*ktitor*" (lay church elder) for his philanthropy.

Bohrer locates these works, like Karamzin, as firmly grounded in the early nineteenth-century refocusing of Enlightenment encyclopedism toward greater depth and accuracy on specific, local subjects at the cost of achieving universal coverage. Shifting attention from centers to peripheries, these works "imagine[d] a new kind of British rural world, not chorographic, topographic, or pastoral, but one consisting of diverse provincial localities, each worthy of study because of their unique environment and local society."[75] Bohrer credits the emergence of these new perspectives to growth in provincial towns thanks to industrialization—a factor quite absent in the Russian case—but also to the "concurrent growth of provincial intellectual communities," communities that are comparable to the Russian Free Economic Society, the Moscow Agricultural Society, and the expansion of printed reading materials available to provincial readers in the first half of the nineteenth century.[76]

Bohrer emphasizes how these works, as compared to earlier rural tales, shift perspective from "a view of the countryside from the country house to a view . . . from the village."[77] While Andrei's writing, both private and public, is by definition based in the country house in the sense that it is written by a landowner sitting in his study looking out at the village (populated by people he actually *owned*), in another way it is possible to see Andrei's various writings as analogous to the British stories. Andrei, as a provincial noble of middling income in a culture (and history) dominated by a tiny minority of much wealthier elites, does in effect shift our attention from the cultural trendsetters of the capitals to rural communities. And, much like the Russian campaign for rational agriculture (in which Andrei took his small part), these British authors, too, imagined their reading audience as ignorant or unappreciative. Finally, like Andrei's writing, these British works were not nostalgic: "They offer ways to think locally in a world increasingly enmeshed in a global economy and culture. In *Annals of the Parish*, local worlds do not persist in unchanging isolation from the global; economic development and social change are intimately tied to exchanges with the broader world."[78]

If it is easy to see traces of Andrei's thinking in various corners of the contemporary landscape of ideas, is it also possible to find echoes of Andrei in the wider public of readers? One of the several fictitious contributors to the *Library for Reading* that its editor, Osip Senkovsky, invented was one Baron Brambeus, whom the Chikhachevs specifically mentioned reading. Melissa Frazier described Brambeus as "a flamboyant provincial with a penchant for personal asides and a lively, earthy sense of humor." His writing was "marked by a chatty, intimate tone and a great deal of apparently personal detail." Frazier argues that "Senkovskii created Brambeus and others to deliberately destabilize identity and authorship."[79] Ironically, faux contributors like Brambeus produced a real one in Andrei Chikhachev.

In the 1770s Nikolai Novikov "produced a gallery of social types" on the pages of his satirical journals, many of whom maintained longevity in the Russian cultural consciousness. Prominent among these was "the province-bound gentry-man," whom Bella Grigoryan describes in her study of the development of this "type" in artistic literature as "a rather flexible figure, his duties debated, his social identity in the process of being formed," a "provincial landowner who communicates with like-minded individuals, members of his social estate," "who opts to mind his estate instead of serving."[80] The "type" was in flux over the many decades he walked across the pages of Russian belles lettres, but in the 1820s and 30s he was formed in part by fictitious contributors to journals and newspapers like Brambeus, and in novels by writers like Faddei Bulgarin.

The "type" of provincial landowner devoted to state service through provincial industriousness, and the "type" who wrote enthusiastically to journals with folksy and excessively detailed anecdotes about his domestic arrangements and private life could not be more clearly embodied in a real-life human being than it is in Andrei Chikhachev. The resemblance is so uncanny that it seems impossible to believe Andrei's natural tendencies in this direction were not strongly encouraged, at least, by his reading of Brambeus and Bulgarin. Andrei consciously took up the pen in emulation of his heroes, and he may have consciously copied their style, but there is more to the resemblance than these factors.

The irony of Andrei resembling so closely the "type" is that the creators and perpetuators of the "type" eventually either abandoned him or developed him in quite different directions out of a sense that real provincial landlords were not living up to the model. But there was Andrei. And on the pages of the journals and newspapers of the 1840s, Brambeus and his ilk gave way to other real people. Andrei and others like him did more than spill ink on ramblings about cheesecloth and toothaches and clean air. They deeply and sincerely believed in their moral and intellectual service to the empire. Print culture in the 1820s and '30s did not create Andrei in the sense of giving him a worldview he did not independently hold, but it seems likely that this print culture reinforced Andrei's inclinations and gave him a vocabulary and a place—newsprint columns—where he could articulate it for himself and others.

Osip Senkovsky wrote much of the content for his journal himself but masked it as coming from a panoply of colorful, pseudonymous others. Frazier argues that Senkovsky was engaging in a deliberate Romantic play with identities and the nature of the relationship between reader and writer.[81] Andrei, on the other hand, argued forcefully in an 1846 article in the *Agricultural Gazette* that all articles should be signed by their real writers, with not only names but addresses too. Andrei's goals being considerably more pragmatic and less complex than those of Romantic writers, he urged contributors to periodicals to be open so that interested readers could engage with writers in further conversation. "How good would it be," he asked, if readers could more readily trust writers, and if those who would normally never meet might become acquainted in writing, perhaps even become close.[82] Andrei maintained this stance as the years passed: in 1848 he published another article titled, "About the Common Participation of the Nobles in the *Agricultural Gazette,*"[83] and toward the end of his publishing career, in 1865, another article appeared, "Acquaintanceship by Correspondence (About the Exchange of Letters from Colleague to Colleague through the Editor)."[84] Here, in the full confidence of having been published for two decades, Andrei used the term "colleague" to describe contributors rather than "nobles"; he had begun to consider himself a professional.

Andrei spoke from experience about the possibilities for acquaintanceship and even close friendship through correspondence about newspaper articles. His good friend the Astrakhan landowner Vladimir Kopytovskii, with whom Andrei revived the "notebook correspondence" system that had lain dormant since his quarrel with Yakov, who referred to Andrei as his "sweet brother," was a man Andrei never actually met. They became acquainted when Kopytovskii wrote to Andrei in response to an article. Other letters from readers survive, and Andrei wrote to other amateur journalists whose work he admired. He also annotated his copies of the *Agricultural Gazette* with little notes of approval, such as "completely agree" and "very interesting!" acting out a dialog as he read.

In 1850 Andrei received a letter from Aleksei Durakovskii of Pskov province, who wrote because he was just embarking on "agricultural pursuits" on an estate inherited from his father. He wanted advice on such topics as how to "order" the most necessary buildings, and how to "teach peasants useful crafts," especially sieve-making, a topic on which Andrei had recently written.[85] Another of Andrei's correspondents was a Elisei Mochalin, who referred to himself as Andrei's "grandson." Either this was a metaphorical relationship because of a significant age difference, or perhaps Elisei was the son of Andrei's godson, so that the relationship was religious rather than by blood. In any case, Elisei Mochalin was another devoted reader of the *Agricultural Gazette*, sharing Andrei's deep concerns—and specific positions—on civic matters, and he even wrote in the same ornate style. In other words, both were products of the same provincial culture bred on the works of Bulgarin and others like him.[86]

And Nikolai Cherepanov, a close friend of Yakov's, wrote to Andrei in April 1850, saying that his favorite author, too, was Bulgarin, but that he enjoyed Andrei's own writing still more: "your letter surpasses in my mind all of his compositions in the pleasantness of its style and engagingness, and for your labors regarding the description of Kovrov county, many and many venerable persons will tell you thanks." He himself thanked Andrei for the loan of some books, mentioning specifically that even though the sixth part of Bulgarin's memoirs was not published in the newspapers, he was able to read it in the *Library for Reading.* [87]

Still another like-minded soul was Andrei's childhood friend N. Saranskii. Saranskii had been out of touch with Andrei for many years, so their similarities were not due to reinforcing each other's ideas over years of friendship, as Andrei and Yakov did. When Saranskii wrote to Andrei in 1850 he described his career in the years since he had left service and busied himself with estate management: "I care not so much about myself as after my peasants," and here he used an affectionate (and paternalistic) diminutive for them, "*muzhichki*." Like Andrei he enjoyed talking with his peasants, but he also knew how much doing so worked to his advantage: "My conversation with them brings me inexpressible pleasure. This tender technique brings me their full trust." Saranskii then asked Andrei for advice, because he wanted to teach his peasants some crafts: "This will benefit peasants because they will spend winter with their families and [it] will benefit him because he'll get the craftsmen he needs."[88]

As Russian print culture matured (even while the numbers of periodicals or their print runs were often decreasing), other real landowners contributed to periodicals as Andrei did. The *Agricultural Gazette* probably saw more of this than others for the obvious reason that it was aimed at an audience of provincial landowners, focused its coverage almost exclusively on agricultural, local, and domestic matters, and perhaps because, as a government-sponsored newspaper, it was relatively uninteresting to more creative writers. The *Agricultural Gazette* actively encouraged submissions, not just from provincial landlords but from peasants as well. According to the son of the newspaper's longtime editor, "peasants often wrote his father with comments on the periodical."[89] So did landowners. Even as early as 1835 the editors thanked a long list of named contributors, none of whom were titled, and boasted of having twice the total number of contributors as in 1834.[90]

Contributions from landlords were often brief and rarely led to the kind of ongoing publishing career that Andrei built for himself, but they do demonstrate that Andrei was not the only real embodiment of the "type." In 1835, for example, a Guards Second Lieutenant Sinelnikov wrote that he "frequently came across questions offered by Mssrs. Subscribers to the *Gazette* and whose solutions served to explain many curious and useful articles in the economic area," so he "endeavor[ed] to offer three questions, whose resolution would without doubt be of benefit." The three questions concerned resin, where one could obtain Spurry seeds, and queried the weight of Spanish wool.[91] Other submissions might be annotated by the editors like this one from the same year: "This article, composed by V. S. Verzhbitskii, landlord of Mogilev province, was submitted to the Editor of the *Agricultural Gazette* from the Imperial St.-Petersburg Free Economic Society for printing." The passing on of the submission confirms that the Free Economic Society was less interested in minor landlords without reputation than was the *Agricultural Gazette*.[92] In addition to articles and short commentaries, the *Agricultural Gazette* printed contributions of data from readers, such as a chart on the seeding and harvesting of grain over fifteen years provided by the landlord Ivan Pleshcheev of the village Ivanopolia in Bakhmutskii County.[93]

Still other examples of men writing and working in the same mold as Andrei abound, although none achieved significant fame, or any interest from intellectual elites (who only occasionally deigned to eviscerate them with words as Ogarev did to Andrei). One such man was Petr Shemiott, an agricultural writer, who like Andrei believed that "[b]lessed Russia . . . makes up one patriarchal, happy family, guided by the Father-Autocrat."[94] Similarly, Alison Smith quotes another writer stating that life in the provinces "might be less brilliant with urban luxury and noise, but it is infinitely more touching, happy, and useful."[95] In 1849 a landowner named V. N. Pogozhen wrote to Bulgarin's journal *Ekonom,* attributing all failures in Russia "to negligence, to bad habits from child-hood, to lack of education, to blind superstitions and attachment to ancient practices . . . despite the fact that education and enlightenment have already penetrated into many parts of Russia." Pogozhen's response to this deplorable state of affairs was identical to Andrei's—he "decided to start with the children of his estate; in his mind, giving them a proper education was the best means to improve matters."[96] Yet another such landowner was I. V. Saburov of Penza province, who wrote "long treatises" published in *Notes of the Fatherland* in 1842 and 1843. Like Andrei, Saburov was an actual person using a real name, though he seems to have been more of a true agriculturalist than a theoretician of the provinces as Andrei was (he corrected the *Library for Reading* on the difference between black earth and humus, for example).[97]

More prominent than these men was V. P. Burnashev, who was briefly successful as an agricultural writer and served in several government ministries. As elite interest in the campaign for rational agriculture waned, so did Burnashev's career. But in the 1830s and '40s he wrote under his own and other names on agriculture and industry as well as on "educational books for children and peasants," along with contributions to *Ekonom* and the journal of the Free Economic Society. His career faded—not coincidentally—after the serf emancipation in 1861, and he died in poverty and obscurity.[98] Alison Smith describes his central goals as: "imagining Russia's best future as a place where modern, rational (and western) techniques, interpreted by a nobility that took seriously its duty to improve agriculture, supported an essentially Russian and essentially agricultural way of life."[99] Burnashev was, like Andrei, a Russian nationalist without denying that valuable lessons could be learned from western Europe (among his many projects, Burnashev supported the importation of French influences in his cookbooks, while organizing them around the Orthodox fasting calendar).[100]

The best-known parallel to Andrei Chikhachev is Andrei Bolotov, a man two genera-tions older who exhibited the same graphomania; he too was obsessed with the minutiae of village life and with propagating its many advantages. His published work reached greater audiences than Andrei's, but it was of a similar type, a jumble of folksy advice and personal anecdotes emphasizing the practical and the everyday over the universalistic "scientific" advice of the Free Economic Society in its earliest days. Bolotov recom-mended foreign teachings when they seemed relevant and useful, without either fetishiz-ing or automatically rejecting anything on the basis of foreignness alone. Some of his advice that may have seemed far-fetched, such as that landlords should teach literacy to all peasant children "through which they will come to know the law," became, decades later, dear to the heart of Andrei and his sympathetic readers and fellow contributors in the *Agricultural Gazette.* [101]

These several counterparts to Andrei Chikhachev shared the characteristics that make him, and them, living embodiments of the imaginary "type" first articulated in print by Novikov. Other writers after Novikov took up his theme in a curious mixture of both fiction and reality, further blurring the lines between art imitating life and life imitating art. Historian John Randolph discussed Derzhavin's "almost fetishistic" description of village minutiae in his 1807 "Russian country house poem," in his study of the private life of the Bakunin family (Aleksandr Bakunin was a friend of Derzhavin's). The Bakunins, though of modest wealth, were far more worldly and well-connected than the Chikhachevs, as Aleksandr Bakunin's friendship with Derzhavin, the great poet of his age, suggests. Randolph portrays the late eighteenth-century Bakunins as part of the process of re-defining noble service to the fatherland as land stewardship, not without difficulty.[102]

A transitional literary figure in the process of working out the nobleman's role in the countryside was Nikolai Gogol. According to literature scholar Bella Grigoryan, Gogol struggled with this question in the late 1840s as he was working on the (never finished) second volume of *Dead Souls*. As part of his struggle to articulate his own vision of the provincial nobleman, Gogol parodied Bulgarin's earnest efforts to present positive provincial role models. In real life, Gogol also appears to have tried to enact the role of the earnest and productive landowner. Gogol may have inadvertently been more accurate than he thought, in that his "work" on his estates consisted of elaborate plans that he passed on to his mother and sisters for implementation. His instructions to his female relations were, according to Grigoryan, "[w]ritten in a familiar, conversational tone. . . . Meant for a very small audience, this is a decidedly private, domestic kind of text that will only be fully understood by someone who knows well the spatial organization of the estate, as well as the markings made by the author prior to his departure from Vasilevka." Among his instructions Gogol insisted that one of the women personally oversee work in the fields (as Natalia Chikhacheva did), though even in this private document Gogol used a masculine pronoun to refer to specific women.[103]

Gogol's dropped thread was picked up in Ivan Goncharov's 1847 novel *A Common Story*, which traces the development of the hero Avduev "from a young provincial with naively misplaced hopes for writerly fame to a practically minded denizen of the northern capital." The path from an ambitious but deluded aspiring writer to a recognized professional writer revolves around a parallel evolution in Avduev's thinking about the provincial estate. He begins his writing career naively imagining provincial life from the safe distance of the capital; he then goes out into the country to discover that much of the advice he had produced was wrong, and he finally returns to "study more and write a book." Grigoryan points out that "his work as a journalist who writes prescriptive texts about model gentry domestic culture is meant to coincide with his turn away from the foggy dreams of an enraptured dilettante-writer towards the more sober-minded sensibility of the Positive Age."[104] Finally, there is even a western European precedent for the imaginary model reader who seemingly comes to life: a French merchant named Jean Ranson was so moved by Rousseau's *Julie* (1761) that he wrote many letters to the author, addressing Rousseau as *"l'Amia* Jean-Jacques," echoing Andrei's imaginary close friendship with his "Faddei my Venediktovich."

Andrei's synthesis of the ideas of his time was thus not unique: he had a community of like-minded peers in the Moscow Agricultural Society and in the readers of his own articles, with some of whom he corresponded.[105] It is not a coincidence that the vast majority of his articles appear in the *Agricultural Gazette*, which catered to his true peers among the middling gentry. The success of Andrei's publishing career may be due to his deft synthesis of these ideas for readers who were likewise concerned with preserving their traditional values, and yet anxious to prosper and to ensure greater opportunities for their children than they had themselves enjoyed. Andrei had found a way of looking at the world that synthesized seemingly disparate ideas and that embraced Russianness, without accepting the many material and moral deficiencies that provincial Russians saw all around them. It should be no surprise that his articles were accepted enthusiastically by the *Gazette* editors. Nor is it surprising that recent studies based on print culture and agriculture reveal many other men who shared Andrei's core values and perspective on the importance of the provincial estate to Russia's future. It would be surprising, indeed, if his point of view on the world were not a fairly common one among the educated, essentially conservative, and economically insecure provincial gentry. Their values have been forgotten not because they were rare or aberrant but because they were unacknowledged or despised by the urban intellectuals who dominated Russian literary and historical narratives.

By the mid-nineteenth century it was probably too late to resolve the tremendous problems of serfdom through education alone, but the significance of Andrei's ideas was that they lacked both the defensiveness and pessimism of the vested establishment and the resentful alienation of the intelligentsia. Being free of the intellectual circles of the capital cities, Andrei arguably lacked the companionship of intellectual peers, but he gained freedom from polarized debate. He was neither a Westernizer nor a Slavophile, neither a liberal nor a classic conservative, neither reactionary nor radical. He was loyal but looked forward to progress through change. He sought to use his westernized education to see Russia more clearly and understand it in greater depth. He wanted social change without sacrificing his social values or the political status quo. This sets Andrei apart from the members of recognized intellectual circles. Although his ideology was cobbled together from many sources and certainly derivative, it was nevertheless independent in that he ascribed to no one school of thought. As he put it himself: in Paris, in St. Petersburg, in Moscow, and in Borduki "there are little articles that are quite good."[106]

Conclusion

DURING THEIR LONG lives together, Andrei and Natalia experienced peace and enough prosperity to invest in capital improvements, which would be enjoyed by their heirs, they hoped, for generations to come. They experienced trials and loss, but they saw two of their children grow to adulthood, they were close to several grandchildren, enjoyed a rich social life, succeeded at their work, and were respected for their efforts by their peers, including, for Andrei, the thousands of readers of his journal articles.

This life story is a marked contrast to the experiences of Andrei and Natalia's children. Aleksei and his wife, Anna, and Aleksandra's widower, Vasili Ragozin, reached full adulthood just as the debates and reforms of the 1860s transformed the bases of the agricultural life they had been reared to inherit. They were better educated than their parents, but their education outdistanced the opportunities the late-imperial Russian state could offer them, while opportunities to lead an independent landowning life became substantially restricted when the end of serfdom upset the precarious financial balance of middling property-holders. Anna Boshniak, Aleksei's wife, had engineering knowledge she would never use. Aleksei worked for the railroad in Vladimir, but by his own admission his duties were far from challenging. Only Aleksandra's widower, Rogozin, was fully employed. He was elected justice of the peace for his county in 1866, which he said would make him "busier than was good for his health."[1] As a local judge, his duties were tasks that were previously performed by landowners—Rogozin's own father among them—before serf emancipation in 1861, but now the relationship between nobles and peasants was bureaucratized, dismantling the paternalistic relationships of the old village.[2]

Provincial landowners like Andrei Chikhachev had had ideas for how the emancipation should come about—slowly and with the gradual education and professionalization of both peasantry and gentry—but they also had an accurate sense that the dismantling of serfdom was beyond their control; it would be decided in St. Petersburg by the emperor, his bureaucrats, and by the wealthiest nobles. The letters Andrei saved from 1860 and 1861 demonstrate that he and his correspondents watched the emancipation discussions from the sidelines, anxiously waiting to find out under what terms their lives would be transformed. A letter from Aleksei to his parents on January 15, 1861 described a trip to Vladimir, where elections related to "the peasant question" were taking place. He wrote that "two nobles" were elected to represent the province and given a salary of 2,000 rubles each.[3] Aleksei did not name the nobles elected; they were not among his or his parents' acquaintances. The central body working out emancipation terms was the Editorial Commission, led by chairman Ya. I. Rostovstev. In 1860 Andrei and his friends pinned their hopes for an emancipation that did not impoverish the countryside on Rostovstev, only to hear of his sudden death. Elisei Mochalin wrote: "General Rostovtsev, the man on whom the hopes of all Russia were resting, died. They say that affairs have passed to Miliutin, for whom there is not much hope. Let His holy will be done! Events are running by themselves and will reach their own definite limit."[4]

Clearly, that "limit" was going to be reached without the input of people like Andrei, Aleksei, and their friends, and equally clearly, they were not optimistic about the eventual result. In an earlier letter, Mochalin had conveyed more encouraging rumors about the Editorial Commission: "They also say that it is supposed to give peasants personal freedom, and with landlords they must voluntarily come to a contractual agreement. In my opinion, this is the best outcome of the peasant question. To a bad lord no one will go— and this will make him be good." At this time Mochalin still optimistically hoped the commission was coming to a conclusion that matched his and Andrei's own ideal. Further, "they are gathering information about members of Economic Societies and landlords who are well familiar with agriculture. For what? So far I don't know!"[5] Mochalin was right to question the rumor—the various organizations and published agricultural writers like Andrei were in fact never given a meaningful voice in the reform.

In addition to serf emancipation, other vast social and cultural changes were occurring around the midcentury, including a reform of the judicial system. And amid overall educational expansion, women were presented with unprecedented opportunities. Discussions of "the Woman Question"—or what women's place in society was or ought to be— were undermining the gender order on which marriages like Andrei and Natalia's were based. As the nineteenth century drew to a close, there was a general awareness of a "marriage crisis," in which "new opportunities for social mobility . . . shook to its foundations Russia's hierarchical social order."[6]

Divorce was not completely unheard of in the decades before emancipation. In fact, Andrei and Natalia knew of at least one unfortunate case among their acquaintance. An unsigned 1829 letter informed "sister" Natalia Ivanovna and "brother" Andrei Ivanovich that "Polonka" was divorcing her husband and "he fleeced her completely, she gave him all of [her] property, only leaving herself 200 souls . . . that are mortgaged and 60 thousand [rubles] of private debt."[7] But the late nineteenth century saw a widespread phenomenon of traditional marriage roles no longer being taken for granted. Those who wrote about marriage began with renewed vigor and urgency to promote domesticity, now increasingly spelling out a female role that was much more strictly limited than it had previously been in Russia.

The flourishing of the cult of domesticity in the post-emancipation period and its connections to aspirations to "culture" and gentility have recently been examined.[8] Barbara Alpern Engel emphasizes the redefining of male behavior, even more than the simultaneous elevating and limiting of the female sphere, as central to this development. The influence of the cult of domesticity on real women was a "contradictory" process, with different ramifications in various contexts.[9] Engel argues that these contradictions reflect the still relative lack of importance of the cult of domesticity on women's roles in the nineteenth century: "Economic conditions persisted in limiting the extent to which the cult of domesticity affected the real behavior of real women."[10] The "importance of the *khoziaika*" persisted, even as domains were shrinking for provincial gentry women in the wake of emancipation. Engel found in her study of divorce petitions that "[i]t is the dignity, status, and authority vested in the position of *khoziaika*, rather than homemaking itself, that stands out in women's plaints and self-presentations and in the responses to them of other people."[11] Furthermore, in the documents Engel examines, women's responsibilities in the household were rarely mentioned, except when men infringed on their sphere, and in one case a husband was criticized for understanding his wife's duties too narrowly.[12]

While over the second half of the nineteenth century domesticity had an inconsistent effect on real women's spheres, men's roles were re-imagined in significant ways in the post-emancipation period: "[Men] spilled considerable ink discussing their role in public life, their success at work or in the widening public sphere."[13] Participation in an intellectual sphere and achieving "culture," (understood to be acquired, not "bred") had already been a strong influence on Russian gentry men's self-definition and understandings of masculinity, as Andrei's story demonstrates. But when emancipation removed (in theory) the imbalance between free nobles and unfree peasants, the male role as state servitor lost its last legal foundation. At the same time, the influence of the intelligentsia through printed media was constantly increasing. In addition, the expansion of education was allowing more people from non-noble estates to aspire to "culture" and intellectual fulfillment. These developments influenced the male side of the cult of domesticity in ways unique to Russian circumstances. Russian men, especially of the middling estates, did emphasize their duties to provide for their families, but they also sought to establish their reputations among their peers and to contribute to the public good. Status among male peers has been shown to be a crucial factor in masculinity in Victorian England as well, but in the Russian case aspirations to public service, clearly linked to a much earlier service ethic, became combined with aspirations to culture and gentility.[14]

Along with the new emphasis on Western-style domesticity came a rediscovery of the sixteenth-century advice manual *Domostroi*, which describes a female head of household in terms nearly as expansive as Natalia's self-definition as *khoziaika*. In the *Domostroi*, however, husbands were advised not only to oversee their wives' morality along with that of children and servants but also to beat them as necessary (perhaps reflecting in part a primarily militaristic early modern understanding of elite masculinity). In the late nineteenth century the *Domostroi* was found by publicistic writers to be a convenient model of what the modern marriage was expected *not* to be. The expansive wifely role was ignored, while the beatings were lampooned, so that modern husbands who expected wives to stay in their kitchens appeared civilized by comparison.[15]

This latter change, too, is reflected in the Chikhachev documents. Aleksei's wife, Anna Konstantinovna Boshniak, left to posterity a notebook "on mechanical engineering," taken from 1848 university lectures delivered by Professor Ostrogradskii (a preeminent mathematician who taught in an number of institutions including the Pedagogical Institute).[16] This education, unimaginable for a woman of her class in Natalia's generation, may well have changed the terms of Anna's marriage to Aleksei. They lived apart for a number of years following her illness in 1860, though the reasons for the separation are unclear.

In July 1860, Anna wrote affectionately to her parents-in-law to explain to them her dilemma of whether to travel to the healthier climate of the Crimea with her relatives and oldest son, Kostya. She hoped to permanently improve her health, but would leave behind her husband, Aleksei, and younger son, "Andryusha," who would live with his Chikhachev grandparents in her absence. Anna explained that her relatives and acquaintances said that she was wrong not to go to Crimea, "and that I am not caring enough about the happiness of my husband, not wanting to use such a convenient opportunity to repair my health." Yet, curiously, in the very next clause she explained that the crux of her decision to travel related to having the funds—right now she was "getting [money] from the common [funds]" while "later during our separation I will not be able to undertake anything." The "our" in "our separation" refers to herself and her husband, and the word she chose for "separation" (*razdel*) was usually used to refer to the legal separation of property between married spouses. If she intended the word to convey only the physical separation they would experience because she was traveling, it would have been an idiosyncratic usage of the word, while her mention of funds supports the notion that *razdel* referred instead to a legal separation. Furthermore, her next sentence hints that she may have had emotional reasons for leaving: "And so I don't know what to do, perhaps I will even dare [to do it] because the returning spasms have shown me for sure that there is more than <u>one</u> cause for my illness, and that I will not get completely well without undertaking something decisive." Anna concluded this letter with the words "don't be angry at your much-loving and much-respectful daughter."[17] Her next, equally emotional missive, with significant passages crossed out, again suggested that her relationship with Aleksei was complicating her decision to travel for her health. She wrote that he had visited, but she was "in no condition" to describe his stay. Indeed, her subsequent attempt at an explanation was so heavily crossed out and so haphazardly written that it is incoherent, but the words "sad to remember," "parted with him," and "see him again" demonstrate that her emotional turmoil centered on Aleksei. She mentioned some hope of happier circumstances in the future but concluded, "but still this parting is very, very hard for me, I don't even know how this year will drag on, but God is merciful!"[18]

By December 1860 Anna complained to her husband's parents that she had had no news from Aleksei for more than three months, and that she was so ill she could not write.[19] Andrei and Natalia then received a letter from Aleksei explaining that "[f]rom Vladimir I also wrote to her but unfortunately forgot to congratulate her [on her birthday or name day], for which I now apologize."[20] Andrei forwarded his letter to Anna and her relatives, and they sent it back with a letter of their own, including a postscript by Anna's son Kostya, but without a word about Aleksei.[21] A few months later, in mid-February 1861, Anna wrote to her in-laws again while Aleksei was staying with them, explaining in her short letter that she was "ill in body and soul" and concluding, "Aleksei, I kiss Your [hands],"[22] using the formal "you" (*Vashi*).

In another letter Anna apologized to her in-laws, saying she was sorry she could not "be useful" because of her health. Surprisingly, she added, "the children . . . to some extent need me, and I tell you positively, my dears, that I can't stay in Ushakovo and do not wish [to;] instead of benefit this will only bring me harm. I have my own family and my own corner where I can live if I can't go away." It is not clear whether she expected her husband and children to reject her, leaving her to her "own corner," or if she was saying she preferred to be there. In any case, she was seriously upset—her letter is incoherently written and nearly illegible, and she concludes, "sometimes I feel so horrified that you can't even imagine."[23] In her next letter Anna begged her father-in-law's forgiveness for her "doubts" about his attachment to her. She apologized for not expressing everything she should have, but "apathy would have taken me over, and therefore I once more ask [you] to forgive your daughter for her mistrust, who is broken by unending suffering and has lost almost all hope for the better; your letters made me more than once regret my mistake." She then described her illness is some detail, saying she had no strength to sit, needed to be carried to the bath, and in addition had an inflammation in her stomach. The fact that she could "barely hold a pencil" explains the incoherency of her letters. She confessed that "grumbling took [her] over more than once" and concludes, "do pray for Your daughter who loves and deeply respects you."[24]

A final letter from this period, from Aleksei, notes only that "I have not written to Annochka for a while and have not had [letters] from her."[25] Whether the causes of Anna and Aleksei's separation stemmed from financial, health, or emotional difficulties (or from all three), the fact remains that by living apart they lacked the stable and amicable partnership from which Andrei and Natalia benefited both financially and emotionally. Moreover, even though Aleksei had inherited Berezovik from his uncle Chernavin already in 1845 and expected to eventually inherit Dorozhaevo also, his letters from this period suggest that the income he derived from his estates in the 1860s was not sufficient to provide for himself and his family, causing him to live in Vladimir for months at a time and eventually semi-permanently, while he worked in various civil offices. Like Aleksei, his son, Kostya, and Kostya's sons would also retain professional positions in addition to the estates they owned at Dorozhaevo and Berezovik, and the other small properties they had inherited, apparently because these lands could no longer produce a subsistence income for their families after emancipation.

While the story of Andrei and Natalia's family comes to a close with the last sets of letters and account books kept in the 1860s, the Chikhachev family carried on through Aleksei's son, Konstantin ("Kostya"), who inherited Dorozhaevo after Andrei's death in 1875. Konstantin still owned the estate at Dorozhaevo when Tsar Nicholas II abdicated the throne in 1917; he died a year later, after the Bolshevik Revolution but before revolutionary events had caught up to Vladimir province. One of Konstantin's sons, Aleksandr (born April 20, 1879), had already become a local magistrate with the rank of titular councilor and a director of a music school in Kovrov, before the Revolution. He emigrated through the Crimea in 1919 and his later fate is unknown. Konstantin's younger son, Anatolii, was educated in mathematics at Moscow University and attended the Mikhailovskii artillery academy. He was an ensign in the field artillery in 1916 and then served in an artillery division in the town of Alatyr in January 1917. Two years later, in January 1919, he was conscripted into the Bolshevik Red Army. Later he settled in Kovrov to teach mathematics. In 1925 he married a Evgeniia Andreevna Tiurina, "of proletarian origins." In 1918 it was Konstantin's daughter Elena who helped the village of Dorozhaevo convert the Chikhachevs' "stone" manor house into the village school. The house—built "sound as a bell"—still stands and until very recently continued to operate as the village school (it is now a museum).[26]

It seems likely that Andrei, obsessed all his life with education and the founder of a serf library, would be pleased at the use of his hard-earned house for a public school—if he could accept the fact of the Revolution, that is. Andrei may have been preoccupied with education to an unusual degree, but for generations the provincial gentry as a group had valued education and family ties highly, as essential means of securing their children's futures. Though their extended noble families were a source of pride, support, and social credit, in their everyday lives they lived with a different kind of extended family that included the serfs they owned, whom they often saw as second set of children. Lower in status and with different needs than their actual children, serfs were nonetheless treated with similar paternalism: they needed to be fed, clothed, and trained toward a practical way of making a living. From Andrei's point of view the peasants of Dorozhaevo could be disobedient or disappointing, but they were a necessary, natural part of his world and could not be avoided or fully controlled. His relationship with them was at its best one of constant negotiation, and it frequently entailed intense daily frustration, no doubt on both sides. As Andrei was aware, it would be up to his children's generation to re-negotiate the relationship between provincial landowners and the serfs who continued to populate the same villages and work the same land—but under new terms.

While a common trope in some early histories of Russia has been to portray Russian society as a system of slavery, in which only the tsar was free and the rest of society was to one degree or another his slave, Augustine in his study of provincial landowner attitudes suggested a different model of authority, based around the family as an organizing principle that was metaphorically re-enacted at every level of society. In this model, *all* the members (including the tsar or father) were to some degree unfree, since they all owed certain obligations to the others, but power was nevertheless highly differentiated, with most of it resting with the father figure: "In such a system a man's worth and standing were not judged by his success or failure in living up to abstract rules of behavior (as in the Western model), but by the internal test of his family relationships with his superiors."[27]

There is evidence from a wide variety of realms to suggest that this family metaphor of authority was a powerful one throughout Russian society in the eighteenth and nineteenth centuries.[28] The family model of authority was not unique to Russia; it was common throughout Europe, and in Russia may have been in part a borrowing of Western rhetoric.[29] The family model was, on its most basic level, a means of justifying the almost unlimited authority of monarchs and aristocrats. At the same time, in theory paternalism was meant to curb the worst excesses of absolute authority. As criticism of old regimes increased over the course of the eighteenth century, the patriarchal ideology this authority was based on also came under attack.[30] However, in Russian society at least, the family model seems to have become reinvigorated, especially at the hands of conservative and nationalist thinkers, in the early nineteenth century. For theorists like Sergei Glinka, for the people who founded the many institutions based on the notion of *vospitanie* in which family models were copied (even while students' literal families were often rejected as insufficiently enlightened to carry out a proper *vospitanie* personally), and for many unremarkable people like Andrei Chikhachev, the family model served as a way of understanding their society and ameliorating some of its worst aspects.

All positive moral values, for Andrei as well as for Bulgarin and other loyal conservatives, lay in knowing and fulfilling one's role, and so it was critical to them that social roles be well defined and stable. Autocracy was meant to be benign—that was *its* role—and so its authoritarian nature could not bode ill insofar as its role was fulfilled. In precisely the same way, a father's role and a husband's role was meant to be benign—nourishing, in every sense—toward children and wife. If an individual father or husband was cruel, the role was not conceived wrongly; rather, the role was not properly fulfilled by that individual, and he was responsible to God for his failings. The same logic applied, as well, to the serf owner (male or female, presumably). Thus, when society failed, it was not because the role of individuals or groups within it was inappropriate, unjust, or oppressive, but merely that those roles were not being embodied completely—"conscientiously"—as they were meant to be by God's law.

There is one way in which this Russian adaptation of the family model of authority seems to have been peculiar. As has been shown in Jessica Tovrov's study of family dynamics and is abundantly evident also in the Chikhachev documents, family roles were understood in elite Russian society as very rigidly *defined,* but they could be filled in any number of flexible ways depending on the practical circumstances: as Tovrov puts it, "activity" was more important to defining one's role than blood relationship. One was a mother (or father, or son, daughter, sister, brother) if one carried out the associated behaviors.[31] This is present throughout the Chikhachev archive when unrelated people were spoken of and behaved as family members—"Grandma" Nesterova in Moscow, "Uncle" Timofei Krylov, "Brother" Nikolai Zamytskii, Andrei's "grandson" Elisei Mochalin and "nephews" M. and N. Stepanov. If roles, no matter how rigid in nature, could be filled as circumstances demanded, then a wife could identify herself and her duty entirely as an estate manager without transgressing the socially acceptable bounds of femininity. Likewise, a father could devote himself to the *vospitanie* of his children and understand this duty as completely consistent with his masculine role "beyond the home."

Families like the Chikhachevs comprised an important bulwark of support for the Russian monarchy, and therefore for the whole traditional system—they were the true believers in "Orthodoxy, Autocracy, Nationality" before it became an official slogan. However, the village at the center of this provincial gentry world was a highly unstable entity, predicated on the social dilemma of serfdom, and surviving only precariously in a seasonal, cash-poor economy. Though the relative social isolation of the village portrayed so vividly in literature (especially from a later period) appears to have actually been far from onerous, at least by the 1830s, the village was nonetheless vulnerable to natural disasters, serf unrest, and the general inadequacy of medical services and basic law enforcement across long distances. Before serf emancipation, conscientious landlords were able to ameliorate some of these problems (while irresponsible landlords could make them a great deal worse).

The dismantling of serfdom took place with little meaningful input from any of those who actually lived all their lives in provincial villages, and in such a way as to leave the peasantry indebted without sufficient means to repay their "redemption," and landlords lacking the power and organized labor force that had maintained relative stability for so long. Land and serf ownership had been the pivot of provincial gentry society, and without it the carefully defined roles of the gentry family and village lost much of their meaning and purpose. The abolition of serfdom, with its concomitant destabilization of the village "family" ruled over by the mother-manager and father-educator, thus also changed the nature of gentry nuclear-family and gender dynamics. The gender roles enacted by Natalia and Andrei in their marriage, specifically, lost much of their purpose for the generation that followed theirs because of emancipation.

The Chikhachevs had understood their respective duties through a lens colored by the needs of their larger, metaphorical family of the estate and all its residents. Natalia mothered her children and all the inhabitants of their various villages and parts of villages by ensuring the provision of bread and clothing for everyone, by keeping the accounts and supervising labor, and by managing the family households at Dorozhaevo and Borduki. Andrei acted his part as the paternalistic authority figure and *vospitatel* or moral educator, doing his best to guide his dependents toward the fulfillment of their various duties (with limited success), and eventually extending his moral leadership into a more public realm through his journalism and philanthropy (with much greater success). Andrei was working as well as he knew how toward the advancement of his society. However, his vision for Russia's future rested on an economic unit and arrangement of space—the serf village integrated into the noble family estate—that very soon ceased to exist.

The underlying presumption of Andrei's worldview, that each individual was born with a God-given duty to fulfill and that all moral qualities stemmed from fulfilling one's duty to the utmost ("conscientiously"), made for a stable and relatively ordered and prosperous life for people like the Chikhachevs, who were able to fit into their prescribed roles fairly comfortably. But the system was unstable over the long term, given external economic and ideological changes undermining rigid definitions of social roles. When, in the 1860s, the combined pressure of social and cultural change, increased capitalistic competition, and industrialization finally began to upset this ancient system, it came tumbling down with astonishing rapidity, precisely because its structure was based on a precarious economic system that hovered always on the brink of failure.

NOTES

PREFACE

1. T. M. Smirnova, *Byvshie liudi Sovietskoi Rossii: Strategii vyzhivaniia i puti integratsii, 1917–1936 gody* (Moskva: Mir istorii, 2003).

2. Susan Smith-Peter, "How to Write a Region: Local and Regional Historiography," *Kritika* 5, no. 3 (2004): 527–42.

3. Most of the local research on Andrei Chikhachev has been conducted by N. V. Frolov and E. V. Frolova. Tatiana Golovina, a literature scholar from Ivanovo State University, has published several articles about Andrei's reading, and O. A. Moniakova published a précis of his articles from the *Vladimir Provincial News*.

4. Susan Smith-Peter, "Books Behind the Altar: Religion, Village Libraries, and the Moscow Agriculture Society," RH 31, no. 3 (2004).

5. Two files of the Chikhachev *fond* were never made available because they were in restoration during the entire period of my research. Both were minor legal documents similar to others that I did see.

INTRODUCTION

1. The term "gender" refers to behavior based on cultural assumptions about sex. Gender is historically constructed: ideas about how men and women ought to behave change over time and place. See Joan W. Scott, "Gender: A Useful Category of Historical Analysis," AHR 91, no. 5 (Dec. 1986): 1053–75. This study examines how gender roles were constructed, and with what consequences and implications, for one real family. Unfortunately, even documents as extensive as the Chikhachev archive leave many impenetrable silences, and the reader interested primarily in women's experiences will be frustrated with the great gaps left in these documents where there

might have been some glimpse into Natalia's opinions as opposed to her activities, or into her mind as opposed to her husband's.

2. Work on domesticity in western Europe and the United States has established the limits of this rhetoric in its native context. Throughout the Victorian period, middle-class British and American women defied the discourse of domesticity in many ways, whether employed as clerks, secretaries, or teachers, or engaged in independent or semi-independent businesses, in large-scale independent charitable and philanthropic endeavors, and the like. See Patricia Branca, "Image and Reality: The Myth the Idle Victorian Woman," in *Clio's Consciousness Raised: New Perspectives on the History of Women,* ed. Mary Hartman and Lois Banner (New York: Octagon, 1976), 179–91; M. Jeanne Peterson, "No Angels in the House: The Victorian Myth and the Paget Women," AHR 89 (1984): 677–708; Cathy N. Davidson and Jessamyn Hatcher, eds., *No More Separate Spheres!: A Next Wave American Studies Reader* (Durham: Duke University Press, 2002) and other works. Similarly, studies of nineteenth-century masculinity have found that the domestic sphere was central to many men's lives and self-identities, especially in their roles as fathers: Stephen M. Frank, *Life with Father: Parenthood and Masculinity in the Nineteenth-Century American North* (Baltimore: Johns Hopkins University Press, 1998); and John Tosh, *A Man's Place: Masculinity and the Middle-Class Home in Victorian England* (New Haven: Yale University Press, 1999).

3. Diana Greene, "Mid-Nineteenth Century Domestic Ideology in Russia," in *Women and Russian Culture,* ed. Rosalind Marsh (New York: Berghahn, 1998); Jessica Tovrov, *The Russian Noble Family: Structure and Change* (New York: Garland, 1987); Mary Cavender, *Nests of the Gentry: Family, Estate, and Local Loyalties in Provincial Russia* (Newark: University of Delware Press, 2007); Olga Glagoleva, "Dream and Reality of Russian Provincial Young Ladies, 1700–1850," *The Carl Beck Papers* 1405 (2000), 1–87; and *Russkaia provintsial'naia starina: Ocherki kul'tury i byta Tul'skoi gubernii XVIII-pervoi poloviny XIX v.* (Tula: Ritm, 1993).

4. Michelle Lamarche Marrese, *A Woman's Kingdom: Noblewomen and the Control of Property in Russia, 1700–1861* (Ithaca, NY: Cornell University Press, 2002).

5. See Greene, "Domestic Ideology"; Tovrov, *Russian Noble Family*; Cavender, *Nests of the Gentry*; Glagoleva, "Dream and Reality."

6. Cavender's study of the middling gentry of Tver province saw language similar to Andrei Chikhachev's, but the absence of comparable private documents by women shed no light on the other sides of these men's lives, as is possible in the Chikhachev case.

7. Simon Dixon, "Practice and Performance in the History of the Russian Nobility," *Kritika* 11, no. 4 (Fall 2010): 763–70. Dixon's article was prompted by Michelle Marrese's important revision of Yuri Lotman's influential essay on Russian noble culture, "The Poetics of Everyday Behavior in Eighteenth-Century Russian Culture," in *The Semiotics of Russian Cultural History*, ed. Alexander Nakhimovsky and Alice Stone Nakhimovsky (Ithaca, NY: Cornell University Press, 1985). "'The Poetics of Everyday Behavior' Revisited: Lotman, Gender, and the Evolution of Russian Noble Identity," *Kritika* 11, no. 4 (Fall 2010): 701–39.

8. PSZ No. 11444; PSZ No. 16187.

9. Marrese, *Woman's Kingdom.*

10. See, e.g., PSZ No. 9267 (1746); Elise Kimerling Wirtschafter, "Legal Identity and the Possession of Serfs in Imperial Russia." JMH 70, no. 3 (September 1998): 561–87.

11. Walter Pintner, *Russian Economic Policy under Nicholas I* (Ithaca, NY: Cornell University Press, 1967), 9–29; Thomas C. Owen, *The Corporation under Russian Law, 1800–1917* (Cambridge: Cambridge University Press, 1991).

12. When the government lowered the interest rate on bank deposits in 1857, investors hurried to withdraw their funds and reinvested in joint-stock companies, thus bringing about Russia's first "stock fever." See Owen, *Corporation*, 30–54; and Steven Hoch, "The Banking Crisis, Peasant Reform, and Economic Development in Russia, 1857–1861." AHR 96, no. 3 (June 1991): 785–820.

13. Marrese, *Woman's Kingdom*.

14. N. M. Shepukova, "Ob izmenenii razmerov dushevladeniia pomeshchikov Evropeiskoi Rossii v pervoi chetverti XVIII-pervoi polovine XIX v.," *Ezhegodnik po agrarnoi istorii Vostochnoi Evropy za 1963 g.* (Vilnius, 1964), 388–419, 393. See also Jerome Blum, *Lord and Peasant in Russia: From the Ninth to the Nineteenth Century* (Princeton: Princeton University Press, 1971).

15. The impoverishment of nobles had been ongoing for centuries. Thomas Esper, "The Odnodvortsy and the Russian Nobility," *Slavonic and East European Review* 45, no. 104 (Jan. 1967): 124–34. According to the report of the charitable Moscow Prison Committee for 1851, of 2,227 beggars arrested in the city during that year, there were thirty-seven male and eighteen female nobles. Gosudarstvennyi Arkhiv Rossiiskoi Federatsii (GARF) F. 123, op. 2, d. 606, l. 12.

16. The statesman Sergei Witte viewed the middling gentry in the post-Emancipation period as useless to the state, because he felt they lacked initiative or ambition. V. I. Gurko, *Cherty i siluety proshlogo* (Moscow, 2000), http://www.historichka.ru/istoshniki/gurko/ (accessed 10/03/2011). On Gogol's representations of the provinces and their enormous influence on subsequent perceptions of the real provinces, see Anne Lounsbery, "'No, this is not the provinces!': Provincialism, Authenticity, and Russianness in Gogol's Day," RR 64 (April 2005): 259–80.

17. On the absence of a Western-style middle class in Russia, see Abbott Gleason, "The Terms of Russian Social History," in *Between Tsar and People: Educated Society and the Quest for Public Identity in Late Imperial Russia*, ed. Edith W. Clowes, Samuel D. Kassow, and James L. West (Princeton: Princeton University Press, 1991), 15–27; Harley D. Balzer, ed., *Russia's Missing Middle Class: The Professions in Russian History* (Armonk, NY: M. E. Sharpe, 1996); Marc Raeff, *Imperial Russia, 1682–1825: The Coming of Age of Modern Russia* (New York: Knopf, 1971), 122; and Elise Kimerling Wirtschafter, *Social Identity in Imperial Russia* (DeKalb: Northern Illinois University Press, 1997). Recent works adding to our understanding of middling groups include Marrese, *Woman's Kingdom*; Cavender, *Nests of the Gentry*; Glagoleva. "Dream and Reality"; Alison K. Smith, *Recipes for Russia: Food and Nationhood under the Tsars* (DeKalb: Northern Illinois University Press, 2008); Catriona Kelly, *Refining Russia: Advice Literature, Polite Culture, and Gender from Catherine to Yeltsin* (Oxford: Oxford University Press, 2001); Catherine Evtukhov, "A. O. Karelin and Provincial Bourgeois Photography," in *Picturing Russia: Explorations in Visual Culture,* ed. Valerie Kivelson and Joan Neuberger (New Haven: Yale University Press, 2008), 113–17.

CHAPTER 1

1. N. V. Frolov, *Vladimirskii rodoslovets* (Kovrov, 1996), 152. Hereafter VR.

2. CH 59, l. 260b. Yakov's ship was the frigate "Princess Lovich," with fifty-four guns. It was "laid down" on December 1, 1827 and launched May 26, 1828. F. F. Veselago, *Spisok russkikh voennykh sudov s 1668 po 1860 god* (St. Petersburg, 1872), 102.

3. The case wasn't concluded until 1840. CH 98, l. 10b.

4. The only personal details provided about Timofei Krylov tell us that painted as a hobby; one day Yakov described how "Uncle was busy all day with painting! [H]e was detailing the <u>waterfall</u>;

provided <u>leaves</u> for the trees; attached <u>branches</u>; now started the <u>sky</u>; his work is proceeding successfully, but he is somehow not happy with the colors!" CH 59, l. 75.

5. CH 57, l. 40.

6. CH 98, l. 250b; 59, l. 58.

7. CH 54, l. 49; 95.

8. CH 59, l. 26.

9. CH 66, ll. 310b–32.

10. Ibid., 143.

11. *Spiski naselennykh mest Rossiiskoi Imperii* 6 (St. Petersburg, 1863), hereafter SNM, and *Voenno-statisticheskie obozrenie Rossiiskoi imperii*, vol. 6, pt. 2 (St. Petersburg, 1852), 174, hereafter VSO.

12. CH 98, l. 260b. Andrei listed the distances from Dorozhaevo of a number of towns and villages, on the cover of one of his notebooks (CH 93).

13. N. V. Frolov and E. V. Frolova, *Kovrovskii krai pushkinskoi pory* (Kovrov, 1999), 6.

14. Ibid.

15. Ibid.

16. VSO, 159, 149.

17. CH 108, l. 271.

18. The lowest and highest available figures are 243 and 419 souls for their combined property. For incomplete figures dating from 1821 to 1861 see CH 57, ll. 80b–11; 90; 98, ll. 170b, 260b, 270b. VR gives the highest number, at 419, which I was not able to corroborate with my sources. In 1836, Andrei contemplated inheriting 269 souls from Praskovia Petrovna Vladykina, though this did not happen. To the prospect of so many souls "on the horizon" Yakov wrote: "I think, for you this is like a Mountain on the shoulders, like a stone on the heart, such trying times? True?" (CH 57, l. 11). My calculations from all the figures available to me are that before Aleksandra's marriage (with property for her dowry) and Aleksei's inheritance of Chernavin's property, Andrei owned about 150–180 souls, and Natalia owned between 88 and 170.

19. CH 122, l. 4. The other named owners were a "Kablukova," a Princess Dolgorukova, and two names that aren't fully legible, seemingly "Rozenmeir" and "Svobodev."

20. SNM.

21. Ibid.

22. CH 59, l. 45.

23. In 1836, before the stone house was begun, Andrei referred to "my wife's hermitage," presumably meaning her favorite room, where she read, wrote, or did needlework. CH 66, l. 1100b, 1400b, et al.

24. CH 57, l. 530b.

25. CH 98, l. 220b.

26. VSO, 184.

27. "O komnatnom vozdukhe," ZG 6, (1845): 44–45.

28. CH 98, l. 260b.

29. CH 129.

30. N. V. Frolov and E.V. Frolova, *Pervaia kovrovskaia biblioteka* (Kovrov, 2000), 13.

31. According to Frolov, Natalia was buried near the church at Berezovik, and Andrei was buried within the grounds of the monastery in Suzdal. VR, 152.

32. CH 41.

33. CH 66, l. 270b.

34. CH 54, l. 200b.

35. CH 105, ll. 330–300b.

36. CH 20, 23–25, 28.

37. CH 128, l.1.

38. CH 66, ll. 144, 150.

39. CH 100, l. 1.

40. CH 57, l. 2. "Rudar'" appears to be an inside joke rather than a misspelling of *sudar'* because it was written in large, carefully shaped letters.

41. Ibid., l. 3.

42. Ibid., l. 830b.

43. Ibid., l. 91.

44. Ibid., l. 430b. "*Likho-chudno-vazhno-slavno-divno-poteshno-chestno-milo-bravo—i sorok raz trakh-tara-rakh-trakh-trakh!!!!—kha! kha! kha! Umoril, prokiiatoi!*"

45. CH 59, l. 690b. Compare the notebook correspondence to early Romantic journals such as the German *Athenaeum*, as described by Melissa Frazier, *Romantic Encounters: Writers, Readers, and the "Library for Reading"* (Stanford: Stanford University Press, 2007), 6–7.

46. CH 57, l. 760b.

47. CH 59, l. 860b.

48. Ibid.

49. Ibid, l. 850b.

50. CH 116, ll. 3–30b.

51. Ibid., l. 18.

52. Bruce Lincoln, *Nicholas I: Emperor and Autocrat of All the Russias* (DeKalb: Northern Illinois University Press, 1989); A. E. Presniakov, *Emperor Nicholas I of Russia: The Apogee of Autocracy, 1825–1855* (Gulf Breeze, FL: Academic International Press, 1974); Nicholas Riasanovsky, *Nicholas I and Official Nationality in Russia, 1825–1855* (Berkeley: University of California Press, 1959); and Richard Wortman, *Scenarios of Power: Myth and Ceremony in the Russian Monarchy* (Princeton: Princeton University Press, 1994), vol. 1, pt. 4.

53. CH 99, ll. 230–310b.

54. Susan Smith-Peter, "The Russian Provincial Newspaper and Its Public, 1788–1864," *The Carl Beck Papers in Russian and East European Studies,* no. 1908 (Pittsburgh: University of Pittsburgh, 2008); Smith-Peter, "Ukrainskie zhurnaly nachala XIX veka: ot universalizma Prosveshcheniia do romanticheskogo regionalizma," in *Istoriia i politika v sovremennom mire,* ed. I. G. Zhiriakov and A. A. Orlov (Moscow, 2010), 447–61; O. E. Glagoleva, *Tul'skaia Knizhnaia Starina: Ocherki Kul'turnoi Zhizni XVIII—Pervoi Poloviny XIX vv* (Tula, 1992).

CHAPTER 2

1. Petr Dolgorukov, *Rossiiskaia rodoslovnaia kniga* 1 (St. Petersburg: 1854–57), 29. Dolgorukov's work is based on government records but is far from complete. Only a few of the gentry families with whom the Chikhachevs associated are mentioned. V. V. Rummel and V. V. Golubtsov, *Rodoslovnyi sbornik Russkikh dvorianskikh familii* (St. Petersburg, 1886), is more inclusive of lesser gentry, although the only Chikhachevs mentioned there are from the Pskov/Voronezh or Yaroslavl/Vologda branches. See also CH 79, an official copy of the Chikhachev coat of arms, which

Andrei received in 1841. The accompanying document confirms the family's rank and origins in the sixteenth century.

2. Brokgauz and Efron, *Russkii biograficheskii slovar': setevaia versiia* (2007, accessed 5/14/07 2007). http://www.rulex.ru/01240253.htm. Two Chikhachev descendants of the Pskov branch enjoy fame as explorers: Petr Aleksandrovich, and Platon Aleksandrovich.

3. Frolov, *Kovrovskaia biblioteka*, 4–5.

4. VR, 151.

5. CH 59, l. 45.

6. S. V. Volkov. *Russkii ofitserskii korpus* (Moscow, 1993), 44–45.

7. Since this is the first appearance of the Saratov land, it may have been Anna's dowry.

8. VR, 152.

9. Ibid.,151.

10. Volkov, 109. See also A. F. Rediger, *Istoriia moei zhizni. Vospominaniia voennogo ministra* (Moscow, 1999); Yu. V. Makarov, *Moia sluzhba v staroi gvardii* (Buenos-Aires, 1951).

11. Frolov, *Kovrovskaia biblioteka*, 6.

12. See Wirtschafter, *Social Identity*.

13. I follow Dominic Lieven's usage: *The Aristocracy in Europe, 1815–1914* (New York: Columbia University Press, 1993), vii. Other foundational texts on nobility in Russia include Aleksandr Romanovich-Slavatinskii, *Dvorianstvo v Rossii ot nachala XVIII veka do otmeny krepostnogo prava* (St. Petersburg, 1870); and Isabel de Madariaga, "The Russian Nobility, 1600–1800," in *The European Nobilities in the Seventeenth and Eighteenth Centuries*, ed. H. M. Scott, 2 vols. (London: Longman, 1995).

14. Blum, *Lord and Peasant in Russia*, 349.

15. Blum suggests their growth was due to overall population growth and grants of peasants by the tsar. He notes that rulers expressed periodic concern about the impoverishment (through partial inheritance) of the lower nobility, and responded with grants of serfs and land in the east, thus allowing some of these families to climb back into the ranks of the *pomestnoe dvorianstvo* while simultaneously colonizing newly acquired or unsettled regions of the Empire. Blum, *Lord and Peasant in Russia*, 355–58. Although there are no equivalent terms for the other two categories of *dvorianstvo* in Russian, for the highest category there is *"aristokratiia,"* or *"znat'"* (wellborn). The third and poorest group can be distinguished as *sluzhiloe dvorianstvo* (though it is not systematically used), conveying the sense that their incomes were dependent on their lifelong service (*sluzhba*), whether civil or military.

16. Blum, *Lord and Peasant in Russia*, 367–70.

17. VSO, 142–43.

18. CH 128, l. 120b. See also CH 54, l. 30.

19. CH 58, l. 182.

20. CH 90, l. 6.

21. Kupreianov lost a leg sometime after 1829, probably during the Polish uprising of 1830–31, but he continued to serve for another two decades, making him something of a war hero by the time he sponsored Aleksei in 1848–50. Brokgauz and Efron's *Russkii biograficheskii slovar'* gives the Kupreianov family a princely title. CH 95, l. 46 mentions the hope that Aleksei would be made an adjutant, but Kupreianov was wounded again and retired before he could do so.

22. CH 83, ll. 39–390b.

23. CH 108, ll. 195–1950b.

24. John LeDonne, "Ruling Families in the Russian Political Order, 1689–1825," *Cahiers du monde Russe et Sovietique* 28 (1987).

25. See J. M. Bourne, *Patronage and Society in Nineteenth-Century England* (London: Edward Arnold, 1986), 114.

26. Ibid., 137.

27. CH 112, ll. 19–190b.

28. CH 66, l. 350b.

29. CH 59, l. 580b.

30. VSO, 171–72.

31. Smith-Peter, "Provincial Public Libraries and the Law in Nicholas I's Russia," *Library History* 21 (July 2005): 112–13. She quotes Frolov in *Kovrovskii krai*, 51.

32. CH 98, ll. 130b, 140b, 170b, 180b.

33. The Izmailovs, the Ikonnikovs, the Kasheevs, a Ragozin, and the Yazykovs.

34. As Michelle Marrese has demonstrated in a wider context, *Woman's Kingdom*.

35. The distinction between related families and unrelated ones is complicated by the fact that they all frequently acted as godparents to the children of friends, and sometimes spoke of those technically related only by these religious ties using familial terms.

36. Through Andrei's branch of the Chikhachev family tree, he and Natalia were related to several other local families: the Vladykins, Naschokins, Kariakins, Aksakovs, and Kupreianovs. The Aleksei Nikolaevich Chikhachev listed on the Chernavin family tree had three daughters in the same generation as Natalia, who settled in Vladimir province, and their families were also friends: the Maikovs, Sleptsovs, and Kostievskiis. Yakov seems to have maintained closer ties with the living Khmetevskiis and Taneevs than Andrei and Natalia did.

37. In 1849 one in twenty-six children in Vladimir province was illegitimate (VSO, 257).

38. VR, 68, 82–84.

39. Frolov, *Predvoditeli dvorianstva*.

40. CH 52. On voting and following the elections, see his collections of letters, 1859–66 (CH 103, 105, 106, 108, 112). According to Frolov, Andrei was elected as a Kovrov County Court judge in 1835 but did not serve out his full term. *Kovrovskaia biblioteka*, 7.

41. CH 108, l. 43–46. Aleksei eventually served as a delegate to the Noble Assembly (VR, 152).

42. Frolov, *Predvoditeli dvorianstva*.

43. CH 58, l. 176.

44. Iuliia Zhukova, "Pervaia zhenskaia organizatsiia v Rossii," *Vse liudi sestry* 5 (1996): 38–56.

45. Cavender, *Nests of the Gentry*, outlines the social activities of gentry men of Tver province, largely centered around provincial assemblies and entirely consistent with Andrei's accounts.

46. Bella Grigoryan, "Noble Farmers: The Provincial Landowner in the Russian Cultural Imagination" (PhD diss., Columbia University, 2011), 73.

47. CH 54, l. 40b; 58, l. 1690b; 71, l. 100b. "Father Lev" borrowed Bulgarin's *History of Russia*.

48. CH 61, 70.

49. Yakov had a smattering of Italian and knew a few phrases in other European languages, with which he impressed and fascinated Andrei (CH 61, l. 710b). He also listed every foreign city he visited in his navy career (ibid., l. 1120b).

50. CH 83, l. 1260b.

51. CH 98, l. 250b.

52. Cavender has analyzed the often formulaic nature of such letters, arguing that while they adhered to a strict pattern that required the use of certain clichés, they nevertheless expressed and reinvigorated close emotional ties between family members. "'Kind Angel of the Soul and Heart': Domesticity and Family Correspondence among the Pre-Emancipation Russian Gentry," *RR* 61, no. 3 (2002).

53. Maarten Fraanje, *The Epistolary Novel in Eighteenth-Century Russia* (Munich: Sagner, 2001). Fraanje is chiefly concerned with the development of literary style and certain themes, which were less diverse or imaginative in Russian letters than in France or England. Apparently, then, if such a difference exists, the cause was not an excessive unreliability of the postal system.

54. Not all post offices were willing to accept the responsibility of mailing cash: Aleksei once wrote that, "because letters with money are not accepted in Lezhnevo, I am forwarding you my letter with a gift, commensurate with my means, for Annochka for her birthday and name day. I humbly request that you read it, seal it, and on occasion send it to the post office in Shuia." CH 106, ll. 32–320b.

55. "They say that there was a detailed letter from Kater. Pavlovna [with whom Natalia was traveling to Moscow], but it seems that it was sent not by mail but with her peasants, and so I did not receive it yet; and in that case [she] should not have written with an occasion [meaning sending the letter by a traveling peasant] at all." CH 54, l. 30. The fact that the Chikhachev archive contains large sets of letters only from 1859 to 1866 should not be taken to mean that they corresponded more in these later years than before. Andrei refers in earlier years to tying up packets of the letters he had received. The archive contains a few unbound letters from earlier years, most of them written to Yakov or exchanged between Chernavin, his mother, Timofei Krylov, and Andrei. The letters from the 1820s and 1830s are very similar in form and content to the letters of the 1860s, though the ones exchanged between Chernavin and Chikhachev are less formal. The only noticeable difference between the two groups of letters is that the quality of paper was vastly reduced once it was mass-produced after the mid-century.

56. See Ian M. Helfant, *The High Stakes of Identity: Gambling in the Life and Literature of Nineteenth-Century Russia* (Evanston: Northwestern University Press, 2001); Marrese, *Woman's Kingdom*, and Sergei Antonov, "Law and the Culture of Debt in Moscow on the Eve of the Great Reforms, 1850–1870," (PhD diss., Columbia University, 2011).

57. CH 36a, l. 29.

58. CH 55, l. 46.

59. CH 57, l. 75.

60. "Neskol'ko myslei sel'skogo zhitelia," ZG 54 (1850): 428–30.

61. Andrei: "12 November 1836, dusk. Today I had a very busy day: . . . . . name day, a river of champagne," CH 66, l. 1360b. See also the family account books, esp. CH 36a, ll. 30b, 50b.

62. CH 58, ll. 1080b (Andrei), 1110b (Yakov).

63. CH 59, l. 480b.

64. Ibid., l. 37.

65. CH 83, l. 560b.

66. CH 59, l. 500b. "*Chetvertak*"—a silver 25 kopek coin.

67. CH 54, l. 210b.

68. CH 58, l. 1740b.

69. When Aleksei bought a few more at a fair in Vilno some time later, that too was significant enough for mention in the diary, CH 83, ll. 70b, 39.

70. CH 58, l. 141.

71. "Kamennoi dom v derevne," ZG 25 (1845):199.

72. The station master was asked to carry reading matter to a neighbor, CH 54, l. 70b. A "coppersmith" carried a note from a neighbor (CH 54, l. 25), and in another instance Natalia's friend was commissioned to buy fabric: "Tatiana Ivanovna [Ikonnikova] became angry at the peddler for allegedly purposely asking several kopeks in excess for the printed cotton with Cupids." CH 54, l. 41.

73. CH 155 is their telegraph signal book. It contains an index of words and phrases that were assigned code numbers because they were frequently used. Perhaps 30 percent of these clearly related to, or might often have been used for, exchanges of goods and favors, not including proper names. See also CH 99 for detailed accounts of exchanges of goods, news, and advice with their neighbors the Kultashevs (l. 77) and the Cherepanovs (ll. 80–81ob) via letters.

74. CH 99, l. 42. The name Stepanov does not appear on the Chikhachev family tree; none of Andrei or Natalia's siblings had children. Andrei's adopted siblings' family names were Zamytskii, Ikonnikov, Yazykov, and Avdulin.

75. In 1819 Andrei assumed 9,700 rubles of his brother's debt, in 1821 another 15,000 rubles, and in 1823 an additional 14,550 rubles. According to a schedule written in the early 1820s, they would have paid off all three loans by 1835, at the exorbitant interest rates of 30 percent, for the 1819 debt, 27 percent for 1821, and 39 percent for the loan taken in 1823. Other notations list smaller debts incurred for their own purposes, e.g., in the early 1820s they sent 1,975 rubles to the Ikonnikovs, "in payment of debt" (CH 36a, ll. 16, 29, 30ob). Yakov recorded at least one major loan taken out in 1827, for 9,200 rubles, on which he was paying 41 percent interest; by 1834, he had paid 1,781.87 rubles of the capital, and a similar proportion of the interest (CH 59, l. 170b).

76. CH 55, l. 45ob. Another accounting of debts from 1842 lists significant sums owed to Nikolai Zamytski, General Kupreianov, A. G. Nosova, and Sergei Ikonnikov (CH 95, l. 1).

77. Antonov, "Law and the Culture of Debt," ch. 2.

78. CH 106, l. 32.

79. Ibid., ll. 95–96. Letter from Kultasheva to Natalia.

80. CH 66, ll. 51–52.

81. CH 99, l. 264.

82. Ibid., ll. 50–52ob.

83. Ibid., ll. 53, 54. Kultasheva was a relation of Andrei's through his mother, and Nosova may also have been related. The initial "A" probably stood for Major's wife Aleksandra Glebovna Nosova, to whom the Chikhachevs owed 3,000 rubles in 1842 (CH 95, l. 1).

84. CH 60, l. 52.

85. VSO, 145–153, 227.

86. Kelly, *Refining Russia,* 99. Kelly refers here to Amanda Vickery, *The Gentleman's Daughter: Women's Lives in Georgian England* (New Haven: Yale University Press, 1998). Tosh (*A Man's Place*) provides a helpful breakdown of the various layers within the Victorian middle class, 13. None of these can be equated to the Russian middling classes for a number of reasons, but it is worth noting that the iconic British middle class was not homogenous either.

87. Vickery, *Gentleman's Daughter,* ch. 1.

88. CH 58, ll. 165, 167, 172. In CH 61, l. 300b, Yakov consults an "apothecary's aide" from Shuia as to the exact definition of the "civic pound" (14 ounces).

89. CH 60, l. 13.

90. CH 99, ll. 124–1240b.

91. Ibid, l. 144.

92. Antonov's account of lawyers in this period suggests this may not have been unusual, 344–62.

93. CH 58, l. 196.

94. CH 70, l. 50.

95. Ibid., l. 8.

96. Ibid., l. 90b.

97. VSO, 144–45.

98. See N. V. Frolov and E. V. Frolova, *Istoriia zemli Kovrovskoi, chast' I* (Kovrov, 1997); N. V. Frolov and E. V. Frolova, *Kovrovskii krai pushkinskoi pory* (Kovrov, 1999).

99. CH 58, ll. 180, 181.

100. CH 98, l. 190b.

101. ZG 25 (1859), 198–99. See Alexander Martin, ed., *Provincial Russia: The Memoir of a Priest's Son* (DeKalb: Northern Illinois University Press, 2002) for a priest who exhibits a conservatism very similar to Andrei's. Though focused on a later period, Laurie Manchester's *Holy Fathers, Secular Sons: Clergy, Intelligentsia, and the Modern Self in Revolutionary Russia* (DeKalb: Northern Illinois University Press, 2011) reveals parallels between Andrei's thinking on *vospitanie* and ideas common to the clergy. David Ransel's *A Russian Merchant's Tale: The Life and Adventures of Ivan Alekseevich Tolchenov, Based on His Diary* (Bloomington: Indiana University Press, 2008) describes a wealthy merchant whose lifestyle is possibly more "aristocratic" than that of the Chikhachevs.

102. CH 59, l. 360b.

103. CH 55.

104. CH 61, l. 117.

105. CH 63, l. 148.

106. CH 99, ll. 262–64.

107. CH 99, l. 219

CHAPTER 3

1. In 1842 Andrei recorded approvingly in his diary an *ukaz* that "explain[ed] to us the way towards the normality of productive forces." The decree established legal procedures for landlords to free peasants by signing a contract for redemption payments. The provision was not widely used, and Andrei himself did not feel able to take advantage of it. CH 95, l. 390b. See PSZ II, vol. 17, no. 15, 462.

2. CH 59, l. 45.

3. See Edgar Melton, "Enlightened Seigniorialism and Its Dilemmas in Serf Russia, 1750–1830," JMH 62, no. 4 (1990): 675–708. Scholarship analyzing relations between landlords and serfs, and the social order that developed between them in eighteenth- and nineteenth-century Russia, is overwhelmingly based on much larger estates where landlords were absent for long periods, if not year-round. The Chikhachev documents (many of them also pertaining to the estates owned first by the Chernavin family and later by Aleksei Chikhachev) contain most of the same types of records as those used in previous studies, though naturally they are different in scale and complexity from those kept by paid managers on the estates of the very wealthy. They include financial

accounts, lists of quitrent payments, land surveys, and census lists of peasant households, full of detail on the names, ages, and relationships of individual serf households. One of the seminal texts on serfdom, Michael Confino's *Domaines et seigneurs en Russie vers la fin du XVIIIe siecle: etude de structures agraires et de mentalites economiques* (Paris: Institut d'etudes slaves de l'Universite de Paris, 1963) is based on publications of the Free Economic Society and concerns only the richest estates. See also Melton, "Enlightened Seigniorialism"; Steven L. Hoch, *Serfdom and Social Control in Russia: Petrovskoe, a Village in Tambov* (Chicago: University of Chicago Press, 1989); Peter Kolchin, *Unfree Labor: American Slavery and Russian Serfdom* (Cambridge, MA: Belknap, Harvard University Press, 1987); Daniel Field, *The End of Serfdom: Nobility and Bureaucracy in Russia, 1855–1861* (Cambridge, MA: Harvard University Press, 1976); Terence Emmons, *Emancipation of the Russian Serfs* (Austin; TX: Holt McDougal, 1970); Iu. A. Tikhonov, *Dvoriankaia usad'ba i krestianskii dvor v Rossii 17 i 18 vekov* (Moscow, 2005); Tikhonov and L. V. Ivanova, eds., *Dvorianskaia i kupecheskaia usad'ba v Rossii XVI–XX vv: Istoricheskie ocherki* (2001), and others.

4. Studies of the nobility and their serfs regularly disregard the presence of village clergy, and often do little to distinguish between household and field serfs, with the important exception of Hoch, *Serfdom and Social Control*. Kolchin, in *Unfree Labor*, argues that Russian landlords were not paternalistic because of their absentee status. Obviously this does not apply to landowners like the Chikhachevs. Cavender's findings in *Nests of the Gentry* confirm that resident landowners' attitudes toward peasants were markedly paternalistic.

5. "Neskol'ko myslei sel'skogo zhitelia," 428–30.

6. See Melton, "Enlightened Seigniorialism." On provincial print culture, I am informed by Smith-Peter, "Russian Provincial Newspaper," and "Ukrainskie zhurnaly."

7. Hoch, *Serfdom and Social Control,* acknowledges the practical differences, but his sources are based on *barshchina* estates in the more fertile *chernozem* region. See also Wilson Augustine's evidence on the differences between *barshchina* and *obrok* estates in the eighteenth century, "Notes toward a Portrait of the Eighteenth-Century Nobility," *Canadian-American Slavic Studies* 4 (1970): 407.

8. Natalia's diaries contain lists of which peasants were on guard duty after the harvest was brought in and also frequent mention of accomplishments of various specialized estate workers, such as weavers, those who tended the cows, carpenters, and plasterers, etc., though not systematically.

9. CH 54, l. 10.

10. This number is based on the total for 1863, published in SNM. In a private notebook from the early 1820s, Andrei listed about forty "household serfs," including young "boys and girls" and those who tended livestock, who were given a monthly allotment in place of a share in the output of the fields. CH 37, l. 140b.

11. CH 98, l. 270b.

12. Andrei did not even want to consolidate his landholdings: in 1850, he explained that his estates were "very scattered, in some places only 5 households, in others less, but I've always been afraid to consolidate them, because of fires, on the one hand, and on the other, in the process of buying and selling—lawsuits! Ach, lawsuits! bbrr!" (CH 98, l. 20b)

13. VSO, 149–52.

14. CH 95, l. 6. In 1835 Yakov wrote condescendingly of a "congress" of three peasant elders, CH 59, l. 430b. But in 1837 he also wrote of an evening "in the girls' room" where the serf girls

were "singing songs" along with which Yakov "distinguished himself." He also mentions frequent *khorovody*, peasant dances, taking place in his house (CH 60, l. 113).

15. Augustine, "Notes toward a Portrait," 409.

16. "Dva slova o rabotakh gospodskikh liudei," MGV 72 (1847), 563.

17. Most peasant memoirists actually lived as merchants or craftsmen. *Vospominaniia russkikh krestian xviii–pervoi poloviny xix veka* (Moscow: NLO, 2006). One memoir confirms the interpretation of historians that peasants often indicated indirectly when a landlord had gone too far, so that an intelligent lord could adjust accordingly, 135–36. Scholarship on peasant life tends to focus on the post-reform period. A notable exception is David Moon, *The Russian Peasantry, 1600–1930: The World the Peasants Made* (London: Addison Wesley Longman, 1999). See also Chris J. Chulos, *Converging Worlds: Religion and Community in Peasant Russia, 1861–1917* (DeKalb: Northern Illinois University Press, 2003); Christine Worobec, *Peasant Russia: Family and Community in the Post-Emancipation Period* (DeKalb: Northern Illinois University Press, 1995); Beatrice Farnsworth and Lynn Viola, eds., *Russian Peasant Women* (Oxford: Oxford University Press, 1992).

18. "Eshche neskol'ko slov o dolgakh," ZG 87 (1848): 692–95.

19. Ibid.

20. Nikolai Gogol, "Selected Passages from Correspondence with Friends," in *Sochineniia N. V. Gogolia*, ed. V. V. Kallash (St. Petersburg, 1915). In the same work, Gogol advised female landowners to take "the entire household economy" on themselves, 139–43. See below, and also Riasanovsky, *Nicholas I*, 89–91.

21. CH 59, l. 320b.

22. "Patriotischeskoe sochustvie k uchilishchu sel'skago khoziaistva dlia potomstvennykh dvorian," VGV 52 (1849): 253. See also CH 98, l. 280b where he used similar language in a private document.

23. "Proizvodstvo prostykh reshet v Kovrovskom uezde," VGV 47 (1848): 267–69.

24. Alexander Martin, "The Family Model of Society and Russian National Identity in Sergei N. Glinka's Russian Messenger (1808–1812)," SR 57, no. 1 (1998): 38.

25. See "O ezhednevnom v slukh domashnem chtenii" ZG 71 (1847); and Smith-Peter, "Books Behind the Altar" on discussions of what kinds of literature should be included in serf libraries. Andrei was a proponent of not limiting the selection to agricultural and religious works.

26. CH 61, ll. 55–550b.

27. Ibid., ll. 79–80.

28. Ibid., l. 950b.

29. CH 59, l. 10.

30. CH 58, ll. 181–82.

31. CH 59, l. 32. It was common among peasants to mistakenly believe that they were allowed to purchase their freedom when their owner died. See many cases to this effect mentioned in *Materialy dlia istorii krepostnogo prava v Rossii* (Berlin, 1872). Perhaps this belief stemmed from the law of November 8, 1847, that granted serfs the right to redeem themselves when their estate was sold at an auction (the law was repealed on July 19, 1849). See PSZ II, vol. 22, no. 21,689 and vol. 24, no. 23,405, Sec. 186.

32. CH 61, l. 1140b.

33. CH 108, l. 239.

34. CH 103, l. 41.

35. Ibid., ll. 270–271ob

36. Augustine ("Notes toward a Portrait") found this attitude prevalent already among the eighteenth-century middling gentry, 422.

37. CH 95, ll. 4–40b.

38. CH 54, l. 400b.

39. CH 53, l. 14.

40. CH 106, l. 32.

41. Ibid., ll. 44, 113ob, 114.

42. The law of May 2, 1833, prohibited the sale of individual serfs without their families. PSZ II, vol. 8, no. 6,163. An earlier law, of August 5, 1771, prohibited auction sales of serfs without land. Although there are indications that these laws were often evaded, at least in the mid-nineteenth century purchase documents for serfs specified that no families were broken up.

43. See Hoch, *Serfdom and Social Control,* on the necessity for this, 102. A more complicated problem arose when a serf expressed a desire to marry a serf from another estate. In one instance, at least, the serfs' wishes were respected: Yakov copied into one of his notebooks a form letter he filled out for a "*vyvodnoe pis'mo*"—a document used to allow a serf to marry a peasant on some-one else's estate. The letter states that both bride and groom were willing, and that Yakov and his heirs disclaimed all rights to the girl and would not interfere in any way in the future. CH 61, l. 1090b.

44. CH 95, l. 4.

45. Ibid., l. 40b. Natalia also took part in these inspections: "in the evening we were talking with Yaroslavl peasants; we appointed brides for two bridegrooms." I. M. Kultashev, their neigh-bor, "had tea" with them, so he may also have been part of the discussion. CH 63, l. 1570b.

46. CH 95, l. 50b. Other references in the same diary, for 1847, discuss similar inspections of peasants, but in that case it was with an eye toward army recruitment requirements rather than marriage: "[I] examined the peasanties [*muzhichki*] from Berezovik," ibid., l. 3.

47. Of course, noble marriages were also arranged with an eye to financial practicalities. The situations, however, were different in several crucial ways. First, young nobles were not inspected as if they were livestock (although young ladies were displayed at social events). Second, noble marriages were generally arranged by the parents, not by an outside and unrelated authority figure. Finally, the young people's wishes were supposed to be respected insofar as these did not threaten their future financial security or the social order. Clearly, the wishes of the couple were treated with considerably less attention or respect in the case of these peasants. On an eighteenth-century trend in noble marriage toward greater individual choice, especially for the bride, see Robin Bisha, "The Promise of Patriarchy: Marriage in Eighteenth-century Russia," (PhD diss., Indiana University, 1994).

48. CH 106, l. 31.

49. CH 66, l. 61.

50. CH 67, l. 6.

51. The Chikhachevs distinguished between "*domashnie*" or "people of the home," which re-ferred to their own family (in other cases this would also have included extended family relations who lived in the same house) and also the nanny, tutors, governess, and any other members of the household who were not quite servants; and "*dvorovye liudi*" or "household serfs," referring both to servants who worked and may have lived in the family house and to other serfs who worked outside the house but had specialized roles and hereditary status.

52. CH 95, l. 10b. Andrei went against the priest in deference to his serf bailiff, Rachok, in this case.

53. CH 54, l. 60b.

54. Ibid., l. 22.

55. CH 53, l. 3. New light on the role of nannies in Russian gentry households is forthcoming in a study by Steven A. Grant, *The Russian Nanny, Real and Imagined: History, Culture, Mythology* (Washington, D.C.: New Academia Publishing, 2012).

56. CH 108, ll. 165–165ob.

57. CH 95, l. 2; 57, l. 58. Cryptically, Andrei also wrote *"Rachok kakov?"* ("What a Rachok!") on nearly all the title pages for the sets of letters he organized and bound in 1850 and the early 1860s (e.g., CH 99, l. 67). In 1842 Andrei admitted to resenting a serf elder because the man had once denounced Rachok. CH 95, l. 10b.

58. "Kamennoi dom v derevne," ZG 25 (1845): 198–99.

59. I am grateful to Boris Gasparov for these insights on the possible uses of *ty/vy* by peasants in the nineteenth century (private correspondence, March 16, 2007). Richard Stites also offered the suggestion that Rachok may have employed *ty* in the same way that peasant nannies used the familiar with their noble charges as children and, sometimes, continued to use it after the children were grown (private correspondence, March 11, 2007). This would be particularly likely if Rachok was old enough to have known Andrei as a child, but unfortunately there is no evidence to indicate Rachok's age relative to Andrei's. He usually referred to peasant elders and the other more responsible and/or talented serfs by their names and patronymics (the patronymic in short form, as in Grigorii Alekseev, not Alekseevich—the long form was reserved for higher ranking people, or, if applied to a peasant, used ironically in the sense of "putting on airs"). When Andrei felt affection as well as respect for a peasant, he often gave them a nickname such as "Monsieur Serge" for a particularly talented serf carpenter; he also enjoyed using nicknames for friends and family members. In contrast, Natalia uniformly referred to all but the most respectable and responsible *starosty* in her diaries by their first names only, in a demeaning diminutive form reserved for members of the lower classes (i.e., "Sashka" rather than "Sasha").

60. CH 58, l. 75.

61. CH 83, l. 13.

62. ibid., l. 46.

63. CH 58, ll. 36–36ob.

64. CH 37, l. 140b. Chernavin's tax assessment for 1835 lists seven peasants living in Borduki, and sixty-nine in Berezovik. Interestingly, they were disproportionately male (forty-two men to twenty-seven women in Berezovik). CH 64, l. 50b.

65. CH 95, l. 4.

66. CH 58, l. 1240b–125.

67. CH 95, l. 1.

68. Some of the letters were written by scribes; of those clearly written by the elder himself, the handwriting varied in sophistication from rudimentary letters closely related to the old church-style forms to handwriting similar to that of educated nobles.

69. CH 95, l. 2.

70. Ibid., l. 70b.

71. CH 99, l. 243.

72. CH 103, l. 14.

73. CH 99, ll. 100b–11.

74. Ibid., l. 310b.

75. CH 54, ll. 33–340b. Andrei later underlined the sentence about beating both the guilty and the innocent, and added a large question mark. When he remonstrated with himself for his temper in that diary, this incident was one of the those to which he was referring. However, Andrei was not the only landlord to find himself facing peasants who refused to say who was responsible for a misdeed, so he may, in his rage, have beaten them all because he did not actually know which ones were "guilty." See a later entry, ibid., l. 500b. In his summary of March's events, under March 11, Andrei writes again about receiving the *starosta* from Yaroslavl village and how he became angry with him, which, he says, was "very bad!!"

76. CH 95, l. 3.

77. Ibid., l. 4. Years earlier, Andrei shouted at the Yaroslavl elder (it is not clear if this was the same man) for "various failures," CH 54, l. 360b.

78. Ibid., l. 46.

79. CH 59, l. 58.

80. Ibid., l. 59.

81. Ibid., l. 61.

82. CH 57, l. 33.

83. "Vernopoddannyi krest'ianin Aleksei Rudenko" ZG 98 (1835): 784.

84. CH 66, l. 57.

85. Augustine, "Notes toward a Portrait," 384.

86. Compare to the case on another estate in their province (apparently not a family they knew), where serfs alleged abuse on the part of a widowed landlady. GAIO F. 207, "Shchulepnikovykh," op. 1, d. 11. Serf unrest was notoriously common under Nicholas I, sometimes occurring on such a large scale that police were required to intervene; in 1848 a noblewoman from Kovrov was killed by her household serfs (VR, 12). Police reports recorded less than a dozen such killings, sometimes as few as three per year in this period. See *Materialy dlia istorii krepostnogo prava v Rossii* (Berlin, 1872).

87. *Vospominaniia russkikh krestian,* 512.

88. CH 66, l. 91.

89. Ibid.

90. Ibid., l. 92.

91. His daughter Olga Alekseevna married Vasilii Lvovich Alalykin, a distant relation of the Chikhachevs (VR, 33). Kascheev had several daughters, who as "young ladies" in the 1830s were frequent visitors of the Chikhachevs and, especially, Yakov.

92. They had good reason to wonder about the procedure; it is unclear by what legal means peasants could complain about their landlords at this time. But this did not mean that such complaints were unheard of; see Marrese, *Woman's Kingdom,* 229–34. For a fascinating case of peasants using the written word to navigate officialdom, see Alison K. Smith, "Authority in a Serf Village: Peasants, Managers, and the Role of Writing in Early Nineteenth Century Russia," *Journal of Social History* 43, no. 1 (Fall 2009): 157–73.

93. CH 53, ll. 22–23.

94. CH 54, l. 22.

95. CH 57, l. 57. Significantly, Natalia used only the singular personal pronoun in reference to herself—the peasants owed *her* personally, and she alone was involved in the negotiation and its consequences.

96. Boris Gorshkov has noted that a series of laws promulgated in the 1820s–50s "challenged the foundation of serfdom by reducing the power of the lord over peasants." These were "direct state responses" to peasant attitudes. Boris B. Gorshkov, "Democratizing Habermas: Peasant Public Sphere in Pre-Reform Russia," *RH* 31, no. 4 (Winter 2004): 385. David Moon writes of peasants negotiating with the law also, "misunderstanding" legislation when it suited them. *Russian Peasants and Tsarist Legislation on the Eve of Reform: Interaction between Peasants and Officialdom, 1825–1855* (Basingstoke: Macmillan, 1992); Moon also writes of serfdom as "viable and workable institutions" that "achieved some sort of balance between the needs and interests of sections of Russian society," "Reassessing Russian Serfdom," *European History Quarterly* 26 (1996): 487.

97. LeDonne, "Ruling Families."

98. Most of these "*donesenie*" that survive are from the last decade before emancipation. If all were not truly well at that time, the serf overseers upon whom Andrei and Natalia relied for these reports were apparently able to resolve the occasional difficulty—incidents of disputes between serfs or minor discontent about conditions are mentioned in some of the reports and solutions also laid out.

99. Despite troubles with serfs and fires, life was still much safer and less chaotic than what memoirist A. N. Engelgardt described in the 1870s, *Iz derevni: 12 pisem 1872–1887* (St. Petersburg, 1999). That said, a list of property left after Yakov's death includes an astonishing arsenal of weapons: two muskets, three pistols, five swords, dagger and four "pig-iron" cannon (2 small, 2 "larger"). CH 94.

100. Augustine, "Notes toward a Portrait," 380.

101. VSO, 152, 257.

102. CH 108, ll. 43–46. Aleksei noted that last time Maksimka had stolen, at a wedding, was because the host did not present him with wine together with the other guests.

103. CH 66, l. 2. Compare these accounts to a theft in an urban and military setting. In Vilno, Poland, while in the army, Aleksei's neighbor and "mentor" Vasilii Andreevich was robbed "and his manservant Lukian was strongly suspected." The loss was considerable—125 silver rubles, all the silver, and a uniform (uniforms were very expensive). No less than two generals came to look into the matter, General Buturlin and Aleksei's "uncle" Kupreianov. They were surprised "how the thief could get in in the middle of the day." CH 83, l. 380b.

104. See CH 95, l. 10b.

105. CH 59, l. 530b.

106. Ibid., l. 51.

107. CH 58, ll. 201–2010b.

108. On the prevalence of infanticide, see David Ransel, *Mothers of Misery: Child Abandonment in Russia* (Princeton: Princeton University Press, 1988).

109. CH 108, l. 440b.

110. CH 57, l. 480b.

111. *ZG* 84 (1836): 668.

CHAPTER 4

1. The root form of the word, *khoziaistvo,* describes the activity in which a *khoziaika* engages, and it has several clusters of meanings according to Dal's definitive dictionary of nineteenth-century Russian. The two relevant ones are differentiated as *domashnee khoziaistvo,* meaning housekeeping and related equipment, and *sel'skoe khoziaistvo,* meaning farmholdings as well as

agricultural activity (the third meaning is "economy" in general, as in *gosudarstvennoe khozi-aistvo*, or state finances, or *narodnoe khoziaistvo,* political economy). *Khoziaistvo* thus includes both economic activity and the totality of property and equipment involved therein. The person who both owned and managed property was a *khoziaika* (female) or *khoziain* (male), as distinguished from a *vladelets* who was merely an owner. Smith translates "*khoziaika*" as "housewife" in *Recipes.* Grigoryan in "Noble Farmers," notes that the term "*ekonom*" was analogous to *khoziaika,* based on the Greek roots for "house" and "law," 57n. Dal's dictionary states that "*ekonom*" and "*domostroi*" are synonyms. On "*khoziaika*" as "mistress of the great Soviet home," see Rebecca Neary, "Mothering Socialist Society: The Wife-Activists' Movement and the Soviet Culture of Daily Life, 1934–41," *RR* 58, no. 3 (July 1999): 396–412.

2. Natalia also did not regularly conduct trade beyond her estate; instead she sent servants or her husband to conduct that part of business according to her instructions.

3. Article 220 of the Napoleonic Code allowed an exception for women engaging in independent commerce, though they needed their husband's permission to begin a business, and their husbands had a right to any profits from said business.

4. See Suzanne Lebsock, *The Free Women of Petersburg: Status and Culture in a Southern Town, 1784–1860* (New York: Norton, 1984) and other works for accounts of how entrepreneurial women either suffered loss of social status or employed intermediaries in order to conduct business.

5. Marrese, *Woman's Kingdom,* 172.

6. Ibid., 4.

7. Ibid., 175.

8. Ibid.

9. The Chikhachevs' major debts were paid off in the late 1830s or early 1840s. Profits from quitrent payments increased significantly in the 1820s, in comparison to the years of Napoleonic wars and their aftermath, when quitrents were depressed. This may help explain how the Chikhachevs managed to pay off their debts. S. A. Nefedov, *Demograficheski-strukturnyi analiz sotsial'no-ekonomicheskoi istorii Rossii. Konets xv–nachalo xx veka* (Yekaterinburg, 2005), 204–6

10. M. Jeanne Peterson, *Family, Love, and Work in the Lives of Victorian Gentlewomen* (Bloomington: Indiana University Press, 1989), 123–31.

11. Joyce W. Warren, *Women, Money, and the Law: Nineteenth-Century Fiction, Gender, and the Courts* (Iowa City: University of Iowa Press, 2005), 3–4.

12. Peterson, *Family,* 123–31.

13. Ibid., 125.

14. Ibid.

15. The postscript contained only a few lines of formal congratulations on the Easter holiday and general well-wishes. CH 102, l. 29.

16. CH 63, l. 1210b.

17. CH 69, l. 6.

18. Occasionally, she made these trips herself, sometimes with her daughter to accompany her, but as her illnesses increased in frequency in the late 1830s she left their estate only rarely, usually for significant social occasions, and almost never without Andrei.

19. CH 63, l. 620b–63.

20. As Tosh, in *A Man's Place,* puts it: "Up-to-date notions of decorum and privacy dictated that servants be kept at arm's length," 20.

21. Amanda Vickery, *Behind Closed Doors: At Home in Georgian England* (New Haven: Yale University Press, 2009), 243–44.

22. On the transformation of middle-class knitting in England and the United States from necessary household work to decorative work pursued for leisure and as a symbol of status, see Richard Rutt, *A History of Hand Knitting* (Loveland, CO: Interweave Press, 1987); and Anne L. MacDonald, *No Idle Hands: The Social History of American Knitting* (New York: Ballantine, 1988).

23. In 1833 they spent slightly more money on clothing for Andrei than for Natalia and much less for their young children. The yearly expenditures were 180.50 rubles for Andrei's wardrobe, 178.92 for Natalia, 40.45 for Aleksei, 48.30 for Aleksandra (only four years old at that time), and 66.50 rubles for "the girls," meaning the serf girls who worked for Natalia in their house. CH 57, l. 6.

24. CH 63, l. 89. The fact that Natalia knitted and sewed clothing for her servants was not unique to provincial Russia. Catharine Clinton has shown that plantation mistresses of the American South were expected to supply their slaves as well as families with knitted stockings; senior women slaves took on all or part of this work only when the total number of slaves was too large for one person to knit all the stockings. Clinton, *The Plantation Mistress: Woman's World in the Old South* (New York: Pantheon, 1982), 28.

25. CH 57, l. 1580b.

26. Ibid., ll. 620b–63. Emphasis added.

27. Ibid., l. 590b.

28. Vickery, *Behind Closed Doors*, 254.

29. CH 58, ll. 1240b–125.

30. Tosh, *A Man's Place*, 20n.

31. Carolyn Pouncy, *The "Domostroi": Rules for Russian Households in the Time of Ivan the Terrible* (Ithaca, NY: Cornell University Press, 1994). See also Smith, *Recipes*; and Darra Goldstein, "Domestic Porkbarreling in Nineteenth-Century Russia, or Who Holds the Keys to the Larder?," in *Russia, Women, Culture*, ed. Helena Goscilo and Beth Holmgren (Bloomington: Indiana University Press, 1996).

32. CH 69, l. 6.

33. CH 63, l. 470b.

34. CH 57, ll. 63–74.

35. Ibid., ll. 880b–89.

36. Ibid., ll. 96, 970b.

37. CH 59, l. 62.

38. CH 57, ll. 8, 11. Andrei, also, was not absent from the larder. He and Natalia simultaneously made their own vinegar. They are listed as "Natasha's vinegar" and " . . . and mine" and marked with the dates they were poured (CH 36a, l. 21).

39. Cf. Goldstein, "Domestic Porkbarreling," which does not address the presence, before 1861, of serf housekeepers and cooks. Andrei's notion of an ideal woman of the house is a class-based notion, and he wanted to see this ideal fulfilled because he saw it as the duty of his class to play this stabilizing role in society.

40. See Smith, *Recipes*, 110–11.

41. CH 59, l. 9.

42. CH 67, l. 20b. Lists of the items they bought, often including the location of purchase and almost always the price, are abundant. Natalia's diaries, account books, including those filled out

by her son and husband in her later years and after her death, and Chernavin account books are all rich sources for the historian of material culture. Andrei also listed in two versions the complete inventory of goods owned by Yakov at his death (CH 94; 93, l. 5–9) and listed his own collection of dishware and other household goods in his notebooks (CH 127 and 36a, ll. 17, 19). These documents deserve separate treatment.

43. CH 63, ll. 240b–25.

44. Ibid., l. 121ob.

45. CH 67, l. 48ob.

46. CH 63, ll. 86ob–87.

47. In the surviving account book (CH 55), Andrei's handwriting appears occasionally, presumably when Natalia was absent or very ill. Unfortunately, most of the surviving notes about finances seem to be drafts, lacking key information, so it is not possible to extract reliable figures about their annual income and expenses.

48. CH 95.

49. CH 63, 67, 69.

50. CH 58, l. 155ob. The sentence continues: "third, at 11 o'clock it's already time to sleep, and fourth, [I] need to send Akulina to Shuia already."

51. The few occasions on which she broke out of the cliched expressions of sisterly affection attest to her sincere, even plaintive, attachment to her brother: "And you, my friend, have been a guest at M[aria] P[etrovna's] for too long. Today Mikhaila did not even bring a quick note from you." CH 58, ll. 124ob–125.

52. Ibid., ll. 110, 111.

53. CH 57, l. 48.

54. Ibid.

55. CH 54, l. 23ob.

56. Though Andrei later claimed not to even know how many serfs he owned, much less their names, he was likely referring to the small villages and parts of villages that he owned but did not regularly visit. CH 98. See also Smith-Peter, "Books Behind the Altar."

57. CH 57, ll. 41ob–42.

58. CH 66, l. 120ob. The repetition of adverbs should not be taken to denote sarcasm; Andrei frequently wrote in this style with complete sincerity.

59. CH 58, l. 143ob.

60. CH 52. Andrei was put in charge of 133 villages by an imperial order (ll. 42–42ob).

61. Andrei's activities are evidenced in his diaries and several "to-do" lists, which pertain almost exclusively to the maintenance of buildings and grounds or to serfs, see CH 36a, ll. 24–24ob.

62. "Vazhnost' khoziaiki v dome," ZG (1847–48). In Georgian Britain the home retained its early modern definition as a household including servants, apprentices, and "resident kin" well into the eighteenth century at least. Vickery, *Behind Closed Doors*, 7. The legal restrictions on women's management of property created a gap between Russian and British women's experiences, even while the realities of both were slow to match the rhetoric model, if they ever did. See Marrese, *Woman's Kingdom*.

63. CH 71, l. 5.

64. Natalia's remarks were recorded by Andrei: "Natasha, having gotten herself busy with yarn, offered me Mr. Bulgarin," referring to Faddei Bulgarin, his favorite author. This typical

passage reads as though Natalia were offering a toy to a bothersome child to keep him out of the way of the grownups. CH 57, l. 72.

65. CH 54, l. 16.

66. See CH 58, l. 106, where Andrei shows more confidence, perhaps in an effort to motivate himself to do better than he had in the past. Referring to a visit he must make to the Marshal of the Nobility about a legal case involving Rykovo, he wrote, "[h]ere it is important to get some advice and to have the time to compose the signature notation, and it is better to do it a day early rather than a minute too late."

67. CH 59, l. 46ob. In this case she referred to Andrei's attempt at writing his own novel.

68. CH 54, l. 12. The second mention of his irritation is on l. 19ob. His temper was a problem for Andrei, and there are several mentions of temper aimed at other people. He even wrote down a list of "laws" for himself, which included #5: "don't get angry—don't get involved in what's superfluous—*toujours le sang-froid*" to which he later added in the margin: "Oh! Wise!" (l. 18). The other incidents of temper recorded in this diary were aimed at his servants, when, on one occasion, they put Aleksei's feet in cold boots and failed to cover him with a blanket (l. 22) and on another, when they allowed him get too near a hot samovar (ll. 33–34ob). On Andrei's use of French as a code for less savory remarks, see also the following French passage in his parallel diary in the middle of an entry otherwise in Russian: "During the night I was obliged to leave six times for bowel movements (*la selle*)," CH 95, l. 5.

69. CH 57, l. 76ob.

70. CH 59, l. 45ob.

71. CH 57, l. 55ob. Inscribed as "noon" in "Paris." It was an inside joke between them for Andrei to pretend he was writing to his brother-in-law from this exotic locale.

72. Ibid., l. 74ob. Emphasis added.

73. CH 71, l. 9.

74. CH 83, l. 69ob.

75. Ibid., l. 71ob.

76. Beverly Wilson Palmer, ed., *A Woman's Wit and Whimsy: The 1833 Diary of Anna Cabot Lowell Quincy* (Boston: Northeastern University Press, 2003), 12.

77. See Robin Bisha, *Russian Women, 1698–1917: Experience and Expression, an Anthology of Sources* (Bloomington: Indiana University Press, 2002) for several short excerpts from Russian women's documents of the period.

78. Laurel Thatcher Ulrich, *A Midwife's Tale: The Life of Martha Ballard, Based on Her Diary, 1785–1812* (New York: Knopf, 1990).

79. Catherine II of Russia, *The Memoirs of Catherine the Great*, ed. Mark Cruse and Hilde Hoogenboom (New York: Modern Library, 2005); E. R. Dashkova, *The Memoirs of Princess Dashkova*, ed. Kyril FitzLyon, Jehanne M. Gheith, and A. Woronzoff-Dashkoff (Durham: Duke University Press, 1995); Nadezhda Durova, *Cavalry Maiden: Journals of a Female Russian Officer in the Napoleonic Wars* (London: Angel Books, 1988).

80. See also Anna Evdokimovna Labzina, *Days of a Russian Noblewoman: The Memories of Anna Labzina, 1758–1821*, ed. Gary Marker and Rachel May (DeKalb: Northern Illinois University Press, 2001); and Gary Marker's insightful interpretation, "The Enlightenment of Anna Labzina: Gender, Faith, and Public Life in Catherinian and Alexandrian Russia," *SR* 59, no. 2 (2000): 369–90.

81. The surviving account book begins with lists of nouns and ends with sentences in its final pages. By date, it ends shortly before the first surviving diary was begun, suggesting that the diary

evolved out of the account book even though she also continued to make separate accounting lists after her diaries began (CH 55). Two notebooks kept by Andrei in the first few years of their marriage (CH 36a, 37) contain estate records similar to those later kept by Natalia and suggest that he may have started out doing some or all of this work. However, his records are incomplete and were soon abandoned. There are scattered notes in Natalia's hand annotating Andrei's records, suggesting that they were either working together or that she took over because he could not attend to the records adequately. Andrei's version is very different from Natalia's in form. Where she wrote daily prose summaries of all transactions on the estate, Andrei dedicated a notebook to record keeping in which he sliced tabs into the sides of the pages and labeled them with the letters of the alphabet. Data was kept in lists, by alphabetized category. This organization was typical of both his and Yakov's obsession with Enlightenment-style reference data, but unlike Chernavin's, Andrei's notebook was quickly taken over by other kinds of notes and pieces of information unrelated to estate management.

82. CH 69, l.450b.

83. Palmer, *A Woman's Wit and Whimsy*, x.

CHAPTER 5

1. CH. 67, l. 40b

2. CH 57, l. 410b.

3. CH 58, l. 1240b.

4. CH 103, ll. 114, 115. From a letter to Elisei Mochalin, 1860.

5. E.g., CH 60, l. 2. Yakov was visited by A. A. Kablukov, then went to S. I. Karetnikov's in the evening, where he enjoyed dancing, singing, "masks" and whist.

6. CH 57, l. 12.

7. Ibid.

8. CH 57, ll. 12–13.

9. CH 57, l. 1090b. See also CH 66, l. 153, Andrei: "We invited guests over, but my wife became very sick and so we had to send them a cancellation."

10. CH 61, l. 1450b.

11. CH 83, l. 790b. A *gusli* is a Russian traditional instrument, similar to a zither or a small, flat harp.

12. CH 60, l. 2.

13. CH 54, l. 4.

14. Frolov, *Kovrovskaia biblioteka*. 7; quote from an 1850 article in ZG.

15. CH 58, l. 162.

16. CH 83, l. 80.

17. CH 155, l. 103.

18. CH 54, l. 50.

19. CH 57, l. 89.

20. CH 98, l. 200b; 54, l. 80b.

21. CH 54, l. 140b.

22. CH 59, l. 8.

23. CH 58, l. 1520b.

24. CH 83, l. 800b.

25. CH 71, l. 100b.

26. CH 83, ll. 780b–790b. This passage is from a brief sojourn at home that Aleksei enjoyed in the middle of his first year of military service. "Breakfast" was taken at around midday or slightly earlier. "Dinner" was in the late afternoon, "tea"—in the English sense, including a light snack— around six p.m., and "supper" was in the later evening.

27. See VR.

28. The date of her wedding is unknown, but Aleksei wrote of her engagement in May, 1848 (CH 83, l. 1250b.), and her first son was born the same year. Her husband, Vasilii Ragozin, the same age as Aleksei, was retired from the Life Guards Moscow Regiment in May, 1847. VR, 116.

29. CH 54, l. 140b.

30. Ibid., l. 16.

31. CH 103, l. 430b.

32. CH 58, l. 179.

33. CH 95, l. 9.

34. CH 112, l. 35.

35. CH 54, l. 220b.

36. VSO, 143. See also Cavender, *Nests,* which demonstrates that the gentry of Tver province were similarly contented.

37. The diarist Anna Labzina and the prominent letter-writer Zinaida Volkonskaia not only found solace in religious faith but also used the cultural power attached to their reputations for piety, in later life, to achieve respect from male peers and a relatively independent lifestyle. Labzina, *Days of a Russian Noblewoman*; Marker, "God of Our Mothers," in *Orthodox Russia: Belief and Practice under the Tsars,* ed. Valerie Kivelson and Robert Greene (University Park: Pennsylvania State University Press, 2003); Marker, "Enlightenment of Anna Labzina"; Maria Fairweather, *Pilgrim Princess: A Life of Princess Zinaida Volkonsky* (New York: Carroll and Graf, 2000); and Bayara Aroutunova, *Lives in Letters: Princess Zinaida Volkonskaya and Her Correspondence* (Columbus, OH: Slavica, 1994). One might also look to popular prototypes of female saints, such as Ulianiia Osorgin (see Brenda Meehan-Waters, *Holy Women of Russia: The Lives of Five Orthodox Women Offer Spiritual Guidance for Today* [San Francisco: Harper, 1993]), to monastic women (see Marlyn Miller, "Under the protection of the Virgin: The Feminization of Monasticism in Imperial Russia, 1700–1923," [PhD diss., Brandeis, 2009]), or to the *Domostroi* model of the female head of household for other ways in which religious vocation could be a means of gaining independence and respect. See also Adele Lindenmeyr, "Public Life, Private Virtues: Women in Russian Charity, 1762–1914," *Signs* 18, no. 3 (1993); William Wagner, "'Orthodox Domesticity': Creating a Social Role for Women" in *Sacred Stories: Religion and Spirituality in Modern Russia,* ed. Mark D. Steinberg and Heather J. Coleman (Bloomington: Indiana University Press, 2007); Isolde Thyret, *Between God and Tsar: Religious Symbolism and the Royal Women of Muscovite Russia* (DeKalb: Northern Illinois University Press, 2001). In John Randolph's *The House in the Garden: The Bakunin Family and the Romance of Russian Idealism* (Ithaca: Cornell University Press, 2007), the author traces the influence of French spiritualist ideas on the Stankevich circle through Mikhail Bakunin's mother.

38. Contrary to Lindenmeyr, G. N. Ulianova argues that up to 80 percent of charitable donations among Moscow merchants after 1860 were what she calls "prestige money" rather than anonymous/religion-driven. See *Blagotvoritelnost moskovskikh predprinimatelei, 1860–1914* (Moscow, 1999).

39. CH 63, ll. 240b–25. Natalia's references to charity are scattered throughout her diaries and account books. Yakov also noted giving 1.75 rubles "to poor nobles" in one of his notebooks (CH 61, l. 117).

40. CH 112, l. 940b.

41. CH 102, l. 29.

42. CH 83, l.3.

43. CH 95, l. 50b.

44. Her participation was mentioned in letters from Father Sila. CH 99.

45. CH 58, l. 99. "*Maloumnyi.*"

46. CH 100, ll. 70b–8.

47. In the list of Yakov's possessions made after his death in 1845, a number of icons of the Mother of God were specifically named (CH 93, ll. 5–9). On Marianism see Vera Shevzov, *Russian Orthodoxy on the Eve of Revolution* (New York: Oxford University Press, 2007), and Christine Worobec, "Lived Orthodoxy in Imperial Russia," *Kritika* 7, no. 2 (Spring 2006): 329–50.

48. CH 58, l. 199.

49. See also Glagoleva, *Tul'skaia knizhnaia starina.*

50. For example, Andrei wrote, "All day I was reading aloud for the second time for my wife the first part of the green manuscript," CH 59, l. 51. Natalia regularly mentioned knitting while listening to Andrei read in her diaries. See also Andrei's article, "O ezhednevnom v slukh domashnem chtenii"; Rutt, *History of Hand Knitting*, ch. 5.

51. CH 66, ll. 21–220b.

52. CH 57, l. 190b.

53. Ibid., l. 290b.

54. Ibid., l. 950b.

55. CH 58, l. 44.

56. Ibid., l. 480b.

57. Ibid., l. 160.

58. Ibid.

59. CH 59, l. 77.

60. Ibid., l. 25.

61. Their copies of the *Agricultural Gazette* were bound for each year, and later donated to Andrei's public library at Zimenki (with an inscription in Andrei's handwriting saying the books were given by "landowner-parishioners Andrei and Natalia"). This collection of bound volumes, with his marginalia, are kept at the town museum in Shuia. Unfortunately, most of the rest of the Zimenki library was lost some time after the 1917 Revolution. An example of his marginalia is the note "Great—good article" on a piece titled "On a few activities in sheep husbandry and field agriculture." ZG 25 (1848): 193.

62. CH 54, l. 17.

63. CH 58, l. 1780b.

64. Other periodicals mentioned only briefly: *Soldataksia beseda, Listok dlia vsekh, Posrednik, Russkaia rech', Strannik,* and *Rassvet.* See CH 103, l. 51 and 106, l. 129 for lists of periodicals composed by Andrei. Other mentions are scattered throughout the *fond.*

65. See Frazier, *Romantic Encounters.*

66. Named booksellers are N. Lutkovskii, also mentioned as an author; Polevoi, probably Nikolai Polevoi, an editor and fixture of middlebrow literature of the period; and Glazunov of Moscow.

67. CH 94; 93, l. 80b.

68. Lists of Yakov's books are incomplete, going only to *D* (CH 61, l. 1540b), and references in the diaries and notebook correspondence are often cryptic. There are also lists of books available from booksellers (ibid.). On Andrei's love for the Lexicon, see CH 57, l. 1100b, where he lists his favorite words under *A*.

69. CH 54, l. 460b.

70. CH 57, l. 30b.

71. Ibid., l. 330b. Yakov disagreed about *The Cuckold* (*Rogonosets*), perhaps because Yakov read it in the original.

72. CH 59, l. 550b. Other foreign works mentioned were tales of exploration or military history (especially relating to Napoleon), a work by Madame de la Fayette (ibid., l. 690b), Greek gospels, and a "Holy History of the Old and New Testaments, decorated with 700 superb drawings" (CH 61, l. 57).

73. CH 95, l. 1200b.

74. CH 86.

75. CH 61, l. 1540b, 570b.

76. CH 58, l. 1690b.

77. CH 83, l. 50b.

78. She mentioned having read something in about forty percent of the entries in her diary, but she named titles or authors only very rarely.

79. The latter two are mentioned in CH 54, l. 9. Andrei read them aloud to Natalia.

80. Ann Wierda Rowland has pointed out that while sentimental novels were famously condemned for featuring women "of excessive, unhealthy, false, or downright silly sensibility," those female characters were often paired for effect with women of "just and natural feeling," as in Austen's *Sense and Sensibility*. Rowland, "Sentimental Fiction" in *The Cambridge Companion to Fiction in the Romantic Period,* ed. Richard Maxwell and Katie Trumpener (Cambridge: Cambridge University Press, 2008), 200–201; In "'A Larger Portion of the Public': Female Readers, Fiction, and the Periodical Press in the Reign of Nicholas I," in *An Improper Profession: Women, Gender, and Journalism in Late Imperial Russia*, ed. Barbara T. Norton and Jehanne M. Gheith (Durham, NC: Duke University Press, 2001), 26–52, Miranda Remnek uses subscription lists, memoirs, and *belles lettres* to demonstrate that other female readers like Natalia were indeed present in the provinces; she concerns herself mainly with their reading of fiction, though not because she sees fiction as gendered female.

81. CH 57. ll. 630b–640b, 690b.

82. See Gary Marker, *Publishing, Printing, and the Origins of Intellectual Life in Russia, 1700–1800* (Princeton: Princeton University Press, 1985); Jeffrey Brooks, *When Russia Learned to Read: Literacy and Popular Literature, 1861–1917* (Princeton: Princeton University Press, 1985); Frazier *Romantic Encounters*; and Grigoryan, "Noble Farmers." Frazier is the most skeptical, writing that "despite the 5,000 subscribers to the *Library for Reading*, there is little evidence in Russia for any real rise of a literary marketplace nor for any corresponding changes in the makeup of the reading public."

83. Grigoryan, "Noble Farmers," 184: "The very fact that Russian authors of domestic manuals offer a variety of conceptions of their readership as people of 'middling estate', 'average means', 'limited or modest means' or members of 'middling circles of society' may be read as a series of attempts to approximate a demographic category, a collective search for a word to call a readership that itself is a discursive construction." See also Frazier, *Romantic Encounters*.

84. See Frazier, *Romantic Encounters,* for a recent in-depth survey of the scholarship on this question in Russia.

85. Maxwell and Trumpener, especially William St. Clair, "Publishing, Authorship, and Reading."

86. A monetary reform in 1839 decreased the price of books, and a series of poor harvests starting from 1838 created a general economic depression. When recovery might have expected by the late 1840s, the revolutionary year 1848 brought instead an increase in censorship. See Frazier, *Romantic Encounters,* 37.

87. Grigoryan "Noble Farmers" and Frazier, *Romantic Encounters.* Frazier quotes critic Vissarion Belinsky as calling the reading public a "terrible invisible master," 100.

88. See Smith, *Recipes*; Marrese, *Woman's Kingdom;* Grigoryan, "Noble Farmers"; Kelly, *Refining Russia.*

89. See Cavender, *Nests of the Gentry*; Glagoleva, *Tul'skaia knizhnaia starina.* On Tver as an "any town" symbolic of the Russian provinces, see Frazier, *Romantic Encounters,* 92–93.

90. Though it was Andrei who wrote frequent encomiums to Bulgarin, Yakov also admired him, and there is no indication that Natalia or any other member of the household or a neighbor disliked Bulgarin. If they had, Andrei would likely have mentioned it, since he would no doubt have found such an opinion aggravating.

91. Grigoryan in "Noble Farmers" restores his significance to the canon as a major influence in the development of the Russian novel.

92. *Ekonom* was mentioned at least once, when Yakov wrote in his notebook that the twelfth issue had "come out." CH 61, l. 57.

93. On Pushkin's role see Frazier, *Romantic Encounters,* 26–29, 30–31. Also Grigoryan, "Noble Farmers," ch. 2, on how Bulgarin and Gogol were also involved.

94. Bulgarin's favorite was "well-intentioned" (*blagonamerennyi*), Grigoryan, "Noble Farmers," 117. Andrei employed similar terms referring to morality and good intentions (the roots *blag-, nrav-, dobr-,* etc.). Grigoryan also quotes the following entertaining critiques of Bulgarin's prose that could equally apply to Andrei's: "here's a labyrinth of chemistry and grammar" and "in what language one may say 'an economic true story', I really do not know," 110, quoted from an 1845 review of Bulgarin's journal *Ekonom, Otechestvennye zapiski* 38 (1845): "Smes," 27.

95. CH 58, l. 174. On the same occasion, Yakov also enthused about an article by Baron Brambeus, a pseudonym of Osip Senkovskii, the editor of *Library for Reading.*

96. CH 57, l. 41.

97. CH 58, l. 1780b.

98. CH 59, l. 330b.

99. CH 54, l. 53.

100. CH 58, l. 1780b.

101. CH 59, l. 490b. Possibly the work under discussion was Konshin's *Graf Oboianskii, ili Smolensk v 1812 godu,* which they seem to have been comparing unfavorably to Zagoskin's novel *Iurii Miloslavskii, ili Russkie v 1612 godu.*

102. Frazier, *Romantic Encounters,* cites typical circulation figures for the eighteenth century as 600–1,200 copies, while the *Library for Reading* "almost immediately achieved an estimated 5,000–7,000 subscribers," 23.

103. Marker, *Publishing,* 177–83.

104. Quoted in Grigoryan, "Noble Farmers," 73. Marker's study found no evidence for or against Karamzin's claim. The Chikhachev evidence can do no better, but it does suggest that the claim is plausible at least by the 1830s.

105. St. Clair, "Publishing, Authorship, and Reading," 33.

106. CH 57. l. 38.

107. Frazier, *Romantic Encounters,* 110.

108. CH 58, l. 1780b.

109. Frazier, *Romantic Encounters,* 91.

110. CH 66, l. 64.

111. Ibid., l. 16.

112. Probably Nikolai Petrovich Lutkovskii, probably also the N. Lutkovskii from whose Moscow bookshop Yakov Chernavin received a package of books, CH 59, l. 330b. Yakov received two novellas, "The Love of My Neighbor" and "Four Fictions."

113. Ibid., l. 300b.

114. Ibid., l. 19–200b. See B. L. Riftin, "Povestvovatel'naia proza: Kitaiskaia literatura XVII v." *Istoriia vsemirnoi literatury* 4:486–97.

115. Grigoryan, "Noble Farmers," 40. It should be pointed out that the *Library for Reading* tried as much as other periodicals to model an ideal provincial reader (see Frazier, *Romantic Encounters*). Its success may perhaps be because it was so eclectic that it hit on something for every taste in each packed issue.

116. Frazier, *Romantic Encounters,* 102.

117. Ibid., 111.

118. CH 57, l. 74.

119. Thomas Newlin, *The Voice in the Garden: Andrei Bolotov and the Anxieties of the Russian Pastoral, 1760–1833* (Evanston: Northwestern University Press, 2001), 87.

120. E. N. Marasinova, quoted in Grigoryan, "Noble Farmers," 53.

121. Cavender, *Nests of the Gentry.* Cavender's research also finds that provincial gentry understood their communities as vertical, encompassing serfs and middling groups in addition to their fellow nobles.

122. CH 57, l. 58.

123. Quoted in Frazier, *Romantic Encounters,* 132. Her translation.

124. Belinsky (like other members of the intelligentsia) was strongly influenced by his stay at the Bakunin family estate. Though a rural setting, it was not a "provincial" one in the sense of being outside circles of wealth and/or influence. See Randolph, *House in the Garden,* 1–2 and ch. 9.

CHAPTER 6

1. CH 63, l. 2. Vera Nikiforovna's last name was underlined but illegible.

2. CH 57, l. 30b. On another occasion, Andrei suggests to his "dear Uncle" that he ought to get better soon, so that Yakov might marry (CH 58, ll. 156–1560b.)

3. CH 58, l. 650b.

4. Ibid., l. 1700b.

5. CH 54, l. 340b.

6. CH 57, l. 20b.

7. CH 59, l. 6.

8. CH 57, l. 20b

9. CH 59, l. 70b.

10. Ibid.

11. Ibid., l. 80b.

12. CH 57, l. 62.

13. Ibid.

14. CH 59, l. 39.

15. CH 57, l. 63.

16. Ibid., l. 74.

17. CH 83, l. 1.

18. CH 95, l. 10b.

19. "Kamennoi dom v derevne," ZG, 25 (1845), 198–99.

20. CH 95, l. 70b.

21. In the West, hysteria was used as a catch-all diagnosis for a vast range of symptoms, but was limited to women and, in some interpretations, was seen to be caused by sexual dissatisfaction. See: Katrien Libbrecht, *Hysterical Psychosis: A Historical Survey* (New Brunswick, NJ: Transaction, 1995); Mark S. Micale, *Approaching Hysteria: Disease and Its Interpretations* (Princeton: Princeton University Press, 1995); Niel Micklem, *The Nature of Hysteria* (New York: Routledge, 1996). According to Dal's dictionary—which, significantly, dates from the later nineteenth century (1863–66)—*isterika* was "a woman's nervous illness, marked by unending, varied fits, noisier than it is dangerous."

22. See also Judith Schneid Lewis, *In the Family Way: Childbearing in the British Aristocracy, 1760–1860* (New Brunswick, NJ: Rutgers University Press, 1986); and Vickery, *Gentleman's Daughter*, ch. 3.

23. CH 60, ll. 3, 9.

24. CH 58, l. 1900b.

25. Ibid., ll. 178, 184, 195–1950b, 200–2000b, 2070b, 2110b. Yakov's diary indicates that his visiting with Andrei was completely curtailed until May, but by June their routines returned to normal, CH 60, ll. 28–53.

26. CH 66, l. 144.

27. CH 71, l. 30b.

28. CH 60, l. 172.

29. CH 100, l. 27.

30. CH 112, l. 57.

31. CH 116, l. 16.

32. Peterson, *Family*, 117–18.

33. CH 59, l. 44. Andrei's term, translated here as "poorly" was *durno*, "poorness" *durnota*, and "crap" *driani*.

34. CH 108, ll. 43–430b.

35. See Antonov, "Law and the Culture of Debt," who describes an elderly Old Believer merchant who cited depression as the major cause of his insolvency during his trial for debt in this period, 130.

36. CH 59, l. 59.

37. Ibid., l. 39.

38. Ibid., l. 610b.

39. CH 66, l. 520b.

40. CH 59, l. 330b.

41. CH 58, l. 2050b.

42. CH 67, l. 90b.

43. CH 98, l. 250b.

44. CH 112, l. 100.

45. Ibid., l. 3. "*Shishichki, chiryshki, pupyshki.*"

46. CH 83, l. 170b. See also a reference to "*lishai,*" a serious rash, CH 58, l. 162.

47. CH 83, l. 160b.

48. CH 106, l. 29.

49. CH 66, ll. 153–55. Andrei added that Shuia was "luring" Dr. Vorobievskii with a house and fine salary, because he "knows his business . . . much better than Mr. Gildebrant."

50. CH 66, l. 35a.

51. CH 58, l. 1980b.

52. CH 102, l. 30.

53. CH 66, l. 143.

54. VSO 3, 344.

55. VSO, 155–56.

56. ZG 41 (1847): 191.

57. CH 99, l. 140b; 54, l. 34; 58, ll. 17, 650b, 1610b, 1960b; ll. 910b–92; 66, l. 520b.

58. CH 99, l. 310b.

59. CH 57, l. 98; 59, l. 62.

60. Ibid., l. 98.

61. CH 66, l. 35. The term was *polynovka*.

62. CH 59, l. 34.

63. CH 58, ll. 184–1840b.

64. CH 95, l. 41.

65. Ibid., l. 570b. The letter was copied into the notebook correspondence, apparently so Yakov's opinion could also be solicited.

66. CH 54, l. 370b.

67. CH 59, l. 48.

68. Ibid., l. 52.

69. E.g., CH 58, l. 17.

70. CH 83, l. 90b.

71. CH 66, l. 49.

72. CH 58, l. 192.

73. VSO, 252.

74. CH 59, ll. 47–470b.

75. VSO, 232. Andrei mentions a Dr. Kikin treating one of his serfs and then breakfasting with Andrei (CH 95, l. 2). Doctors were common enough in early Victorian England; for example, the Tait family lost several children to scarlet fever and in the process consulted an abundance of professional doctors. Peterson, *Family*, 110–14. However, as Ulrich has shown in *Midwife's Tale*, the professionalization of medical practice by university-trained men was just beginning in the United States in the early nineteenth century. It seems unlikely that provincial Russia, with its

very low population density and relatively small number of universities, would be as well supplied with trained physicians as England. G. I. Popov, *Russkaia narodno-bytovaia meditsina: po materialam Etnograficheskogo biuro kniazia V.N. Tenisheva* (Riazan: Aleksandriia, 2010) provides an overview of folk medicine in Russia; Elisa Becker's *Medicine, Law and the State in Imperial Russia* (Central European University Press, 2010) and Charlotte Henze's *Disease, Health Care and Government in Late Imperial Russia: Life and Death on the Volga, 1823–1914* (New York: Routledge, 2011) fill in a wider picture of, apparently, uneven development across the empire.

76. CH 58, l. 168. Other doctors mentioned were Shcherovskii and Bistrom, most often by Yakov, CH 60.

77. CH 60, l. 52, Yakov's left arm was bled by a doctor, and another time a Dr. I. P. Aleksandrov put twenty-six leeches on Andrei's "waist" for chest and stomach pain (CH 95, l. 6).

78. Ibid., l. 178.

79. CH 59, l. 69.

80. CH 108, ll. 308ob–309.

81. CH 70, l. 470b.

82. CH 105, l. 331.

83. CH 95, l.58; 98, ll. 50b, 60b.

84. CH 71, l. 90b.

85. CH 95, l. 58. Between 1838 and 1842 there is a mysterious gap in the documents, coinciding with the quarrel between Andrei and Yakov. The notebook correspondence, Natalia's diaries, and Yakov's parallel diary all end around the close of 1837 (Andrei's diary for that time was, suggestively, lost). It seems likely that the relative dearth of documents is related to the quarrel, or perhaps the coincidence of the quarrel following upon Aleksei's departure for school in Moscow in the autumn of 1837, and the baby Varvara's death in June of the following year. It is also possible that Natalia's and Andrei's diaries did continue, but were destroyed later on, especially if they contained material about the quarrel that they or their descendants later found upsetting. Most of their notebooks were hand-bound, so excisions were possible. Natalia's 1842 diary (CH 71), however, is in a pre-bound book that was taken over by Aleksei, a few years later, with no gap in the pages. Also, Yakov's parallel diary (CH 60) was kept regularly until January 1838 and then left empty for the remaining pre-dated pages through the end of the volume in December of the same year, so he did simply stop diary keeping altogether at this time.

86. Ibid., ll. 350b–370b. Andrei implies that another person may have come between the "brothers," possibly a Petr Alekseevich, who Andrei writes "has revealed himself."

87. Ibid., l. 58.

88. A dialogue between Andrei and Yakov from a few years before their quarrel may shed some light if only by attesting to Yakov's temper being possibly livelier than it appears in his other writing. While discussing the book *The Cuckold,* Andrei jocularly wrote, "I even consider that if I ever decide to make you a cuckold, then the first useful way to do this will be through oratory surpassing that of Demosthenes and Cicero." But Yakov's reply was (seemingly) serious: "You are joking, brother—[yet] you know me, that I will [call you out] for a duel merely for such an insolent thought and then don't hope to go on living without your nose and ears—no, my dear, it will be done simply with pistols at three paces' distance." CH 57, l. 64.

89. The Russian army was engaged against an uprising in Krakow in 1846, in Moldavia and Walachia in 1848 (to defeat a Romanian national movement), and again in Poland in 1849 to

suppress the 1848–49 Hungarian Revolution, which was supported by many Poles. Aleksei went on campaign in early 1848. He saw action, briefly, in Poland that year, but was not severely wounded.

90. VR, 117.

91. CH 105, 106, 108.

92. CH 108, l. 173.

93. CH 99, l. 190, "The death of Sashonochka. The Lord bless [us] August 1850."

94. CH 59, l. 1.

95. CH 99, l. 2500b.

96. CH 54, l. 26. From "The Madmen" by a "Mr. Spisei."

97. CH 99, ll. 232–33.

98. Ibid., l. 273.

99. CH 100.

100. CH 54, l. 460b.

101. CH 66, l. 64.

102. See Susan Smith-Peter, "The Local as Familial Space in the Mid-Nineteenth Century: A. I. Chikhachev's *The District Treasurehouse*" (Mid-Atlantic Slavic Conference, New York, NY, April 4, 2009) for the story of the county reference book, as well as Andrei's plans for its continuation after his death. Her quotes on the latter are from the Kopytovskii notebook correspondence, CH 98.

103. CH 54, ll. 320b–33.

CHAPTER 7

1. CH 116.

2. CH 93.

3. Greene, 79. See also Kelly, *Refining Russia.*

4. Richard Wortman, "The Russian Empress as Mother," in *Family in Imperial Russia: New Lines of Historical Research*, ed. David L. Ransel (Urbana: University of Illinois Press, 1978), 60–61.

5. On the unproblematic reception of imported ideas alongside stable Russian self-identities, see Marrese, "Poetics Revisited."

6. "Vazhnost' khoziaiki v dome," ZG 53 (1847): 417–19.

7. Ibid.

8. Ibid.

9. Ibid.

10. Ibid.

11. His journalism and, even more so, his fund-raising for local religious and educational causes must be considered a real and important public service, especially his founding of the public library. But these activities occupied him only for the ten years between his children's marriages and his declining health in the latter half of the 1860s. The article under discussion was published in 1847, when he had only just begun to engage in public discourse.

12. "Vazhnost' khoziaiki v dome," ZG 53.

13. Ibid.

14. CH 54, l. 35–350b. Emphasis added.

15. Marrese has shown this conception of the "home" as the larger estate to be common to the Russian nobility. Marrese, *Woman's Kingdom*.

16. "Vazhnost' khoziaiki v dome," ZG 37:294.

17. CH 54, l. 12.

18. See Kelly, *Refining Russia*, on modesty and young ladies. The qualities considered necessary to catch a husband were very different from those needed to run an estate.

19. The Russian reads much more smoothly: "*Nezabvennaia moia golubushka—starushka radel'nitsa moia.*"

20. CH 112 l. 94ob.

21. "Kamennoi dom v derevne," ZG 25 (1845): 198–99.

22. "O komnatnom vozdukhe," ZG 6 (1845): 44–45.

23. "Eshche neskol'ko slov o dolgakh." In another article, Andrei wrote that his ideal family life, lived according to "a strict plan" of prayer, reading, and daily conversation, would not be possible "if husband and wife do not think about this completely similarly. Only in their mutual agreement can any good beginning operate." "Sochustvie k mysli o derevenskikh vrachakh" ZG 80 (1848): 635.

24. "Eshche neskol'ko slov o dolgakh."

25. Ibid. Original emphasis.

26. The separation was not, of course, always complete: "Writers and 'men of letters' . . . worked at home, often heavily reliant on the unacknowledged secretarial assistance of a wife or daughter," Tosh, *A Man's Place,*17.

27. Tosh notes that this tendency "must not be overstated," but it was the model on which expectations were formed, *A Man's Place,* 7.

28. Ibid., 13–18.

29. Ibid., 13.

30. Vickery, *Behind Closed Doors*, 7.

31. CH 99, l. 210ob.

32. CH 59, l. 580ob.

33. Galina Ulianova, *Female Entrepreneurs in Nineteenth-Century Russia* (London: Pickering & Chatto, 2009), 41–43, 76, 120–21.

34. Marrese, *A Woman's Kingdom.*

35. Barbara Alpern Engel, *Breaking the Ties That Bound: The Politics of Marital Strife in Late Imperial Russia* (Ithaca, NY: Cornell University Press, 2011), 157. Despite the similarity, the Kupriianovs were probably not related to the noble Kupreianov family.

36. Jared Camins-Esakov, "Mediating Wives: The Role of Women in the Construction of the Russian Canon" (paper presented at the Mid-Atlantic Slavic Conference, New York, March 26, 2011), 10.

37. Randolph, *House in the Garden.*

38. "Ekonomiia. O vvedenii pravil'nago lesnago khoziaistva Grafineiu Sof'eiu Vladimirovnoiu Stroganovoiu," SP 3 (1835): 11–12.

39. Smith, *Recipes*, 140. Gotovtseva's articles appeared in 1822, 1835, and 1836.

40. Peterson, *Family,* 132.

41. Vickery, *Behind Closed Doors*, 127.

42. Ibid., 120.

43. Ibid., 13.

44. Neither did gentry women of the American South. See Clinton, *Plantation Mistress.*

45. Vickery, *Behind Closed Doors,* 9.

46. Ibid.

47. Peterson, *Family.* See her discussion of Eleanor Ormerod (149) or the career of Catherine Tait. This model was present in Russia, too: one "beneficent landlady" of Chernigov province, reported the *Agricultural Gazette* in 1835, used the interest from her fortune of twenty-five thousand rubles to pay the taxes for her 266 peasants in perpetuity. For her generosity Uliana Selivanovich received the "goodwill" of the sovereign, who ordered that her action be publicized ("Blagodetel'naia pomeschitsa" ZG 79 (1835): 631).

48. The example of the curate's wife is from Vickery, *Behind Closed Doors,* 11, plate 1. See also Peterson, *Family,* ch. 5: some women lived outside the mold of domesticity, but in every case their work was feminized, usually couched as charity or educational endeavors even (or especially) when the day-to-day tasks performed were normally considered masculine, such as management or intellectual and creative work.

49. Susan A. Glenn, *Daughters of the Shtetl: Life and Labor in the Immigrant Generation* (Ithaca, NY: Cornell University Press, 1990), 6.

50. Nadieszda Kizenko, "'Orthodox Domesticity': Creating a Social Role for Women," in *Sacred Stories: Religion and Spirituality in Modern Russia,* ed. Mark D. Steinberg and Heather J. Coleman (Bloomington: Indiana University Press, 2007), 123, 124; and Engel, *Breaking the Ties,* 166–67. There is considerable scholarship on both the "strong Russian mother" and "Mother Russia" myths, but these derive from folk culture and, if they have any real-world source, relate to peasant constructions of gender. The myth of the strong Russian mother was taken up as part of various nationalist discourses in the later nineteenth century, but here again it was disassociated from noble or gentry culture. See Johanna Hubbs, *Mother Russia: The Feminine Myth in Russian Culture* (Bloomington: Indiana University Press, 1993); Barbara Heldt, *Terrible Perfection: Women and Russian Literature* (Bloomington: Indiana University Press, 1987); and Linda Edmondson, "Putting Mother Russia in a European Context," in *Art, Nation and Gender: Ethnic Landscapes, Myths, and Mother-Figures,* ed. T. Cusack et al. (Burlington, VT: Ashgate, 2003), 53–63.

51. Glenn, *Daughters,* 10.

52. Frank, *Life with Father.*

53. See Pouncy, *The "Domostroi."* A. V. Belova sees a greater range of activities being conceded to women for the first time in the early nineteenth century, even leading to an occasional case of "an inversion of traditional gender roles," but she discounts the possibility of married women engaging in economic activity while husbands were present, "Povsednevnost' russkoi provintsial'noi dvorianki kontsa XVIII-pervoi poloviny XIX v.," in *Sotsial'naia istoriia: ezhegodnik 2003, zhenskaia i gendernaia istoriia* (Moscow: Rosspen, 2003). Marrese's data convincingly demonstrates wider women's spheres as a norm much earlier (*Woman's Kingdom*).

54. Smith, *Recipes,* 108. On Bolotov and women, see also Glagoleva, "Dream." Bolotov married a much younger woman and attempted to mold her, essentially playing the role of father as well as husband. This very likely colored (or reflects) his expectations of women's roles in the family and society.

55. These teams were largely a fiction convenient to tax collection; non-household serf women on the Chikhachev estates worked the (extensive) vegetable gardens, while the "men"

were mentioned tilling grain fields, but the division between household and field labor was not gendered. There were men and women in both categories.

56. Smith, *Recipes*, 109; Marrese, *Woman's Kingdom*.

57. Smith, *Recipes*, 109.

58. Ibid., 120–22, 199.

59. Ibid., 148.

60. Ibid., 144–45, 148, 154–64.

61. CH 102, l. 290b.

62. Despite the greater emphasis on motherhood in British rhetoric, even middle-class Victorian women may have been no more occupied or identified with motherhood than Natalia was. Peterson has argued that the "mystique" of motherhood—in real families—actually postdates the Victorian period, and that in the nineteenth century "[c]hildren were surely a fact, but they were not always a pleasure, not automatically the objects of love. Children took second place to a woman's husband or even to herself." Peterson, *Family*, 103–4, 131.

63. See Wortman, "Russian Empress as Mother."

64. Rowland cautions against equating "the sentimental and the domestic in these years." Sentimental novels and the elevation of sensibility sometimes gave women, at least in fiction, "the ambition to pursue non-domestic work, and the exercise of their sentimental charity often refuse[d] to confine itself to the bounds or interests of the husband's family." Rowland, "Sentimental Fiction," in Maxwell and Trumpener, 201–2.

65. CH 58, l. 85. See also "Sashinka [was] complaining that her little tummy is hurting, but today thank God she is better," ibid., l. 1240b–125.

66. CH 66, l. 112.

67. CH 57, ll. 73, 74.

68. CH 54, l. 140b.

69. Ibid., l. 140b.

70. Ibid., l. 15.

71. Ibid., l. 40b. The sentence about stomach-pumping was, like most things Andrei wrote that were indelicate, in French.

72. CH 71, l. 11.

73. CH 83, l. 2. "Got up at 8 o'clock. 4 degrees below freezing, and all day a little snow was falling. Par[askovia] Ivan[ovna] and Sasha went to the banya. I knitted a stocking, and in the evening went to Madame Shreier, stopped by to see Alesha at the Institute, and saw there Mrs. Zakrevskii, Aleks[andra] Sem[enovna]—a big chatterbox! Paras[ko'via] Ivan[ovna] and I sat until 11 o'clock. Andrei Ivanovich read us a book, and *The Contemporary*."

74. Ibid., ll. 3, 40b, 5.

75. See CH 128, l. 80b. "Papinka and Maminka praised me because I diligently learn the Catechism and because, waking up every morning, I recall the Catechism before doing anything else." This is the only case where Aleksei mentions his mother having any role whatsoever in his education; it might be significant that the type of study referred to here is religious in nature. See also CH 71, l. 20b; 83, l. 810b.

76. CH 54, l. 34.

77. CH 108, ll. 165–1650b.

78. CH 69, ll. 280b–39. Aleksei was aware of his mother's distress; his diary entry for the day his father decided he would go to Moscow reads: "In the morning I studied French conversations,

and learned by heart two pages and Papinka praised me. On the 6th, Papinka said that it was necessary to take me to Moscow, about which Maminka cried" (CH 128, l. 120b). Though he wrote in his diaries through the end of that month, he made no further mention of his mother or her feelings.

79. CH 60, l. 89.

CHAPTER 8

1. This contradicts Catriona Kelly's conclusion that *vospitanie* was an exclusively feminine role in "Educating Tat'yana: Manners, Motherhood and Moral Education (*Vospitanie*), 1760–1840," in *Gender in Russian History and Culture*, ed. Linda Harriet Edmondson (New York: Palgrave 2001). Kelly's sources are largely from literature (some of it prescriptive). She notes that the "ideology of 'pedagogical motherhood'" was a novel idea in late-eighteenth- and early-nineteenth-century Russia, and that the intellectual (as opposed to moral) element was much less pronounced in Russian tradition, 3–4.

2. CH 54, l. 8.

3. See Kelly, "Educating Tat'yana" and *Refining Russia;* Ransel, *Mothers of Misery;* David D. Bien, "The Army in the French Enlightenment: Reform, Reaction and Revolution," *Past and Present* 85 (1979) on Enlightenment-based understandings of upbringing, and especially the notion of using institutes (from orphanages to the elite Smolny Academy to military cadet schools) to keep children away from their unenlightened parents, to be brought up according to new principles. The Russian Imperial Foundling Homes were set up in 1764 and 1770. Kelly explains that a "[n]etwork of state-run schools began to be set up in Russian cities and towns" in the 1780s. Kelly, *Refining Russia*, 9.

4. Quoted in Tosh, *A Man's Place*, 49.

5. Ibid., 6–7.

6. Ibid., 4.

7. Yakov's parallel diary (CH 60) is an equal mixture of both: it is focused on social visits, agriculture, household repairs, and serf management.

8. See Suzanne L. Bunkers and Cynthia Anne Huff, *Inscribing the Daily: Critical Essays on Women's Diaries* (Amherst: University of Massachusetts Press, 1996); Rebecca S. Hogan, "Engendered Autobiographies: The Diary as Feminine Form," *Prose Studies* 14 (1991), and other works.

9. James L. Rice, "The Memoirs of A. T. Bolotov and Russian Literary History," in *Russian Literature in the Age of Catherine the Great,* ed. A. G. Cross (Oxford: Willem A. Meeus, 1976), 17–43.

10. Andrei and Natalia's grandson's 1883 diary was meant for personal reflection and not intended to be read by the whole family: "We had dinner very late, precisely after 5 pm, and because of that I had a rather strong fight with my wife and a small scene resulted. In the evening put papers in order" after midnight, sitting down to write his diary, Kostya added that his wife was asleep and he needed to go to her—from the context, to sleep with her—to "make peace," but he "does not want to sleep." CH 116, l. 22ff.

11. CH 128, l. 1.

12. CH 71, l. 20b.

13. CH 83, l. 127. Aleksei annotated his "Diary of a schoolboy" to remark that he had re-read it himself in 1845, seven years after writing it (CH 71, l. 14).

14. CH 83, l. 14. "In the morning I occupied myself with a letter to Dorozhaevo. Vasilii Semenovich Rubanov came and requested me to send his regards also to you [*Vam*] Papinka and Maminka."

15. His letters to his uncle in the notebook correspondence are formulaic but not without personality or warmth: "My sweet, dear Uncle Yakov Ivanovich! First I send you my deepest regards and wish you good health and all well-being. About myself I report you that I am, Thank God, healthy, but my dear sister has scrofula in her head. In the catechism I am studying page 42, and the last words of my lesson were: in order that Christ through his death brought salvation to our souls. Farewell sweet dear Uncle. To dear grandfather Timofei Ivanovich my heartfelt regards. Your Aleksei Chikhachev." CH 66, l. 143.

16. CH 71, ll. 20b–5, 6. Emphasis added. Telemachus was a classic children's text of the Enlightenment, used by Catherine II to instruct her grandsons and heirs to the throne.

17. Ibid., ll. 42–420b.

18. Ibid., ll. 42–43.

19. CH 54, l. 100b.

20. Ibid., l. 22.

21. Ibid., l. 4. Interestingly, he knew the peddler personally and addressed him politely (he was "Vasilii Sergeevich from Domnino," an estate owned by the Zamytskiis).

22. Ibid., ll. 40b, 60b, 70b, 19.

23. "Pedogogicheskii zhurnal," SP 9 (1835): 33–35.

24. "Kratkii obzor nekotorykh chastei Gimnastiki i Kalistinii dlia devits," SP 42 (1835): 165–67.

25. Examples from the *ukazatel'* of the 1834 volume of ZG.

26. "Detskaia rabota," ZG 18 (1834): 143.

27. CH 128, l. 14. See also the following entries: "On hired horses, we left at 8 o'clock in the morning, and stopped to feed them in the village of Boloino, 40 *versts* from the Town, and we spent the night in the town of Pokrov in the carriage. . . . Feed-stop was in the village of Bunkovo. Rained all morning. . . . Left at noon. Overnight was in the village of Stegolitsy. When we were passing the village of Vedenskoe, they mistook our carriage for the Archbishop's and started ringing the bells; the priests were standing in their finery at the Church gates." (CH 71, l. 8.)

28. "O detskikh igrakh," VGV 40 (1850): 222.

29. CH 93, ll. 47, 500b. He also drew maps of foreign countries, CH 132.

30. CH 54, l. 200b.

31. See Willard Sunderland, "Imperial Space: Territorial Thought and Practice in the Eighteenth Century," in *Russian Empire: Space, People, Power, 1700–1930,* ed. Jane Burbank, Mark Von Hagen, and Anatolyi Remnev (Bloomington: Indiana University Press, 2007), 53.

32. CH 54, 19–20; "O detskikh igrakh," 222. Emphasis added.

33. Mikhail Avrekh, "'A Motley Mixture of Objects': Russian Geographic Writing in the Final Decades of the 18th Century," draft chapter from a Yale University dissertation, shared privately, August 2011.

34. Grigoryan, "Noble Farmers," 67.

35. CH 98, l. 40b.

36. Sunderland, "Imperial Space," 45–47. See also VSO and SNM, and Smith-Peter, "District Treasurehouse."

37. Sunderland, "Imperial Space," 47.

38. CH 129.

39. CH 61, ll. 85ob–86, 103, 127ob–129, 136ob–137, 153ob; 70, l. 1, 100b–40.

40. CH 71, ll. 80b–9.

41. CH 57, l. 72. One extant letter by Aleksei demonstrates that his French was competent, at least within these strict formulas, at age nine (ibid., l. 56).

42. CH 133. CH 37, ll. 2–3 are French vocabulary lists written by Andrei, perhaps for himself.

43. CH 37, l. 2 features one of the lists of new words Andrei kept while reading a book in French. He also toyed with learning words and phrases in other languages. In one instance, the better-traveled Yakov corrected him on an Italian phrase (CH 57, l. 600b).

44. The seminarian was one Vasilii Vasilevich Smirnov (CH 71, l. 8). Yakov knew a smattering of words in various languages because of his travels in the navy. CH 61, ll. 710b, 1120b.

45. Ibid., l. 8ob.

46. See his complex notations calculating various heights and distances around his estate, in his notebooks, CH 70, ll. 68–69ob, 71; CH 79, l. 68–71.

47. CH 57, ll. 670b–71.

48. Ibid. The world translated here as "field" is "pole-voi"—it could also refer to a famous journalist by that name.

49. Ibid. The "Trifon" and "Simon" in the charades probably refer to serfs.

50. CH 98, l. 160b. Calling Yust an "old Crow" Andrei was actually playing on the man's name and patronymic, changing Ivan Ivanovich to "Voron Voronovich." Andrei's *pansion*'s director, Dmitrii Filipovich Delsal, is recorded in official listings of educational establishments in Moscow as a Titular Councilor who kept male students, the last two of whom left him in the first half of 1846. TsIAM, F. 16, op. 14, d. 546.

51. See also "Alesha began to study the Lord's Prayer," "Alesha . . . read out 11 [times 'Give us this day] our daily bread,'" and "Alesha began to learn a prayer before dinner." CH 54, ll. 70b, 210b, 28; 66, l. 143; 71, ll. 70b, 120b–13.

52. CH 54, l. 8.

53. Ibid., l. 3–30b.

54. Ibid., l. 120b–13. August 22. Aleksei mistakenly identified the occasion as the "SOVEREIGN EMPEROR's coronation." Tsar Nicholas I was crowned in 1826, not 1838. Perhaps Aleksei meant to write "name day" or some other more frequent imperial celebration (indeed, it if had been an actual coronation, there would have been much more than fireworks, and Aleksei and his father would have had difficulty simply taking a walk through the Kremlin garden).

55. See CH 83, l. 50b.

56. CH 58, l. 1350b.

57. CH 57, l. 62.

58. Ibid., l. 610b.

59. CH 59, l. 39.

60. Tosh, *A Man's Place,* 3.

61. CH 71, ll. 50b–70b, 12.

62. Ibid., ll. 6–60b, 70b.

63. Ibid., l. 120b. Nesterova is not on either the Chikhachev or Chernavin family tree but appears occasionally in the documents as a venerated family friend of many years.

64. Ibid., ll. 60b–7, 80b, 90b.

65. CH 60, l. 53.

66. CH 54, l. 29 ob.

67. Ibid., l. 25.

68. Ibid., l. 33.

69. Ibid., ll. 31–310b.

70. CH 71, l. 110b. See also: "They were bringing rye sheaves in from the field, and I was enjoying it when they put them into rounded stacks" (ibid., ll. 100b–11) and: "Dined in Budyltsy, watched the [grain] grinders and butter churners" (CH 128, l. 14).

71. Ibid., l. 6.

72. Ibid., l. 4.

73. CH 54, ll. 310b–320b.

74. The value of play has remained a prominent theme in advanced educational theory to the present. It perhaps begins with Rousseau but reached so far as Bronson Alcott, an American contemporary of Chikhachev. See George E. Haefner, "A Critical Estimate of the Educational Theories and Practices of A. Bronson Alcott" (PhD diss., Columbia University, 1937). There are direct links to contemporary works such as: John Caldwell Holt, *How Children Learn* (Reading, MA: Addison-Wesley, 1995); Alexander Sutherland Neill, *Summerhill: A Radical Approach to Child-Rearing* (Harmondsworth, England: Penguin, 1985); Jean Piaget, "Play, Dreams and Imitation in Childhood," *Developmental psychology 25* (London: Routledge, 1999), as well as the Montessori movement.

75. "O detskikh igrakh," 222.

76. CH 59, l. 34.

77. CH 58, ll. 1970b, 205.

78. CH 54, l. 19.

79. CH 58, ll. 1460b–148.

80. CH 71, l. 50b.

81. CH 63, l. 124.

82. CH 63, 67, 69.

83. CH 71, ll. 40b–5, 90b–10.

84. CH 54, ll. 440b, 200b.

85. Ibid., ll. 24, 280b, 28, 29, 330b.

86. Ibid., l. 430b.

87. Ibid., l. 23.

88. Ibid., l. 25. Another affectionate nickname Andrei used for the children was "*chikhachata,*" an unusual diminutive for "Chikhachevs." He used it when he noted that the children were "in luck" because their teacher was temporarily absent to visit his newborn. CH 58, l. 84.

89. CH 58, l. 14.

90. CH 54, l. 52. The "clock" he refers to is probably the wall clock or wall-mounted sundial that he "invented."

91. See Sergei Aksakov's memoir, *Semeinaia khronika; detskie gody Bagrova-vnuka* (Moskva: Goslitizdat, 1958) for another mother who made jam, visited, but also "conducted a war of emotional attrition with her children," Kelly, *Refining Russia,* 7. For examples of children who were raised with much less exposure to their parents, see V. M. Bokova and L. G. Sakharova, *Institutki: vospominaniia vospitannits institutov blagorodnykh devits* (Moskva: Novoe literaturnoe obozrenie, 2001); L. A. Charskaia and Svetlana Alekseevna Kovalenko, *Zapiski institutki* (Moskva: Respublika, 1993); Barbara Alpern Engel and Clifford N. Rosenthal, *Five Sisters: Women against the Tsar: The Memoirs of Five Young Anarchist Women of the 1870s* (Boston: Allen & Unwin, 1987);

Petr Alekseevich Kropotkin, *Zapiski Revoliutsionera* (Moskva: Mysl', 1966); Nikolai Egorovich Vrangel', *Vospominaniia: ot krepostnogo prava do Bol'shevikov* (Moskva: Novoe literaturnoe obozrenie, 2003).

92. CH 128, l. 5. As an example from the mid-eighteenth century: the memoirist Andrei Bolotov was brought up so much apart from his parents, even when they lived in the same house, that his German teacher could beat him without Bolotov's parents suspecting (although eventually the boy complained to them and the teacher had to stop). *Zhizn' i prikliucheniia Andreia Bolotova: opisannye samim dlia svoikh potomkov,* (Moscow: Terra, 1993), vol. 1, chs. 6–8. Steven A. Grant's recent reassessment of the Russian noble family argues convincingly that distant, authoritarian, or exclusively punitive parents were not the norm, as other scholars have sometimes assumed. The Chikhachev documents confirm what Grant sees in his extensive reading of memoir literature; Andrei not only was close to his children physically and emotionally but deemed parents who acted otherwise as deficient. Steven A. Grant, "The Russian Gentry Family: A Contrarian View," *Jahrbücher für Geschichte Osteuropas* 60, h.1 (2012): 1–33.

93. In addition to Alesha studying well all day, the same entry also notes that while Natalia was away in Moscow Andrei was sufficiently bored to play "Idiot" with the children's nanny "5 times" and that Alesha also "worked in the garden with a little spade." The next page states that, again, Alesha "studied well all day." CH 54, ll. 22–22ob; ibid., ll. 10, 20ob, 23, 24, 27–28ob.

94. CH 58, l. 127ob.

95. Despite his failure to fill his father's formidable shoes, Aleksei was an able student. A copy of the examination certificate states that Aleksei passed and obtained his first "class rank" on the table of ranks on November 28, 1844. He was tested at the Shuia county school, and his certificate was signed by county judge "Ikonnikov," who was also a close friend of Aleksei's parents. His evaluations were as follows: 1. Catechism—quite good; 2. Russian language: exceedingly good; 3. Russian history and World History: good; 4. Arithmetic: very good; 5. Geometry: sufficient; 6. Geography: quite satisfactory; 7. Calligraphy: quite good; 8. Technical Drawing: good. CH 90, l. 2.

96. CH 83.

97. See CH 128, l. 14. "Arrived in Vladimir exactly at three o'clock in the afternoon and stayed with Smolkin": here Andrei made an illegible correction near the name "Smolkin." Other marks throughout the diary are more difficult still to make out but indicate corrections made by someone after the fact.

98. CH 128, l. 13. To this Chernavin added, "Your Papinka's instructions you must remember, sweet Aleshinka; and write to us as often as possible. Your uncle Yakov Chernavin."

99. CH 83, ll. 49ob–50, 83ob.

100. According to Frolov, Aleksei would be retired at the rank of lieutenant, one rank higher than his father had attained, VR, 152.

101. CH 83, ll. 57ob, 73ob, 85ob, 90ob. See also ll. 50ob, 84, and 110ob.

102. Ibid., l. 89.

103. Ibid., ll. 100ob, 38.

104. Ibid., l. 54. Also ll. 60ob ("At Dear Uncle's at 4 o'clock for dinner, and in the courtyard regimental music was played, which I listened to from Vasilii Andreevich's window."), and 108ob ("I went with Evgenii Ivanovich and my French tutor for a walk. We stopped by the sweet shop and listened there to the musicians, one of whom played the violin magnificently.").

105. Ibid., l. 54.

106. Ibid., l. 590b. Also ll. 112–1120b. Aleksei's son, Kostya, would also play the piano. CH 116, l. 120b.

107. His very few mentions of young ladies are circumspect: "At 5 o'clock I went to [visit] Major Shegrin, drank tea there and stayed quite a while. I chatted mostly with Mariia Iakovlevna, and with her brother Budakov" (CH 83, l. 51) and "[I was a]t Vasilii Andreevich's, and together with him we went to Adjutant Firks. His spouse is a beautiful and very educated lady" (ibid., l. 750b). Rebecca Friedman identifies drinking as one of the defining characteristics of masculinity for university students at this time. She recounts the tale of the student Blagov who, like Aleksei, does not drink among his friends. Blagov was feminized by his fellows, and his mother and grand-mother were blamed for his oddity. In the Chikhachev case, Aleksei's appearance of sobriety is almost certainly due to his father's influence. Friedman describes university students as balancing several images of masculinity—"the obedient servitor, the civilized gentleman, [and] the drunken comrade," with the guidance of male mentors (not fathers but institutional father-figures). Andrei pushed Aleksei away from all three masculine images, substituting his own image of domestic moral rectitude, intellectualism, and piety. Friedman, "From Boys to Men: Manhood in the Nich-olaevan University," in *Russian Masculinities in History and Culture,* ed. Barbara Evans Clements and Rebecca Friedman (New York: Palgrave, 2002), 33–34, 46–47.

108. Ibid., ll. 49, 50, 520b, 55.

109. Ibid., l. 54.

110. Ibid., l. 670b–68, 85. He got an officer's ribbon but did not become a real officer—this rank was referred to as *portupei-praporschik.*

111. Ibid., ll. 700b, 88.

112. CH 99, l. 242.

113. CH 95.

114. CH 99, l. 236.

115. Ibid., l. 140b.

116. Ibid., l. 229.

117. Ibid., l. 230. Aleksei's removal was probably also related to his patron's absence. Before Aleksei completed his military service his benefactor Pavel Yakovlevich Kupreianov was removed from service due to injuries. This left Aleksei, signing himself as a cavalry lieutenant, to write a grateful letter to a General Fedor Ivanovich for making up "for the strong loss which [he] incurred" with Kupreianov's removal. Ibid., l. 21.

118. CH 95, l. 80b.

119. CH 71, ll. 8, 100b–11.

120. CH 66, l. 1580b.

121. Ibid., l. 144.

122. CH 59, 480b.

123. Kelly, *Refining Russia,* 26.

124. On young ladies on the provincial Russian marriage market, see Glagoleva, "Dream" and Bisha, "Promise."

125. The significant number of unmarried men and women (but usually women) in Frolov's genealogy of Vladimir province supports this assumption (VR).

126. CH 54, l. 12. Kelly's conclusion that "independence of mind" was a crucial tenet in con-temporary advice on female education, therefore, probably also holds true, as well as her assertion

that girls' education was commonly much broader than historians have often assumed. *Refining Russia*, 27.

127. Bolotov, *Zhizn' i prikliucheniia*, ch. 5.

128. "Russian subject Anna Ivanovna Shreder" (also spelled "Schreider" and "Schneider") lived in "the house of Mr. Shilovskii" in the Miasnitskaia district in this period. Her *pansion* had "25 noble and 3 non-noble girls as of Sept 1 [1841]; arrived 7 and 4; left 10 and 3; on Jan 1, 1842—22 and 4." There were seventeen *pansions* total listed in Moscow, which in September 1841 had altogether ninety-two noble and thirty-three non-noble males (125 males total) and 497 noble females and seventy-eight non-noble females (575 females total), TsIAM, F. 16, op. 12, d. 251 (1841) and d. 881 (1842). In 1846–47 another nine establishments were included, but as of May 1, 1846, there was no Schreder or Shreier, TsIAM, F. 16, op. 14, d. 546.

129. CH 95, ll. 70b, 80b.

130. CH 98, l. 20b. The "little estate" he speaks of was Berezovik, "all ready" for Aleksei to inherit since Yakov's death in 1845.

131. CH 103, ll. 281–2810b.

132. See, however, CH 112, l. 1: Andrei's diary for the time shortly following Natalia's death. He mentioned Aleksei's presence frequently, doing the shopping and other errands, suggesting that Andrei depended a great deal on his son during this difficult time. Also, it seems Aleksei was in Marienbad at some point—Andrei mentioned that he sent slides home from that city. At the end of 1866 Aleksei's son Kostya mentioned books left behind when his father went abroad. CH 112, l. 42.

133. CH 54, l. 18.

CHAPTER 9

1. CH 95, l. 1200b.

2. Frolov stated that Aleksei studied at Moscow University in his genealogy, but I have not been able to confirm whether Aleksei attended, for how long, or what he studied. VR 152.

3. VGV 47 (1851): 313–15; ZG 22 (1859): 169–72; ZG 21 (1846): 178; ZG 72 (1846): 588, ZG 75 (1846): 607–8, and ZG 87 (1846): 709–10; ZG 9 (1848): 65; ZG 26 (1848): 206. I have found 134 of Andrei's articles; internal evidence suggests there were more.

4. The years in which Andrei's collections of letters received were preserved were 1850, 1860–61, and 1866–67. Because the surviving collections are all from years that marked highly significant events (the death of Aleksandra, the serf emancipation, and the death of Natalia), it seems either Andrei or a descendent chose to save only letters deemed significant.

5. Smith-Peter, evaluating Andrei's articles from the perspective of his participation in the wider print culture, sees a conservative phase immediately following the revolutionary year 1848, with more mellow attitudes seeping in in his last decade or so of publication. Here I emphasize the impact of his religious "epiphany" of 1848 (which may not be unrelated to events abroad that same year) and the death of his daughter, which brought on an even more significant religious crisis but may also have tempered some of his earlier stridency. Both external political events and internal religious and emotional experiences were probably intertwined as influences on his writing. Smith-Peter, "District Treasurehouse," "Books Behind the Altar," and "Provincial Public Libraries."

6. CH 54, l. 45.

7. Ibid., l. 370b.

8. CH 57, l. 76. Yakov shared his ambitions, to a point: in 1837 he was working on a memoir of his naval career (CH 60, ll. 74–75).

9. CH 58, l. 1800b.

10. CH 59, l. 450b.

11. Ibid., l. 450b.

12. Ibid., l. 54.

13. See Vickery, *Gentleman's Daughter*, ch. 7.

14. "Mysli sel'skogo zhitelia o gubernskoi gazete," VGV 45 (1850): 249–51.

15. Ibid.

16. "Dva slova o rabotakh," 563.

17. CH 59, l. 570b, "*Vospitanie*" and "*obrazovannost.*"

18. Cf. Smolny and other major imperial educational institutions, where the Enlightenment-based idea that children should be educated by the state, far from their parents' unreliable influence, was giving way at this time to notions of the close-knit family, domestic harmony, and Romanticism that advocated for parents' and children's close emotional attachment.

19. Tovrov, introduction, *Russian Noble Family*.

20. CH 58, ll. 188, 1890b.

21. CH 98, l. 20b. See also "Patrioticheskoe sochustvie," 250: "the establishment of the school of agriculture for hereditary nobles, whose Statute is already confirmed by the Sovereign (SP 1849, no 64)."

22. Smith-Peter, "Books Behind the Altar."

23. "Patrioticheskoe sochustvie," 250–51.

24. "Dva slova o rabotakh," 563.

25. Ibid.

26. CH 98, l. 20b.

27. Ibid., l. 290b.

28. "Dva slova o rabotakh," 563.

29. On the real pace of Russian courts in the mid-nineteenth century, see Antonov, "The Law and Culture of Debt." Intriguingly, Elisei Mochalin wrote to Andrei in 1860 about a fraud against the government and concluded, "my hair is rising from the thought to what extent we are afraid to speak about an abuse of power as if we are talking about some kind of state secret." CH 103, l. 430b.

30. See Smith-Peter, "Books Behind the Altar," and "District Treasurehouse."

31. CH 55, l. 460b.

32. CH 66, ll. 13–130b.

33. CH 60, l. 11.

34. CH 66, l. 120.

35. CH 59, l. 44.

36. CH. 58, l. 135.

37. Ibid., ll. 1600b–161.

38. Ibid., l. 144.

39. Chernavin saw action during the 1831 Greek rebellion. On July 31, a Russian fleet stormed the fortifications of Poros. A group of Russian sailors including Captain-Lieutenant N. Sipiagin and Lieutenant Ya. Chernavin and others boarded the brig *Athena*: "The brig's

task was to approach the fortress at the distance of a musket shot and to open artillery fire to attract attention." *Morskoi sbornik* 3 (2003): 95.

40. CH 66, l. 54.

41. See Smith, *Recipes*, which highlights the contradictions and instabilities in the search for "nationhood" in this period, esp. 160–62.

42. CH 59, l. 36.

43. Ibid., l. 30.

44. CH 54, l. 210b.

45. Ibid., l. 90b.

46. "Dva slova o rabotakh," 563.

47. According to Dal's dictionary, the word Andrei used (*prednaznachenie*) could refer to religious predestination, fate generally, or, interestingly, a bureaucratic appointment, as in "you are fated" to a new post.

48. "Dva slova o rabotakh," 563.

49. Ibid.

50. Ibid. Andrei would have gleaned this militarist attitude through *Russkii invalid* and similar statist periodicals.

51. CH 59, ll. 58–580b.

52. Ibid.

53. CH 99, ll. 2300b–231.

54. CH 59, l. 41. Yakov wrote the word "tavern" broken down into syllables to emphasize his disgust: "*ka-ba-ki.*" See also CH 60, l. 6.

55. CH 57, l. 390b. The word translated here as "nationality" is a straight translation from their "*natsional'nost'.*" Perhaps significantly, they used the Western root rather than the Russian "*narodnost',*" with the root "*narod*" or "people," generally understood as referring to the peasantry, so that "*narodnost'*" refers primarily to ethnicity, with the implication that the uneducated classes are the core of Russian national identity.

56. On early nineteenth-century England as an agrarian/authoritarian society (and the promotion of nationalism in this context), see C. A. Bayly, *Imperial Meridian: The British Empire and the World, 1780–1830* (London: Longman, 1989).

57. Ibid.

58. See "Proizvodstvo prostykh reshet v Kovrovskom uezde." VGV 42 (October 1848): 235–37. In "District Treasurehouse" Smith-Peter links Andrei's interest in the cheesecloth factory with the Yurev Agricultural Society and provincial activities on behalf of rational agriculture in general.

59. "Patrioticheskoe sochustvie."

60. On the varieties of Russian conservatisms in the early nineteenth century, see Alexander Martin, *Romantics, Reformers, Reactionaries: Russian Conservative Thought and Politics in the Reign of Alexander I* (DeKalb: Northern Illinois University Press, 1997).

61. CH 66, l. 49.

62. CH 57, ll. 87–870b.

63. CH 99, l. 273.

64. CH 103, ll. 275–2750b.

65. CH 106, l. 540b.

66. T. N. Golovina, "Iz kruga chteniia pomeshchikov srednei ruki (po dokumentam 1830–1840kh godov iz usadebnogo arkhiva," *Novoe Literaturnoe Obozrenie 93* (2008), magazines. russ.ru/nlo/ 2008/93/g038.html (accessed 10/2/2011).

67. Ibid.

68. Ibid. Golovina also asserts that Natalia did not read travel books, but examination of the entire archive reveals this assumption to be unsupported. The whole family, including Natalia, listened to Andrei reading travel books. Also, Golovina suggests Natalia rarely left the estate for lack of fashionable clothes, because Andrei once joked deprecatingly about her outfit. This, too, is a misreading; context shows that her health and estate management kept her at home.

CHAPTER 10

1. On Chaadaev and the context of his Letters, see Gordon Southworth Cook, "Petr Ia. Chaadaev and the Rise of Russian Cultural Criticism, 1800–1830" (Ph D diss., Duke University, 1973).

2. For context on the construction of national pasts as "imagined," see Benedict Anderson, *Imagined Communities: Reflections on the Origin and Spread of Nationalism* (New York: Verso, 1991). Anderson influentially conceptualized nationalism as communities of shared identity, linking people who would not otherwise interact personally—i.e., the community was a product of imagined connections, often centered on a perception of a glorious shared past. In other words, nationality was socially constructed.

3. "Dva slova o rabotakh," 563.

4. Ibid.

5. Technically, the *Moscow Provincial News* was a regional newspaper while the *Agricultural Gazette* where Andrei published regularly was national in circulation. However, the Moscow paper represented the empire's second capital and largest city, where the cultural elite and wealthiest nobles were certain to spend some time. The agricultural newspaper was mostly limited to the provincial gentry, and would have been seen as intensely boring to most people in the capital cities, especially urban intellectuals.

6. N. P. Ogarev, "Zamechanie na zamechanie g. Chikhacheva," *Izbrannye sotsial'no-politicheskie i filosofskie proizvedeniia* (Gosudarstvennoe izdatel'stvo politicheskoi literatury, USSR, 1952): 101–5.

7. Compare Ogarev's treatment of Andrei to critic Nikolai Dobroliubov, who later eviscerated Sergei Aksakov in a similar vein. Grigoryan, "Noble Farmers," 193.

8. Ogarev, "Zamechanie na zamechanie."

9. Ibid.

10. Ibid.

11. "O barshchine" ZG 4 (1848): 26–27.

12. On Alexander I's views, see Janet M. Hartley, *Alexander I* (New York: Longman, 1994).

13. Susanna Rabow-Edling, *Slavophile Thought and the Politics of Cultural Nationalism* (Albany: SUNY Press, 2006), 2. Her study concentrates on the work of the two principle originators of Slavophile thought, Khomiakov and Kireevskii. The classic English-language work on Slavophilism is Andrzej Walicki, *The Slavophile Controversy: History of a Conservative Utopia in Nineteenth-Century Russian Thought* (Notre Dame: University of Notre Dame Press, 1989). Contrast Rabow-Edling's view with Vera Tolz, *Russia, Inventing the Nation* (London; Oxford University Press, 2001).

14. Rabow-Edling, *Slavophile Thought*, 2–4. She quotes F. C. Beiser, *Enlightenment, Revolution, and Romanticism: The Genesis of Modern German Political Thought 1790–1800* (Cambridge, MA: Harvard University Press, 1987), 8, 206–8. See also Lounsbery, "Provincialism," on the long-term influence, much of it positive, on Russian thought of conceptions of Russia itself as inherently provincial. Lounsbery traces intelligentsia conceptions of provincialism mainly to Gogol, which should be contrasted to Andrei's understandings, based on personal experience and only reinforced by his (selective) reading of literature.

15. Slavophile views on the gendering of *vospitanie* are somewhat contradictory, but Smith-Peter has documented their concern for the religious education of peasant girls and its connection to their roles as mothers: "Educating Peasant Girls for Motherhood: Religion and Primary Education in Mid-Nineteenth Century Russia," RR 66, no. 3 (July 2007): 391–405.

16. Kelly, *Refining Russia*, 130.

17. See CH 36a ll. 17, 19; 55; 93, ll. 5–9; 94; 102. Even their serfs wore Western clothing; see Aleksei's diary, CH 83, l. 46, where he lists a striped summer jacket, pantaloons, and two cotton vests among his new clothes.

18. The early twentieth-century conservative bureaucrat V. I. Gurko accused Minister of Finance Sergei Witte of harboring "hatred" toward struggling middling landowners and allegedly trying to "destroy" their "economic solidarity" with other landowners by encouraging them toward industrial enterprises. Gurko defended these people as "poets of their occupation . . . looking . . . only . . . to feed their families and to provide a *vospitanie* to their children." He accused Witte of "dislik[ing] and even despis[ing] these people precisely for their . . . inability . . . to accumulate capital." Gurko added that local agricultural committees, composed of such landowners, "spoke above all for providing for the peasants' interests, for abolishing their legally separate existence, and in general directed their main attention to meeting the popular needs." V. I. Gurko, *Cherty i siluety*, ch. 3.

19. For a start on the enormous literature, see Marc Raeff, *Origins of the Russian Intelligentsia: The Eighteenth-Century Nobility* (New York: Mariner, 1966). For a recent revisionist look at the origins of the intelligentsia, see Randolph, *House in the Garden,* who argues against the depiction of the intelligentsia as essentially alienated. On the nobility as free of fundamental cultural conflict over Russianness versus a "false" Western identity, see Marrese, "Poetics Revisited." Priscilla Roosevelt's *Life on the Russian Country Estate: A Social and Cultural History* (New Haven: Yale University Press, 1995) emphasizes shared interests between nobles and peasants in the country. In *Nests of the Gentry* Cavender emphasizes provincial nobles' cohesion as a social estate, but without "alienation" from other provincial social groups. Both Roosevelt and Cavender identify a greater tension in nobles' self-identities between Russianness and Europeanness than I see in the Chikhachevs. Instead, the "unproblematic cultural bilingualism" Marrese identifies is most evident in the Chikhachev papers, though as people who were less educated and less well-traveled than others studied by Marrese, it is more accurate to describe the Chikhachevs as unproblematically open to Western influences, without threat to their self-identity as Russians.

20. Among recent works on state formulations of Russian national identity, see Wortman, *Scenarios*, ch. 7; Nathaniel Knight, "Ethnicity, Nationality and the Masses: *Narodnost'* and Modernity in Imperial Russia," in *Russian Modernity: Politics, Knowledge, Practices*, ed. Yanni Kotsonis and David Lloyd Hoffmann (New York: St. Martin's, 2000); M. D. Dolbilov, *Russkii krai, chuzhaia vera: etnokonfessional'naia politika imperii v Litve i Belorussii pri Aleksandre II* (Moscow,

2010); and on the relationship between empire and Russian nationalism, see A. Miller, *Imperiia Romanovykh i natsionalism* (Moscow, 2006).

21. See A. L. Zorin, *Kormia dvuglavogo orla: Literatura i gosudarstvennaia ideologiia v Rossii v poslednei treti xviii-pervoi treti xix veka* (Moskva: Novoe literaturnoe obozrenie, 2001), ch. 10.

22. Smith, *Recipes*, 110. Smith demonstrates how cookbooks and similar instruction manuals were one means through which the "fashions of the time" were disseminated from towns to countryside. The writers of the advice manuals in her study were, like, Andrei, neither Westernizers nor Slavophiles, 9.

23. Translation and relevant discussion of this passage is in Grigoryan, "Noble Farmers," 1–5.

24. Ibid.

25. Smith, *Recipes*, 104.

26. For discussion on the impact of the emancipation of the nobility on conceptions of the provincial landowner, see Smith, *Recipes*; Grigoryan, "Noble Farmers"; and Roosevelt, *Life on the Russian Country Estate*.

27. Newlin, *Voice in the Garden*, 49, quoted in Smith, *Recipes*, 105.

28. See Smith, *Recipes*; Grigoryan, "Noble Farmers"; Kelly, *Refining Russia;* and Cavender, *Nests of the Gentry*, for detailed accounts of this campaign, as well as Joseph Bradley, *Voluntary Associations in Tsarist Russia: Science, Patriotism, and Civil Society* (Cambridge, MA: Harvard University Press, 2009), ch. 2.

29. Smith, *Recipes*, 126.

30. Ibid., 127.

31. Grigoryan, "Noble Farmers"; Frazier, *Romantic Encounters*.

32. Grigoryan, "Noble Farmers," 51; and Smith, *Recipes*. Smith notes that there was a period when publications (and enthusiasm) flagged around the turn of the century as well; a crash in the early 1830s was related to a period of depression in agricultural markets and was followed by a big spike, (110, 123–28). On noble resistance to the campaign to redefine their role as landowners, see Grigoryan "Noble Farmers," for an enlightening discussion of Goncharov's novels as an explicit articulation of such resistance, 24.

33. Grigoryan, "Noble Farmers," 16; Smith, *Recipes*; Marrese, *Woman's Kingdom*.

34. Smith, *Recipes*, 131.

35. In contrast, the *Agricultural Journal* published by the Moscow Agricultural Society—to which for some reason Andrei did not subscribe—folded in 1859. The *Works* of the Free Economic Society continued to 1894 but with interruptions. See Smith, *Recipes*, 128.

36. Newlin, *Voice in the Garden*, 87. See also Randolph, *House in the Garden*, on educated noblemen feeling a compulsion to demonstrate their "distinction." On the seeming contradiction of writing publicly about private life and its connection to sentimentalism, see Andreas Schonle, "The Scare of the Self: Sentimentalism, Privacy, and Private Life in Russian Culture, 1780–1820," *SR* 57, no. 4 (Winter 1998): 723–46.

37. SP 49 (1835): 194–95.

38. On the tensions expressed by Russian writers about the landlord's role, see Grigoryan, "Noble Farmers," 8–9.

39. Curiously, in a passage of the notebook correspondence for April 1836, Andrei referred to a landlord as a *"votchinnyi nachalnik,"* literally a boss or a commander of the land, a terminology that made him sound more like a part of the state hierarchy than an independent property owner. Andrei contrasted this figure with a petty peasant official that he thought belonged to either

Yakov or his neighbor Khmetevskii. Regardless of who he belonged to, Andrei wrote, he "should be beat up." If the landlord, as "boss," refused to do this, then a petition ought to be sent to the police, which would "rip apart" said landlord. Which was apparently deserved "because in service every [illegible] boss is punished." CH 58, l. 850b.

40. On Lomonsov's project, see Grigoryan, "Noble Farmers," 36. In framing a "problem of authority" I follow Smith, *Recipes*.

41. Smith, *Recipes*, 112, 118.

42. Ibid., 103.

43. Rabow-Edling, *Slavophile Thought*, 9. Also see Riasanovsky, *Official Nationality*, for the popularity of the slogan and the ideas it represented, and Cynthia H. Whittaker, *The Origins of Modern Russian Education: An Intellectual Biography of Count Sergei Uvarov, 1786–1855* (DeKalb: Northern Illinois University Press, 1984), on the intellectual origins of the slogan.

44. CH 57, l. 3.

45. CH 58, l. 1790b.

46. Ibid., l. 1040b.

47. CH 58, l. 1040b.

48. Ibid., l. 1790b.

49. CH 57, l. 77 ob. "*Zemskii* court" was actually a rural police authority, not a court in the English sense. Yakov was more sanguine about his brother-in-law's chances, and responded that he should write, but "not in journals, but really to the Northern Bee, because . . . Bulgarin and Grech will print his articles" (ibid., l. 760b).

50. Frazier, *Romantic Encounters*, 76.

51. Ibid., 174–75.

52. Ibid., 75–76.

53. Whittaker, *Origins*.

54. CH 58, ll. 42–420b.

55. CH 54, l. 48.

56. Contrast Andrei's expectation that literature reflect his real experience of the world with the intelligentsia view of the writer as "prophet," "responsible for shaping the spiritual and moral destiny of the nation," in Pamela Davidson, "The Moral Dimension of the Prophetic Idea: Pushkin and His Readers," SR 61, no. 3 (Fall 2002): 490.

57. CH 54, l. 420b.

58. CH 54, ll. 420b–43.

59. Ibid.

60. Ibid.

61. CH 98.

62. Grigoryan, "Noble Farmers," 74.

63. On landscape and nationality see Christopher Ely, *This Meager Landscape: Landscape and National Identity in Imperial Russia* (DeKalb: Northern Illinois University Press, 2002).

64. Mikhail Avrekh, "How to Create a Russian Girl? Or, Karamzin's Heroines and Geographic Writing" (paper presented at the Mid-Atlantic Slavic Conference, New York, New York, March 26, 2011), 4.

65. Rowland, "Sentimental Fiction," 191–92.

66. On Romanticism in Russia, see Frazier, *Romantic Encounters*; Diana Greene, *Reinventing Romantic Poetry: Russian Women Poets of the Mid-Nineteenth Century*, (Madison: University of

Wisconsin Press, 2004); A. M. Gurevich, *Romantizm Pushkina* (Moskva, 1993); I. V. Kartashova, *Romantizm i ego istoricheskie sud'by* (Tver, 1998); Nicholas Riasanovsky, *The Emergence of Romanticism* (New York: Oxford University Press, 1992); V. I. Sakharov, *Romantizm v Rossii: Epokha, shkoly, stili* (Moskva, 2004); Andrzej Walicki, *Russia, Poland, and Universal Regeneration: Studies in Russian and Polish Thought of the Romantic Epoch* (Notre Dame: University of Notre Dame Press, 1991). Andrei's own usage of the words "romantistic" and "sensibility" indicate that he associated both simply with rich emotional experience, e.g.: "[T]he rain was 'romantistic.'" (CH 58, l. 143.) and "We went to [visit] Maksim Mitrofanovich Kalakutskii, and having dined we left for home. His little son Sashinka cried bitterly while saying goodbye to Alesha—even in childhood itself sensibility is strong!" (CH 54, l. 120b.)

67. See Dena Goodman, *Republic of Letters: A Cultural History of the French Enlightenment* (Ithaca, NY: Cornell University Press, 1994).

68. See Frazier, *Romantic Encounters*, on the connection between lending libraries and Romanticism, and on Romantic writers' conceptions of reading publics, esp. 42.

69. See Alexandra Kate Parfitt, "Immoral Lessons: Education and the Novel in Nineteenth-Century France" (PhD diss., Yale University, 2010).

70. CH 59, ll. 51, 53.

71. Ibid., l. 52ob.

72. "Pol'za obshchestvennago chteniia," ZG 21 (1834): 168.

73. "Dva slova o rabotakh," 563.

74. Martha Bohrer, "Thinking Locally: Novelistic Worlds in Provincial Fiction," in Maxwell and Trumpener, *Cambridge Companion*, 90.

75. Ibid.

76. Ibid.

77. Ibid.

78. Ibid.

79. Frazier, *Romantic Encounters*, 53.

80. Grigoryan, "Noble Farmers," 42, 82, 198.

81. Frazier, *Romantic Encounters*, 52, 71.

82. "O stat'iakh bez podpisi," ZG 7 (1846): 56.

83. "Ob obschem dvorian uchastii v Zemledel'cheskoi Gazete," ZG 98 (1848): 781–82.

84. "Zaochnoe znakomstvo (O peredache pisem ot sotrudnika k sotrudniku - chrez redaktsiiu)," *VGV* 1 (1865): 64–67.

85. CH 99, l. 82.

86. E.g., CH 103, l. 275.

87. CH 99, ll. 80–80ob

88. CH 99, l. 251ob.

89. Vladimir Engel'gardt, "Vospominaniia o direktore tsarskosel'skogo litseia Egore Antonoviche Engel'gardte," *Russkii Arkhiv* 10, no. 7–8 (1872): 1487, quoted in Smith, *Recipes*, 225n. See also 129–30 on the *Agricultural Gazette* in general.

90. ZG 1835: 832. The editors note that that year they published 377 articles, of which 307 were original or altered by the editors, leaving seventy translated from a foreign source. The total circulation was 4,837 copies. In 1834 (p. 416) the editors listed 232 total articles, of which 198 were original or altered. Fifty-three were sent in by readers, but over half of those were in German. Twenty-eight contributors signed their names. Of those people, two were princes (a Volkonskii

and a Golitsyn), one a count (Mordvinov), and ten have non-Russian names. Among these is E. A. Engelgardt, who edited ZG from 1838 to 1852 and appears in the Chikhachev *fond* as a correspondent of Andrei's. The total circulation for 1834 was 4,295 copies.

91. "Khoziaistvennye voprosy," ZG 69 (1835): 552.

92. "Rabota na urok," ZG 53 (1835): 417.

93. ZG 84 (1836): 668.

94. Smith, *Recipes*, 125.

95. Ibid., 133.

96. Ibid., 137–38.

97. Grigoryan, "Noble Farmers," 132.

98. Smith, *Recipes*, 123.

99. Ibid, 123–24.

100. Ibid., 155, 124.

101. Smith, *Recipes*, 108. See also Grigoryan, "Noble Farmers," 65; and Newlin, *Voice in the Garden.*

102. Randolph, *House and the Garden.* On Derzhavin's poem and its connection to Randolph's argument, see Grigoryan, "Noble Farmers," 1–7.

103. Grigoryan, "Noble Farmers," 124–27, 147–49. Grigoryan refers here to Marrese's finding that despite the reality that many women were managing estates, written reference to this fact is scarce. *Woman's Kingdom,* 180.

104. Grigoryan, "Noble Farmers," 158; see ch. 3 for a discussion of images of provincial landowners in three Goncharov novels.

105. See Cavender, *Nests of the Gentry;* and Smith-Peter, "Books Behind the Altar" and "District Treasurehouse." At least two of Andrei's close friendships—with Vladimir Kopytovskii and Elisei Mochalin—originated in the pages of the *Agricultural Gazette.* In 1860 Mochalin wrote to Andrei that he read aloud to his wife in the evenings just as Andrei had described doing in one of his articles. Mochalin wrote that for these evening readings, "we particularly like to read your articles, they always contain a lot of instructional things." CH 103, l. 430b.

106. CH 57, l. 92.

CONCLUSION

1. He also mentioned that he could not see well without glasses, which explains why his letters are mostly illegible. CH 112, ll. 670b–68.

2. Daniel Field argues that emancipation finally came about for cultural reasons, including a decline in patriarchal authority and a lack of cohesion in the noble estate. See also Terence Emmons, *Emancipation of the Russian Serfs.* On the development of gentry organizations into an organized political force in the very late imperial period, see Roberta Manning, *The Crisis of the Old Order in Russia: Gentry and Government* (Princeton: Princeton University Press, 1982). Seymour Becker disagrees with Manning on some points about the nobility's adjustment to new roles in this same period; see his *Nobility and Privilege in Late Imperial Russia* (DeKalb: Northern Illinois University Press, 1985).

3. CH 106, ll. 29–320b.

4. CH 103, l. 1140b.

5. Ibid., l. 430b.

6. Engel, *Breaking the Ties*, 1.

7. CH 53, l. 8. There is no indication of a sister or adopted sister who could have been nicknamed Polonka on the Chikhachev or Chernavin family trees. She may have been a cousin.

8. Engel, *Breaking the Ties*, 160.

9. Ibid.; Smith, *Recipes*; Kelly, *Refining Russia*; Marrese, *Woman's Kingdom;* Elena Molokhovets, *Classic Russian Cooking: Elena Molokhovets' a Gift to Young Housewives,* trans. and ed. Joyce Toomre (Bloomington: Indiana University Press, 1992); Goldstein "Domestic Porkbarreling"; Beth Holmgren, "Gendering the Icon," in Goscilo, *Russia, Women, Culture,* 321–46.

10. Engel, *Breaking the Ties*, 160.

11. Ibid., 171.

12. Ibid., 196.

13. Ibid., 180.

14. Tosh, introduction, *A Man's Place*; Engel, *Breaking the Ties*, ch. 6.

15. For a 1905 cartoon satirizing the *Domostroi,* see Engel, *Breaking the Ties*, 32. See also Smith, *Recipes,* 105.

16. CH 96. The notebook contains twenty-four sheets, and they are all definitively in her handwriting, as compared to the letters she wrote to the Chikhachevs in 1860–61. This does not mean that she herself attended these lectures, but at the very least she copied the notes of someone who had.

17. CH 105, ll. 14–15.

18. Ibid., ll. 74–75.

19. CH 106, l. 180b.

20. Ibid., l. 320b.

21. Ibid., l. 120.

22. Ibid., l. 134.

23. CH 99, ll. 208–9.

24. CH 112, ll. 590b–600b.

25. Ibid., l. 149.

26. VR, 150–54.

27. Augustine, "Notes toward a Portrait," 384.

28. Glinka's conception of society was patriarchal in the sense that his preferred metaphor for all social relations was the family. He had been educated at the cadet corps, a milieu saturated with French Enlightenment literature that extolled the relationship between an authoritative yet gentle father and his devoted, loving children—what Lynn Hunt calls the "good father" model of the family—as the only acceptable basis for familial (and, by extension, social and political) authority. Among educated Europeans and Americans, this "good father" conception had largely displaced the inherited old-regime notion that the father's role was to be a stern disciplinarian (Martin, "Family Model," 34). In other words, the rhetoric about family should be seen not as necessarily a "backward-looking" conservative traditionalism, but rather as part of a widely accepted contemporary interpretation of Enlightenment thought. Also see Marrese, *Woman's Kingdom.* Russian institutions in the nineteenth century were not seen as we see institutions today—as faceless entities, run by committee—but as a paternalistic hierarchy. See, for example, F. M. Tolstoi (1827), *Prazdnestvo 29 dekabria 1855 goda, v Pazheskom Ego Imperatorskogo Velichestva Korpuse, v chest' General-Adiutanta kniazia Viktora Illarionovicha Vasil'chikova* (St. Petersburg, 1857), 14.

29. Not that it was not already present in Russia: see Valerie A. Kivelson, *Autocracy in the Provinces: The Muscovite Gentry and Political Culture in the Seventeenth Century* (Stanford: Stanford University Press, 1997).

30. Martin, "Family Model," 28. He cites Gordon S. Wood, *The Radicalism of the American Revolution* (New York: Vintage, 1992), 145–68; and Lynn Hunt, *The Family Romance of the French Revolution* (Berkeley: University of California Press, 1992), 17–52.

31. Tovrov, introduction, *Russian Noble Family*.

SELECTED BIBLIOGRAPHY

For a complete bibliography, see www.kpantonova.com.

ABBREVIATIONS

In the endnotes, "CH" refers to the Chikhachev family archive: Gosudarstvennyi arkhiv Ivanovskoi oblasti (GAIO) *Fond* 107, *opis'* 1. CH is followed by the *delo* (file) and *listok* (page) numbers.

AHR   American Historical Review
GARF   Gosudarstvennyi arkhiv Rossiiskoi Federatsii
GAIO   Gosudarstvennyi arkhiv Ivanskoi oblasti
JMH   Journal of Modern History
MGV   Moskovskie gubernskie vedomosti
PSZ   Polnoe sobranie zakonov
RH   Russian History/Histoire Russe
RR   Russian Review
SNM   Spiski naselennykh mest
SP   Severnaia Pchela
SR   Slavic Review
TsIAM   Tsentral'nyi istoricheskii arkhiv Moskvy
VGV   Vladimirskie gubernskie vedomosti
VR   Vladimirskii rodoslovets (Frolov, 1996)
VSO   Voenno-statisticheskoe obozrenie Rossiiskoi imperii, vol. VI, part 2 (Vladimirskaia guberniia)
ZG   Zemledel'cheskaia gazeta

SUMMARY OF ARCHIVAL SOURCES

Gosudarstvennyi istoricheskii arkhiv Ivanovskoi oblasti (GAIO), Fond 107, "Chikhachevy," opis' 1.

Diaries and account books by Natalia

Delo 55: Acct. book, 1831–34 (72 ll.)
Delo 63: Diary, Jan–Dec 1835 (162 ll.)
Delo 67: Diary, Sept 1836–Mar 1837 (77 ll.)
Delo 69: Diary, July–Oct 1837 (44 ll.)
Delo 83: Diary, Jan 1842 (3 ll.)

Diaries and account books by Andrei

Delo 126: Early acct. book, no date (8 ll.)
Delo 36(a): Acct. book, 1821–23 (35 ll.)
Delo 37: Misc. notebook, 1821–23 (16 ll.)
Delo 46: Acct. book, 1825–26 (44 ll.)
Delo 48: Acct. book, 1826–27 (15 ll.)
Delo 54: Diary, 1830–31 (68 ll.)
Delo 124: Acct. book 1837–45 (begun by Aleksei in 1835) (22 ll. total)
Delo 73: Notebook, 1838 (24 ll.)
Delo 95: "Parallel Diary," 1842–47 (143 ll.)
Delo 100: Unpublished memoir, "Notes from a [monk's] cell," 1852–57 (42 ll.)

Diaries and account books by Aleksei

Delo 128: Diary, 1835–37 (later taken over by notes from Andrei) (38 ll.)
Delo 124: Acct. book, 1835–37 (taken over by Andrei) (22 ll. total)
Delo 71: "Diary of a Student," 1838 (14 ll.)
Delo 133: Student's notebook and exercises in French (n/d) (75 ll.)
Delo 83: Diary, 1847–48 (121 ll.)
Delo 102: Acct. book, 1854–58 (147 ll.)
Delo 109: Acct. book, 1864–67 (4 ll.)

Books of correspondence between Andrei, Natalia, and Yakov

Delo 57: Vol. 1, 1834–36 (116 ll.)
Delo 59: Vol. 2, 1834–36 (78 ll.)
Delo 58: Vol. 3, 1836–37 (211 ll.)
Delo 66: Vol. 4, 1836–37 (158 ll.)

Notebook correspondence between Andrei and his friend, Astrakhan landowner Vladimir Kopytovskii

Delo 98: Apr–Dec 1850 (32 ll.)

Diary and account books by Yakov Chernavin

Delo 47: Acct. book, 1825–34 (42 ll.)
Delo 61: Acct. book, 1834–45 (154 ll.)
Delo 60: "Parallel diary," 1834–41 (235 ll.)
Delo 70: Notebook, 1837 (76 ll.)
Delo 153: Late notebook, n/d (32 ll.)
Dela 31, 50, 51, 88, 89, 149: Various letters (12 ll. total)

Collections of letters sent to Andrei and Natalia, gathered and annotated by Andrei

Delo 53: 1824–30, 1843–44 (23 ll.)
Delo 99: Jan–Dec 1850 (276 ll.)
Delo 103: Dec 1859–June 1860 (404 ll.)
Delo 105: June 1860–Dec 1860 (142 ll.)
Delo 106: Dec 1860–Mar 1861 (172 ll.)
Delo 108: May 1861–Dec 1861 (326 ll.)
Delo 112: Nov 1866–Jan 1867 (110 ll.)

CITED ARTICLES BY A. I. CHIKHACHEV
Zemledel'cheskaia gazeta (ZG)

"O komnatnom vozdukhe." 6 (Jan 1845): 44–45.
"Kamennoi dom v derevne." 25 (Mar 1845): 198–99.
"O stat'iakh bez podpisi." 7 (Jan 1846): 56.
"Kak luchshe ustroit' verkhov pogreb." 21 (Mar 1846): 178.
"O dolgakh." 72 (Septr 1846): 588; 75 (Sept 1846): 607–8; 87 (Oct 1846): 709–10.
"Vazhnost' khozaiki v dome." 37 (May 1847): 292–93; 53 (July 1847): 417–19; 37 (May 1848): 294–95.
"O ezhednevnom v slukh domashnem chtenii." 71 (1847).
"Vopros ob istreblenii volkov." 9 (Jan 1848): 65.
"Otnosheniiakh mezhdu pomeschikami." 26 (Mar 1848): 206.
"Sochustvie k mysli o derevenskikh vrachakh." 80 (1848): 635–37.
"Esche neskol'ko slov o dolgakh." 87 (Oct 1848): 692–94.
"Ob obschem dvorian uchastii v Zemledel'cheskoi Gazete." 98 (Dec 1848): 781–82.
"Neskol'ko myslei sel'skogo zhitelia." 3 (Jan 1850): 20–22; 48 (June 1850): 379–80; 54 (July 1850): 428–30.
"Sel'skoe obrazovanie—o vospitaniia detei." 22 (Mar 1859): 169–72.

Vladimirskie gubernskie vedomosti (VGV)

"Lekarstvo ot zubnoi boli." 41 (Oct 1847): 191.
"Proizvodstvo prostykh reshet v Kovrovskom uezde." 42 (Oct 1848): 235–37; 47 (Nov 1848): 267–69.
"Patrioticheskoe sochustvie k uchilischu sel'skago khoziastva dlia potomstvennykh dvorian." 52 (Dec 1849): 253–54.

"O detskikh igrakh." 40 (Oct 1850): 222.

"Mysli sel'skogo zhitelia o gubernskoi gazete." 45 (Nov 1850): 249–51.

"Neskol'ko myslei (avtobiograficheskoe)." 46 (Nov 1850): 259–60.

"Neskol'ko slov dlia zhelaiuschikh pomolit'sia v Kieve." 47 (Nov 1851): 313–15.

"Zaochnoe znakomstvo (o peredache pisem ot sotrudnika k sotrudniku—chrez redaktsiiu)."
   1 (1865): 64–67.

Moskovskie gubernskie vedomosti (MGV)

"Dva slova o rabotakh gospodskikh liudei." 72 (June 1847): 563–64.

OTHER PUBLISHED SOURCES

Antonov, Sergei. "Law and the Culture of Debt in Moscow on the Eve of the Great Reforms,
   1850–1870." PhD diss., Columbia University, 2011.

Augustine, Wilson R. "Notes toward a Portrait of the Eighteenth-Century Russian Nobility."
   Canadian-American Slavic Studies 4 (1970): 373–425.

Bisha, Robin. "The Promise of Patriarchy: Marriage in Eighteenth-Century Russia." PhD diss.,
   Indiana University, 1994.

Blum, Jerome. *Lord and Peasant in Russia: From the Ninth to the Nineteenth Century.* Princeton:
   Princeton University Press, 1971.

Bolotov, A. T. *Zhizn' i prikliucheniia Andreia Bolotova: opisannye samim dlia svoikh potomkov.*
   3 vols., S. Ronskii, P. Zhatkin, and I. Kravtsov, ed. Moscow: Terra, 1993.

Bourne, J. M. *Patronage and Society in Nineteenth-Century England.* London: Edward Arnold,
   1986.

Brokgauz, and Efron. *Russkii biograficheskii slovar': setevaia versiia* 2007, accessed 5/14/07 2007;
   Available from http://www.rulex.ru/01240253.htm.

Cavender, Mary. *Nests of the Gentry: Family, Estate, and Local Loyalties in Provincial Russia.*
   Newark: University of Delaware Press, 2007.

Clinton, Catherine. *The Plantation Mistress: Woman's World in the Old South.* New York:
   Pantheon, 1982.

Emmons, Terence. *Emancipation of the Russian Serfs.* Austin, TX: Holt McDougal, 1970.

Engel, Barbara Alpern. *Breaking the Ties That Bound: The Politics of Marital Strife in Late Impe-*
   rial Russia. Ithaca, NY: Cornell University Press, 2011.

Field, Daniel. *The End of Serfdom: Nobility and Bureaucracy in Russia, 1855–1861.* Cambridge,
   MA: Harvard University Press, 1976.

Frank, Stephen M. *Life with Father: Parenthood and Masculinity in the Nineteenth-Century*
   American North. Baltimore: Johns Hopkins University Press, 1998.

Frazier, Melissa. *Romantic Encounters: Writers, Readers, and the "Library for Reading."* Stanford:
   Stanford University Press, 2007.

Frolov, N. V. *K iugu ot Kovrova.* Kovrov: N. V. Frolov, 1995.

———. *Pervaia Kovrovskaia biblioteka.* Kovrov: Mashteks, 2000.

———. *Predvoditeli dvorianstva i predsedateli semzkoi upravy Kovrovskogo uezda.* Vladimir:
   Vladimirskaia obl. nauch. universal'naia biblioteka, 1994.

———. *Predvoditeli dvorianstva Muromskogo uezda.* Vladimir: Vladimirskaia obl. nauch.
   universal'naia biblioteka, 1996.

———. *Predvoditeli dvorianstva Viaznikovskogo uezda*. Vladimir: Vladimirskaia obl. nauch. universal'naia biblioteka, 1997.

———. *Predvoditeli dvorianstva Vladimirskoi gubernii*. Vladimir: Vladimirskaia obl. nauch. universal'naia biblioteka, 1995.

———. *Sel'tso Ievlevo i ego okrestnosti*. Kovrov: Best-V, 1996. *Vladimirskii rodoslovets*. Kovrov: Best-V, 1996.

———. "Sem'ia Chikhachevykh i istoriia pervoi obshchestvennoi biblioteki Kovrovskogo uezda v s. Zimenki." In *Voroninskie chteniia-94: materialy oblastnoi kraevedcheskoi konferentsii*. Vladimir: Vladimirskii obl. fond kul'tury, 1995.

Frolov, N. V., and E. V. Frolova. *Istoriia zemli Kovrovskoi*. Kovrov: Best-V, 1997.

———. *Iz istorii sela Pavlovskogo*. Kovrov: Best V, 1998.

———. *Kovrov pravoslavnyi*. Kovrov: BEST-V, Mashteks, 1999.

———. *Kovrovskii istoricheskii sbornik*. Kovrov: Mashteks, 2000.

———. *Kovrovskii krai Pushkinskoi pory*. Kovrov: BEST-V, 1999.

———. *Liubets na Kliaz'me*. Kovrov: Mashteks, 2000.

———. *Pervaia kovrovskaia biblioteka*. Kovrov, 2000.

———. *Vladimirskie namestniki i gubernatory, 1778–1917 gg*. Kovrov: BEST-V, 1998.

Glagoleva, O. E. "Dream and Reality of Russian Provincial Young Ladies, 1700–1850." *The Carl Beck Papers in Russian & East European Studies* 1405 (2000): 1–87.

———. *Tul'skaia knizhnaia starina: ocherki kul'turnoi zhizni XVIII-pervoi poloviny XIX vv*. Tula: Izd-vo Tul'skogo gosudarstvennogo pedagogicheskogo instituta, 1992.

Glenn, Susan A. *Daughters of the Shtetl: Life and Labor in the Immigrant Generation*. Ithaca, NY: Cornell University Press, 1990.

Goldstein, Darra. "Domestic Porkbarreling in Nineteenth-Century Russia, or Who Holds the Keys to the Larder?" In *Russia, Women, Culture*, Helena Goscilo and Beth Holmgren. ed. Bloomington: Indiana University Press, 1996.

Golovina, T. N. "Chitateli Pushkinskoi pory." In *Sovremennoe prochtenie Pushkina: mezhvuzkovskii sbornik nauchnykh trudov*, V. V. Tikhomirov. ed. Ivanovo: Ivanovskii gos. universitet, 1999.

———. "Gazeta dlia odnogo chitatelia." In *Potaennaia Literatura: issledovaniia i materialy*, Dmitri i Lakerbai, et al. ed. Ivanovo: Ivanovskii gos. universitet, 2000.

———. "Golos iz publiki: chitatel'-sovremennik o Pushkine i Bulgarine." *Novoe literaturnoe obozrenie* 4 (1999): 11–16.

———. "Iz kruga chteniia pomeshchikov srednei ruki (po dokumentam 1830–1840kh godov iz usadebnogo arkhiva." *Novoe Literaturnoe Obozrenie* 93 (2008), magazines.russ.ru/nlo/2008/93/go38.html (accessed 10/2/2011).

———. "Pis'ma literatorov A. I. Chikhachevu." In *Folklor i literatura Ivanovskogo kraia: stati, publikatsii, materialy*, V. A. Smirnov. ed. Ivanovo: Ivanovskii gos. universitet, 1994.

Goscilo, Helena, and Beth Holmgren, eds. *Russia, Women, Culture*. Bloomington: Indiana University Press, 1996.

Greene, Diana. "Mid-Nineteenth Century Domestic Ideology in Russia." In *Women and Russian Culture*, Rosalind Marsh. ed. New York: Berghahn, 1998.

Grigoryan, Bella. "Noble Farmers: The Provincial Landowner in the Russian Cultural Imagination." PhD diss., Columbia University, 2011.

Gurko, V. I. *Cherty i siluety proshlogo*. Moscow, 2000, http://www.historichka.ru/istoshniki/gurko/ (accessed 10/3/2011).

Hoch, Steven L. *Serfdom and Social Control in Russia: Petrovskoe, a Village in Tambov*. Chicago: University of Chicago Press, 1989.

Kelly, Catriona. *Refining Russia: Advice Literature, Polite Culture, and Gender from Catherine to Yeltsin*. Oxford: Oxford University Press, 2001.

Labzina, A. E. *Days of a Russian Noblewoman: The Memories of Anna Labzina, 1758–1821*, Gary Marker and Rachel May. ed. DeKalb: Northern Illinois University Press, 2001.

LeDonne, John. "Ruling Families in the Russian Political Order, 1689–1825." *Cahiers du monde Russe et Sovietique* 28 (1987): 233–322.

Lounsbery, Anne. "'No, This Is Not the Provinces!' Provincialism, Authenticity, and Russianness in Gogol's Day." *Russian Review* 64 (2005): 259–80.

Marker, Gary. "The Enlightenment of Anna Labzina: Gender, Faith, and Public Life in Catherinian and Alexandrian Russia." *Slavic Review* 59, no. 2 (2000): 369–90.

———. *Publishing, Printing, and the Origins of Intellectual Life in Russia, 1700–1800*. Princeton: Princeton University Press, 1985.

Marrese, Michelle Lamarche. "'The Poetics of Everyday Behavior' Revisited: Lotman, Gender, and the Evolution of Russian Noble Identity." *Kritika* 11, no. 4 (Fall 2010): 701–39.

———. *A Woman's Kingdom: Noblewomen and the Control of Property in Russia, 1700–1861*. Ithaca, NY: Cornell University Press, 2002.

Martin, Alexander M. "The Family Model of Society and Russian National Identity in Sergei N. Glinka's Russian Messenger (1808–1812)." *Slavic Review* 57, no. 1 (1998): 28–49.

Materialy dlia istorii krepostnogo prava v Rossii. Berlin, 1872.

Maxwell, Richard, and Katie Trumpener, eds. *The Cambridge Companion to Fiction in the Romantic Period*. Cambridge: Cambridge University Press, 2008.

Melton, Edgar. "Enlightened Seigniorialism and Its Dilemmas in Serf Russia, 1750–1830." *Journal of Modern History* 62, no. 4 (1990): 675–708.

Newlin, Thomas. *The Voice in the Garden: Andrei Bolotov and the Anxieties of Russian Pastoral, 1738–1833*. Evanston, IL: Northwestern University Press, 2001.

Ogarev, N. P. "Zamechanie na zamechanie g. Chikhacheva," *Izbrannye sotsial'no-politicheskie i filosofskie proizvedeniia* (Gosudarstvennoe izdatel'stvo politicheskoi literatury, USSR, 1952): 101–5.

Owen, Thomas C. *The Corporation under Russian Law, 1800–1917*. Cambridge: Cambridge University Press, 1991.

Peterson, M. Jeanne. *Family, Love, and Work in the Lives of Victorian Gentlewomen*. Bloomington: Indiana University Press, 1989.

Pouncy, Carolyn. *The "Domostroi": Rules for Russian Households in the Time of Ivan the Terrible*. Ithaca, NY: Cornell University Press, 1994.

Rabow-Edling, Susanna. *Slavophile Thought and the Politics of Cultural Nationalism*. Albany: State University of New York Press, 2006.

Randolph, John. *The House in the Garden: The Bakunin Family and the Romance of Russian Idealism*. Ithaca, NY: Cornell University Press, 2007.

Ransel, David L. *Mothers of Misery: Child Abandonment in Russia*. Princeton: Princeton University Press, 1988.

Riasanovsky, Nicholas V. *Nicholas I and Official Nationality in Russia, 1825–1855*. Berkeley: University of California Press, 1967.

Roosevelt, Priscilla. *Life on the Russian Country Estate: A Social and Cultural History*. New Haven: Yale University Press, 1995.

Rutt, Richard. *A History of Hand Knitting*. Loveland, CO: Interweave Press, 1987.

Smith, Alison K. *Recipes for Russia: Food and Nationhood under the Tsars*. DeKalb: Northern Illinois University Press, 2011.

Smith-Peter, Susan. "Books Behind the Altar: Religion, Village Libraries, and the Moscow Agriculture Society." *Russian History/Histoire Russe* 31, no. 3 (2004): 213–33.

———. "Educating Peasant Girls for Motherhood: Religion and Primary Education in Mid-Nineteenth Century Russia," *Russian Review* 66, no. 3 (July 2007): 391–405.

———. "The Local as Familial Space in the Mid-Nineteenth Century: A. I. Chikhachev's *The District Treasurehouse*." Mid-Atlantic Slavic Conference, New York, NY, April 4, 2009.

———. "Provincial Public Libraries and the Law in Nicholas I's Russia." *Library History* 21 (2005): 103–19.

———. "The Russian Provincial Newspaper and Its Public, 1788–1864." *The Carl Beck Papers in Russian and East European Studies,* no. 1908. Pittsburgh: University of Pittsburgh, 2008.

———. "Ukrainskie zhurnaly nachala XIX veka: ot universalizma Prosveshcheniia do roman-ticheskogo regionalizma." In I. G. Zhiriakov and A. A. Orlov, eds., *Istoriia i politika v sovre-mennom mire.* (2010): 447–61.

Sunderland, Willard. "Imperial Space: Territorial Thought and Practice in the Eighteenth Century." In *Russian Empire: Space, People, Power, 1700–1930*, Jane Burbank, Mark von Hagen, and Anatolyi Remnev. ed. Bloomington: Indiana University Press, 2007.

Tosh, John. *A Man's Place: Masculinity and the Middle-Class Home in Victorian England*. New Haven: Yale University Press, 1999.

Tovrov, Jessica. *The Russian Noble Family: Structure and Change*. New York: Garland, 1987.

Spiski naselennykh mest Rossiiskoi Imperii, vol. 6 (Vladimirskaia guberniia). St. Petersburg, 1863.

Ulrich, Laurel Thatcher. *A Midwife's Tale: The Life of Martha Ballard, Based on Her Diary, 1785–1812*. New York: Knopf, 1990.

Vickery, Amanda. *Behind Closed Doors: At Home in Georgian England* (New Haven: Yale University Press, 2009).

———. *The Gentleman's Daughter: Women's Lives in Georgian England*. New Haven: Yale University Press, 1998.

Voenno-statisticheskie obozrenie Rossiiskoi imperii. St. Petersburg, 1852.

Volkov, S. V. *Russkii ofitserskii korpus*. Moscow, 1993.

Vospominaniia russkikh krestian xviii – pervoi poloviny xix veka. Moscow: NLO, 2006.

Whittaker, Cynthia H. *The Origins of Modern Russian Education: An Intellectual Biography of Count Sergei Uvarov, 1786–1855*. DeKalb: Northern Illinois University Press, 1984.

Wirtschafter, Elise Kimerling. *Social Identity in Imperial Russia*. DeKalb: Northern Illinois University Press, 1997.

Wortman, Richard. "The Russian Empress as Mother." In *Family in Imperial Russia: New Lines of Historical Research*, David L. Ransel. ed. Urbana: U of Illinois Press, 1978.

———. *Scenarios of Power: Myth and Ceremony in Russian Monarchy*. 2 vols. Princeton: Princeton University Press, 2006.

INDEX